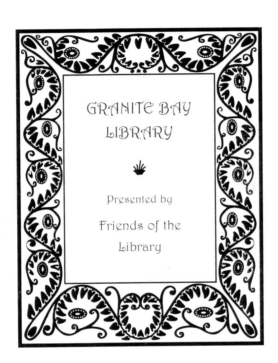

Money and Government

ROBERT SKIDELSKY

Money and Government

The Past and Future of Economics

Yale UNIVERSITY PRESS
New Haven and London

First published in the United States in 2018 by Yale University Press.
First published in the United Kingdom in 2018 by Penguin Books Ltd., London,
as *Money and Government: A Challenge to Mainstream Economics*.

Yale University Press books may be purchased in quantity for educational, business, or
promotional use. For information, please e-mail sales.press@yale.edu (U.S. office) or sales@
yaleup.co.uk (U.K. office).

Typeset in 10.5/14 pt Sabon LT Std by Jouve (U.K.), Milton Keynes.
Printed in the United States of America.

Library of Congress Control Number: 2018954397
ISBN 978-0-300-24032-0 (hardcover : alk. paper)

This paper meets the requirements of ANSI/NISO Z39.48-1992
(Permanence of Paper).

10   9   8   7   6   5   4   3   2   1

Contents

CONTENTS

Figures

FIGURES

Preface

We are at a junction where the whole of macroeconomic policy is up for grabs. Everything we thought settled by the Great Moderation of the fifteen pre-recession years, a period of exceptional stability in Western economies, has been thrown into turmoil by the scale of the collapse of 2008–9 and the feebleness of the recovery from it. That poses a mighty challenge for the ruling economic doctrines. Policy will shift, is already changing; textbooks will have to be revised. Economics in the future will need to reflect much more on where it has come from and what it needs to do.

This book aims to build a new audience for economics while, at the same time, being of interest to the professional economist. It attempts to bridge the gap between popular books inspired by the crisis, which economists don't read, and economists' analyses of the crisis, which non-economists cannot understand.

It started off as a series of lectures to third-year economics students at the University of Warwick, and I am grateful to the Department of Economics for allowing me to put into practice my ideas of how economics should be taught. The book seeks to enfold technical issues in what, for want of a better term, may be called political economy. I am interested in the interplay between economic ideas and the circumstances in which they rise, flourish and decay. My account of what went wrong in 2008–9 is grounded in the historical debates on economic policy. The proposals in the last chapter for a new framework for economic policy are derived from the lessons I draw from both this history and the Great Recession itself.

Britain has been my chief witness for the defence and prosecution. This reflects the limitations of my own knowledge, but it is not the entire reason for my focus. For much of the period, and for many of the events covered by this book, Britain was the pacemaker and rule-setter for the global economy, an amazing achievement for a country with just 1 per cent of the world's population (it went briefly up to 2 per cent in the 1850s). David Hume, Adam Smith, David Ricardo, John Stuart Mill, Alfred Marshall and John Maynard Keynes towered over the economics of their day; Britain was the first modern gold-standard nation, the first commercial society, and the first industrial nation. The City of London bestrode the world of international finance; the Victorian fiscal constitution provided a universal model of good government; and Britain possessed adequate hard power to enforce the rules of a liberal international trading order. It was from the 'Manchester system' that Karl Marx and Friedrich List, the great nineteenth-century continental dissidents, tried to distil their lessons; and, much later, Karl Polanyi took Britain as his case study of the wrenching effects of the market economy.

I am talking here about the mainstream – classical and neo-classical – economics tradition. Nineteenth-century economic practice was always much more pluralist than mainstream doctrine. But though there were many dissenters from the Smith–Ricardo school, there were no serious analytical challengers – that is, until Keynes in the twentieth century.

In the first half of the twentieth century, economics became much more pluralist in parallel with the convulsions of the world wars, the Great Depression, and the decay of British power. Keynes was the last economics leader from Britain. After the Second World War, the centre of gravity in Western economics shifted decisively to the United States, the new political hegemon, while the dissenting voices of Marxism and Protectionism continued to hold sway in developing countries, and the communist world built a Pharaonic system that dispensed with Western economics altogether. By the 1990s, with the fall of communism, economics had become an almost wholly American-owned subsidiary, the charter of globalization. Today, with the decay of American power and following the Great Recession of 2008–9, another geopolitical – and intellectual – shift is taking place.

I have not attempted a general history of economics, which would certainly include many great thinkers and important schools not mentioned here, but only that part of it which seemed most important for understanding the economic collapse of 2008–9; hence my focus on the 'unsettled issues' of money and government. In my approach, I have been chiefly influenced by Keynes, whose biography I have written. However, as the book progressed I became increasingly drawn to the insights of Karl Polanyi, with his insistence that, to be viable, a market order has to be 'embedded' in a framework of rules, policies and institutions. This insight has been somewhat neglected by the dominant school of Anglo-American economics.

My debts have accumulated. I would in particular like to thank Spencer Boxer, Gordon Brown, Oliver Bush, Andrea Califano, Tim Congdon, Paul Davidson, Michael Davies, Meghnad Desai, Tommaso Gabellini, Jamie Galbraith, Simone Gasperin, Andy Haldane, Geoffrey Harcourt, Michael Kennedy, David Laidler, Laurie Laybourn Langton, Toby Lewis, Felix Martin, Vladimir Masch, Marcus Miller, George Peden, Atanos Pekanov, Philip Pilkington, Edward Skidelsky, Leanne Stickland, David Sturrock, Thomas Tozer, Christopher Tugendhat, Paul Westbrook and Christian Westerlind Wigstrom. Their help has been invaluable; the approach is my own.

Introduction

I. UNSETTLED ISSUES

Macroeconomics is about money and government, and their relationship. The unsettled questions in macroeconomic policy stem from disputes about the part money plays in economic life, and the part government should play. For 250 years, the dominant view of the economic profession has been that money is of no importance except when it gets 'out of order', and that government interference with the market usually makes things worse. 'You can't buck the market,' Mrs Thatcher famously declared. A competitive market economy, it was claimed, has an automatic tendency to full employment. Disturbances to employment are the result of interference, usually by or at the behest of governments, creating or promoting monopolies, impeding price adjustments or, crucially, by 'monkeying around' with the money supply, thus inducing people to trade at the wrong prices. At first it was believed that control of money should be entrusted to the gold standard; when the gold standard broke down, to independent central banks. Government should be limited to ensuring the conditions required for efficient market exchange. The only task of macro policy was to control the money supply.

This view of policy was successfully challenged by the Keynesian revolution, which, starting as a new theory in the 1930s, dominated macroeconomic policy until the 1970s. The Keynesians denied that a monetary economy – one in which contracts are made in money, not goods – had any automatic tendency to full employment. This was because people could choose to hold money, rather than spend it, and the reason they might wish to do so was the omnipresence of uncertainty; as Keynes put it, the possession of money 'lulls our disquietude'.

Given the role of money as a 'store of wealth', the macroeconomy was inherently unstable, and was liable to settle down in a position of 'under-employment equilibrium'. It was therefore the task of government to maintain a full employment balance between supply and demand, which included the management of money as part of the management of the economy. But it was not money that had to be kept in order; it was the market system itself. If it was left free of management and regulation, it would be socially and politically disruptive. In the Keynesian era, stretching from the end of the Second World War to the 1970s, the free world economy experienced a unique period of stability and growth.

In the 1970s, however, the Keynesian system succumbed to 'stagflation' – the simultaneous rise in inflation and unemployment – and the Keynesian attempt to manage the macroeconomy was abandoned. The core idea behind the new classical economic policy that succeeded it was that central banks should be mandated to control inflation, with unemployment left to settle at its 'natural' rate. This was taken to be a rate on which macroeconomic policy could not improve. The unemployed should get on their bikes and look for work.[1]

In technical terms, familiar to economists, the question about the relationship between money and government is a question about the relationship between monetary and fiscal policy. The Keynesian innovation was that the government should influence the level of total spending through fiscal policy, with monetary policy made consistent with the aims of fiscal policy. By contrast, in new classical economics, monetary policy – keeping the economy supplied with the right amount of money – is the whole of macroeconomic policy, since fiscal policy cannot influence the level of total spending, only its direction. This was the doctrine 'in power' in 2008.

The collapse of 2008 and its aftermath was a test of the two theories of macroeconomic policy, not under laboratory conditions but in as close to a real-life experiment as we are likely to get. According to the mainstream view of the time, the collapse should not have happened and, even if it had, recovery should have been swift. In the second, Keynesian, hypothesis, its happening was always a possibility, and recovery was never likely to be fast or full. However, the old Keynesian recipe for running economies at full employment through fiscal policy had succumbed to inflation, and has not been rehabilitated, so policy for the future remains unsettled.

The proximate cause of the collapse of 2008 was the accumulation of private debt, much of it the result of fraud on the part of the lenders and myopia on the part of the borrowers. A vast, global, inverted pyramid of bank, business and household debt was built on a narrow base of underlying assets – American real estate. When the base tottered, the pyramid fell. The failure of the sub-prime mortgage market in the United States triggered a collapse in the prices of financial assets. The fall in the net wealth of banks in 2007–8 produced a global financial crisis. This was transmitted to the real economy through a tightening of credit by the banks and a fall in demand by consumers and businesses, whose wealth and confidence had evaporated.

It all developed with astonishing speed. The bankruptcy of Lehman Brothers on 15 September 2008 precipitated a stock market collapse in October. Once banks started to fail and stock markets to fall, the 'real' economy started to slide too. Banks stopped lending. Creditors foreclosed on loans to debtors. Businesses laid off workers. Total spending shrank. This brought about generalized conditions of slump throughout the world by the fourth quarter of 2008. It was eerily reminiscent of what happened in the Wall Street Crash of 1929.

The worst of the storm passed after a year. Unlike in 1929, governments intervened to prevent disaster. Governments and central banks around the world vigorously pumped money into their deflating systems. But in some European countries, governments were virtually bankrupted by the excesses of their banking systems. The collapse of state revenues brought public debts to unprecedented peacetime levels, reviving the most persistent of the economic orthodoxies: that governments are the problem, not the solution. As economies stabilized, policies of austerity were adopted to put governments back into the fiscal cage from which the severity of crisis had temporarily released them. Today, monetary expansion is being eased, in recognition that it has done as much as it can, while austerity is being eased in recognition that monetary policy is not enough. The future of the fiscal–monetary mix is unsettled.

The standard account of the origins of the crisis starts with an (unexplained) shock to the financial sector, which is then transmitted to the non-financial sector through the freezing of credit. However, it is possible that the trouble was rooted in the non-financial economy. Despite the rosy retrospect of the so-called Great Moderation years of the early 2000s, the Western economies that collapsed in 2008 were not in pristine condition. Unemployment was about double what it had been in the Keynesian era. The huge accumulation of household and corporate debt – in the advanced economies, average private-sector debt as a percentage of GDP went up from 50 per cent in 1950 to 170 per cent by 2008 – was one indication that large sections of the pre-crash economy were not 'paying their way'. This was partly a consequence of a marked growth in inequality. Real wages were stagnant or falling; investment was down from its historic levels, and with it productivity growth. The finance sector was growing faster than the economy, and financiers were getting much richer than anyone else. Signs of 'secular stagnation' were not hard to see, after the event. I have singled out the stagnation of real earnings as the deep cause of the crisis, the result of which was transmitted to the financial sector through the build-up of unsustainable debt. The Great Moderation is known chiefly for its low inflation and cyclical stability. It now seems more of a lull before a storm bound to break. It leaves the fate of advanced capitalist economies in limbo. At the time of writing, a resurgent financial system and a mediocre real recovery threaten a repeat crash at no distant date.

II. THE CULPRITS

'Why did no one see it coming?' asked Queen Elizabeth II of a group economists at the LSE in October 2008.[2] This book is an attempt to answer that question and suggest how to avoid such foul-ups in the future. This will not be easy. It will not be enough to strengthen so-called financial 'resilience' to shocks. It is economies which need to be made resilient to shocks.

It is natural to start with the financial institutions, which egregiously over-borrowed and over-lent, and which were heavily into all kinds of fraudulent practices. Gripped by a collective hubris, the institutions were oblivious to the rocks ahead. The lure of present gains drove out the fear of future losses.

But to stop with the banks would be a mistake. The banking sector was freed up to do its best and worst by national governments and regulators, who held a benevolent view of the financial system. Finance was viewed essentially as an intermediatory, bringing together willing buyers and sellers of goods and services. In the language of the day, the financial market was an 'efficient' market, which needed no more regulation than any other market. The peculiar property of finance as a vent for speculation and fraud was ignored.

This benign view of finance extended to the financial innovations of the 1990s. Securitization – the process of transforming non-marketable assets into marketable ones – led to a continuous lengthening of the chain of indebtedness. This 'financialization' of the economy – the growing share of money being made from purely financial operations – was praised (or at least justified) as 'making capital allocation more efficient' and therefore maximizing growth. Business school professors set up their own hedge funds to test their theories.

But how, the enquirer may ask, did so many governments come to hold views which were plainly absurd in retrospect? He is led inexorably to the source of these beliefs, to the 'intellectual climate', the Zeitgeist, the tide of thought and feeling that liberated our financial markets from national controls. The enquirer will discover that at the heart of today's mainstream macroeconomics is the belief that unimpeded competitive markets deliver optimal welfare, and that the financial institutions which create money, and through which money is allocated, have no independent effect on the real equilibrium of the economy, but are only acting on behalf of well-informed sovereign consumers. He will discover that the forecasting models of finance ministries and central banks lacked a financial sector. The assumption that future prices would move in line with current expectations removed any need to take precautions against financial collapse, despite a continuous history of financial manias and panics. Aiming to minimize the interference of the state, mainstream economics ignored the financial wolves on the prowl.

Surely it is here – in the world of economic ideas – that the original flaw in the regulatory design is to be found. Governments believed things about the economic system that were not true, or at least not true enough. In the name of these ideas, finance was allowed to spin out of control; and its implosion produced a world depression.

Practical people usually pooh-pooh the influence of academic scribblers. The English famously feel themselves to be healthily exempt from intellectual influences. In fact, academic thought and policy were not so closely linked in the past. But today, economic ideas penetrate much more deeply into economic policy, because economic policy-making is largely in the hands of professional economists. Most of them work not in universities, but in treasuries and central banks, in commercial banks, businesses and newspapers, in political parties and think-tanks, or as business consultants and lobbyists. The days are long past when a Governor of the Bank of England could welcome one of its first academic economists with the words: 'you are not here to tell us what to do, but to explain to us why we have done it'.[3] Now economists do tell decisionmakers what to do.

This is supposed to make policy more expert, less partisan. However, economics is by no means the scientific citadel that many of its practitioners claim it to be. It displays a silent ideological slant while sticking to the accepted canons of scientific method. Since the 1980s, the dominance of new classical theory in economics has coincided with the neo-liberal capture of politics. The connection is not fortuitous. New classical economics has provided an economic-theoretic justification for neo-liberal policies; neo-liberal ideology has shaped the way economists 'model' the economy. Both readily sign up to Ronald Reagan's distillation of two centuries of conventional wisdom: 'The government is the problem, not the solution.'[4]

However, to say that economics is inherently ideological is not quite to get to the root of the puzzle of what went wrong in 2008. Why *this* ideology and not *that*?

Ideology is highly influenced by the structure of power, as well as helping to bring about a structure of power favourable to it. This is the important element of truth in Marx's claim that the dominant ideas of any epoch are those of its ruling class. The crash of 2008 revealed the power of financial interests.

A huge puzzle in the pre-crash situation is the weakness of democratic government in face of the structural power of finance. Orthodox political science tells us that in democracies accountability runs from government to the people. But one cannot get a grip on the history of the crisis without realizing that it is the financial community, far more

6

than 'the people', that decides both the terms and the conditions on which government gets its money. The money–power nexus works both indirectly, through its influence on election finance and the presentations of the media, and directly through its role in financing government borrowing. What the 'efficient allocation of capital' means in practice is the allocation which is efficient for the financial sector. In the last twenty to thirty years, the chief economic role of Western governments has been to provide the financial system with a nice environment for it to maximize its profits. This has included being prepared to bail out banks when their excesses made them insolvent, and being prepared to cut their own spending on social welfare to retain the confidence of the bond markets. Following the crash, the financial sector has turned the brave words of politicians about the need for reform into rhetoric largely without substance.

The Marxist claim that big business controls politics rests on the twin claim that the business class is a monolith and that it is effectively unchecked by countervailing forces. In fact untrammelled business power is the exception rather than the rule. On the one side business power itself is divided, notably between exporters and importers, creditors and debtors, small and big businesses, and 'finance' and 'industry'; on the other side, business power has been checked by varieties of popular power. The more equal the balance of forces, the less likely we are to get a single story about the way the economy works.

A central claim of this book is that there was a balance of power between capital and labour from the 1920s to the 1970s which enabled the emergence of a Keynesian state relatively free from the vested interests. It was in this period that the idea of the state as a benevolent guardian of the public interest gained currency. But in the last forty years the balance of power has shifted decisively from labour to capital; from the working class to the business class; and from the old business elites to new financial, partly criminal, elites. How this has come about deserves a profound study of its own, of which only hints can be given in the pages that follow. What can be claimed is that the main homage which mainstream economics pays to power is to render it invisible.

Finally, theory and policy are moulded by the conditions of the times. These produce what John Hicks called 'concentrations of attention',[5] by which he meant the problems that economists choose to study. What causes shifts in attention? In the interwar years persistent mass unemployment was *the* problem; in the 1970s it was inflation. Such changes in facts disturb the kaleidoscope; they determine what the viewer sees. (For a further discussion of the relationship between ideas, power and circumstances, see the appendix to this Introduction, p. 11.)

What follows will attend primarily to macroeconomic doctrines as they developed until 2007, and the way these have been tested and found wanting by the crisis and its aftermath. The book is an essay in political economy, since it pays attention at all times to the context of the rise and fate of different economic doctrines. Knowing what economists thought in the past, and how and why they came to think as they did, is, as Hicks has pointed out, an essential part of 'keeping watch' on the discipline as, unlike in the natural sciences, it can record no unambiguous progress in knowledge. It is perhaps natural for me to embrace a political economy approach, since I was originally trained as a historian, and no historian can be oblivious to the historical forces that produced the stories by which economic events are understood.

III. A BRIEF SKETCH OF THE BOOK

The book is divided into four parts. The first takes the reader through the historical debates on monetary and fiscal policy before the First World War. This history is crucial to an understanding of the pre-crash orthodoxy. The second investigates the rise and fall of the Keynesian revolution, showing how this episode ended with the partial restoration of Victorian monetary and fiscal policy. The third part shows how this restoration was itself tested by the collapse of 2008–9 and its aftermath, reopening issues formerly considered settled. Part Four concludes with reflections on the whole and a sketch of a new macroeconomics.

Part One starts with three chapters on the history of monetary theory and policy. Chapter 1 surveys the debates on the origins of money, on the nature of money, on what determines its value, and on the consequences of disturbances to its value. Chapter 2 covers the three great nineteenth-century debates about how money might be 'kept in order', which, starting in the era of the gold standard, culminated in the 'scientific' Quantity Theory of Money at the start of the last century, the subject of Chapter 3. This chapter pinpoints the rupture in monetary theory, represented by the two versions of the Quantity Theory of Money developed by Irving Fisher and Knut Wicksell, respectively.

Chapter 4 examines the nineteenth-century theory of fiscal policy. The point of special emphasis is that fiscal rules and monetary rules were considered complementary. Their joint purpose was to prevent governments from issuing too much money. With Britain setting the pace, by 1900 all 'civilized' countries had linked their domestic currencies to the gold standard and their governments balanced their budgets at the lowest level of taxes and spending possible. But the theory of the 'minimal state' was never wholly accepted outside Britain. The idea of the state as the indispensable actor in a nation's economic development survived in the 'pre-scientific' doctrine of mercantilism. Specifically, free trade, though preached by economists, was never widely accepted on the continent of Europe, or even in the United States. By the 1880s and 1890s, the doctrine of laissez-faire had started to be challenged by the rise of democracy, the depressions of the 1880s and 1890s, and the emergence of the welfare state. The appearance of the word 'unemployment' in the *Oxford English Dictionary* in 1888 marked the arrival of a 'problem' that would dominate economic theory and policy for the next eighty years.

Part Two traces the rise, triumph and fall of the Keynesian revolution, a period stretching from the publication of Keynes's *General Theory of Employment, Interest, and Money* in 1936 to the 1970s. Chapter 5 shows how the Keynesian theory of economics and policy were a response to the Great Depression of the 1930s. It was seemingly vindicated by the achievement of full employment and stable growth in the thirty years that followed the Second World War, the subject of Chapter 6. The Keynesian regime ran into trouble in the stagflationary 1970s and was superseded by 'monetarism', which was in fact a reversion to pre-Keynesian orthodoxy about both money and governments. Chapter 7 ends with an account of the 'New Consensus' – a mixture of 'new' classical and 'new' Keynesian economics, which was in turn brought down by the collapse of 2008.

Following the theoretical twists and turns of this economic saga, no one can fail to be impressed by the persistence in economic theory of the core idea that an unimpeded market system tends to full employment equilibrium, unless obstructed by 'spanners in the works', generally thrown by governments. First suggested by Adam Smith's metaphor of the 'invisible hand', this insight was formalized in the general equilibrium theory of Leon Walras in 1874. Much later, as late as in our own day, the microeconomics of Walras begat new classical macroeconomics. The main storyline has been heavily modified and qualified in face of disconfirming events, but has always re-emerged, in more or less unchanged form. This leads to the conclusion that there has never been a real 'paradigm' shift in economics comparable to those occasionally experienced in the natural sciences (by paradigm shift I mean a fundamentally different way of looking at the material being studied). The Keynesian revolution came closest to it. Mostly, it has been a story of persistence without progress. This persistence can be explained by the fact that the rise of scientific economics coincided with the rise of capitalism, and the logic of economics as we know it is not easily separable from the arguments in support of capitalism.

Part Three of the book is about theoretical and policy responses to the downturn of 2008. It relates these responses to the historical debates covered in Parts One and Two and shows how they carried the baggage of the past with them. Chapters 8 and 9 show how fiscal and monetary policy met, or failed to meet, the challenge of the downturn. The main theme is that with fiscal policy quickly disabled by ballooning government debts, the task of stabilizing economic life fell to unconventional monetary policy. Chapter 8 examines the theory and practice of 'fiscal consolidation': the effort by governments to liquidate deficits and reduce national debts to restore 'confidence'. Chapter 9 surveys the rationale, and limited success, of 'quantitative easing', the attempt by central banks to offset the deflationary effects of fiscal consolidation by injecting large amounts of money into the financial system. My broad conclusion is that the post-crash monetary–fiscal mix was successful in preventing the collapse of 2008–9 from turning into the rout of another Great Depression, but has not succeeded in restoring durable economic prosperity. Indeed, the methods by which it rescued damaged economies from the financial excesses of the pre-crash years have set the scene for the next financial crash. Our economies are still on life-support systems, and the withdrawal of these will be exceptionally challenging.

Chapters 10, 11 and 12 look at the structural causes of financial instability. Chapter 10 analyses the macroeconomic impact of the growth of inequality of income and wealth. The focus of Chapter 11 is on financial innovation, partly in response to the explosive increase in the demand for credit. Chapter 12 examines the contribution of current account imbalances to the instability of the pre-crash economic system.

And so to the topic of the final part: what is to be done? The central question of political economy today is as it has always been: what does a government need to do to secure the relatively smooth – and socially and morally tolerable – functioning of a decentralized, money-using, largely privately owned economy?

Technical material is presented, as far as possible, in appendices to individual chapters, so as not to break up the flow of ideas.

APPENDIX 1.1: IDEAS, VESTED INTERESTS AND CYCLES

Ideas versus Vested Interests

Keynes ended *The General Theory of Employment, Interest, and Money* with the famous words: 'But, soon or late, it is ideas, not vested interests, which are dangerous for good or evil.'[6] Anyone involved in the production of ideas has to believe this, unless they are being paid by someone to produce the ideas. In today's world, the chief manufactory of ideas is the Academy. Pure research has long been recognized as an independent intellectual pursuit; its hallmark, disinterestedness; its purpose, the search for truth. The pecuniary interest of scholars is not directly involved in either the direction of their enquiry or its results.

At the same time, there is what Joseph Schumpeter called the 'sociology of success'. Put crudely, why are some ideas acceptable, and others rejected or marginalized? In the natural sciences this question is relatively easy to answer: newer ideas bring us closer to reality than the older ones. For this reason, quantum physics replaced classical physics. Reality is unchanging, only the theory changes as it improves our understanding of reality. Predictive power is the ultimate test of the truth of a scientific hypothesis.

In social sciences this is much less true. The natural world does not interfere with one's observation of it; the social world does. It is the changeability of the object being studied which demarcates social sciences from natural sciences. Social reality is constantly shifting, problems crucial at one time become irrelevant at another. As a result, propositions in social science do not satisfy the 'universality criterion'. They are limited in time and place. As Amir Kumar Dasgupta points out, theories in economics are independent of each other, they do not supersede each other.[7] Theories in the social sciences cannot be successfully confirmed or falsified, except briefly. Progress in economics consists of greater precision in stating ideas, not the greater explanatory power of the ideas themselves; and the precision may be at the expense of the explanation. In economics, much more than in physics, the research agenda and structure of power within the profession reflect the structure of power outside it. Economic research programmes have the character of ideologies. And this, of course, was precisely Marx's contention when he wrote: 'What else does the history of ideas prove, than that intellectual production changes in proportion as material production is changed?'[8]

The relationship between ideas, circumstances and power is one of the most complicated questions in social science. Ideas are not at the mercy of circumstances in any straightforward way. The disciplines which produce theories exhibit stability through time, in their concepts, techniques and language. That is why paradigm shifts are rare. It is true that disciplines turn to new topics. But there is no need to relate all new topics to changes in the world. Theorists might simply get bored with the old topics, feeling that debate about them has reached a dead end. Change of topic is also connected with generational change within a discipline.

It is nearer to our theme to say that ideas change when large facts of the world change. Dasgupta talks of 'epochs of economic theory'. He wrote: 'A system of economic theory evolves in response to questions that are provoked by a given set of circumstances in the economy. As circumstances change, or people's attitude to them changes, questions are revised, and a new system springs up.'⁹ Dasgupta is right to distinguish between changes in circumstances and changes in people's attitudes to these changes. A large shock can upset existing ideas, and policies based on them. But the nature of the adjustment of the ideas and policies is not determined. The Great Depression of the 1930s, coming on top of the First World War, benefitted rival claims to the liberal succession in the different forms of communism, fascism and Keynesian social democracy. The travails of the world economy since 2008 have led to outbreaks of populism of both the left and right, whose ideological and political potential is as yet undetermined.

Thus there is no direct relationship between ideas and problems. Facts can be interpreted in different ways. He who controls the interpretation controls the story. This brings us to the question of power.

Adapting Steven Lukes, one may think of ideas as a form of 'soft power', which structure our debates about reality.¹⁰ Alternatively, and more comprehensively, they may be seen as shaping our consciousness – the way we interpret our world.

Ideas are therefore an independent source of authority. Practical men – politicians, businessmen, civil servants – are consumers, not producers, of ideas. This gives the producers of ideas considerable latitude vis-à-vis their users. The vested interests are in no position – even were they capable of it – to dictate the precise form of the intellectual defence offered for their practices. Thus the economist's justification of the free market is likely to be both more general and also more circumscribed than that offered by the business class. For example, economists have almost always opposed protectionism and monopoly: business has generally been in favour. Ideas are thus capable of making self-interest seem more enlightened.

The fact that ideas are produced in non-profitmaking institutions doesn't, though, dispose of the question of the hard power behind the soft power. Who finances the business schools that produce the MBAs of contemporary business life? Who finances the dissemination of ideas in the media and think-tanks? What are the incentives facing the producers, disseminators and popularizers of ideas even in a society in which discussion is 'free'? In short, what is the agenda of business?

One must avoid over-simplifying. It is much harder – and I would say fruitless – to try to relate philosophical, artistic and literary productions to the structures of power. They are just as likely to be critiques of the status quo as homages to it, even though many subtle and not-so-subtle mechanisms, social and pecuniary, exist, for co-opting cultural elites into the business system.[11] More importantly, the cultural critique of capitalism, while persistent and often profound, has had very little influence on economics and economic policy. Nor is the state simply (or always) an agent of the bourgeoisie. Notionally, at least, it stands for the public interest. There is a bigger role for 'public intellectuals' in a mixed economy of public and private sectors than in one in which business calls the shots.

Assertion of the independence of ideas is a necessary modification of crude Marxism, and one which I dare say Marx himself would have accepted. Nevertheless, in the Marxist scheme, the intellectual class, like the state, attains only 'relative autonomy', and ideas rarely overturn the perception or promotion of self-interest, however much they may modify its expression. Practical men like nothing better than to have their prejudices dressed up in scientific language. Ultimately, the ideas in power serve the interests of the class in power; since the 1980s this has been overwhelmingly the financial class.

Cycles

Economics, taking its cue from physics, is an equilibrium system. Disturbances are said to be brief and self-correcting. But economists, as well as historians, have been fascinated by the rhythmic character of economic life, the waves of innovation and destruction, the rise and fall of systems of political economy. The most famous economic theory of cycles is the Kondratiev cycle, a long wave of forty or fifty years, which starts with a cluster of new technologies and exhausts itself when they have been used up. Schumpeter drew on this idea in his depiction of capitalism's cycles of creation and destruction. Within the long cycles are shorter cycles of boom and bust, lasting eight to ten years. Lacking proper scientific explanation (Paul Samuelson called cycle theories 'science fiction'), cycles have nevertheless had a great influence on macroeconomic policy. Typical macroeconomic constructions, such as the 'cyclically adjusted budget deficit', refer explicitly to short cycles of definite duration, which oscillate round some 'normal' or 'long-run' situation.

Historical cycles refer to disturbances of a moral/social, rather than technological, equilibrium. That is to say, they embed technological innovation within the wider frame of political and social change. Societies are said to swing like pendulums between alternating phases of vigour and decay, progress and reaction, prodigality and puritanism. Each expansive movement produces a crisis of excess that leads to a reaction. The equilibrium position is hard to achieve and is always unstable.

In his *Cycles of American History* (1986) Arthur Schlesinger Jr defined a political economy cycle as 'a continuing shift in national involvement between public purpose and private interest'. The swing he identified was between 'liberal' (what we would call social democratic) and 'conservative' epochs. The idea of the 'crisis' is central to both. Liberal periods succumb to the corruption of power, as idealists yield to time-servers, and conservative arguments against rent-seeking win the day. But the conservative era then succumbs to a corruption of money, as financiers use the freedom of deregulation to rip off the public. A crisis of under-regulated markets presages the return to a social democratic era.

This idea fits the American historical narrative tolerably well. It also makes sense globally. The era of 'conservative' economics opened with the publication of Adam Smith's *Wealth of Nations* in 1776. Yet despite the early intellectual ascendancy of free trade, it took a major crisis – the Irish potato famine of the early 1840s – to produce an actual shift in policy: the repeal of the Corn Laws in Britain in 1846 ushered in the free trade era.

In the 1870s, the pendulum started to swing back to what the historian A. V. Dicey called the 'age of collectivism'. The major crisis that triggered this was the first great global depression, produced by a collapse in food prices. It was a severe enough shock to produce a major shift in political economy. This came in two waves. First, all the major countries except Britain put up tariffs to protect agricultural and industrial employment. (Britain relied on mass emigration to eliminate rural unemployment.) Second, all industrial countries except the United States started schemes of social insurance to protect their citizens against life's hazards. The Great Depression of 1929–32 produced a second wave of collectivism, now associated with the 'Keynesian' use of fiscal and monetary policy to maintain full employment. Most capitalist countries nationalized key industries. Roosevelt's New Deal in the United States regulated banking and the power utilities, and belatedly embarked on the road of social security. International capital movements were severely controlled everywhere.

This pendulum movement was not all one way, or else the West would have ended up with communism, which was the fate of large parts of the globe. Even before the crisis of collectivism in the 1970s, a swing back had started, as trade, after 1945, was progressively freed from tariffs and capital movements liberalized. The rule was free trade abroad and social democracy at home.

The Bretton Woods system, set up with Keynes's help in 1944, was the international expression of liberal/social democratic political economy. It aimed to free foreign trade after the freeze of the 1930s, by providing an environment that reduced incentives for economic nationalism. At its heart was a system of fixed exchange rates, subject to agreed adjustment, to avoid competitive currency depreciation.

Liberalism, or social democracy, unravelled with stagflation and ungovernability in the 1970s. This broadly fits Schlesinger's notion of the 'corruption of power'. Keynesian/social democratic policymakers succumbed to hubris, an intellectual corruption that convinced them they possessed the knowledge and the tools to manage and control the economy and society from the top. This was the malady against which Hayek had inveighed in his classic *The Road to Serfdom* (1944). The attempt in the 1970s to control inflation by wage and price controls led directly to a 'crisis of governability', as trade unions, particularly in Britain, refused to accept them. Large state subsidies to producer groups, both public and private, fed the typical corruptions of behaviour identified by the New Right: rent-seeking, moral hazard and free-riding. Palpable evidence of government failure obliterated earlier memories of market failure. The new generation of economists abandoned Keynes and, with the help of sophisticated mathematics, reinvented the classical economics of the self-correcting market. Battered by the crises of the 1970s, governments caved in to the 'inevitability' of free market forces. The swing back became worldwide with the collapse of communism in 1989–90.

A conspicuous casualty of the reversal was the Bretton Woods system, which succumbed in the 1970s to the refusal of the US to curb its domestic spending. Currencies were set free to float, and controls on international capital flows were progressively lifted. This heralded a wholesale shift to globalization. Globalization was, in concept, not unattractive. The idea was that the nation state – which had been responsible for so much organized violence and wasteful spending – was on its way out, to be replaced by the global market. The promise of globalization was set out by the (highly sceptical) Canadian philosopher John Ralston Saul, in 2004:

> That in the future, economics, not politics or arms, would determine the course of human events. That freed markets would quickly establish natural international balances, impervious to the old boom-and-bust cycles. That the growth in international trade, as a result of lowering barriers, would unleash an economic-social tide that would raise all ships, whether of our western poor or of the developing world in general. That prosperous markets would turn dictatorships into democracies.[12]

Today we are living through a crisis of conservative economics. The banking collapse of 2008 brought to a head a growing dissatisfaction with the corruption of money. Neo-conservatism had sought to justify fabulous rewards to a financial plutocracy, while median incomes stagnated or even fell. In the name of efficiency it had promoted the offshoring of millions of jobs, the undermining of national communities, and the rape of nature. Such a system needed to be fabulously successful to command allegiance. We shall see in the next few years whether the repairs made to the economic structure after the collapse have been sufficient to arrest the swing back to collectivism and nationalism that has already started.

PART ONE

History of Economic Thought

In 1844, John Stuart Mill published his *Essays on Some Unsettled Questions of Political Economy*. In his sights was a famous doctrine, Say's Law, which then defined – and for many economists still does define – the central theorem of macroeconomics: supply creates its own demand. Everything that is produced is bound to be consumed, because otherwise there would be no point in producing it. The problem that obsessed the first generation of 'scientific' economists was the pressure of population on resources, especially food supply. Such a world of scarcity seemed to rule out the possibility of what Mill called a 'general glut' of commodities.[1] The problem was a general glut of people. Yet economic life exhibited cycles of boom and bust. In the bust period, masses of commodities were produced *for which there was no market*.

How could this experience of the real world, Mill asked, be reconciled with a doctrine which held that a general surplus of goods was impossible?

Mill argued as follows. Say's Law depended on 'a supposition of a state of barter'. In barter, buying and selling are 'simultaneously confounded'. But money offers the possibility of postponing purchases. Instead of spending money people may want to hoard it. Such postponement of purchase may arise from a 'general anxiety'. So all that is produced for consumption need not be bought. However, if money is a commodity, like gold, an excess demand for money will lead to resources being switched to gold production. Thus Say's Law, that 'every increase of production, if distributed without miscalculation among all kinds of produce in the proportion which private interest would dictate, creates, or rather constitutes, its own demand', was valid as a general principle. By this fudge, Mill escaped from the dilemma he had posed.[2]

Nevertheless, his essay raised the most fundamental issue in macroeconomics: the relationship between money and the production economy. Following hard on its heels was a second issue, also raised by Mill, which lies at the heart of macroeconomic policy: how to stop money 'getting out of order'. The two are interlinked, in the sense that they involve the conditions under which money can be made to serve rather than disturb production. They are unsettled in the sense that people have been arguing about them ever since money started to be used. Our own attempt to make sense of these arguments takes us back to the origins of money itself. Why did people start using money? Was it inseparable from production, or was it something added on? What is its place in the scheme of social life?

I

The Mysteries of Money:
A Short History

'Money's a matter of functions four,
A medium, a measure, a standard, a store.'

Nineteenth-century jingle

'[Money] only exerts a distinct and independent influence of
its own when it gets out of order.'

J. S. Mill, 1848[1]

I. THE CLASSICAL DICHOTOMY

The story starts with the classical dichotomy: the division of economics into the theory of value and the theory of money. The dominant
question in economics has been: why do things cost what they do?
The first generation of scientific economists held that the price of
things was determined by the number of hours' work it took to produce a quantity of stuff. A later generation concluded that the price
of goods is determined by their value to the consumer. The cost of
labour adapts itself to the preferences of buyers. Value is simply
market price. This is today's theory. The point to note, for our purposes, is that neither of these explanations of value involves money.
Goods cost goods: they are bartered for each other. Money, according to the classical story, plays no role in the determination of 'barter'
prices, i.e. there is no desire for money as such.

The theory of money is concerned with something else: what determines the value or price of money, or its inverse, the general or average

price level? The answer given by the elementary textbook is its quantity. The more money there is, the more goods as a whole will cost; the less there is, the lower the average price. The important claim of the theory of money is that the quantity of money makes no difference to the *relative prices* of goods and services. All it does is to explain the average price of all of them, and that affects nothing 'real'.

So what is the role of money in this story? The answer is it 'oils the wheels of trade'. It enables more trade to take place than otherwise would have. But it has no effect on the terms of trade. In Aristotelian terms, it is 'barren': it creates and destroys nothing. Today's textbooks on banking and finance do little more than echo Aristotle. Banks simply 'intermediate' between buyers and sellers. This arcane phraseology serves the protective purpose of disguising the actual power of finance – and financiers – in the economy.

Philosophically, the underlying idea of the classical dichotomy goes back to Descartes' famous distinction between appearance and reality, and his rejection of induction as the method of discovering truth. In medieval times, the general view was that the way things appear is the way they are: we observe God in nature. This was what Descartes rejected. Observation can reveal only how things appear to be; behind the appearance lies the reality. The task of science is to get 'under the surface of things'. Adopting this standpoint, 'scientific' economics set itself the task of penetrating beyond the money values that we observe to the underlying world of real values. In the persistent language of economics, money is a 'veil' that hides from us the knowledge of real relationships. Economics must strip away the veil of money; or, more accurately, make the veil transparent, so we never confuse appearance and reality.[2] The Cartesian distinction runs from David Hume to Milton Friedman, and underpins the axiomatic structure of mainstream economics.

In the 1930s, the economist John Maynard Keynes challenged the classical dichotomy with what he called 'the monetary theory of production'. He wrote, in 1933:

> [In the classical view] money . . . is not supposed to affect the essential nature of the transaction . . . between real things, or to modify the

motives and decisions of the parties to it. Money, that is to say, is employed, but is treated as being in some sense *neutral* . . .

The theory which I desiderate would deal, in contradiction to this, with an economy in which money plays a part of its own and affects motives and decisions and is, in short, one of the operative factors in the situation, so that the course of events cannot be predicted . . . without a knowledge of the behaviour of money between the first state and the last. And it is this which we ought to mean when we talk of a *monetary* economy.[3]

In other words, we cannot separate the theory of value from the theory of money. Money enters into the 'motives' for trade. Goods cost money, not goods. So it is the 'behaviour of money' in the time between trades that we have to attend to. Money cannot be 'neutral', in the required sense that its value has no effect on the prices at which people want to trade, because the only prices people know are money prices. By the same token there is no such thing as a barter equilibrium – what goods would exchange for in the absence of money. There is only a monetary equilibrium.

So what affects the behaviour of money? This should be a key point of enquiry into the behaviour of a monetary economy. Why did money come to exist? What purpose does it serve?

II. THE ORIGINS OF MONEY

No one knows exactly where, how or why money started, so people are free to invent stories. The main aim of the storytellers has been to elucidate, by reference to a hypothetical past, the nature of money in their own time. Two such stories have dominated the literature of money. Adam Smith's eighteenth-century story tried to explain why money consisted of gold and silver. The chartalist theory, dating from the end of the nineteenth century, tried to explain why money consisted mainly of credit. We can call these the metallist theory and the credit theory.

Adam Smith's story, which goes back to Aristotle, is still the textbook favourite. It is certainly the easiest story to understand, which accounts for its popularity. Before money, it is claimed, there was barter – direct exchange of goods for goods. But barter requires a 'double-coincidence' of wants. Both partners need to want what the other has, at the same time. So money was invented to enable one of the parties to pay the other in something which the other could use to buy something else. Adam Smith conjectured that the 'something' which became the 'medium of exchange' must have been 'some one commodity . . . [which] few people would be likely to refuse in exchange for the produce of their industry'.[4] Though cattle, salt, shells and the like were used, metals, and especially the precious metals gold and silver, came to be preferred, for their divisibility, but even more for their durability and scarcity. It was these qualities which fitted them to be the measure of perishable things.

At first 'rude bars' of iron, copper, gold and silver sufficed, because of their greater relative stability of value. To avoid having to weigh a lump of metal for each transaction, it became customary to affix a public stamp upon certain quantities of metals, certifying their weight and quality. 'Hence the origin of coined money, and of those public offices called mints.' The essence of this fable is that though it was convenient to make contracts in money, behind the veil of the contracts were real things being traded for each other at their real (i.e. barter) prices.

The theory of the bartering savage is heavily indebted to the classical anthropology of Adam Smith's day, at the heart of which is the figure of *homo economicus*, who pursues his self-interest in isolation from society. That this still underlies neo-classical psychology is made clear in Paul Samuelson's famous textbook, where we read: 'A great debt of gratitude is owed to the first two ape-men who suddenly perceived that each could be made better off by giving up some of one good in exchange for some of another.'[5] Most economists have favoured the bartering savage story, because it leaves out society and government.

By contrast, the *credit* story, which took root at the end of the 1800s, makes money start life as a *debt contract* – a promise to pay in the future for something bought today. The credibility of the promise depends on trust in the debtor. But trust is not bestowed on a stranger, so it is the existence of a social bond which makes money possible. The language of money is the language of promises: 'my word is my bond'. As Alfred Innes writes: 'By buying we become debtors and by selling we become creditors.'[6] The credit theory of money does not automatically upset the classical dichotomy, if it is assumed that credit is simply an advance on money, which is itself an advance on goods. But it greatly weakens it by placing expectations at the centre of its account of 'real' transactions.

This seemingly recondite dispute about the origins of money reflects a deep divergence about the purpose of money. Was money to be thought of primarily as a means of effecting two transactions barely separated in time? Or was it also, and distinctively, to be seen as a link between the present and the future? The first led to the view that the only important demand for money was as a 'means of payment'; the second that its significant economic role was as a 'store of value'. It was the motives for holding money independently of the desire for goods – the positive preference for liquidity – which interested Keynes. The 'fetish for liquidity', he reasoned, could have only one cause: uncertainty about the future. For if everyone knew for certain what the morrow would bring, there would be no rational reason for hoarding lumps of metal or pieces of paper. In fact, there would be no need for money at all. So, the dispute about the origins of money was, at its heart, an epistemological one: how predictable were future events?

III. THE VALUE OF MONEY

As one might suppose, the metallist and credit theories give different answers to the question of what gives money its value.

According to the metallist theory, the value of money inheres in the value of the thing of which it is composed, namely the metal. The 'essential' value of gold and silver is determined by properties intrinsic to them, such as their attractiveness, scarcity and durability. In the credit theory, money is simply a token of what is promised; its value is conferred by the degree of trust in the promise of its issuer.

The credit theory offers three possible issuers of money. By far the most important is the chartalist theory. This holds that the main issuer of money is the state. According to Georg Friedrich Knapp (1905) and Innes (1913), the state issues receipts (tokens of liability) for goods it commandeers. Coins (with the head of the ruler on them) are stamped tokens of state debt. These receipts circulate as currency, because the state's ability to ensure that taxes are paid in the money it itself issues makes its 'promises to pay' uniquely reliable. Adam Smith acknowledged that:

> A prince, who should enact that a certain proportion of his taxes should be paid in a paper money of a certain kind, might thereby give a certain value to this paper money; even though the term of its final discharge and redemption should depend altogether on the will of the prince.

Similarly, Innes argued that 'the redemption of government debt by taxation is the basic law of coinage and of any issue of government "money" in whatever form'.[7]

The chartalist story reflects the fact that the earliest economies of which we have record – those of the Egyptian and Mesopotamian empires, a few thousand years before the birth of Christ – were tributary economies, economies in which the flow of goods and services was mainly between rulers and ruled. The subject owed the ruler tribute; the ruler owed the subject services in return. For example, in Egypt, a certain proportion of agricultural produce was delivered to the temple granaries, from which were paid the 'wages' of workers employed on public works, such as the building of pyramids and temples. One of the earliest purposes of money was to make it easier to 'render tribute [taxes] unto Caesar' (Matthew 22: 17–21). Reciprocal obligations could be discharged by tokens of purchasing power, rather than by actual transfers of physical goods, the tokens expressing customary valuations of the physical obligations. If this model of the earliest economies is accepted, the origin of money is related primarily to the operations of public finance, not of markets. Promises come before coins: coins are merely tokens of promises.

Neo-chartalists of 'modern monetary theory', such as Warren Mosler and Randall Wray, go further: the state doesn't need to tax in order to spend; it needs to spend in order to tax. Neo-chartalists tantalize you with such questions as: how can you pay taxes if the government has not already spent the money? The state's debts are the source of its revenue: the more it spends the more revenue it can collect. This is the simplest justification for deficit finance in a slump: the debt creates the revenue to discharge it.[8] It is curiously blind to the thought that people may choose to withhold the taxes they owe the state if they disapprove of the purposes for which they are being raised.

The state is not the only possible issuer of debt. Any debt may serve as a means of payment if the security (trust) in the debtor's promises is great enough. Privately created liabilities have always circulated alongside public liabilities. Of these by far the most important are the debts of banks. Banks would issue loans to borrowers in the form of promissory notes (notes promising to pay cash on demand) backed by their deposits. These notes could circulate as currency. However, the liabilities of banks were never as secure as those of the state, because of the danger of a run on the bank if the bank was seen to be over-indebted. The value of the notes, in short, depended on trust in the solvency of the bank.

Supporters of the credit theory, like Felix Martin, deny the state or banks an exclusive role in determining the value of money. Its value, they say, is negotiated between creditors and debtors, and determined by the balance of power between the two.[9] Creditors can keep up the value of money if they are in a position to enforce full payment of the debts owing to them; debtors can reduce it by evading repayment.

The metallic or essentialist theory of money should not be dismissed too readily. Money may be a token of trust, but not all monies are equally trustworthy. Behind the supremacy of gold lies the fact that it *can't go bad*. It is the ultimate guarantor of value. Since gold disappeared as money there has always been something unreliable about the currency.

Even when state money became paper, and therefore intrinsically worthless, it was thought desirable to maintain belief that government notes – promises to pay the bearer – were in fact debt certificates backed by gold. Until 1971, the value of the American dollar was widely believed to depend on its convertibility into gold, as though the value of gold guaranteed the value of paper dollars. After 1971, the central bank's high-powered money was deemed 'good as gold'. Monetary history is full of such fictions, but all fictions have their basis in experience and human psychology.

IV. CREDITORS AND DEBTORS

There has always been a tension between the convenience of having a fixed, unchangeable yardstick of value and the desire of creditors and debtors to have a money which suits their own interests. This is the class-struggle theory of money. In the industrial age, the conflict between capitalists and workers overlapped the older conflict between creditors and debtors without ever replacing it.

To historical sociologists like David Graeber, much of the history of the world can be interpreted in terms of the struggle between creditors and debtors. Whatever the loan or wage contract says, there is always a risk in an uncertain world that promises will be devalued or revalued; hence the intensity of the conflict to control the value of the promises.[10]

The state has only a limited incentive to guarantee the value of money. The reason is that it can always produce the money necessary to defray its expenses, either by debasing the coinage when money is metal or by printing more of it when it is paper. So, throughout history rulers have cheated on the amount of money they were manufacturing. While claiming to maintain the value of money, they have reduced the weight and fineness of the gold and silver in their coins, or issued too much paper. By imposing an 'inflation tax' they can get hold of extra real resources without openly raising taxes. 'A government can live by this means', wrote Keynes, 'when it can live by no other. It is the form of taxation which the public find it hardest to evade and which even the weakest government can enforce, when it can enforce nothing else.'[11]

Throughout history too, reformers have directed their efforts to preventing the state from debasing the coinage: in Ricardo's words, inflation 'enriches . . . the idle and profligate debtor at the expense of the industrious and frugal creditor'.[12] The main purpose of essentialist monetary thought was to stop the state from debasing the coinage. That is why it insisted that the value of money lay in the value of the metal in the coin.

A good example of this argument was the claim by the seventeenth-century mercantilist William Petty that a reduction in the silver content of the coin was bound to be self-defeating. It would diminish the amount of goods people were willing to give up for it, except among 'such Fools as take Money by its name, and not by its weight and fineness'.[13] Petty was wrong. The debased coins issued by the royal mint continued to circulate at their face value. The key to their acceptability lay in the fact that they were the only legal tender. As Aquinas had realized four centuries before Petty, money was the 'one thing by which everything should be measured . . . not by its nature, but because it has been made a measure by men'.[14] The convenience of using the state's money as a means of payment for goods and obligations outweighed the losses, actual and potential, suffered by creditors through debasement, unless the debasement was carried to extremes, at which point the state's money ceased to be used for any purpose.

By the start of the nineteenth century it was realized that a stronger defence against 'over-issue' of money was needed. This could be secured by limiting the quantity of the state's money to the quantity of gold bullion in the country – the subject of Chapter 2 – and placing strict limits on the operations of the state itself. If the state could be confined to a narrow range of activities, its incentive to expand the money supply would be correspondingly circumscribed. This was the main object of the Victorian fiscal constitution, which we describe in Chapter 4. The rule that the state's spending should be annually balanced by taxation at the lowest possible level was designed precisely to limit the state's ability to 'debase the coinage'.

The other main danger to the value of money was the clamour of the debtor class to be relieved of its debts.

In *Hamlet*, Shakespeare has Polonius enjoin his son, Laertes:

> Neither a borrower nor a lender be;
> For loan oft loses both itself and friend,
> And borrowing dulls the edge of husbandry.

Polonius's advice, more recently echoed by Angela Merkel, has always been an old wives' tale, if applied within a single jurisdiction. The chief way of starting or carrying on a business is by borrowing money, despite its fearful moral pitfalls. Polonius's instruction makes a lot more sense if applied across country borders, because that raises much more acutely the question of the security of loans.

The age-old question for monetary policy was, whose interests should it protect? Those of lenders or borrowers, creditors or debtors? Creditors demanded of money above all that it keep its value between transactions. But debtors simply wanted to have enough money to enable them to carry on their business, and expected the state, the bank or the money-lender to produce it. These requirements were far from coinciding. Creditors are natural essentialists – they want principal and interest to be paid back in full-weight coin. Debtors are natural nominalists – they want to pay back less than they borrowed if they can.

Because of their importance in stabilizing expectations, promises need the support of both punishment and forgiveness.

Creditors assert a moral right to be repaid in money of equal value to that which they lent and a moral duty of the debtor to repay it, at whatever sacrifice. The root of credit is the Latin word *credo*, 'I believe'. A lender is someone who trusts that the borrower will pay them back in money of equivalent value.[15] Lenders assert that, without such trust, lending will cease, and trade will languish. To ensure the necessary trust, creditors have always created as many obstacles to default as government or convention allow. They have kept interest rates as high as possible against risk of default. They have imprisoned or enslaved defaulting debtors, or taken their property. They have invaded, or refused loans to, states that repudiate their debts. Economists talk of the 'moral hazard' of making life too easy for debtors. The more cynical see loans to impecunious debtors as a kind of asset-stripping, a substitute for armies to obtain land and resources.

However, the debtor position is not without moral support. All religions have supported 'debt forgiveness' and abhorred 'debt-bondage'. It was customary for new rulers to declare a debt amnesty, as in the Jubilee law of the Babylonians, recorded in the Bible. Solon (*c*.638–558 BC) was the famed lawgiver who cancelled the debts of Athenian farmers. (Throughout history farmers have been the biggest debtor class, because of the seasonal character of their business and the unreliability of harvests.) The line in the Lord's Prayer – 'Forgive us our sins as we forgive those who have sinned against us' – can be rendered: 'Forgive us our debts, as we also forgive those in debt to us.'[16] The recent bail-outs of bankrupt banks are examples of debt forgiveness.

Shakespeare vividly dramatized the moral resistance to the creditor who claims his 'pound of flesh' for failing to repay a loan. In *The Merchant of Venice*, the money-lender Shylock suggests as a 'merry sport' that, in the event of a default, the merchant-borrower Antonio must satisfy him with a pound of his own flesh, 'to be cut off and taken in what part of your body pleaseth me'. Then the joke goes horribly wrong. Antonio's ships carrying his goods for sale are wrecked; he cannot repay the loan on the appointed day, and Shylock claims his forfeit. Shylock's downfall – he loses all his money – expresses the popular attitude towards the money-lender, who, in medieval Europe, was often a Jew. Anti-Semitism was part of a generalized debtor hostility to the rentier class – the class that lives off interest and rents.

The position of debtors was further strengthened by the Abrahamic-Christian prohibition of usury, or taking interest on the loan of money. Anti-usury laws ran from the earliest times until the nineteenth century (in Britain they were only abolished in 1835), and still exist in Islamic countries. Medieval folk believed usurers were prematurely carried off to hell, or that their money turned to withered leaves. They occupy the seventh circle of hell in Dante's *Divine Comedy*.

Two moral considerations lay behind the anti-usury legislation. The first stemmed from the idea that a debt contract is a kind of unfair trade. Since the lender is nearly always in a stronger position than the borrower, it was felt that the borrower needed protection from the lender's rapacity. Put simply, a farmer faced with a ruined harvest, or a trader with the loss of his goods, may have to borrow to stay alive, however high the interest he has to pay on the loan; a lender is under no compulsion to lend and, unchecked by law, may ask whatever interest he wants for loaning out his money. Therefore state and custom tried to keep the interest on lending money as low as possible.

But, secondly, there was also a long-standing moral hostility to 'making money out of money'. This goes back to Aristotle's view that money is, by its nature, 'sterile', so that interest on money rewarded no productive activity.

Scientific economics dropped the moral taboos and legal restrictions against taking interest. It treats interest as a justified payment for the cost of saving – denying oneself present consumption – and the risk of investment. If interest were denied or limited, there would be less incentive to save, and a disincentive to lend, therefore less investment and slower growth of wealth.

Modern developments have eased the intensity of the ancient struggle between creditors and debtors. Stock markets and limited liability have provided an alternative to bank borrowing for raising capital, and the penalties for default have been progressively relaxed. We no longer demand labour services of defaulting debtors, or send them to prison. Debt-bondage is a shadow of its old self.

With the rise of modern tax systems, the state's need to issue debt to finance its expenditure has also declined. Its incentive to debase the coinage therefore decreased. Because governments had less recourse to their subjects for loans, people became much more willing to hold government debt. The nineteenth century was the golden age of the bondholder, with the state paying its debts in full-value money. This cosy world was horribly upset by the two world wars of the twentieth century and the triumph of democracy. The state became a huge net borrower for the first time since the Napoleonic wars, and the new voters came from the debtor, not creditor, class. Following the Second World War the debasement of money – inflation – was more or less continuous. But in the 1980s there came a reversal. Inflation was reined in, as the creditor class regained something of its old ascendancy. As unemployment rose and wages stagnated, loan sharks offering 'pay day loans' at usurious interest rates proliferated. In the Eurozone debt crisis of 2010–12, a 'troika' of creditors, in a return to nineteenth-century methods, demanded of Greece islands, gas extraction rights and museums – their 'pound of flesh' – as surety for loans they knew would never be repaid.

The truth is that any monetary policy will always produce winners and losers, depending on the terms of access to credit. The modern answer – placing monetary policy in the hands of an 'independent' central bank – does not make money 'neutral', because monetary policy is bound to have distributional effects.

V. THE ORIGINS OF THE QUANTITY THEORY OF MONEY

The Quantity Theory of Money is more accurately termed the Quantity of Money Theory of Inflation, because it was invented to explain inflation, and (much later) became the basis of policy to prevent it. Although both inflation and deflation are consequences of having the wrong quantity of money, the quantity theory was never specifically aimed at explaining deflation, deflation being considered an inevitable consequence of the previous inflation. Therefore, if you could prevent inflation, you would automatically prevent the deflation that followed the pricking of the inflationary bubble. In our own day, this argument is associated with Friedrich Hayek.

It was the sixteenth-century French philosopher Jean Bodin who turned the common understanding of inflation as 'too much money chasing too few goods' into something like a theory, in order to explain the century-long rise in prices which, starting in the middle of the 1500s, ran parallel with the importation into Europe of newly discovered and mined silver from South America. The influx of silver from South America, which started in 1550, was the first great *monetary* disturbance of modern times, the price level in Spain doubling between 1550 and 1600.[17] This unsettled all customary relations of the medieval world, and gave birth to speculation, both intellectual and financial.

In his *Réponse aux paradoxes du M. de Malestroict* (1568), Bodin wrote that 'The principal & almost only [cause of rising prices] is the abundance of gold & silver, which is today much greater in this kingdom [France] than it was four hundred years ago.'[18] This conjecture is said to be the start of the quantity theory of money.[19] However, an early version of it may already have existed in China in the middle of the fourth century BC.[20]

Bodin's conjecture seemed reasonable enough. If there is suddenly more money to spend on a fixed supply of goods it seems obvious that competition to buy them will force up their prices; the same competition with less money will cause their prices to fall.

This condition has been the basis of the quantity theory ever since. However, though in pre-industrial societies there was little economic growth, the supply of food would vary with the harvests. Prices of foodstuffs would go up and down without any prior impulse from money. It is true that more money would be needed to pay the higher prices. But it is precisely at this point that the role of money as *credit* enters the picture, as in the phrase 'buying goods on tick'. Here money functions simply a means of account, without any physical substance. Medieval economies responded to the dearth of coin by expanding the supply of 'tick money'. This then would be paid back in cash when prices came down.[21]

The invention – in fact rediscovery – of banking in northern Italy in late medieval times was key to making the supply of money more 'elastic', especially for rulers faced with rising costs and declining revenues.

Banking started up in Florence around 1300, the era of Dante. This financial innovation was soon followed by banking crises – the Bank of Bardi and that of the Peruzzi family crashed in 1345. 'Early banks', explains Hicks, 'were very *unsound*, over-anxious to accept deposits, and not yet conscious of the conditions under which alone it can be prudent to push such deposits to profitable use.'[22] What's changed?

The way modern banking grew up has been described by Nicholas Kaldor:

> Originally goldsmiths (who possessed strong rooms for holding gold and other valuables) developed the facility of accepting gold for safe-keeping and issued deposit certificates to the owners. The latter found it convenient to make payments by means of these certificates, thereby saving the time and trouble of taking gold coins out of the strong room only to have them re-deposited by the recipient of the payment, who was likely to have much the same incentive of [sic] keeping valuables deposited for safekeeping. The next step in the evolution towards a credit-money system was when the goldsmiths found it convenient to lend money as well as to accept it on deposit for safekeeping. For the purpose of lending they had to issue their own promissory notes to pay cash to the bearer (as distinct from a named depositor) on demand; with this latter development the goldsmith became bankers, i.e., financial intermediaries between lenders and borrowers.[23]

The language of banking – 'taking' deposits and then 'lending' them out – reflects the original function of banks as storehouses and intermediaries. But most 'deposits' today are created by the banks themselves when they make loans. These loans are often 'unsecured': made on trust in the borrower's promise to repay. The loans, when spent, create fresh deposits, out of which new loans can be made. Unlike the quantity theory of money, which is a 'supply of money' story, the credit theory of money is a 'demand for loans' tale. The amount of money fluctuates with the demand for loans and the creditworthiness of borrowers; and both fluctuate with the state of business.

There has never been complete agreement about what constitutes the 'money supply'. Today most money is credit, without physical existence: it is created by electronic transfer between deposits. The state's paper money ('cash') is only a tiny fraction of a country's payments system. Monetary economists distinguish between cash, whether held under the bed, in current accounts or by banks as reserves, and money loaned to customers by banks, held in deposit accounts. They call the first 'high powered' or 'narrow' money, and the second 'broad' money, and distinguish them by somewhat confusing and inconsistent acronyms: Mo, M1, M2, M3, M4.[24] To preserve the fiction that commercial banks cannot create money 'out of nowhere', orthodox theory posits a mathematical relationship between narrow and broad money, known as the 'money multiplier'. This fiction persists to this day in mainstream academic economics, though central banks themselves have never paid much attention to it.[25]

Thus the question of whether the source of money is external to the economy (*exogenous* in economics-speak) or created and destroyed in the course of making transactions (*endogenous*) remains unsettled. A reasonable way of looking at the matter is to say that endogenous money is the rule, with exogenous money as a windfall – such as happened to Europe with the discovery of silver in South America.

VI. THE DEMAND FOR MONEY

The quantity theory of money ignored the possibility that people might want to hoard money. Economists say there is no 'demand for money' as such, only for consumables. They have usually treated the demand curve for money as the demand curve for goods and services. It slopes downwards, as the more of something one has, the less one is said to want it. Saving is construed as a demand, not for money but for future goods, with the rate of interest measuring the discounted present value of the future stream of anticipated utility.

But money, said the philosopher John Locke, thinking of gold and silver, 'is a lasting thing a man may keep without spoiling'.[26] By the same token, it can keep without spending. But why should anyone want to *keep* money? Gold and silver were used as stores of value (as well as signs of power, prestige and wealth) before they acquired their monetary use as means of exchange. King Midas of the ancient legend hungered after gold, not gold coins.[27] Already in Roman times, India was seen as the 'sink of the world's gold', much of it absorbed in jewellery and display. Its value, that is, was independent of its use as money.

But why should people wish to hoard *money*? Economists have associated the propensity to hoard money with periods of uncertainty and unsettlement. Thus J. B. Say – of the infamous Say's Law, which says that supply creates its own demand – recognized that from time to time 'capitals [may] quietly sleep in the pockets of their proprietors'.[28] It was this propensity which led John Stuart Mill to consider Say's Law an 'unsettled question' in his essay of 1829.[29] Speculators, too, have always known that in disturbed times they can profit from being liquid. Increased propensity to hoard, what Keynes called the 'speculative demand for money', thus arises from increased uncertainty. It slows down the economy by slowing down the spending of money on currently produced goods and diverting it into financial operations.

Thus money earned in producing goods may be unavailable for spending on those goods, causing unemployment. If the government could ensure that all the money earned producing goods was spent on buying them, there need never be unemployment.

VII. MONEY, THE GREAT DECEIVER

The central claim of the classical dichotomy is that the value of money (or *average* level of prices) makes no difference to the relative prices of goods and services. If all prices go up together, it makes no difference to the price *ratios* at which goods exchange. If this is so, attention to the quantity of money might seem redundant. However, experience showed that while the value of money or price *level* itself didn't matter, *changes* in it did. Rising prices were associated with prosperity; falling prices with dearth. This correlation led a group of seventeenth-century thinkers called mercantilists to identify money with wealth. The more money a kingdom had, the wealthier it was; the less, the poorer. The mercantilists were the first to challenge the classical dichotomy – the absolute separation of money from the real economy.

The 'scientific' economists who followed the mercantilists pointed out the flaw in mercantilist reasoning. The association of money with wealth, they said, was the result of 'money illusion'. As the economic historian Eli Heckscher put it: 'Everyone under natural economy (barter) recognized that exchange was the more favourable the larger the amount of goods which could be got in exchange for one's own. But then came the monetary system which drew a "veil of money" over the interconnected factors in exchange.'[30] That money was a veil that obscured accurate knowledge of barter values became a standard trope in classical economics. To remove the veil (or equivalently, to make a money economy behave like a barter economy) was at the heart of the twentieth-century monetary reform movement.

The eighteenth-century philosopher David Hume gave the first precise rendering of the phenomenon of money illusion. It is inserted into his essay on the balance of trade.[31] Here he considers the influential mercantilist argument that a country with no domestic sources of gold and silver needs to aim for a continuous trade surplus, if it is to have enough money to support a growing population. This required restricting imports, and therefore domestic consumption, and aggressively promoting exports, often through wars aimed at excluding competitors from domestic and foreign markets.[32]

Hume demonstrated that the mercantilist attention to the trade balance was fallacious. Trade between two countries, he says, automatically balances itself. This was a logical implication of the barter theory of trade: goods trade for goods. Money does not fundamentally alter the picture. A temporary imbalance between exports and imports produces countervailing gold flows, which, through their effects on price levels (up in the surplus country, down in the deficit country), restores the balance. This is his famous 'price–specie–flow' mechanism. Just as it is impossible to keep water flowing uphill, so 'it is impossible to heap up money, more than any fluid, beyond its proper level'.[33] Hume was the first clearly to identify a payments mechanism that ensured that trade would be balanced. This achievement was crucial to the free trade case developed by Smith and Ricardo.[34]

Hume, however, introduced a critical qualification: in the 'short-run', an inflow of money could, by creating money illusion, stimulate business activity by increasing the rapidity, or velocity, of circulation.[35] This insight made him the originator of the short-run Phillips Curve (see pp. 205–8), later taken up by Milton Friedman. Ever since

Hume, economists have distinguished between the short-run and the long-run effects of economic change, including the effects of policy interventions. The distinction has served to protect the theory of equilibrium, by enabling it to be stated in a form which took some account of reality. In economics, the short-run now typically stands for the period during which a market (or an economy of markets) temporarily deviates from its long-term equilibrium position under the impact of some 'shock', like a pendulum temporarily dislodged from a position of rest. This way of thinking suggests that governments should leave it to markets to discover their natural equilibrium positions. Government interventions to 'correct' deviations will only add extra layers of delusion to the original one. That Hume's distinction between the effects of short-run and long-run changes in the quantity of money destroys the practical utility of the theory for short-run stabilization policy was not realized until much later, and has still not been fully accepted by true believers.

Adam Smith also recognized that a growing economy required that the supply of money should increase roughly in line with demand, if 'the average money price of corn' was to stay the same. That is why he supported the issue of paper money as a supplement to gold money; paper would provide 'a sort of waggon-way through the air, [which enables] the country to convert . . . a great part of its highways into good pastures and corn-fields, and thereby to increase very considerably the annual produce of its land and labour'.[36] Later monetary theorists also recognized that gold money, whose increase depended on the discovery of new gold mines, could not guarantee the desirable stability of the price level. But they went further than Smith in arguing for cutting the link between money and gold completely.

VIII. CONCLUSION

The sketch above has revealed two contrasting patterns in the theory of money, which may be called the 'hard' and 'soft' money schools. They run through the history of monetary thought and policy to our own time.

Figure 1. Beliefs of the hard and soft money schools

Beliefs of the money schools	The two money schools	
	Hard/Metallist	Soft/Nominalist
Origin of money	Barter	Credit
Nature of money	Commodities	Tokens of credit
Value	Intrinsic/Objective	Political/Social
Theory of money	Exogenous	Endogenous
Use of money	Transactions	Transactions/Store of value
Favours	The creditor	The debtor
Epistemology	Risk	Uncertainty

The next two chapters will show how these contrasting clusters of thinking worked themselves out in the theory of monetary policy.

2

The Fight for the Gold Standard

'Whoever, then, possessed the power of regulating the quantity of money can always govern its value.'

David Ricardo, House of Commons, 1821

'Nearly every theme in the [contemporary] monetary debate is a replay . . . of the controversies between the Currency and Banking Schools over a century ago.'

Tim Congdon, 1980[1]

Figure 2. Four key monetary debates

Chronology of monetary debates	The two sides of each debate (and their proponents)	
Recoinage, 1690s	Commodity / essentialist (Locke, Newton)	Credit / nominalist (Lowndes)
Convertibility, 1797–1821	Bullionists (Ricardo)	Real bills [BoE] (Thomas Attwood [Birmingham School])
	(Henry Thornton)	(Henry Thornton)
Currency vs Banking School, 1840s	Currency School (Overstone, Torrens)	Banking School (Tooke)
Bimetallism, 1880s–1890s	Gold standard	Gold and Silver standard (William Jennings Bryan)

I. PRELUDE TO THE GOLD STANDARD: THE BRITISH RECOINAGE DEBATE OF THE 1690s

In the 1690s, Britain, then on a silver standard, was at war with France. Full-weight silver coins were being exported to pay for foreign military expenses; 'clipped' or lighter-weight coins with the same face value but less silver were informally substituted in domestic circulation. By 1695, it was estimated that the vast majority of domestically circulating coins contained only 50 per cent of their official silver content.[2] Prices rose by 30 per cent over the 1690s as the purchasing power of coins declined. The monetary authority (then the Treasury) had lost control of the money supply.

What was to be done to stop the country running out of money? William Lowndes, the Secretary to the Treasury, proposed devaluation. The Treasury would mint new coins of the same face value as the older coins but containing 20 per cent less silver, equivalent to a devaluation of 20 per cent, and declare them to be legal tender. Unless a limit was placed on counterfeiting, the result might be hyperinflation.

However, the philosopher John Locke, who was also asked to advise on the currency, rejected devaluation in favour of revaluation. Locke distinguished between intrinsic value and market value. It was because of its intrinsic value that metallic money could serve as a standard of value for all marketable things. A 'pound' sterling was simply a definite weight of silver. Its price, once settled, 'should be inviolably and immutably kept [the same] to perpetuity'.[3] Lowndes's proposal was as deceitful as claiming 'to lengthen a foot by dividing it into fifteen parts ... and calling them inches'.[4] The answer to Locke is that a quantity of silver is not an objective measure of value, but just a less fluctuating one than cows. His argument for fixing the currency in terms of a weight of silver was political: a fixed metallic standard was a token of the government's integrity, not a property of the metal itself.

Locke's proposal to revalue the currency reflected his political aims. In his social contract theory, the state was given a duty to maintain its citizens' property. Silver coin was property, therefore its devaluation was akin to robbery. Behind Locke's proposal to keep the value of money constant was the ideology of the creditor. The creditor should be repaid in coin of the same value as the coin lent. Any other course would defraud him. Such a 'hard' money regime would prevent the state 'stealing' the property of its citizens by devaluing the currency in which it settled its debts.

Locke had a practical argument for keeping the value of money (or price level) constant. He said that the previous standard had served England well for nearly a hundred years. The harm came from changes in the standard, which 'unreasonably and unjustly gives away and transfers men's properties, disorders trade, puzzles accounts, and needs a new arithmetic to cast up reckonings, and keep accounts in; besides a thousand other inconveniences'[5] – certainly valid concerns.

Both sides in the debate accepted the fact that changing the quantity of money would have real effects. Isaac Newton, then Master of the Mint, accepted the case for devaluation, arguing that if the coinage was revalued, as Locke wanted it to be, the money supply would fall, resulting in trade depression: fixed costs required flexible money. Locke, too, understood that halving the money supply would lead either to the halving of output and employment or a halving of wages, prices and rents, though he did not say which. More important to him was the thought that devaluation would lead to inflation. Inflation, by reducing the real burden of debt, would defraud creditors.

Locke won the day. Parliament ordered that clipped coins be handed in to the mint by a due date, the seller receiving (fewer) heavy-weight coins in return. The result was chaos. Since their revaluation took much of the existing coinage out of circulation, it resulted in an 'immediate and asphyxiating coin shortage'.[6] The bullion price of silver remained obstinately higher than the new mint price, so many of the new coins were exported. Those shopkeepers left holding the light coins rioted. Prices fell, business confidence collapsed, trade contracted. Within a generation so much silver had disappeared from circulation that the silver standard had to be replaced by the gold standard.

The recoinage crisis did lead to two permanent innovations in monetary policy. The Bank of England was set up in 1694 with the authority to issue notes. The Jacobean state was, in the words of Gladstone, 'a fraudulent bankrupt', which had to offer special inducements to get anyone with money to lend to it. These induce-ments were enshrined in the Bank's first charter. The proprietors were given a monopoly of lending to the government, in return for 8 per cent interest, with the loans secured on earmarked revenues. (Locke saw an independent Bank of England as a critical bulwark for constitutional monarchy.)

Secondly, in 1717 Newton, as Master of the Mint, fixed the value of the pound at £3 17s 10½d per standard ounce of 22 carat gold, equiva-lent to a fine gold price of just under £4 4s 11½d. The Bank was obliged to convert its notes into gold on demand at this price. This remained sterling's gold price for two hundred years, except for its suspension in the Napoleonic wars. Sound money triumphed, and the record was one of long-run price stability; between 1717 and the First World War, the average annual rate of inflation was just 0.53 per cent. But there were considerable short-run fluctuations; the average *magnitude* of annual price changes was 4.42 per cent.[7]

The establishment of the Bank of England and Newton's rule made it much safer to lend to the state. The superior ability of the British state to mobilize the funds of its subjects for war was an important factor in its victories over France (a much more populous country) in the eighteenth century. A new social contract came into existence: merchants would lend to the state provided the state so conducted its affairs that its promises to pay were credible. As we shall see, this con-tract was the monetary counterpart of the fiscal contract whereby Parliament granted the government supply for approved purposes, including war, on condition that it balanced its budget in peacetime.

For the first time the British state was in a position to issue long-term debt. Its 3% Consols (consolidated debt raised on the revenues of the kingdom) were treated as liquid reserves by the banks, and over time became the safest form of security-holding for the new class of rentier bourgeoisie. The superior credibility of sterling would make it, over time, the world's main vehicular currency for trade and pay-ments: sterling, being 'as good as gold', minimized the need for gold transfers.

Older theorists had recognized that the standard of value was a pol-itical question, because it decides the distribution of wealth, income and the risks of uncertainty. Locke's followers successfully insisted that it had to be fixed to avoid economic and, therefore, social disruption. Like all social scientific analysis that claims to reduce the political to the natural, it was largely a cover for vested interest.[8]

II. NINETEENTH-CENTURY MONETARY DEBATES: AN OVERVIEW

In the nineteenth century there were three grand discussions of monetary policy: the bullionist versus 'real bills' controversy from 1797 to 1821; the Currency School versus the Banking School debate of the 1840s; and the bimetallist controversy of the 1880s and 90s. British economists and bankers led the first two; bimetallism was an American cause. The focus of the first two debates was on the causes of inflation. This reflected – as it still does – the long-standing bias in monetary theory to treat inflation ('too much money') as the cause of most economic evils. On this view, the prelude to a crisis was the over-issue of money by governments and/or banks, feeding speculative bubbles that were bound to collapse. Thus, deflation was viewed as an inevitable consequence of the collapse of the inflationary boom. By the mid-1800s, the gold standard had triumphed as the indispensable anti-inflationary anchor, for the reason given by Locke and repeated by Adam Smith: provided the currency was firmly linked to gold, gold's natural scarcity would stop any over-issue of money. But no sooner had the gold standard won the anti-inflationary battle than it was itself challenged, at the end of the century, by those who started to argue that scarcity of gold was a major defect in the system, because this prevented an expansion of the money supply in line with the growth of production. This set the scene for the monetary reformers to advocate cutting the link between money and gold altogether.

Running through the debates, but by no means clearly, was the question of the relationship of money to the economy. Both those who wanted a 'hard' currency to stop inflation and those who wanted a more 'elastic' currency to accommodate business and population growth, believed that the money supply was independent of the real economy of production and trade, and could therefore 'get out of order'. The alternative claim that money, being created by bank loans and liquidated by their repayment, could neither exceed nor fall short of business conditions, while popular among businessmen and some bankers, was rejected by the professors of political economy as false reasoning: political economy taught that money, while it facilitates barter, can be a veil which hides from the eye the true value of the goods being traded. Therefore money could not be assumed to be automatically proportioned to real economic need: it had to be kept proportional by rules governing its issue.

III. BULLIONISTS VERSUS THE 'REAL BILLS' DOCTRINE

The first of the debates came about as the result of the Napoleonic wars. War brought heavy military outlays, at home and abroad. In 1797, the Prime Minister William Pitt authorized the Bank of England to suspend the convertibility of the Bank's notes into gold, as gold drained out of the country. The exchange rate of the pound against other currencies immediately dropped by 20 per cent. Gold was hoarded, causing the price of gold bullion to rise. The government resorted to printing notes to offset the fall in prices and to pay for ever-enlarging expenditure. The national debt soared to 260 per cent of GDP.[9]

The suspension of convertibility coincided with increases in agricultural prices. The average price for a 'Winchester quarter' (eight Winchester bushels, or just under a quarter of a ton) of wheat, for example, rose from 45s 9d in 1780–89 to 106s 2d in 1810–13.

The inflationary boom raised directly the question of the direction of causation. Did more paper money cause prices to be higher? Or did higher prices cause more money to be produced?

In *The High Price of Bullion* (1810), David Ricardo blamed the Bank of England for issuing more paper money than the economy could usefully absorb. Prices, he argued, would go up, and the exchange rate down, 'to the same amount' as the increase in money. The over-issue of money, in turn, had provided people with the means to buy government debt, issuance of which would have been impossible had the Bank not been relieved of its obligation to convert its liabilities into gold. Ricardo stated that 'the necessity which the Bank felt itself under to guard the safety of its establishment [gold reserve], therefore, always prevented, before the restriction from paying in specie [i.e. the suspension of convertibility], a too lavish issue of paper money'.[10] Once the gold convertibility obligation had been removed, the Bank's directors were 'no longer bound by *"fears for the safety of their establishment"* to limit the quantity of their notes to that sum which should keep them of the same value as the coin which they represent'.[11] Ricardo went further, arguing that without a gold check there might be 'no amount of money' which banks 'might not lend'.[12] The ever-present danger of over-issue required convertibility into gold. From the Bullionist argument sprang an idea that was to be central to the modern quantity theory of money: the stock of money could be effectively regulated through the control of a narrowly defined monetary base.[13] The prescription that it should be so controlled was the essence of the doctrine of sound money.

In its defence against Ricardo's charges, the Bank of England denied that its policy had caused the depreciation of the pound: banks had simply lent, as always, on the basis of good security; this included the Bank of England's loans to the government. The inflation was caused by the rise in agricultural prices following poor harvests and by the government's claims on national resources to fight the war. The falling exchange rate was partly a consequence of the extra food imports that the crop failures required, and partly a result of the outflow of funds to cover the subsidies to Britain's foreign allies. Neither was the consequence of any 'over-issue' of notes by the Bank of England.

In making this case, the Bank of England promoted the 'real bills' doctrine. The Bank, explained the Governor, 'never force a note into circulation, and there will not remain a note in circulation more than the immediate wants of the public require'. The Bank's lending, secured by 'real bills' (collateral), was self-liquidating on completion of the projects which gave rise to the asset: a theory known as the 'law of reflux'.[14] Ricardo attacked the real bills doctrine on the ground that 'real capital' could be created only by saving, not by credit: a claim notably revived by Hayek and the Austrian School in our own day.

Henry Thornton's attack on the real bills doctrine was superior to

46

Ricardo's. As he pointed out in his *Enquiry into the Nature and Effects of the Paper Credit of Great Britain* (1802), the Bank's argument had a major technical weakness. It assumed that the issue of bills was independent of the price at which they were discounted, a price which lay in the power of the Bank of England to regulate. In fact, economic activity was jointly determined by the demand for credit and the price of credit. But Thornton failed to spot two other flaws in the real bills doctrine. The Bank never explained what determines the 'needs of trade' – lurking in the real bills doctrine is an assumption of full employment. And the Bank failed to distinguish productive investment from speculation.[15]

Thornton was the most remarkable monetary theorist of the early nineteenth century. To Smith and Ricardo, the rate of interest played no part in determining the quantity of money, the money rate of interest being merely a 'shadow of the "rate of profit" on real capital'.[16] Thornton was the first to distinguish between the rate of interest as the price earned from lending money, and the rate of profit earned on capital investment. He therefore anticipated Wicksell in appreciating that the supply of money is determined by the interaction of the 'current rate of mercantile profit' with the market rate of interest.[17] He was the first to describe the cumulative process of credit creation. The only control the central bank had over the quantity of money was to 'limit its paper by means of the price at which it lends'.[18] By setting a 'bank rate', the central bank could control the interest rate structure and thus the quantity of domestic credit.

Ricardo won the argument, because his explanation of inflation was creditor-friendly, and because the Bank was unable properly to explain the inflation that had followed the suspension of convertibility. The 1810 Bullion Report concluded that a 'rise in the market price of gold above its mint price will take place if the local currency of this particular country, being no longer convertible into gold, should at any time be issued to excess'; the Bank, a private corporation, had failed to restrict its loans out of concern for its own profits.[19] It was vain to think that the issue of a discretionary currency could be limited. The Report advocated an immediate resumption of convertibility of notes into gold at the pre-suspension price set by Isaac Newton a hundred years previously – 'the only true, intelligible, and adequate standard of value', as Robert Peel called it.[20] Bank lending would be automatically curtailed; most of the notes issued in the period of suspension would simply cease to be legal tender. (The equivalent of the recoining of 1697.) Wisely, however, the House of Commons decided to delay implementation of its findings.

The end of the Napoleonic wars was followed by deflation and depression. The depression was caused not so much by the resumption of gold convertibility itself as by anticipation of it. The depression lasted twenty years, with the commodity price level falling 59 per cent between 1809 and 1849.[21] Agriculture was hit by renewed competition; arms manufacturers round Birmingham went bust. Political reactions to the deflation of prices included the radical Chartist movement in Britain and revolutions on the Continent. Orthodoxy, wedded to the commodity theory of money, attributed the fall in prices to a decline in the production of precious metals. But Thomas Attwood, a Birmingham banker, attributed the depression partly to the curtailment of state orders for arms. The exchange rate, he said, should only be stabilized after five to ten years of full employment. He urged the need for 'accommodating our coinage to man, and not man to our coinage';[22] Britain should have a paper currency that was not tied to gold. Ricardo rejected Attwood's arguments. 'A currency may be considered as perfect, of which the standard is invariable, which always conforms to that standard, and in the use of which the utmost economy is practised.'[23] Gold convertibility was restored in 1821. All this was a rehearsal of the debate which followed the end of the First World War, with the arguments and sequence of policies being almost identical.

Jacob Viner noted that Ricardo was blind to the short-run consequences of the policies he advocated. The Ricardian vice of abstraction from reality is beautifully illustrated by an exchange between Ricardo and his friend Thomas Malthus in January 1821 concerning the causes and consequences of the great depression in trade which had followed the Napoleonic wars. Ricardo accused Malthus of having 'always in your mind the immediate and temporary effects of particular changes – whereas I put these immediate and temporary effects quite aside, and fix my whole attention on the permanent state of things which result from them'.[24] Malthus admitted his tendency to 'refer frequently to things as they are, as the only way of making one's writing useful to society' and of avoiding the 'errors of the tailors of Laputa, and by a slight mistake at the outset arrive at conclusions most distant from the truth'.

This argument has run through economics, with Keynes taking up Malthus's baton in the 1920s. As we will have further reason to emphasize, the short-run/long-run distinction has had a baleful effect on economics and economic policy. It has served to protect its long-run equilibrium thinking from the assault of disruptions, and to justify policies of inflicting pain on populations. One may feel that insistence on the need for short-run pain (e.g. austerity) for the sake of long-run gain, when the short-run can last decades and the long-run may never happen, testifies to a refined intellectual sadism.

IV. CURRENCY SCHOOL VERSUS BANKING SCHOOL

The second of the grand monetary discussions of the 1800s was really a continuation of the first, but this time in the context of the restored gold standard and a business cycle connected with railway speculation. The Currency School, led by Lord Overstone, George Norman and Robert Torrens, expanded on the arguments of the Bullionists. While the Bullionists regarded convertibility into gold as a sufficient safeguard against the over-issue of notes, the Currency School argued that the drain of gold from the central bank wouldn't immediately curtail issue of credit by the country banks, who were not subject to specie reserve requirements.[25] The Bank of England had to have control over the whole note issue in order for domestic currency to behave like a metallic currency.

The Banking School pooh-poohed these arguments. Their spokesmen, Thomas Tooke, John Fullarton and James Wilson, argued that the policies of the Currency School imposed undesirable limitations on the central bank's ability to adjust the quantity of money to changes in the demand for money. Tooke claimed to show that in the period 1762 to 1856 fluctuations in the note issue had followed fluctuations in business activity, not preceded them. Fullarton said that commercial transactions didn't require a prior issue of money, but could be carried out by book credits transferable by cheque.[26]

Despite the objections raised by the Banking School, the Currency School won the day, because it provided a practical foundation for maintaining the gold standard. The Bank Charter Act of 1844 gave the Bank of England a legal monopoly of note-issue in England and Wales.[27] New notes (or cheques) could be issued only if the Bank received an equivalent amount in gold. The 'fiduciary issue' – the part of the note-issue not backed by gold – was to be frozen at its 1844 level. The purpose of the Act, as stated by one of its backers, 'was to make the currency, consisting of a certain proportion of paper and gold, fluctuate precisely as if the currency were entirely metallic' – i.e. to fluctuate very little.[28]

Yet the Currency School's triumph was less overwhelming than it seemed. In exceptional circumstances, the government retained the power to suspend the Act. Moreover, it was in the second half of the nineteenth century that the Bank of England started to develop its modern function as 'lender of last resort' to the banking system, a duty codified in Walter Bagehot's 1873 classic, *Lombard Street*. Bagehot argued that it was the Bank's duty to keep large-enough reserves to be able, in a crisis, to lend freely to all solvent banks at a very high rate of interest. Widely resisted at the time on the high ground of 'moral hazard', it led to the Bank organizing the rescue of Barings in 1890. This was the doctrine that the US Federal Reserve signally failed to apply in the Lehman Brothers crisis of September 2008, and which the European Central Bank was debarred by law from applying in the European banking crisis that followed.

V. BIMETALLISM

Until the early 1870s, the international monetary system was bi-metallic: some countries, like Britain, were on a gold standard, and other countries, like France, were on both gold and silver standards. The customary ratio of exchange between gold and silver was 1:15. But both France (in 1873) and America (in 1879) de-monetized silver, and went on to a full gold standard.[29] Other states aspiring to be 'first class' countries with first class credit ratings also joined the gold standard.[30] By the 1880s the gold standard had gone international.

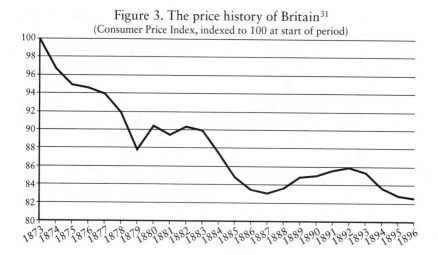

Figure 3. The price history of Britain[31]
(Consumer Price Index, indexed to 100 at start of period)

The increased trust in international money helped trigger the first age of globalization.

But no sooner had the gold standard won its victory than its position was undermined, by the continuous fall in wholesale prices which lasted from 1873 to 1896. This was known as the Great Depression, before the second one usurped its place in the history of economic misfortunes.

It was not a depression in the modern sense, rather a lingering deflationary disease, punctuated by bursts of excitement. Nevertheless, it started the third grand monetary discussion. There was much debate about whether the causes of the deflation were monetary or 'real'. Just as it had explained the mid-century's rising prices by the Californian and Australian gold discoveries, orthodoxy now explained the fall in prices by the exhaustion of existing mines and the de-monetization of silver. The successors of the Banking School attributed it, instead, to the collapse in agricultural prices following the fall in transport costs and increased supply from the Americas. For instance, the English statistician Robert Giffen argued that 'it is the range of prices as part of a general economic condition which helps determine the quantity of money in use, and not the quantity of money in use that determines prices'.[32]

The orthodox school won the analytical battle, as it had ever since the time of Jean Bodin. Falling prices were due to scarcity of money.

But by the same token the role of gold as money came under attack. Statesmen and economists had united in support of the gold standard and currency convertibility, because they regarded convertibility as the only safeguard against inflation. Yet the gold standard was now exposed as an important cause of deflation.

Bimetallism – a monetary system in which both gold and silver would be legal tender, with a fixed rate of exchange between them – won its greatest popular support in the United States. American farmers, with loans denominated in gold, were squeezed by falling prices which raised the real price of their debts. They agitated for a reintroduction of a silver-backed currency to expand the money supply and stave off deflation. William Jennings Bryan, the (unsuccessful) Democratic presidential candidate of 1896, declared: 'you shall not crucify mankind upon a cross of gold'. Bimetallism was championed by Bryan and others as a way to increase the money supply. The bimetallic cause lost not just because of bimetallic currency's inherent unsteadiness – it was likened by the economist Irving Fisher to 'two tipsy men locking arms'[33] – but because cheaper ways of mining gold, enabling the development of South African gold mines, relieved the gold shortage.

But the analytical debate was far from over. To prevent monetary shocks it was necessary for gold production to keep pace with productivity growth. However, new gold production was very imperfectly correlated with a growing economic system's need for money. Central banks started to see their function as to smooth out price cycles, raising interest rates and hoarding gold to dampen price rises, and lowering them and allowing reserves to fall to check downward pressure. But would not a better way to secure an elastic currency be to cut the link between money and the precious metals once and for all? The time had come to free monetary conditions from erratic gold movements.

VI. HOW DID THE GOLD STANDARD ACTUALLY WORK?

The gold standard linked the volume of a country's currency to its gold stock. Its essential feature was that all the domestic currencies of the trading partners could be converted into gold at a fixed price.

Currencies were just names for different weights of gold; they were 'as good as gold' because they could be converted into gold.[34] This meant they could be freely traded with each other. A system of this kind required both freedom for individuals to import and export gold and a set of rules relating the quantity of domestic money in circulation to the amount of the central bank's gold reserve. Without freedom to import and export gold, gold could not serve as an international means of payment; without rules to limit the issue of paper money to the quantity of their gold reserves, central banks could easily run out of gold.

The gold standard was designed to force governments and countries to 'live within their means'. The fact that it put money creation beyond the reach of governments was widely seen as its chief virtue. As Herbert Hoover put it in 1933: 'we have gold because we cannot trust governments'. The gold standard also forced countries to live within their means by depriving them of gold if they didn't. As David Hume had pointed out, a country which imported more than it exported would, literally, run out of money. It could, of course, borrow, but loans had to be repaid. Gold was the risk-free collateral for loans, the guarantee against default. For a country to be 'on gold' – to commit to paying its debts in gold – was the smooth path to borrowing; the nineteenth-century equivalent of an AAA-rating. The gold standard was well suited to the interests of creditors, because it prevented inflation being used as a method of reducing the real burden of debts. Its disciplines were onerous and it was thought that only 'first class' countries could accept them. Britain was first to link its currency to gold in 1721, but by the end of the 1800s all 'civilized' countries had followed suit.

The great mystery of nineteenth-century monetary history is the success of the gold standard. It was designed to keep both governments and countries from over-spending and did, on the whole, work. 'Civilized' countries no longer defaulted on their debts. But a correlation is not a cause. The question is: was it the rules of the gold standard which kept money 'in order'? Or did underlying conditions make it relatively easy to follow the rules? Exactly the same question would arise in the Great Moderation years of the 1990s and 2000s: was it central bank inflation-targeting which kept inflation low, or was it what the Governor of the Bank of England Mervyn King described as a 'nice' environment?

David Hume's price–specie–flow mechanism originated the story of how the gold standard was supposed to work. Domestic prices would fall in gold-losing countries and rise in gold-gaining countries, restoring equilibrium in their trade balances. This left 'central bankers [with] little to do besides issuing or retiring domestic currency as the level of gold in their vaults fluctuated'.[35]

In fact, gold flows were only a tiny element in the nineteenth-century adjustment mechanism. To settle trade imbalances by shipping bullion round the world was much too costly. Nor did individual country prices vary inversely with each other. They tended to move in tandem.

If countries didn't play by the Hume rules, perhaps they played by the Cunliffe rules? The influential Cunliffe Report of 1918 presented a two-stage model of adjustment which had been extracted from the history of the gold standard (Figure 4). In the first stage, the drain from the central bank's gold reserves (G) causes it to raise Bank Rate (r) – the rate of interest at which it lends money to its member banks. This is adjustment 1 in the diagram. The result is a capital inflow sufficient to finance any temporary – typically seasonal – deficit on the trade account. Bank Rate can then come down again (adjustment 4 in the diagram).

However, if the adverse current account balance persists after adjustment 1 then the second stage of Cunliffe's model, involving two further adjustments (2 and 3), will come into play before the interest rate goes back down (adjustment 4). In the second adjustment, the higher

Figure 4. The Cunliffe Mechanism

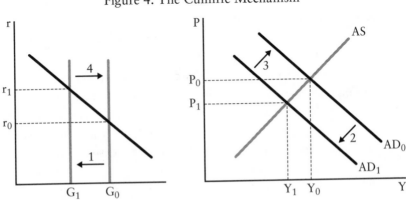

interest rates cause a drop in aggregate demand for domestic goods (AD), which exerts downward pressure on the price level of domestic goods (P) and on the level of output (Y), along the aggregate supply curve (AS). The drop in prices then leads aggregate demand for domestic goods and for the country's exports to shift back up, leading to a higher level of output and prices (adjustment 3). This, in turn, prompts gold outflows to reverse, which eventually causes Bank Rate to drop back down to its original level (adjustment 4).

The Cunliffe model improves on the simple Hume account by treating Bank Rate, not gold flows, as the operational adjustment tool, and by emphasizing the difference between short-run and long-run adjustment mechanisms. That temporary imbalances under the gold standard were financed by short-term borrowing, not gold flows, is clear; but there is little evidence of the price and income changes which were supposed to bring about the permanent adjustment of imports and exports. Current account imbalances tended to persist.[36] So what was the gold standard's secret?

Monetary historians such as Barry Eichengreen emphasize the importance of the *commitment* to convertibility.[37] This was the moral rule of the system. 'Promises must be kept,' thundered the bankers; to 'go off' gold was a breach of faith. Like marriage vows, promises of fidelity to gold were designed to keep doubt at bay, because it was recognized that humans were frail and that the more their pledges were treated as sacred, the less likely they were to be broken.

There is obviously something in this. Commitment to convertibility eliminated, or greatly reduced, exchange risk and this facilitated the financing, hence expansion, of trade. But it is also true that in the heyday of its authority, no onerous adjustments of the Hume or Cunliffe type were needed; had they been, the gold standard might well have collapsed much sooner. Adjustment was certainly eased by the fact that in the nineteenth century new discoveries of gold, as well as financial innovation, occurred frequently enough to keep pace with production, keeping the price level stable. More importantly, the direction and character of the trade, capital and population flows in this, the first age of globalization, obviated any systemic threat of system collapse. To put it simply: debtors were not subjected to sufficient strain *ex ante* to force painful adjustment *ex post*. Virtue was relatively cheap.[38]

Five different aspects of the incentive to virtue can be noted:

1. Barry Eichengreen has argued that the commitment to currency convertibility was not endangered by democracy, since suffrage was limited and trade unions were weak.[39] This implies a tolerance of unemployment. In fact, cheap grain imports from the New World caused huge unemployment among agricultural labourers in Europe from the 1880s onward, but it did not persist. This is because the unemployed in Europe got, not on their bikes, but on ships to the New World. Between 1881 and 1915, there was a net emigration of 32 million people from Western and Central Europe, about 15 per cent of its population, most of whom went to the thinly populated New World. The non-persistence of unemployment fed the belief of the classical economists that, given flexible labour markets, unemployment would be transient. But this particular type of labour flexibility depended on having excess supplies of labour in one part of the world and excess supplies of land in another.

2. The predominantly commodity structure of international trade, and the low share of non-tradable services in domestic GDPs, meant that, on the whole, the law of one price prevailed, limiting the need for price adjustment. The wedge between domestic and foreign prices, which made the adjustment problem so politically fraught in the twentieth century, was much less pronounced before 1914.

3. International trade was relatively non-competitive. The massive reduction in transport costs enabled a long-distance trade to build up between the core European countries and their overseas or transcontinental peripheries. To put it at its simplest, capital goods from Western Europe built the railways and harbours in the peripheries from which were transported foodstuffs and raw materials to Western Europe. The fact that most international trade resulted in a complementary exchange of manufactures for raw materials reduced the pressure on individual core countries to 'be competitive'.

4. Current accounts were balanced by capital flows. The gold-standard world was divided into a developed centre and developing peripheries. From the 1870s to 1914 an increasing

volume of capital flowed from the 'core' of developed countries to the 'periphery' of developing ones. The growth of capital exports coincided with, and was facilitated by, the incorporation of the main trading countries into the gold-standard system between 1870 and 1900. Sovereign states joined the gold standard independently; they made their colonies and dependencies part of their monetary systems. The gold standard offered investors a cheap and efficient credit-rating agency. Provided they practised monetary discipline, balanced their budgets and were free of arbitrary regime change, developing countries could go on borrowing to finance their 'catch-up' at low interest rates.

5. The gold standard worked in tandem with empire. The golden age of the gold standard was also the golden age of imperialism. Imperialism cemented globalization. Between 1880 and 1900 the whole of Africa and parts of Asia were incorporated into the European empires. Thus the spread of the gold standard coincided with the political division of the world into sovereign and dependent states. A high proportion of European loans went to colonies and semi-colonial dependencies. The colonies provided sheltered markets for the exports of the colonial power and important sources of their foodstuffs and raw materials. Exports of capital tended to be directly tied to the exports of machinery and manufactures from the lending country, with the colonist following in the footsteps of the trader and investor.

By 1870, 70 per cent of British foreign investment was going to its empire, whose territories were, in effect, on a sterling standard. Even in 'independent' Latin America, creditors could enforce their will because state borrowers were weak sovereigns. Thus, imperialism, formal and informal, lowered the cost of development capital. Lenin would later see imperial rivalry as the seedbed of war, but before 1914 imperialism was the means by which the developing world was enabled to accumulate capital goods. It was the treble outward movement of trade, investment and population under the imperial umbrella which gave an upward thrust to global economic activity.

These structural supports of the international gold standard are widely recognized. More debatable is the role of Great Britain in sustaining the system. The gold standard has been called a 'British-managed' or 'sterling' standard; Keynes called London 'the conductor of the international orchestra'. The argument has been between those, like Eichengreen, who argue that the gold standard was a co-operatively managed system, and those, like Kindleberger, who claimed that it was a hegemonic system, with Britain as the hegemon.[40]

Eichengreen is undoubtedly right to say that, as far as Europe is concerned, the system rested on central bank co-operation, made possible by the relative absence of political conflict. Despite all the tensions, there wasn't a major war in Europe from 1871 to 1914, a period of forty-three years. However, Britain did play a leadership role, not just because of the global reach of the British Empire, but also – and connected with this – because of the dominant position of Britain in international trade, finance and migration. Over the course of this period, it provided around two-fifths of the world's capital exports;[41] in 1900, Britain took just under a quarter of the world's imports;[42] the City of London was the world's undisputed financial centre, 'through which flowed all the transfers between borrowers and lenders, creditors and debtors, and buyers and sellers that were not internal to a single country';[43] and much of the New World was populated by emigrants from the British Isles.

These features, according to Charles Kindleberger, enabled Britain to take on the support of the global system in periods of adversity 'by accepting its redundant commodities, maintaining a flow of investment capital, and discounting its paper', the three essential countercyclical services.[44] The importance of the Kindleberger thesis is that it explains better than any other how the adjustment problem – who adjusts to whom? – was solved under the classic gold standard. Broadly speaking, it was the chief creditor country, Britain, which took on the onus of adjustment. Britain, or more precisely the City of London, provided the world with a surrogate sovereign, akin to an international central authority, offering some of the services of a world government or bank. (The United States would take on this role after the Second World War.)

For example, a small rise in Bank Rate would attract foreign funds to London at will. Britain's uniquely maintained free trade policy meant that it could run commodity import surpluses when the terms of trade moved in its favour, and beef up capital exports and exports of people when the terms of trade turned against it. These were crucial balancing functions.[45]

Britain's fiscal constitution reinforced sterling's hegemonic role. The idea that 'the pound was as good as gold' expressed not a mechanical link between gold and currency, but the belief that the British state would so conduct its fiscal affairs that the purchasing power of a pound note would remain stable.

The first age of globalization was not the frictionless paradise depicted in free trade models. The average height of tariff barriers rose in the forty years before the First World War, as competitive trade became a larger fraction of total trade. Britain allowed its arable farming to be destroyed by cheap imports from the Americas: France and Germany protected theirs. Banks tended to hoard gold if it was abundant, allowing their reserves to rise. The gold standard often cracked at the peripheries, as Latin American and southern European governments defaulted on their bonds: Greece was in default for much of the time. At such times capital flows turned into capital flight, and new loans were made conditional on guaranteed revenue streams.

Nevertheless, Cairncross's summary is apt:

> The conditions of the period seemed to work together for the unstable maintenance of stability. A qualified stability admittedly, for there were repeated and severe depressions; and an insecure stability, since it required the constant opening of new fields for investment and the free movement and rapid increase of population which these openings encouraged; but none the less, by interwar standards, stability.[46]

3

The Quantity Theory of Money:
From History to Science

'For it is the part of man to be master, not slave, of nature, and not least in a sphere of such extraordinary significance as that of monetary influences.'

Knut Wicksell, 1898[1]

'The theory of the interest rate mechanism is the center of the confusion in modern macroeconomics. Not all issues in contention originate here. But the inconclusive quarrels ... largely do stem from this source.'

Axel Leijonhufvud, 1979[2]

I. THE QUANTITY THEORY OF MONEY:
THE TWO BRANCHES

In the twentieth century, gold lost the battle to control money. There was either too much or too little of it. In the first case it was blamed for inflation; in the second, for deflation and unemployment. Instead of control by gold, there would be control by experts in the central bank, equipped with 'scientific' theory. The battle between the supporters of gold and the monetary reformers dominated the monetary history of the first third of the new century.

The reformers took their stand on a mathematical version of the Quantity Theory of Money (hereafter QTM). The QTM is the first theory of macroeconomics; it is also very muddled. On the one hand it depicts money as being a paltry thing, hardly worth writing about;

on the other, it sees it as a mighty monster, which has to be kept under lock and key if it is not to wreak havoc. These two views are inconsistent, the cognitive dissonance arising from trying to account for the real-world impact of monetary disturbances with an analytic structure that abstracts from the use of money. The realization that money needs to be treated as an independent factor of production had to wait until the coming of Keynes. And even Keynes had to emancipate himself from the quantity theory before he felt he could accurately analyse the economic problem to which money gave rise.

The key belief of the pre-1914 monetary reformers was that instability in the price level generates not just economic but social instability, by producing unanticipated shifts in the level of activity and distribution of wealth. The aim of economic policy ought therefore to be price stability. This policy prescription rested on the belief that, in a system of fiat money, the central bank has ultimate control over the quantity of money in circulation. If the central bank can control the quantity of money, either directly or indirectly, it has the power to make the price level what it wants it to be. And if it can make the price level what it wants it to be, it can control economic fluctuations. Thus the QTM went beyond explanation to prescription. It was intended for use. It was the scientific cure for price fluctuations, which were regarded as the main cause of business fluctuations.

The two principal versions of the QTM are associated with the American economist Irving Fisher (1867–1947) and the Swedish economist Knut Wicksell (1851–1926), respectively. For Fisher, changes in the price level are directly caused by the expansion and contraction of central bank or 'narrow' money. Wicksell, while accepting the causal relationship between money and prices, argued that the money supply was created by commercial banks in the course of making loans; and that the central bank could exercise indirect control only by regulating the price of loans (interest rate). These two versions of the QTM have contested the ground of monetary theory ever since, with many doubting whether Wicksell was really a quantity theorist at all. The American version of the QTM derives from Fisher via Milton Friedman; the European version is more Wicksellian. Keynes was a Wicksellian until the early 1930s, when he broke with the QTM altogether.

II. FISHER'S SANTA CLAUS

In 1911, Fisher produced his famous equation of exchange:

$$MV = PT$$

On the left we have M for the money supply and V for velocity of circulation – the number of times a unit of money changes hands in a period of time. P is the weighted average of all prices and T the sum of all transactions in the specified period. (For a technical discussion, see Appendix 3.1, p. 71.)

The equation of exchange is true by definition. If the number of dollars in the economy is $5 million, and each dollar changes hands twenty times a year, then the total amount of money changing hands is $100 million. This, by definition, must equal the total value of transactions in the economy. In plain English, 'things cost what is paid for them'. But this tells us nothing about causation.

Fisher turned his equation of exchange into a theory of the price level by assuming, first, that the price level is 'normally the one abso- lutely passive element in the equation of exchange'[3] (i.e. money is *exogenous*), and secondly, that the velocity of money and the volume of transactions (V and T respectively) stay the same in the relevant period. Given the ground rules of the discussion, 'there is no possible escape from the conclusion that a change in the quantity of money (M) must normally cause a proportional change in the price level'.[4]

Fisher then proceeded to test the logic empirically. Studying the two-thirds rise in US prices between 1896 and 1909, he concluded that most of it could be explained by a doubling in the quantity of money (due to increased gold mining), a tripling of deposits (due to increased business activity) and a slight increase in velocity (due to a growing concentration of people in cities). That money supply increased ahead of prices, while velocity stayed relatively constant, heavily shaped Fisher's conclusion that but for the growth of the money supply, the price level would have gone up only by about half the amount it did.[5]

Fisher's model exhibited the classic form of model construction: a hypothesis, a presumed set of relationships linking the hypothesis to the other model variables, the logical conclusion, and the empirical testing of the conclusion.

There was also the 'Cambridge' equation, derived from Alfred Marshall:[6]

$$M = kPT$$

Here k, the demand for cash to hold, is the reciprocal of V, its rate of turnover.

The Fisher and Cambridge statements of the QTM both present a transactional view of money (deriving from the barter theory considered in Chapter 1). But there is a subtle difference of emphasis. The Cambridge economist Marshall introduced marginal utility into the demand for cash function: people 'balance at the margin' the advantage of holding money and buying investments. But this was a purely decorative concession to the new-fangled marginal productivity theory of value. It had no operational significance for his own monetary theory. The Marshallian k is merely a 'temporary abode of purchasing power'. He gave as an example keeping enough money in the bank to pay the weekly wages. He would also have recognized holding reserves for contingencies. He did not consider these to be major leakages from the spending stream. So, for control purposes, the two equations came to the same thing, confirming the view that people acquired money only to spend it.

How does new money get into the system? If the QTM is to provide a rationale for monetary policy, the answer to this question is important. Fisher (like Marshall) assumed that individuals have a 'desired ratio of money to expenditure', this amount being given by 'habit and convenience'.[7] He then argued: 'If some mysterious Santa Claus suddenly doubles the amount [of money] in the possession of each individual', the recipients would spend the excess money in buying goods of various kinds, leading to a 'sudden briskness in trade' as people try to restore their money–expenditure ratio. But the only way individuals can get rid of money is by handing it over to other people; society as a whole cannot be rid of the extra money. Thus, 'the effort to get rid of [surplus cash] . . . will continue until prices have reached a sufficiently high level'; that is, until the increased spending of the community would cause prices to double, thus restoring the real value of their cash balances. This is the source of Friedman's idea of 'helicopter money'. In technical terms, the demand for 'real balances' is brought into equality with the increased supply of money by a change in the price level.[8]

Evidently, the simple Fisher story needs no 'transmission mechanism': Santa Claus (or the helicopter) drops the money straight into the pockets of potential consumers. The need to specify a transmission mechanism arises from the existence of a banking system. Marshall explicitly assumes that the new money comes through the banks, via its effect on interest rates. The first effect of an influx of gold into the banking system, he says, is to lower interest rates. This increases the demand for loans. The increased demand for loans will 'carry off' the larger supply of loanable funds available. The spending of these loans will cause prices to rise until, with the extra funds being exhausted, interest rates rise again.[9] This is known today as the 'bank lending channel'. However, interest rates play no independent part in determining the quantity of money: they are merely the means by which, in a banking system, the helicopter money gets into the pockets of those who will spend it. This is because Fisher and Marshall still thought of money as cash rather than credit: it was the injection of cash which determined the interest rate structure.

Both the Fisher and Cambridge versions assume a stable money multiplier, that is, a stable ratio of reserves to deposits.[10] Similarly, they presuppose a stable velocity of money, unaffected by changes in its supply. In holding V constant, they ruled out the possibility of fluctuations in the demand for money.

However, like previous monetary theorists, Fisher did distinguish between the short-run and long-run effects of a change in the quantity of money. If everyone adjusted instantly and equi-proportionally to a change in the money stock, money would affect only the price level. But relative prices don't adjust instantly, because people don't know what the new equilibrium price is – i.e. they are uncertain about how much prices will go up or how much they will fall.

It was a common observation that when the price level is rising (or as we would say today, when inflation is rising) people will spend their money faster; if it is falling (or expected to fall) they will hoard it. Thus Nassau Senior in 1819: 'Everybody taxed his ingenuity to find employment for a currency of which the value evaporated from hour to hour. It was passed on as it was received, as if it burned everyone's hands who touched it.'[11] This had happened with French *assignats* in the 1790s. The reason is that rising prices impose an 'inflation tax' on the holders of existing currency notes: each note buys less than before. To avoid having to spend more money on their desired goods, holders of these notes increase the speed or velocity with which they spend them.

Falling prices have the reverse effect: people delay spending their cash, expecting to get their goods cheaper a little later. Marshall's seemingly innocuous k, the proportion of their wealth which people hold in cash, rises and falls with 'each turn of the tide in prices'. But the QTM is valid only if velocity stays constant. And velocity only stays the same if the price level resulting from the change in the money stock is perfectly foreseen. Thus, although the QTM comes out of that stable of thought which believes that money affects only prices and nothing else, policy based on the QTM was set the task of keeping prices stable to avoid arbitrary shifts in activity and distribution. Uncertain expectations enter the monetary story for the first time, with the management of expectations becoming an implicit part of monetary control.

Uncertainty about the future course of prices is Fisher's explanation of the business cycle. In equilibrium, the quantity of money has a fixed ratio to bank deposits, and to the quantities and prices of goods offered for sale. In 'periods of transition', though, from one price level to another, these ratios vary, causing the real economy to malfunction. Fisher singled out the misbehaviour of the rate of interest as 'largely responsible for . . . crises and depressions'.[12] The nominal rate of interest doesn't adjust quickly enough to changes in the quantity of money, causing the price level to 'overshoot' or 'undershoot', and consequently the real rate of interest (seen as the result of the price level changes) to stay either too low or too high for the equilibrium of saving and investment. In the upswing, falling real rates enable businessmen to make windfall profits; so bank deposits increase faster than the quantity of money, increasing the velocity of circulation, and driving interest rates still lower. There will be a temporary increase in trade and employment. Eventually banks are forced in self-defence to raise interest rates because they can no longer stand an abnormal expansion of their balance sheets. Rising nominal rates then bring about a crisis and depression, as loan portfolios contract, and velocity slows down; 'the collapse of bank credit brought about by loss of confidence is the essential fact of every crisis'.[13] Fisher's 'swing of a pendulum' can last ten years. But these disturbances to the pre-existing equilibrium, while grave, have entirely monetary causes, and therefore monetary remedies. Fisher thus remained faithful to the classical dichotomy: the separation of monetary from 'real' events.

Fisher had a remedy. Pendulum swings in prices and trade can be avoided (or at least mitigated) by *knowledge* and *policy*. On the side of knowledge, Fisher anticipated the main point of the 'rational expectations revolution' sixty years later: if bankers had the correct model of the economy (the QTM) they would be able to anticipate price changes from knowledge of monetary data and adjust the quantity of loans promptly.

On the side of policy, a theoretically perfect solution to price fluctuations would be an inconvertible paper standard. Paper currency would be expanded in the same proportion to the increase in business activity.[14] But unlimited power of note-issue would be subject to political manipulation, especially on behalf of the debtor class.[15]

To limit the discretion of the monetary authority, Fisher toyed with the idea of a tabular standard (price-indexed contracts), but in the end settled for the 'compensated dollar', a scheme to vary the quantity of notes obtainable for a unit of gold so as to keep their purchasing power steady. Instead of getting a fixed price of $20.67 for an ounce of gold, a person seeking to convert gold into dollars could get either more or fewer paper dollars for it, depending on whether the price of gold was rising or falling. As a counter to deflation, this was like the medieval practice of debasing the coinage, but now put forward as a scientific method of monetary management. Fisher pursued this project indefatigably for the rest of his life.

The rate of interest played no operative role in Fisher's control system. Control of the price level was to be effected by varying the quantity of notes, with the rate of interest adjusting passively (though with a lag) to changes in bank reserves. Money was liable to play an independent disturbing role only in periods of transition, when the rate of price increases was uncertain. This was an additional reason for ensuring that the price level was kept stable.

The increasingly rigorous formulation of the QTM associated with Fisher made it clear even to quantity theorists that changes in monetary conditions had real and not just nominal effects. During the 'transition periods' from one price level equilibrium to another, interest rates, profits, wages and velocities would stray from their equilibrium values, thereby disturbing the proportionality theorem. Moreover, unforeseen changes in prices brought about arbitrary redistributions of wealth and income. Prevention was better than the cure of boom and bust.

III. KNUT WICKSELL'S CREDIT MONEY VERSION OF THE QTM

Like Fisher, the Swedish economist Knut Wicksell was appalled by the social damage wrought by fluctuations in the price level. All monetary investigations, he wrote, 'are ultimately concerned with creating and maintaining a monetary system which is reliable and elastic, in other words a medium of exchange whose purchasing power in relation to commodities changes either not at all or only very slowly in either direction'.[16]

Wicksell also identified himself as a quantity theorist, and agreed with Fisher about the QTM as applied to a purely cash economy – one where the only money in circulation is notes and coins. However, money in an economy with a developed banking system is mainly created by the banks, and it is disturbances to the credit system – to the supply of, and demand for, loans – not exogenous money shocks, which give rise to the business cycle. The business cycle is a 'credit cycle'.

The banks have a double role in Wicksell's model. On the one hand they are loan intermediaries between the savings of households and the investments of business. But they also supply credit to the business sector. The 'circular flow' thus consists of savings and credit, both flowing in and out of the banks.

Wicksell's circular flow displays the now standard macroeconomic identity:

$$Y = C + I$$
$$S = Y - C$$
$$S = I$$

Figure 5. Leijonhufvud's circular flow diagram[17]

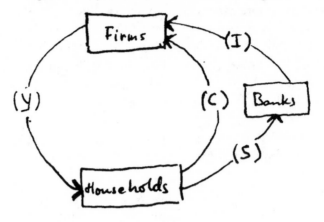

where Y is output, C is consumption, I is investment and S is savings. In equilibrium, banks intermediate between the (real) savings of households and the (real) investment decisions of firms. In a period of rising prices, firms get both bank credit and household savings. By lending more to the business sector than flows in as savings from the household sector, the banking system will cause the circular flow to expand, and the price level to rise.

When banks are lending more than the public wishes to save, there is no check to the expansion of money and rise in prices. Wicksell asks us to imagine a giant bank that is the source of all loans and in which all the community's money is deposited. In giving customer A a loan, the bank creates money out of nothing. When A spends the loan, he increases customer B's deposits in the same bank, the spending of which increases customer C's deposits, and so on. In other words, the first loan enables prices to rise without limit. As Wicksell said, the upward movement of money 'creates its own draught'.[18]

The conclusion suggested by this thought experiment is that governments *do not have direct control of the money supply*; money in modern economies is created by commercial banks when they make loans.

Echoing Thornton, Wicksell reasoned that the expansion and contraction of credit (and thus the price level) can take place only if the market rate of interest deviates from the 'natural' rate, or what Wicksell calls the real rate of return on capital.

> Now let us suppose that the banks and other lenders of money lend at a different rate of interest, either lower or higher, than that which corresponds to the current value of the natural rate of interest on capital. The economic equilibrium of the system is *ipso facto* disturbed. If prices remain unchanged, entrepreneurs will in the first instance obtain a surplus profit ... over and above their real entrepreneur profit or wage. This will continue to accrue so long as the rate of interest remains in the same relative position. They will inevitably be induced to extend their businesses in order to exploit to the maximum extent the favourable turn of events. As a consequence, the demand for services, raw materials and goods in general will be increased, and the prices of commodities must rise.[19]

In this passage is to be found the source of Wicksell's mistake. Highly original as Wicksell was, his roots were in the barter theory of exchange, in which banks simply intermediate between buyers and sellers. He thought that by raising and lowering the price of credit the central bank could make money 'neutral' in relation to the 'real' or 'natural' rate of interest on capital. But the 'rate of interest on capital' is just as much a money rate as is bank rate. The so-called natural rate is, as Keynes was later to insist, an *expected* rate, and the expectations were of a money return for a money outlay. There is no escape from the circle of money.

Nevertheless, Wicksell goes on to his conclusion that 'the maintenance of a constant level of prices depends, other things being equal, on the maintenance of a certain rate of interest on loans'.[20] This paved the way for modern monetary policy: monetary authorities should aim to keep the short-term interest rate equal to the estimated movements of the natural rate of interest on capital, plus an inflation target. Pre-2008 crash monetary policy was broadly Wicksellian.

Leijonhufvud summarizes Wicksell's argument as follows:

i) the circular flow of money income and expenditures will
   expand if and only if there is an excess demand for commodities;

ii) 'investment exceeds savings' implies 'excess demand for commodities' and conversely;

iii) investment will exceed saving if and only if the banking system lengthens its balance sheet at a rate in excess of that which would just suffice to intermediate household saving;

iv) the economy will be on its real equilibrium growth path (capital accumulation path) if and only if savings equals investment;

v) the value of the interest rate that equates saving and investment at full employment is termed the 'natural' rate.[21]

IV. WAS WICKSELL A QUANTITY THEORIST?[22]

Because Wicksell thought that changes in the 'natural' interest rate arise from real factors (such as wars, technological innovations, etc.), it is tempting to conclude that he was not a quantity theorist – that he thought that price movements were ultimately explained by changes in the real economy.

This is not how Wicksell saw himself. Real shocks could not lead to price level changes *without* an increase or decrease in bank deposits. 'In short, changes in the stock of deposits were to Wicksell the one absolutely necessary and sufficient condition for price level movements.'[23] This was later echoed by Milton Friedman. Only if the central bank accommodated supply-side shocks by changing the price of credit could there be any price level changes. This was to lead to a hundred years of futile debate about what caused inflation: did the supply shocks cause money to expand, or did monetary expansion cause the supply shocks?

Why did Wicksell need the QTM? The quick answer is, for therapeutic purposes. He wanted the central bank to be able to offset fluctuations in the economy, and the only way it could influence the market rate was through the bank rate. Since the gold standard could not guarantee the appropriate bank-rate policy it should be replaced by an international paper standard, controlled by a committee of central banks.[24]

V. CONCLUSION

Two developments started to make the QTM operational for short-run stabilization purposes. The first was the development of the index number method of measuring the value of money. Secondly, by 1900 the gold standard was on the way to becoming a 'managed' standard, as central banks started to use changes in bank rate, variations in reserve requirements, open-market operations and central bank co-operation to offset gold flows.[25] It was increasingly recognized that commercial banks could manufacture money by creating bank deposits. But as long as the central bank had the means of regulating the rate of money creation by the commercial banks, the existence of credit money seemed to pose no danger to its ability to control prices.

The heroic faith in the QTM as a short-run stabilization policy instrument, even though the QTM was palpably untrue in the short-run, is explained by the urgency of its therapeutic ambitions. Even economists such as England's Dennis Robertson and the Austrian Joseph Schumpeter, for whom the business cycle was caused by 'real' shocks like technical innovations, thought that intelligent monetary policy could prevent the rocking tendency from becoming too violent. But as Eprime Eshag wrote, the QTM was 'somewhat wanting and to a large extent irrelevant as an instrument of analysis of short-run unemployment and production problems which became the primary concern of the economists during and after the [Great Depression]'.[26]

APPENDIX 3.1: FISHER'S EQUATION

Fisher built up his equation as follows:[27]

$$MV = \Sigma pQ$$

On the left, we have M for the money supply and V for the velocity of circulation. On the right, we have a summation of all the goods sold in an economy over a given period multiplied by their price. That is, we have:

$$MV = p_1 Q_1 + p_2 Q_2 + p_3 Q_3 + \ldots + p_n Q_n$$

Here, Q_1 and p_1 might stand for the number of bottles of milk sold and their price, Q_2 and p_2 for the number and price of textbooks, and so on.

Fisher defines the Qs as 'goods' very broadly, to include 'wealth, property, and benefits'.[28] What counts as a 'good' is non-trivial, and can severely impact the usefulness of the equation of exchange and the validity of the QTM: this will cause trouble when we come to Milton Friedman and the 2008 crisis.[29]

We can then simplify things by giving P as a weighted average of all prices, and T as the sum of all the Qs, yielding:

$$MV = PT$$

Finally, Fisher distinguished between two kinds of currency. First, there is money proper (e.g. bank notes), and secondly, there are bank deposits. We can distinguish then between M (money proper) and M' (bank deposits) and their respective velocities, giving us the final version of his equation:[30]

$$MV + M'V' = PT$$

4

Theories of the Fertile and Barren State

'Taxes which are levied on a country for the purpose of supporting war, or for the ordinary expenses of the State, and which are chiefly devoted to the support of unproductive labourers, are taken from the productive industry of the country; and every saving which can be made from such expenses will be generally added to the income, if not to the capital of the contributors.'

David Ricardo, 1817[1]

'Institutions that initially existed to serve the state by financing war also fostered the development of the economy as a whole . . . In the beginning was war.'

Niall Ferguson, 2001[2]

I. INTRODUCTION

The second unsettled issue in macroeconomic policy concerns the economic role of the state. What part does the state play in creating wealth? Although this question was discussed in Han Dynasty China (81 BC) and by the fourteenth-century Arab scholar Ibn Khaldûn,[3] it was not asked in Europe before modern times, partly because there was no state in the modern sense, partly because the growth of earthly wealth was not considered a justified (or feasible) object of human striving. The economy simply had to be kept productive enough to reproduce the social order. It was only from the sixteenth century onwards, with the voyages of discovery, the establishment of national states, the breakdown of the feudal economic system, and the emancipation of thought from religious doctrine that it became possible to envisage a future very different from, and better than, the past. The idea that wealth might deliberately be made to grow led a new school of political economists to question the economic practices by which humans had hitherto lived.

Their historical reflections led them to conclude that previous institutions had been severely dysfunctional from the point of view of wealth creation. In the past there had been great accumulations of wealth, but these had never led to self-sustaining growth. Rather, history disclosed a cyclical, not a progressive pattern: wealth expanded for a time and then contracted. Why was this? The political economists found the answer in the fact that the monarchs, soldiers and priests who made up 'the state' in traditional societies had appropriated, and then squandered, the wealth created by producers in wars, conspicuous display and great building projects to the glory of God and themselves. Even the richest states of old had been ruined by the extravagance and myopia of their ruling classes. Pre-modern rulers had invested too much in God, not enough in Mammon. Political economy set itself the task of providing the intellectual tools for breaking the mould.

Adam Smith contended that the growth of wealth depended on the spread of commerce (division of labour) and the accumulation of stock (investment). This was a distillation of post-medieval economic speculation, as was the view that a strong central state was needed to break down local barriers to trade and create a unified domestic market. However, two views emerged about the role of the state in economic development.

First in the field were the mercantilists, who gave the state a continuing role in trade promotion and accumulation. The mercantilists believed that state activity and spending could galvanize the growth of national wealth. War was an investment decision by the state: the state needed sufficient revenue to conquer foreign markets. Mainstream political economy, following the lead of Smith and Ricardo, rejected this programme. The state's two essential economic tasks were to remove barriers to trade and to secure private property rights. It should be granted power and revenue proportional to these tasks, but no more.

Central to this view was that trade sprang up spontaneously if obstacles were not placed in its way. This was as true of international as of domestic trade. From this point of view, resources devoted to wars of conquest were not an investment, but unproductive consumption. As Adam Smith put it in 1755: 'Little else is requisite to carry a state to the highest degree of opulence from the lowest barbarism but peace, easy taxes, and a tolerable administration of justice; all the rest being brought about by the natural course of things.'[4] Put simply, the state should get out of the way of private production for market. As the French merchants put it to the mercantilist minister Colbert, '*laissez-nous faire*' – 'leave it to us'. The mercantilist and laissez-faire views have fought it out ever since the birth of economics.

The Keynesian revolution of the twentieth century cut across this divide between mercantilism and laissez-faire by introducing an argument about state investment absent from both camps: the inability of a market system to maintain continuous full employment. Whereas all the disputes of pre-Keynesian economics were, at heart, about how most efficiently to create wealth from given resources, Keynes argued that, in normal circumstances, the limitation of effective demand prevented the full utilization of *potential* resources. The state should be allowed money not just to fight wars, but to bring into play additional resources.

In introducing an investment role for the state, Keynes also introduced a new division in economics, between *macroeconomics* and *microeconomics*. The essential claim of macroeconomics is that the study of the individual parts of the economy, i.e. microeconomics, even in combination, does not explain its total size. Put simply, the parts do not add up to the whole, because they are mutually dependent on each other.

We can classify these different positions, in roughly chronological sequence, by the simple criterion of how much the state should constitutionally be allowed to tax and spend:

1. The mercantilists saw the state as a wealth galvanizer, with the national debt and the accumulation of 'treasure' from export surpluses as its main instruments. The mercantilist outlook was general in the seventeenth and eighteenth centuries and has never disappeared, despite its repeated 'refutation' by later mainstream

economics. Germany was the chief mercantilist nation in the nineteenth century; and Germany, China and Japan are examples of contemporary mercantilism.

2. Mainstream economists from Adam Smith onward believed that state spending, far from adding to 'the national revenue', subtracted from it. The loss should be minimized by keeping public spending as low as possible. Budgets should be balanced annually at the lowest possible level. The only trade policy should be free trade: the balance of trade was automatically self-correcting. Mainstream political economy dominated British fiscal policy in the Victorian age.

3. Keynesians believed that the state budget should be used to secure the full employment of potential resources. The Keynesian fiscal constitution ran roughly from 1945 until 1975.

4. The neo-Victorian fiscal constitution, running roughly from 1980 to 2008, marked a partial return to the Victorian fiscal ideal. The budget should normally be balanced at the lowest level of spending and taxes that politics allowed. An expanding national debt was the road to ruin. Insofar as economy-wide balancing was needed, this was to be done by monetary policy.

The economic collapse of 2008 threw both the theory and practice of fiscal policy into disarray. Government deficits spiralled all over the Western world and countries' national debts crept up to 100 per cent of GDP or higher. Mostly this was an ad hoc response to the severity of the recession. But the slump severely damaged the consensus on fiscal policy, which had been taken for granted until recently, without producing any agreement on an alternative. On one side, there are the neo-Victorians, the fiscal hawks who want to get back to limited states and properly balanced budgets. On the other are the fiscal doves, who not only believe in the value of deficit spending in a slump, but who want fiscal rules flexible enough to dampen business cycles, secure full employment and boost economic growth.

This chapter will explore how the debate between the mercantilists and the political economists played itself out in the eighteenth and nineteenth centuries. But first, Figures 6 and 7 give a bird's-eye view of Britain's fiscal experience over the last three hundred years.

Figure 6. UK public spending as a proportion of GDP[5]
(per cent)

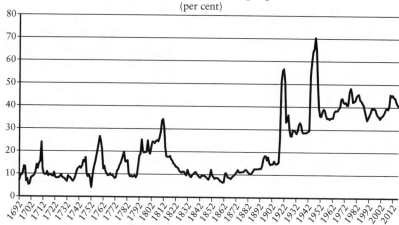

Figure 7. UK public debt as a proportion of GDP[6]
(per cent)

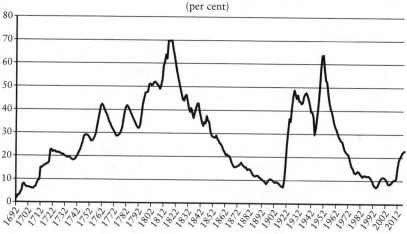

II. THE FERTILE STATE OF
THE MERCANTILISTS

Economies for most of history have been 'state-led' in the sense that the activities of rulers have determined whether they grew, stagnated or declined. But increased wealth (what we now call economic growth) only became the explicit object of state policy in the seventeenth and eighteenth centuries. Mercantilism was the first attempt to discover, by scientific reasoning, what it was that caused wealth to grow. In this endeavour, the mercantilists focused on the role of money and trade, and the state's role in both. Foreign trade was regarded as the main impetus to wealth, but only if it produced a surplus of money for the nation. Hence mercantilism's obsession with the 'balance of trade'. Its leading features, according to Denis O'Brien, were 'bullion and treasure as the key to wealth, regulation of foreign trade to produce a specie inflow, promotion of industry by inducing cheap raw material imports, export encouragement, [and] trade viewed as a zero-sum game'.[7]

Mercantilism was based on a fallacy, though quite a fruitful one: like pre-modern medicine, it had elements of truth and falsehood. The fallacy was the belief that exporting is better than importing, and that the object of economic policy should therefore be to secure a favourable balance of trade. This was the prevailing doctrine of most European states in this period. Of course, all countries cannot achieve a surplus simultaneously, so the pursuit of these policies involved continuing trade wars between the leading European powers.

Adam Smith accused the mercantilists of equating 'wealth' with 'gold'. The more sophisticated of them never believed this. What they did believe was that accumulating gold was a means to increase a country's share of the world's wealth by fighting successful wars. This seems circular: a trade surplus was required for war; and war produced a trade surplus. But the mercantilists believed that for each state the benefits of having trading monopolies would outweigh the cost of acquiring them. In addition, some mercantilists believed that the influx of precious metals would reduce the rate of interest, and so stimulate domestic manufacturing.

The practical policy of mercantilism was to deprive rivals of trade opportunities. In a classic move, Britain passed a series of Navigation Acts, starting in 1651, and aimed mainly at the Dutch carrying trade; the Acts, among other prohibitions, restricted trade between Britain and its colonies to British-owned ships. 'What we want is more of the trade [that] the Dutch now have,' said the Duke of Albermarle. Another example was the Methuen Treaty of 1703, which allowed English textiles to be admitted into Portugal free of duty in return for a preferential tariff on the import of Portugese wine to England.

Mercantilism can thus best be seen as a policy of increasing the relative power and, by means of power, the wealth of individual states through manipulation of trading relations. Adam Smith's claim to be the founder of scientific economics rests on his demonstration that trade need not be a zero-sum game, and that mercantilist policies, by restricting the size of the market, reduced the growth of wealth, and engendered the wars which justified them. David Ricardo put the case for free trade on a theoretically robust basis by proving arithmetically that, if countries were to specialize in producing and trading goods in which they were *relatively* more efficient, the real income of all the trading partners would be maximized – a logical demonstration that has stood the test of time, against all its critics, and provided a powerful normative argument for free trade policy. However, Ricardo's arithmetic proof that specialization was best offered cold comfort to those domestic producers who were as efficient as their situation and endowments allowed them to be. Against his scientific demonstration we can cite the spirit of King James I's proclamation: 'If it be agreeable to the rule of nature to prefer our own people to strangers, then it is much more reasonable that the manufactures of other nations should be charged with impositions than that people of our own kingdom should not be set to work.'[8] This argument for protectionism has always resonated, despite proof that free trade would be better.

There were some favourable consequences of mercantilist policies. They encouraged the centralization of state power, and this increased security of private property and fostered the unification of the internal market. They promoted manufacturing, exporting capacity and the growth of a merchant class (usually by grants of crown monopolies to chartered companies). They built up naval power. It is certainly a tenable view that the reduced cost of money engineered by the inflow of gold, together with the monopoly profits of commerce, helped finance Britain's industrial revolution. The successful players in the mercantilist game (Britain was the most successful) did establish very powerful trading positions in Asia and North America, which survived the end of mercantilism; Britain's imperial economic system, created in the mercantilist era, continued well into the twentieth century.

Niall Ferguson has provided a splendid picture of Britain as the model of the eighteenth-century fiscal warrior state.[9] Constitutional limitations robbed the British state of its arbitrary character, but, paradoxically, its enhanced legitimacy made it a more effective agent of national purpose than the absolute monarchies of the continent of Europe. Navies were also much cheaper to run than armies. You can use the same ships and sailors for either trading or military purposes, and it was through its merchant marine that Britain built up its overseas trading empire from the 1600s onwards. Countries striving to emulate Britain's economic performance placed more emphasis on the state's creative power than on the constitutional limitations prescribed by British liberal thinkers like John Locke, or the precepts of fiscal finance adumbrated by Adam Smith.

Britain's fiscal constitution was based on the idea that wealth was generated through the competitive struggle of nations. The edge lay not with the states with the largest resources, but with the states that could most efficiently mobilize resources for their foreign policy goals. The constitutional character of the British monarchy gave it an enhanced revenue-raising power. Additionally important was the centralization of tax collection in a paid bureaucracy, instead of relying on tax farming – leasing out tax collection to private agents – and the sale of offices. This enabled the British government to raise 12.4 per cent of GNP in taxes in 1788, compared to France's 6.8 per cent.[10]

As Ferguson tells it, the institutions for mobilizing resources were Parliament, the tax bureaucracy, the national debt and the central bank. The superior development of this financial 'square of power' in eighteenth-century Britain gave it not only a decisive military advantage over its main rival, France, but also a faster rate of economic growth.[11]

However, the principal fiscal weapon for the struggle was the national debt, and the main issue for fiscal policy, then as later, was the sustainability of this national debt. 'In a fiscal state, a steady and secure flow of tax revenues forms the basis for large-scale borrowing without the threat of default and hence the need for the state to pay high interest rates to obtain funds.'[12] Britain 'out-taxed, out-borrowed, and out-gunned' France in the Napoleonic wars.[13] Ferguson traces the origins of modern debt finance to a series of financial innovations in England, starting with the establishment of the Bank of England in 1694 (France only got its central bank in 1800) and the adoption of the gold standard in 1717, and culminating, in 1751, in the birth of 'Consols' – the consolidated debt of the British government in the form of liquid, but perpetual, bonds redeemable at par.[14] The effect of these innovations was to increase the size of the sustainable public debt. Undertaken for warlike motives, the measures not only enabled Britain to beat France in a long struggle for dominance, culminating in the Napoleonic wars, but they also stimulated the growth of commerce. The key point here is that the proliferation of tradable public debt instruments 'effectively created the private market for private sector bonds and shares' by spreading risk.[15] Moreover, 'the emergence of the bondholders as an influential lobby within parliament reduced the risk of default by the British state and thereby increased the state's capacity to borrow cheaply'.[16]

In short, Hanoverian England was a brilliant war machine and commercial engine. The wealth accumulated through commerce enabled it to become the 'first industrial nation'. Succeeding generations paid off its huge public debt out of the proceeds of its economic growth. The mercantilist policy of Britain's eighteenth-century Hanoverian monarchy, which laid the basis for the *Pax Britannica*, was abandoned by Britain itself, but became the model for successful state performance of all those countries trying to 'catch up' with Britain.

III. THE WASTEFUL STATE OF THE POLITICAL ECONOMISTS

The late eighteenth century saw a turning away from the warlike state. Adam Smith may have written that 'defence ... is of much more importance than opulence', but he saw the mercantile system of his time, and its wars, as having 'not been very favourable ... to the annual produce'.[17] Like his contemporaries, the French 'physiocrats', he believed that the source of wealth was 'produce' – though he extended the meaning of this term to include manufacture as well as agriculture. Against the protectionism of mercantilism, Smith roundly asserted that consumption was 'the sole end and purpose of all production'.[18] From this point of view, restricting domestic consumption in order to achieve an export surplus was irrational. The national debt incurred to pay for the mercantilist wars restricted the growth of wealth, and therefore consumption.

An important part of Smith's case for the wastefulness of state spending rested on his argument that trade, left free, conferred benefits on both trading partners. One did not need wars and monopolies to have a great commerce. It would come about organically under conditions of 'natural liberty'. Book IV of Smith's *Wealth of Nations* is devoted to an attack on the mercantilist system. Mercantilist wars were fought for the benefit of the sovereign and vested interests, at the expense of the consumer.

The analytic basis of the doctrine of state frugality is straightforward. According to Smith, wealth is increased by the accumulation of capital through saving and investment.[19] Taxation diverts income from private accumulation to state consumption, and therefore subtracts from wealth creation. The state is, by definition, unproductive. Smith and his followers saw strengthening Parliament's control of revenue at the expense of the monarchy's as the way to reduce state consumption.

Classical economists aimed to limit, not abolish the state. According to Smith, the system of 'natural liberty' leaves the state four duties: defence of the country; administration of justice; responsibility for education; and

> erecting and maintaining certain public works and certain public institutions which it can never be for the interest of any individual, or small number of individuals, to erect and maintain, because the profit could never repay the expense to any individual or small number of individuals, though it may frequently do much more than repay it to a great society.[20]

In modern parlance, these works and institutions are called 'public goods': goods which, for one reason or another, cannot be supplied by the market, and for Smith included those which 'facilitate the commerce of any country, such as good roads, bridges, navigable canals, habours, etc.', as well as a system of national education to repair the ravages to human intelligence wrought by the division of labour.[21] For these duties, but only these, the state had to be provided with revenue. Having only a modest list of duties, the state's revenue should also be modest. 'Be quiet' was Bentham's famous prescription for government: leave economic growth to the natural desire for improvement.

Smith ignored mercantilist concern with money and employment.

Money was simply a lubricant. The economists who followed Smith believed that in conditions of natural liberty all savings would be invested, resources fully used.

Taxation does not appear in the index of *The Wealth of Nations*, but there is a large section on the national debt, the growth of which in the 1700s Smith regarded as the main impediment to increased prosperity. 'Like an improvident spendthrift, whose pressing occasions will not allow him to wait for the regular payment of his revenue, the state is in the constant practice of borrowing of its own factors and agents, and paying interest for the use of its own money.'[22] Issuing debt was a way of extracting money from the citizen by stealth. 'There is no art which one government sooner learns of another than that of draining money from the pockets of the people.'[23]

Through borrowing, the sovereign was enabled to fight expensive and unnecessary wars. Smith had little faith that a sinking fund for repayment of debt would solve the problem of 'perpetual funding', since the reduction of public debt in peace had never been proportional to its expansion in war.[24] In the past, liberation of the public revenue from debt burdens had been brought about by open default or 'a pretended payment' (inflation).[25] But Smith denounced this as a 'treacherous fraud', which destroyed the state's creditworthiness.[26]

The only possible advantage of borrowing to finance wars was that it might make more saving possible than if the whole cost of wars was raised by taxation alone.[27] Indeed, Smith attributed the prosperity which, contrary to his polemic, had accompanied the big expansion of the national debt in the eighteenth century, to the fact that state borrowing had not impeded the growth of saving. By their inherent frugality, the British had been able to repair 'all the breaches which the waste and extravagance of government had made in the general capital of society'.[28]

The only honest way to pay off the national debt was by increasing taxation or cutting spending. Smith thought the colonies should be taxed to pay for their defence. But if they couldn't be made to pay, Britain should rid herself of the delusion of empire 'and endeavour to accommodate her future views and designs to the real mediocrity of her circumstances'.[29]

Smith's argument, that state spending 'crowded out' productive private spending, was reinforced by Ricardo. Ricardo regarded all state expenditure as inherently wasteful. Taxes and public loans equally destroy capital. But, unlike Smith, Ricardo thought that raising loans to pay for state expenses 'tends to make us less thrifty', by deceiving us that we only have to save to pay the interest on the loan, rather than our share of its full tax equivalent.[30] This is interesting, because while Ricardo's analysis led him to believe that borrowing was simply deferred taxation, he did not believe that the taxpayer necessarily understood it to be so.[31]

Countries, said Ricardo, should use periods of peace to pay off the national debt as quickly as possible, and 'no temptation of relief, no desire to escape from present, and I hope temporary, distresses, should induce us to relax in our attention that great object'.[32] So a proper sinking fund should be set up. Writing after the Napoleonic wars had left Britain a national debt of 260 per cent of national income, Ricardo asserted that if, by the time of the next war, the national debt had not been considerably reduced, either that war must be paid for by taxation, or the British state would be bankrupted. In the period covered by this book we shall encounter four big spikes in the national debt: post-1815, post-1918, post-1945 and post 2008–9; the first three were caused by war, the last by government's response to economic collapse. Each 'excess' led to the restoration of 'virtue' in the form of fiscal austerity.

The repudiation of mercantilism outlined above reflects the turn of economics from a monetary to a 'real' analysis. The mercantilists (and most other 'pre-scientific' economic thinkers) stressed the role of money, credit and public finance in fertilizing economic activity, whereas in the 'real' analysis of Smith and Ricardo the growth engines are thrift and productivity, with money as a mere 'veil' which hid from people their true circumstances, and taxation and public borrowing subtractions from both.[33] As Mill wrote in 1844, no one any longer argued for the 'utility of a large government expenditure, for the purpose of encouraging industry'.[34] Earlier, David Hume had pointed out that the mercantilist concern with ensuring, through an export surplus, a sufficiency of the precious metals, was a delusion (see above, p. 37). The economic task was to ensure the most efficient allocation of 'real' resources. This was best left to the market.

In the rejection of mercantilism by the classical economists it is not clear whether ideas or circumstances were in the driving seat. George Stigler believed it was 'the absence of major wars' in the nineteenth century which caused the state's role to recede and the 'reign of liberty' to expand.[35] However, it is possible that the change in economists' views about how to obtain wealth caused the incidence of war to decline. It may also be that peace and war, progress and decay, are subject to long cycles, with economic theory adapting to each phase of the cycle.

IV. THE VICTORIAN FISCAL CONSTITUTION

Put into practice from the mid-nineteenth century onwards, the classical economists' view of the state's role dominated British fiscal policy until the First World War, and it limped on afterwards into the 1930s. The views of Smith, Ricardo and Mill, though not cited directly, were part of the mental equipment of the frugal Victorian Treasury. Deficit finance was shunned; budgets were to be annually balanced. Central government was to be kept small in relation to the economy. 'A Chancellor was judged not only on his ability to balance his budget but also to reduce the National Debt.'[36] Maintaining a regular sinking fund for debt redemption was considered part of 'balancing the budget'. Surpluses were to be used only to reduce the national debt and not spent the following year. Free trade triumphed after 1846, when Parliament repealed the Corn Laws protecting British agriculture.

Ricardo would have been pleased with the progress in reducing the national debt shown in Figure 8; by the outbreak of the First World War, the debt–GDP ratio had fallen to a fifth of its peak in the aftermath of the Napoleonic wars. In a recent analysis of debt reduction between 1831 and 1913, Nicholas Crafts argues that much of this success can be attributed to a strong commitment to balancing the budget. The British government ran persistent primary budget surpluses over the course of almost a century, with only six instances of a deficit higher than 1 per cent of GDP. There was no inflation, and

Figure 8. The rise and fall of UK war debt[37]
(public debt as a proportion of GDP, per cent)

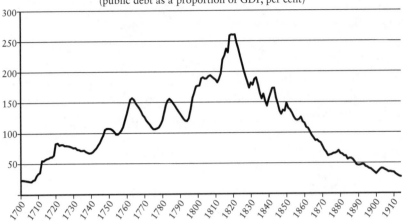

the government would not have been able to rely on buoyant growth alone, since real interest rates on the debt in this period were consistently higher than real growth rates.[38]

A crucial innovation was income tax, first levied in 1814, and renewed by Peel in 1842. By 1911–14, this had become the principal source of government revenue. Income tax had the double benefit of giving the British state a secure revenue base, and aligning voters' interests with cheap government, since only direct taxpayers had the vote. Legitimacy of the taxation system was enhanced by strengthening Treasury control and giving responsibility for assessing tax liability to the Inland Revenue, independent of government. 'Fiscal probity', under Gladstone, 'became the new morality.'[39]

Public spending as a share of GDP fell from 1830 to 1870, then remained flat, before the Boer wars and increased military spending in the run-up to the First World War caused a rise. In 1900, the British government spent 14 per cent of GNP, the proportion having been under 10 per cent for most of the nineteenth century. Spending on social services came to 2.6% of GNP; economic services (agriculture, forestry, fishing, industry, transport and employment) took 1.9% of GNP; defence, law and order 7.4%; interest on the national debt 1%; with the rest spent on administration, overseas services and environmental services (the provision of basic services such as roads, lighting and water).[40] The government owned no industries except the post office and a few ordnance factories; income tax was tiny, and most people were below the direct tax threshold, though there were indirect taxes ('excise duties') on working-class 'sins' like drink and gambling. Municipal utilities such as gas and water were financed by loans from central government to local authorities. But most of what we now think of as welfare was still provided by voluntary insurance and private philanthropy. The state was thus too small to have much direct influence on aggregate demand, either through discretionary spending or built-in stabilizers. Not that it was expected to.[41]

Though limited borrowing was permitted in times of war, this exception was not to be taken lightly; as far as possible, war was still to be financed out of current tax receipts. When this was not possible, current budget deficits were to be financed by long-term debt, repaid as soon as peacetime allowed current budget surpluses again.[42] However, with the British Navy ruling the waves, and free trade replacing protectionism, peace came to be regarded as the norm.

The Victorian minimal-expenditure constitution was challenged by the Liberal government's social reforms in the 1900s, as well as by the need to increase defence spending to meet the German threat. Social reform was partly driven by a desire to ensure a workforce that could compete with the United States and Germany, partly by the extension of the suffrage. Lloyd George's 'People's Budget' of 1909 proposed increasing the standard rate of income tax to 1s in the pound (a rate of 5 per cent) for incomes between £2,000 and £3,000, and to 1s 2d (5.8 per cent) for incomes over £3,000, as well as introducing an additional super tax of 6d (2.5 per cent) on the amount by which incomes over £5,000 exceeded £3,000. He also proposed raising death duties (inheritance tax) and introducing a 20 per cent tax on any increase in land value when that land changed hands – all to a torrent of execration from the wealthy. These taxes were partly to pay for an enlarged social budget, which now included grants for education, old-age pensions and 'social' insurance against sickness and unemployment.[43] Yet diverging from the expenditure-minimization tradition did not mean abandoning the balanced-budget rule: 'the desire to obtain a budget surplus to reduce the Debt remained as strong as ever'.[44] And, despite the emergence of business cycles, there was no hint yet of a state duty to maintain a high level of employment.

V. THE PERSISTENCE OF MERCANTILISM

Historians have dubbed Britain's fiscal constitution 'precocious' or 'exceptional'.[45] Having fought the wars of the eighteenth century to become 'top dog', Britain had no need for an energetic state, and preached laissez-faire and free trade. Latecomers to the feast learned more from Britain's eighteenth-century practice than from its nineteenth-century precepts. Catch-up economics was explicitly national.

The most important theoretical criticism of the Smithian system came from the German economist Friedrich List, who, in turn, had picked up many of his ideas from Alexander Hamilton, theoretician of American protectionism. Ricardo's doctrine of comparative advantage, a sophisticated argument for free trade, was a theory of static equilibrium, which left the first successful trader in any free trade world with the most valuable advantages. But, as List pointed out, the *'power of creating wealth* is infinitely more important than *wealth itself'*.[46] And the power of creating wealth belonged to power proper, because – as history had amply shown – 'a nation, by means of power, is enabled not only to open up new productive sources, but to maintain itself in possession of former and recently acquired wealth'.[47]

What mattered to List (and in this he spoke for most German economists) was not the riches of individuals, but the nation's well-being. List criticized Adam Smith's school of thought for (i) its 'boundless cosmopolitanism', which ignored national interests; (ii) its 'dead materialism', which ignored mental and moral aims; and (iii) its 'disorganising particularism and individualism', which ignored social cohesion.[48] The German Historical School of economists redefined mercantilism as 'nation-building'. They introduced the important, but now neglected, idea that the validity of economic doctrines depends on circumstances. What might be good for a nation at one time might be quite unsuitable for it at another. Free trade, List remarked scornfully, was the doctrine of a country which, having 'attained the summit of greatness . . . kicks away the ladder by which [it] has climbed up . . . In this lies the secret of the cosmopolitical doctrines of Adam Smith.'[49] So List added to the state's four duties, listed by Smith, the development of the 'productive forces'.

Economics (just about) recognizes List's 'infant industry' argument as an exception to the general case for free trade. It fails to recognize that he founded a general theory of economic development, of which free trade is a special case.

German policymakers took List's teaching to heart. The financial, commercial and industrial machine that Britain had developed haphazardly over two hundred years, Germany built deliberately in half a century. First came the *Zollverein*, or customs union, of the separate German states between 1834 and 1866, linked together by a bond-financed railway system, and capped by the establishment of the German Empire in 1873. In 1879, following the Great Depression (see above, p. 51), Bismarck liquidated Germany's free trade moment by imposing tariffs on foreign grain and industrial products, and starting compulsory social insurance for health, accidents and old age. Under cover of Protection, German industry surged ahead on all fronts: heavy industry – machine-building, electrical engineering and construction – followed by chemical engineering, precision mechanics and optics. The giant Kiel Canal, linking the North Sea to the Baltic, was built with funds from the naval budget between 1887 and 1895. Before the end of the century Germany had overtaken Britain in industrial production, and 'Made in Germany' rivalled 'Made in Britain' as the protected home market became the springboard for Germany's assault on world markets. With its deliberate attention to product innovation and vocational training (theoretical and practical), its network of research institutes, its corporatist business structure linking big business and investment banks, and its social insurance schemes, Germany's organized capitalism bore little resemblance to Manchester liberalism. As a contemporary French journalist explained: 'The Germans . . . looked ahead in a broad-minded, far-sighted manner.'[50]

In the United States, too, the needs of catch-up subverted the aggressive business ideology of laissez-faire. Tariffs on foreign goods were seen both as a means of economic growth *and* as providing the government with revenue in a federal system.[51] Tariffs shielded industry throughout the nineteenth century; the state funded big infrastructure projects, such as the Erie Canal linking the Great Lakes to the Hudson river. Because of the 'wild west' character of American business expansion, the Federal government were also pioneers in the legal regulation of business life. By the end of the 1800s, the United States, too, was forging ahead of Britain industrially. Its conversion to free trade and deregulation came only in the 1940s, when it had replaced Britain as 'top dog'.

Most developing countries in the twentieth century learned their economics from Hamilton and List rather than from Smith and Ricardo. That is to say, they set about, under state direction, shaping their trading advantages, rather than passively accepting those supposedly bequeathed by the first-starters. They were unashamedly mercantilist, believing in free exports but controlled imports. And, in a reprise of the nineteenth century, they came under increasing pressure from the already rich countries to abandon their policies of import substitution.[52]

Of most concern to us here is the attitude of different countries to the national debt. For most countries, public borrowing was a necessity. Lacking efficient tax systems, they had to borrow to finance even routine activities, let alone wars, relying on the yields of customs duties and other state monopolies to pay back their creditors. The survival of tariffs in the nineteenth century is partly explained by the state's need for revenue.

The combination of huge public debts left over from the Napoleonic wars and the lack of reliable sources of tax revenue gave private money-lenders like the Rothschilds their dominant position in the middle years of the nineteenth century.[53] The Rothschilds created the international bond market. Nathan Rothschild's loan to Prussia in 1818 set the pattern for future loans. It was a fixed-interest sterling loan, with investors being paid in London, not Berlin; this removed both the risk of loss on the exchange rate and the inconvenience of collecting interest from abroad. Nathan Rothschild insisted that the 'good faith' of the borrowing government had to be underpinned by a ceiling on state debt and a mortgage on the royal estates – the first time that such conditions had explicitly featured in contracts between money-lenders and sovereigns, anticipating the modern concern with the problem of debt sustainability.[54] As Nathan Rothschild explained to the Prussian state Chancellor: 'Without some security of this description any attempt to raise a considerable sum in England for a foreign Power would be hopeless.'[55] In Niall Ferguson's words, 'If investors bid up the price of a government's stock, that government could feel secure. If they dumped its stock, that government was quite possibly living on borrowed time as well as money.'[56] This was the classical creditor position.

The Rothschilds certainly talked as if they had a vested interest in peace. They reiterated that 'it is the principle of our house not to lend money for war'.[57] Yet, a glance at their balance sheet shows that they made most of their money by financing preparations for war and the international transfers that tended to follow. The 'golden age' of the Rothschilds, from 1852 to 1874, spanned the Crimean War and the four wars of Italian and German unification. The reason is clear: the wars of the 1850s and 1860s were fought by states that were, by and large, strapped for cash. Wars and war scares might depress the prices of existing bonds, but they greatly increased the yield – and hence attractiveness to investors – of new debt. On 30 April 1859, Rothschild's London house cabled its Paris partner: 'Hostilities have commenced. Austria wants a loan of 200,000,000 florins.' With the rise of competitor banks, the Rothschilds knew that they had no 'veto on bellicosity'. If they failed to underwrite loans to states, others would. The fatal weakness of banking pacifism was that profits came before peace.

The Rothschilds were also drawn into 'lending money for war' by their involvement in railway bond issues. The railway lines that linked Austria to Germany, Italy, Hungary and the Balkans, paid for by the Vienna Rothschilds and their subsidiary, the Creditanstalt, were largely built for military purposes. In the 'war of the railways' in the 1850s, the multinational resources of the Rothschilds triumphed over the resources of their Parisian rival, the Péreire brothers. But their railways were thereafter hostage to state policy.

Reliance on international bond markets imposed a discipline on the fiscal and exchange-rate policies of states, just as it does today. Although the merchant banks were rivals, they could agree on what made a particular state creditworthy. It was their business to do so, for had they not been able to secure their loans, no one would have invested in them. So the bond markets played a crucial role in pro-moting 'sound finance'. The bankers were equally ardent advocates of 'sound money'. By the end of the nineteenth century, foreign state loans were usually made conditional on their recipients joining the gold standard. With Britain's example before them, the bankers understood that constitutional monarchies were more likely than absolute ones to repay debt, and tried to make constitutional reform a condition of loans – for example, in the Rothschild loan to Austria in 1859. But the spread of constitutional government had a paradox-ical consequence. By making states more efficient in collecting taxes, it weakened their need for international bankers.

With the improvement of state revenues, the development of deposit and joint-stock banking, and the growth of domestic capital markets, there was less demand for the financial services supplied by the 'Jews of Kings'. In the last third of the nineteenth century, the bankers' power weakened as nationalism came to the fore and as governments' fiscal positions strengthened. The introduction of income tax in Prus-sia between 1891 and 1893 made it possible for Germany to adopt Britain's balanced-budget rule.[58] But governments in Latin America continued to rely on the services of international bond markets to finance their needs until well into the twentieth century, their fre-quent defaults not deterring the optimism of investors for long.

State borrowing was not just a matter of necessity; necessity alerted people to its advantages. Alexander Hamilton, America's first Secretary of the Treasury, wrote: 'a national debt, if it is not excessive, will be to us a national blessing, an "invigorating principle"'.[59] His rationale was that public debt enlarged the pool of private credit, thus enhancing invest-ment. This argument faded with the deepening of private credit markets. But another argument for public debt survived. Throughout the 1800s Prussia made public investments in technical education, roads, key industries, railways and an overseas trading corporation, as part of its policy of 'catching up' Britain. In this, the state worked closely with industrialists and was able to staunch the emigration of young Germans to America. As W. O. Henderson concludes in his assessment of German economic development, Bismarck 'realised the influence which the cen-tral Federal governments could exercise over industrial developments through their control over the public sector of the economy'.[60]

VI. CONCLUSION

The difference between mercantilists and classical liberal economists was one of means, not ends. Both wanted to increase national wealth through state action, but whereas mercantilists favoured direct intervention through investment and trade policy, liberals sought to confine the state to creating the background conditions for a free market. The latter's self-presentation as 'anti-state' was a deception, springing partly from lack of historical perspective and partly from ideology: clearly a market order looks more attractive if presented as the result of a spontaneous growth rather than as an artefact of state power. The deception persists to this day, with the neo-liberals loudly proclaiming their faith in the free market, even though in reality it would not exist for a day without continued state support.

The history of fiscal theory shows that, far from being the scientific paragon it claims to be, it is highly ideological, reflecting economic circumstances, historical mythology and class forces, with the enabling concept of public goods waxing and waning with circumstances and the size of the franchise.

PART TWO

The Rise, Triumph and Fall of Keynes

In the twenty years of peace following the First World War, the macroeconomic policy rules of the previous half century broke down. This was because the conditions making it possible to keep them disappeared. The old macroeconomy (in the days before macroeconomic *policy*) rested on a tripod of gold, balanced budgets and free trade. All three were unhinged by the war. Quite simply, the gold standard became the transmitter, rather than dampener, of external shocks, while domestic adjustment to shocks became more costly. It was a period of experiment in theory and policy. Nationalist economics replaced free trade. As Keynes wrote in 1933: 'Not believing we are saved already, we each would like to have a try at working out our own salvation.'[1]

The nineteenth-century gold standard had worked after a fashion owing to special conditions. After the war, it became completely dysfunctional. Barry Eichengreen paints a compelling picture of 'an international monetary system disturbed by misaligned exchange rates, insufficient and unhelpfully distributed reserves ... and at the same time incapable of responding to disturbances due to rigidities in wage structure, rising tariffs, and the failure of cooperation'.[2] London's ability to act as 'conductor of the international orchestra' was fatally weakened by the war; Britain could stay in the war only by borrowing heavily from the United States, the new creditor. The problem of 'global imbalances' reared its head for the first, but by no means the last, time, with the United States' permanent trade surplus, unmatched by an equivalent export of capital, exerting deflationary pressure on much of the rest of the world.

Universal suffrage, the welfare state and mass trade unionism were the legacies of total war, at least in Europe: the quid pro quo for the carnage inflicted on populations by their governments. Both the left and the right accepted that the economic mechanism was blocked. In *The Decay of Capitalist Civilisation*, Beatrice and Sidney Webb, leaders of pre-war Fabian socialism, wrote in 1923: 'There can be no permanence in a situation in which we abandon production to capitalism, and yet give the workers the political power to enforce demands on the national income which capitalism has neither the ability nor the incentive to supply.'[3] A voice on the right of politics said much the same ten years later:

> Instead of allowing economic forces to operate freely, the tendency [in the UK] since the War, has everywhere been in the opposite direction. The dole policy, the activities of the trade unions, and the employers' associations, and the various hindrances to migration have all inter-fered with the freedom of the labour markets. At the same time the activities of trusts, cartels, and marketing schemes have all retarded or suppressed the indispensable movement of prices. In a word, the organism has been drugged and paralysed. Hence the present deplor-able situation.[4]

In this blocked system, unemployment became the chief expression of market sclerosis, and the main challenge to economic policy. Unemployment among the insured workforce in Britain averaged about 10 per cent in the 1920s, double what it had been before the First World War.

Persistent mass unemployment was also a challenge to economic theory. There was no theory of output and employment as such, since classical theory presupposed a state of full employment. Experience validated this to some extent. Economies might be knocked over for a short time, but they got up again without government help. Workers moved not from town to town, but from continent to continent. Say's Law was not mortally challenged. This changed with the (second) Great Depression, which started in 1929 and from which the world did not fully recover until the Second World War.

Theory and policy alike were slow to recognize that conditions had changed. Under the slogan 'back to normalcy', determined attempts were

Figure 9. UK unemployment through to the Second World War[5]
(per cent)

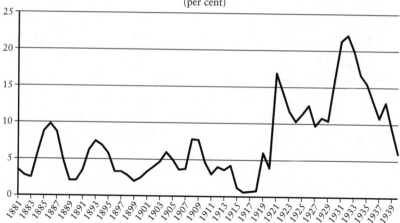

made in the 1920s to retrieve the pre-war system. At their heart was the restoration of the international gold standard. Orthodoxy saw this as the indispensable framework for domestic monetary discipline. Further, a gold anchor was proof against inflation. To restore the gold standard, suspended in the war, it was essential for governments 'to balance national budgets by contraction of expenses rather than by increase in taxation, to stop inflation by ceasing to cover budget deficits by recourse to paper money, and to cease borrowing for unproductive purposes'; in short, to liquidate war finance.[6] This was a return to the old post-Napoleonic Ricardian programme, which became the consensual position of all governments.

Then, on 24 October 1929, Wall Street collapsed, starting the worst depression since the industrial revolution. It was world-wide. Falls in agricultural prices and industrial production, and rises in unemployment, were colossal, with the United States and Germany worst hit of the industrial nations. In the USA the volume of production fell by a third; unemployment rose to a quarter of the labour force. Investment stopped completely. German industrial production was halved; unemployment rose to 6 million – an unemployment rate of 24 per cent. Britain escaped comparatively lightly, since, having missed out on the boom of the 1920s, its economy had less far to fall. The downward slide continued for three years, shattering economies and political systems. The chief beneficiary in continental Europe was fascism. Recovery, which started in 1932, never returned economies to full health, and there was a further steep collapse in the United States in 1937–8. It took another world war to restore full employment in the two major Western democracies.

The Great Depression set off a period of experiments in thought and policy. Keynesian economics was the most successful of the results.

David Laidler has shown that many hands went into 'fabricating' the Keynesian revolution.[7] It was partly a revolution in monetary policy, involving a break with the gold standard. It was partly a revolution in fiscal policy, which involved abandoning the balanced-budget rule. Monetary policy was henceforth to be subordinated to the government's primary responsibility for maintaining full employment. Keynes's name is rightly attached to this revolution because only Keynes offered a convincing theoretical explanation of persistent mass unemployment. He did so by offering an alternative to the dominant price-adjustment theory of his day and an operational policy for preventing or recovering from economic collapses. Whether his alternative of 'quantity adjustment' was a long-run or short-run process was of less concern to policymakers than its implication that massive unemployment could last long enough to endanger the social order.

5

Keynes's Intervention

'[Central banks should] employ all their resources to prevent a movement of [the price level] by more than a certain percentage in either direction ... just as before the war they employed all their resources to prevent a movement in the price of gold.'

J. M. Keynes, 1923[1]

'... very little additional employment and no permanent employment can in fact and as a general rule be created by State borrowing and State expenditure.'

Winston Churchill, 1928[2]

'In the case of any new proposal all one can do is to show there are some theoretical reasons for thinking it might be effective, and then ... to make the experiment and see how successfully it is carried out.'

J. M. Keynes, 1924[3]

I. THE TROUBLE WITH MONEY

Before the First World War, monetary reformers such as Fisher and Wicksell had urged that central banks should deliberately use monetary *policy* to stabilize the price level, and not just be automatic transmitters of international gold flows. The 'management' of the gold standard had started, but it had not got very far. The democratic innovations of the war, which involved extending suffrage and trade union control over wages, increased the urgency of the task. With industrial economies losing their 'elasticity', a more elastic currency was required.

Once it came to be accepted as prudent, for social reasons, to use monetary policy to mitigate dislocating economic fluctuations, all the unsettled questions in monetary theory were reopened. Was the money supply exogenous or endogenous? What was the transmission mechanism from money to prices? Was the task of the central bank to control currency or credit? Was it possible to combine price stability with exchange-rate stability? The context of these discussions was the radical volatility of prices, very different from the muted modulations of the previous century: post-war hyperinflation in some countries being followed by price collapses.

John Maynard Keynes and Edwin Cannan debated the causes of the wartime and post-war inflations in a re-run of the Currency versus Banking School debates of the early nineteenth century. Cannan, a professor of economics at the LSE, denied that banks create money. To him they were simply cloakroom attendants, who issued tickets for money deposited with them. It was the central bank that produced the 'extra' money. Thus the problem of stopping inflation boiled down to limiting the issue of central bank notes. Cannan wrote as much in his book *The Paper Pound*, first published in 1919: 'Burn your paper money, and go on burning it till it will buy as much gold as it used to do!'[4]

Keynes restated the credit theory. Banks created deposits in response to the 'needs of trade'. Money could not, therefore, be in 'over-supply'. Old-fashioned theorists like Cannan claimed that credit expansion followed currency expansion. But, wrote Keynes, in a modern community with a developed banking system, expansion of notes was 'generally the *last* phase of a lengthy process of credit creation'. To reverse the credit expansion after it had occurred by preventing the quantity of notes from increasing would only bankrupt the business world – 'a course often followed in former days when Professor Cannan's doctrine still held the field'. Control of credit, not control of currency, was the key to price – and, by extension, economic – stability.[5]

How was credit to be controlled? In the *Tract on Monetary Reform* (1923), Keynes wrote down the following equation:[6]

$$n = p(k + rk')$$

where n is currency notes, p is the cost of living index, k is the amount of real 'purchasing power'[7] people keep as cash (outside banks), k' the amount they keep in bank deposits, and r the fraction of these deposits in bank reserves. In equilibrium, k and k' (velocity) are stable, but when the 'mood of business' is changing, it will be the task of the central bank to deliberately vary n and r (the banks' ratio of reserves to liabilities) so as to counterbalance the movements of k and k'. In short, the Bank of England needed to vary the stock of high-powered money to offset changes in the supply of, and demand for, credit. Managing expectation plays the key role in Keynes's scheme of monetary therapy. The central bank must create a confident expectation that the price level will not move more than a certain percentage either way from the price of a standard composite commodity.[8] The message was clear: he who would control money has to control expectations about future prices. This, as we shall see, was the rationale for the inflation targeting adopted in the 1990s.

Like his predecessors, Fisher and Wicksell, Keynes encountered the problem of the gold standard. Bank Rate could be used to stabilize either domestic prices or the exchange rate. It could not do both. Not surprisingly, he condemned the gold standard as a 'barbarous relic', thwarting the beneficent purposes of 'scientific' monetary policy.[9]

In the textbook account, a country's money stock bore a fixed proportion to its banking system's gold reserves, and was inflated or deflated as gold flowed in and out of the country. The problem of keeping domestic prices fairly stable had, to some extent, been finessed by the flexibility of the central bank responses to gold movements, but mostly by the hegemonic role of sterling in the international payments system. After the war, however, the system was rendered unstable by 'British inability and United States unwillingness' to assume these responsibilities.[10]

Because of the wartime inflation, the British government suspended convertibility in 1919, for the first time since 1797. Prices skyrocketed; the exchange rate plummeted. Bank rate was put up to 7 per cent in

1920 to check the inflationary boom, a reasonable step in the circumstances, but it was then held at this now punitive rate in the subsequent year and a half of collapsing prices, output and employment in order to prepare for a resumption of convertibility at the old sterling–dollar exchange rate. This was the Cunliffe adjustment mechanism (see pp. 54–5) being applied not just to liquidate the inflation, but to restore the previous gold value of the pound, in an echo of Locke and Ricardo.

In the spirit of the monetary reformer, Keynes attacked the aim of forcing up the value of sterling. It was to no avail. The aim of policy-makers was to put the tried and tested anti-inflation anchor back in place as soon as possible. Germany went back on to gold in 1924, Britain in 1925, and France and Italy in 1927.

Keynes's *Treatise on Money* (1930) explicitly showed the influence of Wicksell.[11] The business cycle, or what Keynes called the credit cycle, was caused by the deviation of the market rate of interest from the natural rate of interest, or, equivalently, of saving from investment. Keynes now proposed a 'dual method' of controlling the credit cycle: old-fashioned variation in bank rate and the newer technique of open-market operations. Bank rate set the short-term rate; but direct action on the term structure of rates was needed to enforce the official rate in the market. By buying and selling securities (open-market operations) the central bank could vary the amount of cash reserves held by member banks, which they used as the base of a superstructure of credit. Keynes wrote in 1931:

> A central bank, which is free to govern the volume of cash and reserve money in its monetary system by the joint use of bank rate policy and open-market operations, is . . . in a position to control not merely the volume of credit but the rate of investment, the level of prices and in the long run the level of incomes, provided that the objectives it sets before it are compatible with its legal obligations, such as those relating to maintenance of gold convertibility or to the parity of the foreign exchanges.[12]

Keynes's espousal of the credit theory of money was, as can be seen, limited. He needed a cash base – exogenous money – for open-market operations to be feasible. In a modern monetary system, paper cash is the substitute for gold cash and the central bank does the job of the gold standard, only 'scientifically'. In short, Keynes did not entirely jettison the Quantity Theory of Money.

Unfortunately, Britain was in no position to try out the ideas of the monetary reformers. The mistaken policy of relinking the pound to gold at an overvalued exchange rate had resulted in a low employment trap. The worst of all possible worlds, Keynes wrote, is one where

> spontaneous changes in earnings tend upwards, but monetary changes, due to the relative shortage of gold, tend downwards, so that ... we have chronic necessity for induced changes [in wage levels] sufficient not only to counteract the spontaneous changes but to reverse them. Yet it is possible that this is the sort of system which we have today.[13]

Between 1925 and 1929, Keynes wrestled with ways of relieving unemployment within the constraints of the gold standard: curbing capital exports, public investment schemes, co-ordinated money wage reductions. But the scope for action within the golden cage was limited.

Because it did not have to worry about the balance of payments, the United States was the only country in a position to try out the ideas of the monetary reformers. Its current account surpluses produced a steady inflow of gold into the Treasury's strong box, Fort Knox. By 'sterilizing', or hoarding, these inflows, the Federal Reserve System, established in 1913, could prevent them from raising domestic prices, and thus insulate the domestic value of the dollar from that of gold.

Influenced by Keynes, the Fed subscribed to what is known as the 'Reserve Position Doctrine'. This held that the first effect of an increase in a central bank's open-market investments will be to cause an increase in the reserves of the member banks. Hence, by injecting or withdrawing cash reserves the Fed would be able, by altering the reserve base of member banks, to cause them to lower or raise the interest rates they charged on loans. This, explained Paul Warburg in 1923, would enable the Fed to exert a 'strong regulatory effect' on the economic system.[14]

Maintaining stable prices at full employment between 1923 and 1928 by means of open-market operations (OMOs) was considered a triumphant vindication of the 'scientific' monetary policy pursued by the US Federal Reserve Board, and particularly its Governor, Benjamin

Strong. However, a less noticed consequence of the sterilization of gold inflows was that it blocked David Hume's price–specie–flow mechanism. The dollar became progressively undervalued, as did the French franc, which had stabilized the gold–franc exchange rate in 1927 at a large discount to the pound. These two gold 'hoarders', which, by 1929 had amassed 60 per cent of the world's monetary gold stock, exerted a deflationary pressure on the rest of the gold standard world, only partly mitigated by US loans to Germany and Latin America and French loans to Eastern Europe.

Triumph turned to ashes when the Fed failed to prevent the collapse of the US economy in 1929. Following the Wall Street stock market crash of 23 October that year, US output, employment and the money supply plummeted. The world economy was soon reeling from the worst depression since the industrial revolution.

The causes of the crash of 1929 have been much disputed. Friedrich Hayek claimed that it was a result of excessive credit creation in the United States. In his account, the price stability of the mid-1920s, so much praised by the monetary reformers, was an indicator of inflation, not of equilibrium, since productivity gains would have naturally produced a falling price level. Rather than central bank policy, compelling banks to hold 100 per cent reserves against deposits was the only secure way to prevent an inflationary boom, bound to turn into bust. 'Excessive credit creation' became the standard 'Austrian' explanation of the 1929 collapse. It resurfaced to explain the crash in 2008. Keynes's alternative view was that it was the Fed's misguided raising of its discount rate, from 3.5 per cent to 5 per cent in January 1928, which led to the collapse of a healthy investment boom. It turned him permanently against the use of 'dear money' as a boom-control mechanism.[15]

'Never waste a recession,' Joseph Schumpeter is said to have said. On the Austrian analysis, recessions give a chance to re-allocate 'mal-invested' productive factors to efficient uses. They should therefore be allowed to run unhindered until they have done their work. Economists whose common sense had not been completely destroyed by their theories rejected the drastic cure of destroying the existing economy in order to rebuild it in the correct proportions. Milton Friedman, heir of the monetary reformers of the 1920s, would later claim that the Fed could and should have prevented the slide into a 'great' depression by expanding its open-market operations – buying government bonds – to whatever extent was needed to offset the flight into cash. In practice, OMOs on a large scale started only in 1932.

In *The Great Contraction* (1965) Friedman and Schwartz write:

> The drastic decline in the quantity of money during those years and the occurrence of a banking panic of unprecedented severity ... did not reflect the absence of power on the part of the Federal Reserve System to prevent them. Throughout the contraction, the System had ample powers to cut short the tragic process of monetary deflation and banking collapse. Had it used those powers effectively in late 1930 or even in early or mid-1931, the excessive liquidity crises ... could almost certainly have been prevented and the stock of money kept from declining or, indeed, increased to any desired extent. Such action would have eased the severity of the contraction and very likely would have brought it to an end at a much earlier date.[16]

Friedman and Schwartz blamed the monetary debacle on weak leadership by George Harrison, who had succeeded Benjamin Strong as President of the Federal Reserve Bank of New York. Their conclusion had a powerful effect on those in charge of central banks in 2008, especially Ben Bernanke, Chairman of the Fed in 2007–8. According to Tim Congdon: 'The monetary interpretation of the Great Recession pivots on the proposition that the collapses in economic activity seen in the worst quarters of 2008 and 2009 were due to falls in – or at any rate sharp declines in the growth rate of – the quantity of money.'[17]

At the time, Keynes agreed with Friedman's retrospective analysis. In 1930 he advocated 'open-market operations *à outrance*' – buying government securities to whatever extent necessary – to 'saturate' the desire of the public to hoard money.[18] This presupposed that the central bank had the power to expand the quantity of money without limit. But the Bank of England had never shared the confidence of the monetary reformers that the Bank could control the volume of credit at will, as Keynes was soon to discover.

Friedman wrote that '[t]he quantity of money in the United States ... fell not because there were no willing borrowers – not because the horse would not drink ... [but] because the Federal Reserve System forced or permitted a sharp contraction in the monetary base'.[19]

Critics pointed out that the monetary base (currency held by the public plus the reserves of the banking system) *increased* by 10 per cent during the period when broad money, which includes loan deposits, fell by 33 per cent. So it may well have been a case of 'an insufficient demand for loans – of the horse *refusing* to drink'.[20]

There is no secure way of settling this argument. Laidler believes that the Fed did not inject enough cash into the system to offset increased liquidity preference. In contrast, Krugman argues that any additional cash injection would have been passively absorbed into inactive balances.[21] This argument was to be re-run in the 2000s. There was the same confidence that, because 'scientific' monetary policy had supposedly kept inflation low during the years of the Great Moderation, it could raise the rate of inflation to offset the collapse of 2008–9.

II. THE PROBLEM WITH FISCAL POLICY

The First World War challenged not only the traditional view of monetary policy, but also the Victorian ideal of the minimal state. The two were related: sound finance was needed to maintain sound money. As a result of the war, state expenditure, fiscal deficits, inflation and the national debt all rose to heights not seen since the Napoleonic wars. Viewed through Victorian spectacles, they all seemed part of the same disorder.

This 'involuntary' growth of the state was initially assumed to be a wartime anomaly. But enhanced social provision was plainly here to stay. After the war military spending was slashed, but UK central government spending in the 1920s, at 25 per cent of GDP, was almost double its pre-war level. This meant that the government's fiscal operations had a larger impact on the economy, for good or ill. However, although budgets were larger, governments continued to believe that they should be balanced, the balance including a sum set aside to repay a national debt hugely swollen by the war. Interest rate payments on the debt, and sinking fund, now claimed over 30 per cent of the budget. Adherents of the balanced budget believed that only by confronting advocates of new expenditure with the need to raise the money from taxes could there be a check on the inexorable growth of public spending.

The state of the British economy made it increasingly hard to maintain this approach. Pre-war Britain was accustomed to a 'normal' unemployment rate of about 5 per cent. In the interwar years, unemployment among insured workers averaged 10 per cent. Superimposed on this were three cyclical downturns, in 1921–2, 1929–32 and 1937–8. Much of the core unemployment was structural, resulting from a decline of British staple exports – coal, textiles, metals, shipbuilding – and the failure of new products to establish themselves. There would have been severe problems of structural adjustment in any case. But the fragile economy was hit by both supply and demand shocks. A once-and-for-all increase in unit labour costs between 1919 and 1922 was never reversed; and aggregate demand was reduced by the policy of deflation to regain and then maintain the gold standard. Structural adjustment would have been easier had Keynes's recipe of low interest rates and a 'managed' exchange rate been followed, but for most of the interwar years 'abnormal' unemployment was treated as a cyclical problem that would soon disappear. Policies most frequently recommended were to remove the obstacles to adjustment such as war debts and reparations, tariffs, and the over-generous unemployment benefits which hindered labour mobility and wage flexibility. Otherwise it was a matter of emergency measures.

By June 1921, 2.2 million people were out of work – an unemployment rate of 22 per cent – and Britain experienced a then record peacetime budget deficit of 7 per cent of GDP. The Lloyd George coalition government set up a Cabinet Committee on Unemployment, which made several proposals for increasing public spending. Particularly striking was one in December 1921 by Sir Edwin Montagu, Secretary of State for India, that the government should deliberately budget for a deficit by reducing income tax, with the expectation that the borrowing requirement would decline as the tax cuts revived the economy, and therefore the government's revenue.[22] Lloyd George's own preference was to invest in large public works programmes; these counted as capital expenditure and so would not affect the Chancellor's budget for current spending. It was against these supposedly improvident plans that the 'Treasury View' defined itself. In a note to Lloyd George's Committee, Sir Otto Niemeyer, Controller of Finance at the Treasury, explained that unemployment was not due to insufficient demand, but excessive wage costs. 'The earnings of British industry are not sufficient to pay the present scale of wages all round. Consequently if present wages are to be maintained a certain fraction of the population must go without wages. The practical manifestation of which is unemployment.' Niemeyer also warned that a 'very large proportion' of any additional borrowings would be diverting money which would otherwise have been used 'soon' by private industry.[23]

These arguments carried the day. Under intense pressure to cut taxes while simultaneously balancing the budget, the government in 1921 appointed Sir Eric Geddes to head a committee charged with finding additional savings of £100 million a year (over £3 billion in today's money). In what became known as the 'Geddes Axe', government spending was slashed over the next five years, thereby undermining an already fragile economy.[24] Defending the Axe, Stanley Baldwin, the new Chancellor, repeated that 'money taken for government purposes is money taken away from trade, and borrowing will thus tend to depress trade and increase unemployment'.[25] But, contrary to the reasoning behind the Geddes Axe, the cuts in government spending, by causing a depression, *increased* the national debt – from 135 per cent of GDP in 1919 to 180 per cent in 1923. The economy bounced back after a year, but never regained anything like full employment for the rest of the 1920s. Budget balance, as it was then understood, was never restored, because the sinking fund was either reduced or suspended.[26] This dismal sequence was to be repeated after the crash of 2008.

But what is meant by balancing the budget? The difficulties of doing so in the 1920s, in the face of stagnant revenues and rising social expenditures, led to an increase in 'off-budget' accounting. Local authorities and quasi-government agencies borrowed for houses, telephones, roads and public utilities. There was an Unemployment Insurance Fund, which was supposed to 'balance' in normal times. These extra-budgetary expenditures were not counted as part of the deficit. The budget that the Treasury concentrated on balancing was the current spending budget. The Treasury's condition for authorizing borrowing by local authorities and public utilities until at least 1935 was that the money return on investment should be enough to pay both interest and capital on the loan, and therefore not add to the national debt. There was no published figure of Net Public Sector Borrowing until 1968. So the real question was not whether there should be a budget deficit, but what the effects of borrowing outside the central government's budget would be on the economy. This was the issue raised by the Lloyd George 'pledge' of 1929.

In the run-up to the General Election of 1929, the Liberal leader Lloyd George promised that a Liberal government – the Conservatives then being in power – would borrow £250 million for a three-year programme of infrastructure development. This, he claimed, would reduce unemployment 'in the course of a single year' to normal proportions, that is, get rid of what was then called abnormal unemployment. This borrowing was to be 'off budget', most of it coming from the Road Fund, which would borrow £145 million against its income of £25 million. Much of the road programme and associated land use improvements would produce no direct financial return, but the increase in the Road Fund's revenue from motor vehicle taxation year by year would be enough to 'meet the interest and sinking fund on the loan'.[27] Keynes and his fellow-economist Hubert Henderson wrote an enthusiastic endorsement, 'Can Lloyd George Do It?'[28] The extra spending, they argued, would create a 'cumulative wave of prosperity'. The Conservative Chancellor, Winston Churchill, turned to the Treasury for advice. He thought the Lloyd George–Keynes proposals made a lot of sense.

To refute the expansionist argument, the Treasury dusted down a half-forgotten article of 1925 by its only professional economist, Ralph Hawtrey.[29] Hawtrey is credited with crystallizing the traditional Treasury prejudice against 'wasteful' government expenditure into a formal 'Treasury View'. He had stated one part of the Ricardian doctrine with Ricardian clarity in 1913: 'the Government by the very act of borrowing for [state] expenditure is withdrawing from the investment market saving which would otherwise be applied to the creation of capital'.[30] This was dubbed at the time a 'fallacy' by no less an authority than Arthur Pigou, Professor of Political Economy at Cambridge. Pigou asserted that in a slump capital lies idle.[31]

In his more nuanced exposition in 1925, Hawtrey claimed that government borrowing of 'genuine savings' would crowd out an equivalent amount of private investment.[32] The government could create additional employment only by 'inflation' (expanding the quantity of money), because this would create additional bank 'savings', allowing banks to expand credit to private borrowers. But in this case it was the monetary expansion which was crucial. Public works were simply a 'piece of ritual'.[33] Taking its cue from Hawtrey, the Treasury equipped Baldwin's government with a standard response to the Lloyd George proposals: 'we must either take existing money or create new money'. State spending on public works would either be diversionary or inflationary. And inflation was ruled out by adherence to the gold standard. Suitably primed, the Chancellor rubbished the Lloyd George plan by stating:

> The orthodox Treasury view . . . is that when the Government borrow[s] in the money market it becomes a new competitor with industry and engrosses to itself resources which would otherwise have been employed by private enterprise, and in the process raises the rent of money to all who have need of it.[34]

Neither of Hawtrey's alternatives was correct. If private capital is asleep, as Mill, and even Say, recognized might happen, extra borrowing by government need neither produce inflation nor divert 'savings' from existing uses. However, the Treasury adopted the hardest (Ricardian) version of Say's Law, which was well below the analytical standard of even the orthodox economists of the day.

Could Lloyd George's plan have reduced unemployment to its 'normal' level? The argument turns on the size of the so-called fiscal multiplier: the ratio between an increase in government spending and the corresponding change in national income (see below, p. 133). There are two views. On the one hand, the extra money the government spends will go into the pockets of workers, contractors, suppliers, etc., who will then go on to spend this extra money, 'multiplying' the impact of the original injection. On the other, government spending might simply replace, discourage or otherwise 'crowd out' private expenditure and cancel out its own impact, especially if the economy is operating at full capacity. In this case the multiplier would be zero; or even negative, if the government spending caused a crisis of confidence.

How big was the multiplier? In 1929, no one knew. Keynes wrote in 1933 that 2 was the most realistic estimate of the multiplier at that moment. Every pound spent by the government would increase total output by two pounds.[35] But this was four years into the slump, when unemployment had ballooned. In 1929 the multiplier would have been lower, but still positive. Lloyd George's £250 million might well have created the 500,000 extra jobs claimed for it at the time, enough to have mitigated the impact of the world depression.

This is denied by Nicholas Crafts and Terence Mills, who estimate that the government expenditure multiplier in the late 1930s was 0.3 to 0.8, much lower than previous estimates.[36] They admit their conclusion is 'model dependent'. A key assumption of their model is that economic behaviour can be characterized by 'optimizing behaviour by forward-looking households', which 'typically expect consumer expenditure to fall rather than increase in response to an increase in government expenditure', the expenditure 'shock' which they have in mind being the announcement of a big rearmament programme. Since these forward-looking households presumably have the correct model of the economy, they will increase their saving in line with their expectation, producing the predicted results. That the size of the fiscal multiplier partly depends on business and household reactions is undeniable. But it is hard to believe that a programme of public investment, targeted on areas of exceptionally heavy unemployment, would have had the nugatory effects claimed by these authors. It is true that in the 1930s a much bigger programme than that envisaged by Lloyd George would have been needed to restore anything like full employment. But that hardly warrants the conclusion that 'at that point [which point?] there was no possibility of a Keynesian solution to the unemployment problem'. The authors fail to explain how Hitler managed to reduce abnormal unemployment in Germany (from a much higher level than in Britain) to 'normal' proportions in the four years 1933–7.[37]

The minority Labour government elected in 1929 implemented a small part of the Lloyd George programme – far too small to reduce appreciably the rising numbers of unemployment, but enough to alarm

Figure 10. Unemployment rates[38]
(per cent)

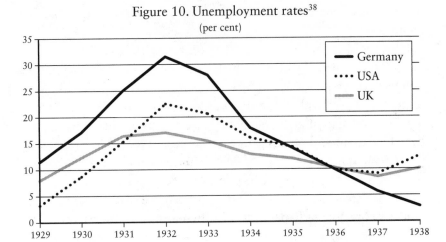

the Treasury. In December 1929, the Treasury's new Controller of Finance, Sir Richard Hopkins, warned against borrowing for road construction: 'A road, however useful it may be, produces no revenue to the State; it does not provide the interest and Sinking Fund on any loan raised. Accordingly, therefore, according to time-honoured principles of public finance it should be paid for out of revenue.'[39]

The deepening depression, with unemployment rising from 10.4 per cent in 1929 to almost 20 per cent in 1931, left Philip Snowden, Chancellor of the Exchequer, with a rising budget deficit. He appointed the May Committee to advise him on fiscal retrenchment, and the Committee reported that the government faced a prospective deficit for 1931–2 of £120 million, approximately 2.5 per cent of GDP. It included the prospective deficit of the Unemployment Insurance Fund in the total.[40] The Conservative opposition blamed the deficit on the extravagance of the Labour government and demanded cuts in 'wasteful' public spending, especially on unemployment benefits. Labour maintained that the hole in the budget was due to the hole in the economy, and the minority government refused to implement the full scale of the spending cuts recommended by the May Committee. As a consequence, Prime Minister Ramsay MacDonald and his Chancellor joined the Conservatives and Liberals in a National Government in August 1931, while Labour went into opposition.

Faced with a prospective deficit for 1931–2 that had been revised upward to £170 million, the National Government legislated a £81.5 million increase in taxes, and spending cuts of £70 million, leaving a projected deficit of £18.5 million. According to Chancellor Snowden, 'An unbalanced budget is regarded as one of the symptoms of national financial instability.' This was the end of the attempt to pay back debt. It also marked the end of the gold standard. Sound finance was supposed to maintain confidence in the currency, but the government's economy measures failed to prevent a continuing flight from sterling, as the merchant banks of the City of London were seen to have borrowed short, and lent long to failed and failing banks on the continent of Europe. No foreign funds were available to 'bail out' the City of London, and the obligation to exchange sterling for gold was suspended on 21 September 1931, never to be restored. Release from the 'golden fetters' liberated monetary policy. Bank Rate came down from 6 per cent to 2 per cent in 1932. Free trade was also abandoned with the Import Duties Act of the same year. Thus the three pillars of Victorian finance – sound finance, sound money and free trade – crumbled, not from conviction but under the pressure of extreme events.

A combination of devaluation, cheap money and protectionism led to a recovery. Recovery produced balanced budgets from 1933 to 1937, but unemployment was slow to come down (though it was increasingly confined to the north of England, Wales and Scotland). Lloyd George went on trying, campaigning for a big public works programme in 1935. But the Conservative Chancellor, Neville Chamberlain, stuck to the older orthodoxy that state spending was *au fond* wasteful, and refused to allocate more than a tiny dollop of money to the 'special areas' of exceptionally high unemployment. And the Treasury itself was still worried in 1937 that borrowing might lead to a spike in interest rates. There was another economic collapse in 1937–8. A £400 million, five-year loan-financed rearmament programme, representing about 5 per cent of GDP, finally lifted Britain out of semi-slump, ten years after the start of the Great Depression. A threat to national security can always be relied upon to abolish worries about the deficit. With Hitler on the prowl, patriotic citizens rushed to invest in war bonds.

Roger Middleton has argued that the tenacity of the balanced-budget rule was based on four beliefs:

1. that 'all factors of production are normally and inevitably utilized by private business';
2. that unbalanced budgets, especially if incurred for 'wasteful' public works, would reduce business confidence;
3. that unbalanced budgets were likely to be inflationary; and
4. that the national debt implied a deadweight loss to productive enterprise.[41]

These were the arguments of Ricardo, and almost exactly the arguments used by George Osborne's Treasury in 2010. However, the Treasury's ability to run budget surpluses in the mid-1920s was critically dependent on 'window dressing' the accounts. The Sinking Fund Act of 1875 required the setting aside of *ex ante* planned surpluses to redeem the national debt. By manipulating the estimated sinking-fund target, the Chancellors of the 1920s were able to accommodate the demands for greater social expenditure under the constraints of the balanced-budget rule. The budget identity 'had become an amorphous hybrid, an amalgam of current and capital accounts, devoid of any internal consistency or tangible economic significance'.[42]

In 1931 Keynes struck a new note. 'Look after unemployment,' he said, 'and the budget will look after itself.'

III. THE MACMILLAN COMMITTEE

The Great Depression of 1929–32 marks the divide between the pre-Keynesian and post-Keynesian worlds of policymaking. Keynes had been appointed a member of the Macmillan Committee on Finance and Industry, set up to enquire into the causes of the deepening slump. His interrogation of officials of the Bank of England and the Treasury in May 1930 was a key confrontation between the old and the new theories of macroeconomic policy.

The chief importance of the Macmillan Committee hearings for Keynes's thinking was that it shook his faith in monetary policy. Hitherto he had regarded monetary policy as key to preventing or modifying the 'credit cycle'; fiscal policy was 'second best', necessitated by the constraints of the gold standard. Now, his emphasis shifted to fiscal policy, with monetary policy in a purely supporting role.

Much to Keynes's surprise, representatives of the Bank of England stolidly denied that the Bank had the power over credit conditions that Keynes, like other monetary reformers, had claimed for it. Bank rate, declared the Governor of the Bank, Montagu Norman, affected only 'short money', leaving the 'whole mass of credit' little changed. Another Bank official, Henry Clay, elaborated on Norman's laconic performance:

> while the conditions of sound banking impose a limit on the amount of credit, the *origin* of credit is to be found in the action of the businessman, who approaches the bank for assistance with a business transaction, and the *basis* of credit is the probability that the transaction can be done at a profit.

'What you are saying', Keynes objected to the Bank official Walter Stewart, 'is that there is always the right quantity of credit?' Stewart doubted whether 'the expansion of bank credit in quantity was a determining factor in prices and trade activity . . . there are a great many things that people can do with money besides buying commodities. They can hold it.' All that meant, Keynes rejoined, was that the Bank would have to 'dose the system with money' and 'feed the hoarder', in order to bring down long-term rates. To which Stewart responded: 'I should not have thought that bank credit determines the long-term rate.' Keynes admitted that when a depression had got too deep, a 'negative rate of interest' might be required to bring money out of hoards, but normally 'a reasonably abundant supply of credit would do the trick'. Stewart persisted: 'Only if borrowers saw a prospect of making a profit and of repaying debts.' Keynes was driven to arguing that 'though [the supply of credit] may be only a balancing factor, it is the most controllable factor'. To which Stewart replied, 'It may be the only thing that the Central Bank can do; but it does not strike me as being the only thing that business men can do . . . I regard wage adjustments as ever so much more important . . . [than] anything bankers can do.' The Bank was denying that, unaided, it could rescue an economy from a slump.[43] Exactly the same issue, with the same arguments on both sides, re-emerged with quantitative easing (QE), following the economic collapse of 2008–9. Such is progress in economic science!

Keynes's belief in monetary therapy was shaken, but not shattered. He still believed that when interest rates were lowered a new range of investment projects would become profitable. But he admitted that bank rate was a weaker instrument for securing lower rates than he had believed. It was all very well to talk of 'feeding the hoarder', but suppose his appetite was insatiable? The result would be a credit deadlock. By 1932 he was writing:

> It may still be the case that the lender, with his confidence shattered by his experience, will continue to ask for new enterprise rates of interest which the borrower cannot expect to earn . . . If this proves to be the case there will be no means of escape from prolonged and perhaps interminable depression except by direct state intervention to promote and subsidise new investment.[44]

This passage marks the defeat of the hopes of the monetary reformers. It is not money which controls expectations about the economy; it is expectations about the economy which control expectations about money. In a deep slump it was no longer enough to manage expectations about the future of the price level; the expectations which needed managing were about the future of output and employment. This required fiscal policy.

But fiscal policy to fight the slump offered its own obstacle in the form of the Treasury View, presented at the Macmillan Committee by the formidable Sir Richard Hopkins. Keynes thought he knew what the Treasury View was, and that he was in a position to refute it. The Treasury had claimed that loan-financed public spending could not add to investment and employment, only divert them from existing uses. This was true, Keynes was prepared to say, only on the assumption of full employment. But Hopkins had foreseen this.

The Treasury was not opposed to government borrowing as such, Hopkins told Keynes; it was not even claiming that all private capital was being used. Its objection was to the particular plan put forward by Lloyd George. This plan, 'far from setting up a cycle of prosperity' as Keynes had hoped, would much more probably 'produce a great cry against bureaucracy' and capital would flee the country, so the loans would have to be 'put out at a very high price'. Was not the Lloyd George plan likely to retard the necessary fall in interest rates? Well, Keynes persisted, suppose instead of borrowing the money from the public, the government borrowed it from the Bank of England. That was 'fantastic', Hopkins replied: 'If I am right in thinking that a great loan directly raised in the ordinary way would carry with it a bad public sentiment and adverse repercussions . . . what would happen if it were raised by what is ordinarily called plain inflation I cannot imagine.' The chairman, Lord Macmillan, concluded: 'I think we can characterize it as a drawn battle.'[45]

Let's stand back for a moment. What Hopkins had done was to invoke what Paul Krugman in 2010 called 'the confidence fairy':[46] the view that the effects of a budget deficit on the economy depend on the expectations of the business community. More broadly, any policy had to take into account the psychological reaction to it. This is to say that the success of a policy depends on the model of the economy in the minds of the business community. If they believe that a government loan-financed programme of capital investment will make things worse, they will react in a way that *will* make things worse. It was not the state's borrowing per se, but loss of confidence in government finance implied by that borrowing, which would create the 'hole' in private capital.

There is no doubt that Keynes was disturbed by Hopkins's confidence fairy. Experience of slump was not itself sufficient to loosen the hold of the old religion. That could be done only by a different model of the economy. Keynes's *General Theory* of 1936 was the attempt to create that different model.

IV. THE GENERAL THEORY OF EMPLOYMENT, INTEREST, AND MONEY

In a letter to a correspondent, dated 22 November 1934, Keynes wrote that the differences between economists 'strike extremely deep into the foundations of economic theory'. He continued:

> The difference is between those who believe in a self-adjusting economy and those who don't. Those who do will always argue for

non-intervention in order to allow freedom to economic factors to bring about their own self-adjustment ... But just because the differences go so deep there is no chance of convincing the opposition until a new scheme of economic theory has been developed and worked out. In the past we have been opposing the orthodox school more by our flair and instinct than because we had discovered in precisely what respects their theory was wrong.[47]

It was to explain precisely why the classical theory was wrong that Keynes wrote his new book. It was Depression itself which gave a radical edge to his critique. The classical theory, he mused, abstracted from the problem of unemployment by assuming there was no unemployment to explain.

The simplest, easiest to understand and, therefore, generally most acceptable version of Keynes's argument is his demonstration that economies adjust to a 'shock' to investment demand by a fall in income and output, leading to 'under-employment equilibrium'. 'Quantities adjust, not prices' was the headline version of Keynes's model. In the classical models, adjustment always means a restoration of a unique (optimal) point of equilibrium through movements of relative prices. The theoretical novelty in Keynes's treatment lay in the claim that, when the desire to save exceeds the desire to invest, the only adjustment path open is through a change in aggregate income and output. The excess saving at the initial equilibrium level of income is eliminated by the fall in income, creating a situation of stable output at less than full employment.

Although in this under-employment equilibrium saving equals investment, as in the classical equilibrium, the causation is reversed. In the classical scheme, the amount of investment is governed by the amount of real resources that households are willing to withhold from current consumption to secure greater wealth in the future. In Keynes's theory, saving is a consequence, not a cause, of investment. The amount of investment determines the level of income; and the level of income determines the amount of saving, via the marginal propensity to consume.

In the *General Theory* there are no banks. The action moves directly from a shock to investment to a fall in income. But Keynes understood that the volume of investment is determined by the expected rate of return on investment – what he called the 'marginal efficiency of capital' (MEC) – compared with the terms on which banks provide finance for it (the market rate of interest). Investment will be pushed to the point where the marginal efficiency of capital equals the market rate of interest. If the rate of interest is 3 per cent, no one will pay £100 for a machine unless he expects to add £3 to his annual net output, allowing for costs and depreciation. So how much new investment takes place in any period will depend on those factors which determine the expected rate of return and the market rate of interest. Here, Keynes distinguishes between the borrower's risk and the lender's risk. The borrower's risk 'arises out of doubts in his own mind as to the probability of his actually earning the prospective yield for which he hopes'. But in any system of borrowing and lending one must take into account the lender's risk, which arises from the possibility of a default. Thus the financing of investment by the banks involves a duplication of risk which would not arise if the investor were venturing his own money. A shock to confidence could reduce both the supply of finance from the banks and the demand for it. Nevertheless, Keynes regarded changes in the borrower's expectation of risk as much the most important in explaining fluctuations in investment. It is through the MEC that 'the expectation of the future influences the present'; and it is the dependence of the MEC on changes in expectations which renders it 'subject to . . . somewhat violent fluctuations'.[48]

Keynes comes to the heart of his explanation of economic collapse in his discussion of Say's Law. Paul Krugman rightly says that the 'demolition of Say's Law' that 'supply creates its own demand' is the 'crucial innovation' in the General Theory. The law is 'at best a useless tautology when individuals have the option of accumulating money rather than purchasing goods and services'.[49] But 'why should anyone outside a lunatic asylum wish to use money as a store of wealth?' Keynes asks. His answer is that investment falls with the rise of uncertainty – the rise of which is signalled by the increased demand for cash.[50] Uncertainty in the General Theory is not just confined to those transition periods when the value of money is changing. It is present in all transactions of a forward-looking character.

In his account of the psychology of investment, both in chapter 12 of the *General Theory* and in a *Quarterly Journal of Economics* article ('The General Theory of Employment') of February 1937, Keynes breaks decisively with the neo-classical model of rationality, in which agents with perfect foresight accurately calculate the risk they run by committing present funds to secure future income streams. Because investors do not know the risks they are running (but only pretend to), investment is subject to steep and sudden collapses when their false confidence in the pretence evaporates. 'New fears and hopes will, without warning, take charge of human conduct. The forces of disillusion may suddenly impose a new conventional basis of valuation.'[51] With investment governed by flimsy 'conventions' and 'animal spirits', full employment is reached only in 'moments of excitement'. 'Thus', Keynes wrote, 'if the animal spirits are dimmed and the spontaneous optimism falters, leaving us to depend on nothing but a mathematical expectation, enterprise will fade and die; – though fears of loss may have a basis no more reasonable than hopes of profit had before.'[52]

Keynes used the example of a newspaper beauty contest to illustrate the conventional character of investment decisions. Here the prize goes to the reader who chooses not the face he thinks prettiest, but the face which he thinks likeliest to be chosen by the other readers. What we think of as objectivity is trapped within the circle of expectation. Speculation, though, is more like the Victorian parlour game of Old Maid. In this game, the aim of each player is to avoid being left holding the Old Maid (a card without a match) when the music stops. No one wants to be left with the bad investment, but no one knows when it will turn up. So the aim of each player is to make a profit and run.[53]

It is tempting to relate Keynes's 'conventions' to what orthodox economics calls 'fundamentals', and 'animal spirits' to 'irrationality'. According to this view, agents price share values 'correctly' on average, with deviations being mistaken or irrational. But this was not Keynes's view. Conventions and animal spirits alike are grounded in uncertain expectations concerning the future money value of transactions. In a monetary economy, they never escape the circle of money to reach supposedly underlying 'fundamentals'.[54]

If a collapse is characterized by a situation in which the supply of saving exceeds the demand for investment, it would be reasonable to expect, as did the orthodox theory, that a fall in the price of saving (the rate of interest obtainable from lending out saving) would rebalance (or equilibrate) the two at an unchanged level of income. Households will save somewhat less and consume more; businesses will take advantage of lower interest rates to borrow more. Keynes's crucial insight was that the rate of interest reflects the demand for money, not the supply of savings. In Keynes's terms, if liquidity preference rises, a higher rate of interest will be required to induce lenders to part with money, and this will prevent the interest rate falling sufficiently to restore a full employment level of investment. As Keynes explained, the interest rate is 'a measure of the unwillingness of those who possess money to part with their liquid control over it'. It is 'the inducement *not* to hoard'.[55] Thus the rate of interest cannot play the equilibrating role assigned to it in the neo-classical theory.

In his discussion of the role of money, Keynes takes a view of the nature of money that is diametrically opposed to the 'real analysis' of the classical school, as set out in Chapter 1 of this book. For exponents of the 'money as veil' view, there can be no such thing as liquidity preference, or a desire for money distinct from a desire for the goods that money can buy. According to Keynes, though, money *'in its significant attributes* [my italics] is, above all, a subtle device for linking the present to the future'.[56] People accumulate money rather than spend it, because they regard the future as uncertain and therefore hoard money as security against uncertainty. If the future were perfectly known, there would be no rational – as opposed to a psychological-neurotic – reason for 'holding money', or indeed for money at all. It follows from this view of money that the role of financial institutions is not to intermediate between savers and investors, but to provide liquidity, as and when it is needed – at a price. The rate of interest in Keynes's theory is the price of liquidity, not saving.

Keynes also explained why flexible money-wages would not maintain full employment. In the orthodox scheme, the price of labour was assumed, like the price of everything else, to fluctuate with the quantity demanded. Classical economists reasoned that the demand curve for labour, like the demand curve for apples, was downward sloping: the lower the price the more would be sold. Unemployment could thus be explained by the existence of 'sticky' wages: the refusal or slowness of labour in adjusting their wage demands to the new situation. However, wages were not uniformly 'sticky'. Between 1929 and 1932 money-wages in the United States fell by 33.6 per cent, but unemployment kept rising the whole time. 'It is not very plausible', Keynes commented, 'to assert that unemployment in the United States was due ... to labour obstinately refusing to accept a reduction of money wages.'[57] The classical view that if wages fell employment would be increased referred to real wages (W/P – nominal wage divided by price level). But workers bargained for money, not for real wages. They were in no position to reduce their real wage as a whole in a slump by accepting a reduced money-wage, because an all-round reduction in money-wages would simultaneously reduce prices 'almost proportionately', leaving the real wage, and therefore the labour surplus at that wage, unchanged.[58] Unless employers had reason to believe that a reduction in money-wages would be followed by a rise in the price level, they would have no reason to provide additional employment.[59] The argument had a flaw, for a fall in the general price level would increase the value of cash holdings (M/P – money divided by price level), which would, at least to some extent, offset the depressive effect of the fall in money-wages. As we shall see, the non-Keynesians were able to exploit this gap in Keynes's analysis to reinstate the logical integrity of the neo-classical wage-adjustment story. Keynesians were left with a 'sticky wage' story, which was certainly sufficient to justify short-run Keynesian policy to increase money demand, but left the neo-classical theory free to continue to assert that, with perfectly flexible money-wages, economies would always recover naturally from shocks.[60]

Keynes did not condemn the whole corpus of inherited economics; he only wanted to to fill the 'gaps' in what he called 'the Manchester system'. He wrote:

> If we suppose the volume of output to be given, i.e. to be determined outside the classical scheme of thought, then there is no objection to be raised against the classical analysis of the manner in which private self-interest will determine what in particular is produced, in what proportions the factors of production will be combined to produce it, and how the value of the final product will be distributed between

them. Again, if we have dealt otherwise with the problem of thrift, there is no objection to be raised against the modern classical theory as to the degree of consilience between between public and private advantage in conditions of perfect and imperfect competition. Thus, apart from the necessity of central controls to bring about an adjustment between the propensity to consume and the inducement to invest, there is *no more reason to socialise economic life than there was before.*[61] [my italics]

This passage deserves more contextual consideration than it has received. Keynes was not identifying 'modern' (i.e. neo-) classical economics with laissez-faire. He implicitly conceded that within this corpus were to be found some arguments for 'socialising' economic life, to do with the existence of imperfect competition and public goods; only these were not the arguments which concerned him, because they were irrelevant to the problem which did concern him – namely, the existence of continuing mass unemployment.

Keynes's concessions to neo-classical economics were not enough to placate some of his supporters. Economists like Roy Harrod, who wanted to reconcile Keynes's theory to neo-classical theory, tried to persuade him that the important difference between the two concerned the relative speed and strength of income adjustments and price adjustments. Keynes stuck to his guns, by denying that there were any price adjustments at all, however weak and slow-moving, capable of restoring a shocked system to full employment in any reasonable period of time. Only at the bottom of the slump, after income adjustment had done its work, did relative prices start to move, though only to a limited extent. In the controversies following the publication of the *General Theory*, he was moved to observe ironically: 'I hear with surprise that our forebears believed that *cet. par.* an increase in the desire to save would lead to a recession in employment and income and would only result in a fall in the rate of interest in so far as this was the case.'[62]

Keynes's economics was deeply embedded in his ethics. His insistence on maintaining maximum employment was driven by the thought that the quicker the accumulation of wealth could be made to happen, the sooner people would be able to escape from the burden of drudgery – or mechanical work – into fulfilling lives. He looked forward to the day when capital would be so abundant that people would no longer be compelled to 'work for a living'.[63]

V. POLICY IMPLICATIONS

Keynes called his book the 'general' theory, because he took uncertainty to be the general case, with full information as the special case. Thus, under-employment was not a lapse from a normal condition: it *was* the normal condition, interrupted only by 'moments of excitement'. The task of policy was to move the economy from the inferior equilibrium it naturally gravitated towards if 'left to itself', to the superior equilibrium which was available by purposive public action. Provided the aggregate supply curve was not completely inelastic, the government could, by an injection of autonomous demand, move the economy to a superior equilibrium. The *General Theory* thus marked the birth of macroeconomic policy as it was pursued until the 1970s. (The contrast with the classical theory of economic policy is modelled in Appendix 5.1, p. 132.)

By what set of instruments was this improved equilibrium to be brought about? In conventional macroeconomics the government can act on the level of activity through monetary policy, fiscal policy and exchange-rate policy. Reacting against the inordinate hopes of the monetary reformers, Keynes discarded monetary policy as the primary economic regulator. He now doubted the ability of the monetary authority to get interest rates low enough and prices high enough to offset a marked rise in liquidity preference. However, there *was* a role for monetary policy in 'normal' times, which was to maintain continuously low long-term interest rates. For this reason, Keynes opposed the use of 'dear money' to check a boom. The effect of a rise in the interest rate on the yield curve would be very difficult to reverse.

A low enough long-term rate of interest cannot be achieved if we allow it to be believed that better terms will be obtainable from time to time by those who keep their resources liquid. The long-term rate of interest must be kept *continuously* as near as possible to what we believe to be the long-term optimum. It is not suitable to be used as a short-period weapon.[64]

In arguing for the continued (if now limited) power of monetary policy over interest rates, Keynes reverted to the ideas of the *Tract on Monetary Reform* and *A Treatise on Money*. The Quantity Theory of Money continued a ghostly existence in the *General Theory*, as seen in Keynes's liquidity preference equation

$$M = L(Y,r)$$

where the demand for money (L) is assumed to vary with the rate of interest (r) and money income (Y), but where the supply of money (M) is exogenously given, as in the quantity theory.[65] At a given level of money income, the rate of interest equilibrates the demand for cash with the supply of cash. By feeding the hoarder with money, the central bank can prevent the rate of interest rising to choke off investment. Contrary to most Keynesians, Keynes himself believed that some important classes of investment, particularly real estate, were interest-elastic (sensitive). He therefore welcomed the policy of cheap money made possible by leaving the gold standard in 1931, which helped, by starting a housing boom, to lead the way out of the slump. However, unlike the monetary reformers, he did not believe that a policy of low interest rates alone was enough to bring about complete recovery from a slump. Real interest rates in the UK were negative from 1932 until 1937, but unemployment was still 10 per cent in the latter year.

Despite Keynes's obeisance to his past as a monetary reformer, the main policy message of the *General Theory* was that the most powerful and direct way a government could influence the level of spending in the economy is through fiscal policy. The crucial tool for fiscal policy was the multiplier, whose logic Keynes sketched out in chapter 10 of his book, and which is conventionally written:

$$M = 1/(1-MPC)$$

where M is the magnitude of the multiplier and MPC the marginal propensity to consume.

By use of the formula, policymakers could calculate how much extra spending needed to be injected into, or withdrawn from, the circular flow of spending to maintain full employment. The multiplier theory is the fiscal equivalent of the Quantity Theory of Money, and, at full employment, is identical to it. (For technical discussion of the multiplier, see Appendix 5.2, p. 133.)

In advocating loan-financed public spending to maintain full employment, Keynes jettisoned the orthodox policy of cutting public spending to balance the budget in a slump. He wrote:

> it is a complete mistake to believe that there is a dilemma between schemes for increasing employment and schemes for balancing the budget – that we must go slowly and cautiously with the former for fear of injuring the latter. There is no possibility of balancing the budget except by increasing national income, which is much the same as increasing employment.[66]

Keynes's scorn for the reasoning of the deficit hawks spurred him to the following passage:

> It is curious how common sense, wriggling for an escape from absurd conclusions, has been apt to reach a preference for *wholly* wasteful forms of loan expenditure rather than for *partly* wasteful forms, which, because they are not wholly wasteful, tend to be judged on strict 'business' principles. For example, unemployment relief financed by loans is more readily acceptable than the financing of improvements at a charge below the current rate of interest; whilst the form of digging holes in the ground known as gold mining, which ... adds nothing to the real wealth of the world ... is the most acceptable of all solutions.
>
> If the Treasury were to fill old bottles with bank-notes, bury them at suitable depths in disused coalmines which are then filled up to the surface with town rubbish, and leave it to private enterprise ... to dig the notes up again ... there need be no more unemployment and, with the help of the repercussions, the real income of the community, and its capital wealth also, would probably become a good deal greater than it actually is. It would, indeed, be more sensible to build houses and the like; but if there are political and practical difficulties in the way of this, the above would be better than nothing.
>
> ...

Ancient Egypt was doubly fortunate, and doubtless owed to this its fabled wealth, in that it possessed *two* activities, namely, pyramid-building as well as the search for the precious metals, the fruits of which, since they did not serve the needs of man by being consumed, did not stale with abundance. The Middle Ages built cathedrals and sang dirges. Two pyramids, two masses for the dead, are twice as good as one; but not so two railways from London to York. Thus we are so sensible, have schooled ourselves to so close a semblance of prudent financiers, taking careful thought before we add to the 'financial' burdens of posterity by building them houses to live in, that we have no such easy escape from the sufferings of unemployment.[67]

There was a theoretical and social radicalism in Keynes, obliterated in standard post-war Keynesian discussions. Keynes thought insufficient demand was chronic and would get worse; and that, in consequence, the longer-term survival of a free enterprise system depended on the redistribution of wealth and income and the reduction in hours of work. I will return to these points in Chapters 10 and 13.

On exchange-rate policy, the *General Theory* offered a powerful implicit argument against the gold standard. As Keynes would later point out, under the gold standard, adjustment was '*compulsory* for the debtor and *voluntary* for the creditor . . . The debtor *must* borrow; the creditor is under no such compulsion [to lend].'[68] These golden fetters prevented central banks in the debtor countries setting rates of interest geared to domestic needs. The increase in creditor 'hoarding' of countries such as the United States and France as the slump deepened prevented a global fall in long-term interest rates that would have helped revive the 'animal spirits' of investors.

Keynes's International Clearing Union plan of 1941 was designed to remedy this defect. The essence of his plan was that creditor countries would not be allowed to bury their gold in the ground, or charge usurious rates of interest for lending it out; rather, their surpluses would be automatically available as cheap overdraft facilities to debtors through the mechanism of an international clearing bank, whose depositors were the central banks of the Union. Creditor countries would be charged rising interest rates on their bank deposits with the Union; persisting credit balances would be confiscated and transferred to a reserve fund. Keynes explained that no country needed to be in possession of a credit balance 'unless it deliberately prefers to sell more than it buys (or lends)'.[69] So no creditor country would suffer injury by having its credit balance actively employed. Keynes's long-term aim was to replace gold by an international reserve currency, which he called 'bancor'. By increasing or reducing the quantity of bancor, the clearing bank's managers would be able to vary it contracyclically and ensure enough global money for trade expansion.[70]

The *General Theory* divided the economics profession. Older economists thought Keynes was wrong, or had nothing new to say. Younger economists eagerly embraced the new doctrine as offering hope that full employment could be maintained without recourse to the dictatorships then on offer in Germany and Soviet Russia.

Where does the *General Theory* fit into the history of thought? The answer is that Keynes was much more of a classical than a neoclassical economist. His interest was in long-run growth, leading to the stationary state in which everyone could give up painful work. He wanted to get there as quickly as possible, which is why he was so keen to secure maximum investment. The classical theory was wrong only in one respect: in insisting on maximum saving rather than maximum investment, in the mistaken belief that the first was the cause of the second. Corrected for this, it was a serviceable guide for thinking and policy. It is true that Keynes's 'model' was a short-run model, but that's not because he was interested only in short-run stabilization. He wanted a full employment level of investment in the short-run, so as to get to the long-run quicker.

However, there was a serious political-economy gap in Keynes's thought, which critics would exploit to undermine the Keynesian system. His flows of aggregate income and output were unrelated to the decisions of any actors in the economy. That is to say, they were not 'micro-founded' in any individual or class behaviour. On the one side, it was very hard for the older generation of classical economists to see how 'under-employment equilibrium' could be a meaningful state of affairs. Surely workers could always get as much employment as they wanted at the going wage? If they refused job offers it was their choice. On the other side, Marxists pointed out that Keynes had failed to realize that capitalists needed a 'reserve army of the unemployed' to keep down wages. From both points of view, Keynes had not so much captured the adjustment process as frozen the film at a moment in time. One needed to keep it running to capture the full behavioural dynamics of the economic system.

VI. CONCLUSION

The story of the Keynesian revolution opens with gold losing the battle to control money. There was either too much or too little of it, causing inflation or unemployment. The monetary reformers of the 1920s had a noble cause. If money could be freed from its golden fetters and control of its issue vested in an independent central bank, there would always be just the right amount of money for the needs of trade. Such a system would be just as good as gold in stopping a government 'monkeying around' with the money supply.

What the monetary reformers failed to realize was that the money supply could not be controlled without keeping economic activity steady, because unsteadiness in economic activity would be reflected in swings in the velocity of circulation. This was pointed out by Keynes with great clarity in the *General Theory*, and it remains the most telling critique of monetary stabilization policy prior to the crash of 2008–9 and the policy of quantitative easing that followed it.

Classical economists said that full employment was the natural condition of a capitalist market economy. Marxists said unemployment was inevitable. Keynes's great achievement was to demonstrate that unemployment was likely but not inevitable. By inventing macroeconomics, he restored the relevance of economics for a free society.

To be sure, 'Keynesian' policy existed both before and apart from Keynes, if by Keynesian one means simply government spending, whose effect is to provide work. The state had been spending money and providing employment ever since government started, a great deal of it for war purposes.[71]

In Keynes's own time, Hitler, as Joan Robinson remarked, cured unemployment in Germany before Keynes had finished explaining why it existed; Roosevelt's New Deal can also be called Keynesian. But the inspiration of such work-providing programmes was political, not economic. Hitler wanted Germany to be at full capacity to prepare for a war of conquest. Roosevelt's New Deal is an example of pragmatically and politically driven experimentation. As FDR explained in 1936, in language whose eloquence no leader today can match:

> To balance our budget in 1933 or 1934 or 1935 would have been a crime against the American people ... When Americans suffered we refused to pass by on the other side. Humanity came first ...
>
> ... We accepted the final responsibility of Government, after all else had failed, to spend money when no one else had money left to spend.[72]

In such cases, public works programmes were not backed by any theory which showed why they were needed; the classical theory demonstrated they were unnecessary and harmful. Before Keynes, Marxism alone had a theory of unemployment. So Keynes was overthrowing not only existing classical theory but the politics of communism.

The economic context was right for a new theory. Mass unemployment of 20 per cent or more of the workforce demanded intellectual as well as political attention. Marx believed that capitalism's requirement for a 'reserve army of the unemployed' would become intolerable and lead to the overthrow of capitalism. But Marx failed to see the unavoidable consequences of the economic and technological revolution that was going on before his eyes. These consequences, as summarized by Lowe, were

> the shift of political power to the middle classes and the rise of strong labour unions ... capable of making their growing aspirations felt under a system of widening franchise ... This not only democratized the spirit of modern government but created the new administrative key position for a progressive control of economic by political forces.[73]

In short, Marx missed the growth of a social balance between business, labour and government, which took the revolution off the agenda. At the same time, the business class lost its ability to enforce the real-wage reductions that it believed to be necessary to its continued profitability. As a result, mass unemployment became endemic in the developed world. This was the setting in which Keynes's analysis of the economic problem in terms of 'under-employment equilibrium' could gain traction. It promised to break the social stasis by invoking the economic

power of the state. Both capital and labour would gain from the elimination of under-employment. Although Keynes's theory undercut the case
for state socialism, it opened up the road for government 'management'
of the macroeconomy to ensure at least a quasi-optimal equilibrium.

Keynes's theory also undercut the argument for fascism. This aspect
of its political work has been little noticed, because few have bothered
to study fascist ideology. Fascism distinguished between 'good' and
'bad' capitalism, a division corresponding roughly to that between
national industrial and international financial capitalism. Its attack
on international finance was explicitly or implicitly anti-Semitic. It
was to this kind of politics that Keynesian thinking offered an antidote, by providing a rationale for keeping banking under national
control. Few paused to ponder the political consequences of releasing
finance from national regulation in the 1980s and 1990s.

Keynes's theory could have become the basis of policy only under
conditions of social balance. His was the economics of the middle
way; the best deal that liberal capitalism could expect in a world
veering towards the political extremes. He thought of his economics
as the economics of the general interest, for it encompassed, while
transcending, the sectional interests of both capital and labour. This
is true: it was the least ideological of all economic doctrines, the least
dependent on class interest. His political genius was to see that when
the problem was one of unused capacity, redistribution was a minor
question, which could be postponed until later.

But by the same token, his economics threw little light on what
would happen to class income shares when his own policies achieved
full employment, in conditions of trade-union control of the supply of
labour. In such a situation, would capitalism need to recreate Marx's
'reserve army of the unemployed' to restrain wage demands, or would
the government be forced to inflate the economy to keep profits racing
ahead of wages? The latter is what the economist Jacob Viner assumed
would happen when society got accustomed to full employment.[74]
Keynes himself admitted that he had 'no solution . . . to the wages
problem in a full employment economy'.[75] Marxists, too, believed
that attempts to overcome the class struggle by inflation would bring
only temporary relief. So the great question which Keynes believed he
had settled for his own day remained for the future.

APPENDIX 5.I: CONTRAST BETWEEN THE CLASSICAL AND KEYNESIAN MODELS

In the classical model, the economy is always at full employment. Because wages and prices are fully flexible, the aggregate supply curve (AS) is vertical. Government intervention is undesirable as any attempt to raise aggregate demand (AD) has no effect on output/employment, but just causes inflation.

In the short-run Keynesian model, wages and prices are highly sticky so the AS curve is horizontal. The level of output/employment depends entirely on the AD curve, so government intervention is desirable, and in fact necessary. The easiest interpretation of Keynes's message is that, in the face of a negative shock, supply fails to adjust to the fall in nominal demand, so unemployment could develop, and even persist. Eventually supply would adjust (in the long-run, the AS is vertical, as prices have fully adjusted), but it would be better for

Figure 11. Keynes's short-run supply and demand curve

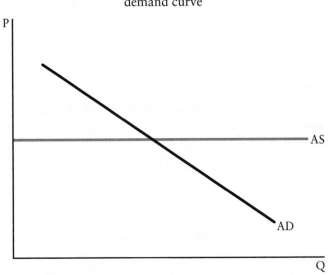

the government not to allow any fall in nominal demand in the first place.

The minimum doctrine to justify policy intervention to stabilize economies can be summarized as follows:

> For Keynes, it was the tendency for the private sector, from time to time, to want to stop spending and to accumulate financial assets instead that lay behind the problems of slumps and unemployment. It could be checked by deficit spending . . .
>
> . . . In the standard Keynesian economic model, when the economy is at less than full capacity, output is determined by demand; and the management of economic activity and hence employment is effected by managing demand.[76]

APPENDIX 5.2: THE FISCAL MULTIPLIER

The fiscal multiplier measures the effect of a change in fiscal policy on real national income. Let us consider a closed economy:

$$Y = C + I + G$$

In the Keynesian framework the consumption equation takes this form:

$$C = C_0 + cY$$

Where C_0 is autonomous consumption and cY is the part of consumption which is explained by the level of disposable income. c represents the marginal propensity to consume, and it takes a value between 1 (all available income is consumed) and 0 (all available income is saved).

Investments are supposed to be dependent on exogenous factors (i.e. expected profitability or 'animal spirits'):

$$I = I_0$$

Government spending is autonomous by definition:

$$G = G_0$$

Inserting the functional forms of C, I and G in the expenditure identity, and rearranging, gives:

$$Y = \frac{1}{1-c}(C_0 + I_0 + G_0)$$

Every variable within the parenthesis represents an autonomous component of aggregate demand. Therefore, with a variation in one of these (e.g. fiscal expansion $+\Delta G_0$), the expression $\frac{1}{1-c}$ captures the value of its multiplier effect on Y. As $0 < G < 1$, the denominator also takes a value lower than 1, but still positive. The overall multiplier will therefore take a value ≥ 1.

Numerical example I

$Y = 100$, $C_0 = 30$, $I_0 = 10$, $G_0 = 10$ and $c = 0.5$ so that the expression $\frac{1}{1-c} = 2$.

Let us assume an increase in fiscal spending so that $G_0 = 12$, implying $\Delta G_0 = +2$. Aggregate demand and income $+\Delta G$ will increase by $+4$ units, not only by the 2 additional ones implied by $+\Delta G_0$.

The result will be $Y = 104$, as $104 = 2(30 + 10 + 12)$.

The value of the multiplier is 2:

$$\left(\frac{\Delta Y}{\Delta G} = 2 \right)$$

and it affects positively and more than proportionally an increase in the autonomous components of demand.

The Neo-classical 'Multiplier'

Let us consider again a closed economy:

$$Y = C + I + G$$

In the neo-classical theoretical framework the consumption equation might take this form:

$$C = C_0 + C(i) + cY$$

The new variable $C(i)$ represents the part of overall consumption which is determined by the rate of interest. Consumption falls as the interest rate increases, and vice versa:

$$\frac{\Delta C}{\Delta i} < 0$$

In the pure form (without any accelerator effect of AD on I), investments are negatively dependent on the rate of interest

$$\frac{\Delta I}{\Delta i} < 0$$

$$I = I(i)$$

Government spending remains as the only autonomous component of demand:

$$G = G_0$$

Inserting again the functional forms of C, I and G in the expenditure identity, and rearranging, gives:

$$Y = \frac{1}{1-c}\left(C_0 + C(i) + I(i) + G_0\right)$$

This time, $\frac{1}{1-c}$ represents only the multiplier effect of a variation in the autonomous component of consumption C_0, as the other component G_0 is supposed to produce changes in the value of $C(i)$ and $I(i)$.

In particular, an expansionary fiscal policy is supposed to produce a 'crowding out' effect on consumption and investment, by negatively impacting on the rate of interest.[77]

The effect of $+\Delta G_0$ is therefore mitigated, if not nullified, by an increase in the rate of interest, which affects negatively both consumption $(-\Delta C(i))$ and investment $(-\Delta I(i))$. Therefore, depending on the magnitude of the crowding-out effect, the multiplier effect of an increase in fiscal policy can be < 1 and even negative.

Numerical example II

$Y = 100$, $C_0 = 20$, $C(i) = 10$, $I(i) = 10$, $G_0 = 10$ and $c = 0.5$ so that the expression $\frac{1}{1-c} = 2$.

Let us assume again an increase in fiscal spending so that $G_0 = 12$, implying $\Delta G_0 = +2$.

This time, this increase will have a crowding-out effect on investment $\Delta I(i) = -1$ and on the component of consumption dependent on the interest rate $\Delta C(i) = -0.5$.

The result will be $Y = 101$, as $101 = 2(20 + 9.5 + 9 + 12)$.

The value of the multiplier is 0.5:

$$\left(\frac{\Delta Y}{\Delta G} = 0.5 \right)$$

and it affects positively and, but less than proportionally, an increase in government spending.

6

The Keynesian Ascendancy

'I believe myself to be writing a book on economic theory,
which will largely revolutionise ... the way the world thinks
about economic problems. When my new theory has been
duly assimilated and mixed with politics and feelings and
passions ... there will be a great change and, in particular,
the Ricardian foundations of Marxism will be knocked away.'
J. M. Keynes, 1935[1]

I. KEYNESIANISM ASCENDANT

Keynes was only partly right, and then only for thirty years. He expected his theory to be qualified by 'politics and feelings and passions', but not that it would eventually be qualified out of existence.

Keynes proposed that in normal circumstances there is not enough effective demand from private firms and households to ensure the use of all potential resources: resources which could be brought into use by existing technology and business organization. Therefore, government policies should add to private demand, not just in a downturn, but in normal times.

In the ideal Keynesian policy system, ensuring the right amount of demand for goods and services was to be done by fiscal rather than monetary policy. This is because Keynesians (unlike Keynes himself) assumed that investment was unresponsive to changes in interest rates. But Keynes had a specific objection to the use of interest-rate policy, which was that a continuous low long-term rate could not be maintained if the policy rate was used to control a boom.

The budget's proper job was not to balance the government's accounts, but to balance the nation's accounts (aggregate supply and demand) at full employment.[2] Whether this required a budget surplus, zero balance, or a deficit depended on the state of aggregate demand. In principle, therefore, the budget could be used to restrain demand as well as to increase it, with the fiscal multiplier giving a precise arithmetical estimate of both. What seemed to make this balancing task feasible was the development of national income accounts, and the technique of economic forecasting. Governments could calculate the difference between potential and actual output and adjust taxes and spending accordingly. Monetary policy was to support fiscal policy. Interest rates were to be kept permanently low, their main purpose being to minimize the 'cost of capital' and enable the government to borrow as cheaply as possible.

It was hardly likely that the ideal policy regime would ever be adopted in pure form. It presupposed not just agreement on how the economy worked, but agreement on the size and purposes of the state. The first was only partial; the second non-existent.

On the theoretical side, economists found it hard to accept that the market economy had no natural tendency to full employment. Such a view ran counter to what James Tobin called the 'theoretical paradigm central to our discipline', that of 'general competitive equilibrium, in which rational individuals optimize and markets for all commodities are simultaneously cleared by prices'.[3] However, economists agreed that price adjustment might be sticky. Thus there was a role for 'stabilizing' the business cycle. Far from being a 'general theory', Keynes's theory was interpreted as a 'special case' of the true general theory of perfectly adjusting prices – an interpretation first suggested by J. R. Hicks in a famous article in 1937.[4]

The political implications of Keynesian policy were always contentious. The ideal Keynesian constitution required a fairly large state ('state' meaning here all those economic activities financed by taxes or borrowing), since the larger the state budget, the greater its influence was bound to be on total economic activity.[5] But the question of the size and scope of the state was a dividing line between the right and the left. The right wanted a smaller state to protect liberty and private property; the left a larger one to limit what it saw as the depredations of capitalism. Conservative politicians, committed to reducing taxation, gravitated naturally towards monetary policy as part of their long-term goal of minimizing the state's role in allocating capital. But this was to limit the radical potential of fiscal policy, and assign the regulation of the business cycle to the weaker of the two possible instruments.

Keynes's 'ideal' system was also designed to remove international obstacles to full employment policy, such as had bedevilled the gold standard. As we have seen, his International Clearing Union plan of 1941 set up a system of sanctions against persistent creditor hoarding. But the United States rejected the Keynes plan, and at the Bretton Woods conference of 1944 substituted an institution of its own devising – the International Monetary Fund – which upheld the orthodox policy of debtor adjustment, finance for deficits being confined to short-term help. The American motive was clear: they had no wish to place their hard-earned dollars automatically at the disposal of profligate debtors. The IMF thus provided no limit on persistent reserve accumulation. Bretton Woods laid the intellectual basis for the 'structural adjustment' programmes which the IMF would insist on as the condition of its loans to Latin America and East Asia in the 1980s and 1990s, and which the 'troika' of the IMF, European Central Bank and European Commission would demand as the condition of financing the foreign debt of Mediterranean countries following the crisis of 2008–9.

Schumpeter has argued that the Keynesian revolution was a response to a particularly British problem, one of an old country with plentiful savings and declining investment opportunities.[6] But this must be partly wrong. Certainly the British were exceptional in the importance they attached to unemployment as the indicator of overall balance. But Schumpeter's assessment cannot account for the widespread diffusion of Keynesian ideas, both in the textbooks and in policy, starting with the United States and then spreading, with a time lag, to Europe. The war had subordinated capitalism to society. Keynesianism was part of the democratic attempt to keep control over the capitalist economy in peacetime.

All Western governments were committed to AROM – activist real output management[7] – but there were big differences between the kind of activism they thought was needed. Sweden practised a form of supply-side Keynesianism derived from the Stockholm School. A high level of welfare spending was married to active labour market measures to force up labour productivity: a policy tailor-made for a small export economy. The French state, which emerged from the war as the nation's chief investor, did not have to learn its statism from Keynes: Colbert had pointed the way in the eighteenth century. In Germany, on the other hand, the statist implications of Keynesian policy biased post-war policy against Keynes. In the Nazi period, Freiburg University provided a haven to a small group of intellectuals who rejected both Nazism and state socialism. The Freiburg School was the 'matrix of a new brand of liberal thought'. It accepted the original liberal belief in a competitive market system, but thought that the gaps in classical thought needed to be filled not by the state budget, but by a constitutional framework. This was necessary to protect competition from distortion, see benefits equitably distributed and protect markets from the encroachment of government. These ideas coalesced in 'ordo-liberalism' and the 'social market economy'. The independent Bundesbank became the monetary pillar of the new German constitution. Ordo-liberalism blended with industrial co-partnership in a German version of incomes policy.[8] Nevertheless, even the Germans became explicitly Keynesian in the 1960s, though only fleetingly.

Taking the advanced countries as a whole, a Keynesian commitment to full employment was a common element in a wider mix of national compromises between right and left, capital and labour. Countercyclical policy, improved protection for labour, partial state ownership, active supply-side policy, enlarged welfare spending, indicative planning, the social market economy, short-term lending facilities through the newly established IMF: all were promoted, in the different countries, as 'middle ways' between laissez-faire and central planning. These social compromises – condemned by Marxists as attempts to bamboozle the workers – left substantial scope for private enterprise and the market economy, but were compatible with a range of socialist aspiration, since they could be slanted towards a large public sector and high marginal tax rates to pay for an enlarged welfare state. In the Cold War era they did important political work in protecting Western societies from communism. But the post-war settlement fell far short of a political consensus; it just happened to fit the condition of the times.

Keynesianism benefitted from the success of post-war capitalism, which was in marked contrast to capitalism's dismal record between the wars. The period running from 1950 to 1975 was a golden age for the global capitalist economy in terms of employment and growth. But was it Keynesian policy which made it golden? Or were conditions, unlike in the interwar years, sufficiently stimulating to make possible full employment and rapid growth without the need for deliberate Keynesian stimulants? And was the attention Keynesians paid to maintaining near-zero unemployment in an environment exhibiting strong secular tendencies to economic growth responsible for the upsurge of inflation which brought the golden age to an end? We shall discuss these questions at the end of this chapter.

The Keynesian age charts a neat parabola of rise and fall. It went through three phases: Full Employment Keynesianism, Growth Keynesianism and Stagflation Keynesianism.

II. FULL EMPLOYMENT KEYNESIANISM: 1945–60

It was Britain and the United States that first adopted Keynesian policy. In both countries, Keynesian economic management was validated by the wartime experience of full employment with relative price stability.[9] Unlike in the previous conflict, the economic policymakers (at least Allied ones) seemed to know what they were doing. And no one in 1945 wanted to get back to the 1930s.

In its 1944 Employment White Paper, the British Government accepted responsibility for securing 'high and stable levels of employment' by ensuring that 'total expenditure on goods and services [is] prevented from falling to a level where general unemployment appears'. Pointedly, it emphasized the need for wage restraint and sufficient labour mobility as a condition of success.[10] In the United States, the Full Employment Act, passed by Congress in 1946, made the Administration responsible for maintaining 'a high employment level of labor and price stability'. There were similar, less explicit commitments in other countries. In the light of experience, full employment came to be defined as 2 per cent unemployment in the UK, 4 per cent in the USA. These then became targets. What did having such targets mean for policy?

The UK's Employment White Paper stated that 'none of the main proposals contained in the Paper involves deliberate planning for a deficit in the National Budget in years of sub-normal trade activity'.[11] The budget that the Treasury expected to be balanced in 'normal' times was the budget of current spending. In sub-normal times, a natural deficit would arise through the reduction in revenues and increases in unemployment payments (the 'automatic stabilizers'), and the government should not attempt to offset this effect by raising taxes and/or reducing spending as Labour Chancellor Philip Snowden had done in 1931. But the government should also be willing to accelerate its capital programmes in sub-normal years. It was the capital account, not the current account, which should be used to maintain full employment.

The post-war fiscal formula recognized that the British state was now a major investor in the economy. It had nationalized key industries like coal and the railways. It owned public utilities like gas and electricity. It built houses, roads, schools, hospitals. The enlarged post-war state meant that government spending was *bound* to have a much greater influence on total demand than before the war, irrespective of specific Keynesian inspiration.

The Conservative Party, elected to power in Britain in 1951, promised, like its Labour predecessor, to make 'the maintenance of full employment' the 'first aim of a Conservative Government'. Yet the Keynesian Treasuries of the post-war years followed Keynes's prescriptions only up to a point. Unlike Keynes's original plan for full employment through capital spending, the governments of the 1950s and 1960s primarily relied on discretionary changes in taxation to achieve this goal. This suited the boom conditions in the first post-war decades better, since movements in output tended to be small and short-term rather than the all-encompassing slump of the kind Keynes had experienced.[12] Fiscal policy aimed to moderate the rate of economic expansion by nudging consumer spending downwards in response to periodic balance of payments crises, by measures such as raising hire purchase deposits, and placing higher duties on tobacco, alcohol and petrol. This 'fine tuning' gave British economic performance a juddering aspect called 'stop-go', spurts of rapid growth reversed by restrictive measures: stop 1951–2, go 1953–5, stop 1956–7, go 1958–9, stop 1960–61. It was alleged that 'budgetary and monetary policy failed to be stabilising, and must on the contrary be regarded as having been positively destabilising'.[13] However, this is too extreme. Whatever the tinkering on the margins, public sector net investment was remarkably stable at about 4–5 per cent of GDP, compared with under 2 per cent before the war. Employment was hardly affected in the 'stop' periods, and, until the 1960s, output growth only modestly. The main casualty of 'stop-go' may have been a slower growth rate than that of competitor countries, though it is doubtful how far this can be attributed to macro-policy.

Fine tuning was not the prefered method in the USA. This was partly because it couldn't be: the British Chancellor controlled his budget, whereas the American President had no guarantee that his tax-and-spend proposals would pass Congress. But it was also partly because the United States, with a continuous surplus on its balance of payments, did not have to adjust domestic spending to the requirements of external balance.

American fiscal technique was based on the full employment budget. The agreed American fiscal formula between 1945 and 1961 was: 'Set tax rates to balance the budget and provide a surplus for debt retirement at an agreed high level of employment and national income. Having set these rates, leave them alone unless there is some major change in national policy or condition of national life.'[14] A rise in the full employment budget surplus would indicate that the actual budget was too restrictive.

American policy laid great stress on the automatic stabilizers. As Paul Samuelson pointed out in what became economics' standard textbook: 'the modern fiscal system has great inherent automatic stabilizing properties'. This is largely because of the much greater role of fiscal transfers as compared to before the war. When the economy turns down, government tax receipts fall and spending on unemployment benefits and other transfers rise, creating an automatic deficit that mitigates the fall in private spending. When the economy recovers the budget automatically re-balances. To preserve this built-in stability, no attempt should be made to balance the budget in a downturn. However, as Samuelson noted, 'a built-in stabilizer acts to reduce part of any fluctuation in the economy, but does not wipe out

100 per cent of the disturbance. It leaves the rest of the disturbance as a task for fiscal and monetary discretionary action.'[15] The stabilizers don't expand demand, they make recessions lighter.

In the fourteen years from 1947 to 1960, inclusive, the *actual* US federal budget was in overall surplus for two years (1948 and 1951); for the rest of the period, there were small deficits (the maximum, in 1959, was 2.7 per cent of GDP) resulting from the operation of the automatic stabilizers.[16] These deficits, which were paralleled by a gradual growth in the full employment budget surplus, were taken by the Keynesian economists as indicating the existence of a small but growing output gap. In Western Europe, as a whole, budgets were in balance: in France large increases in public spending were balanced by large increases in taxation.

By the mid-1950s, Keynesian economists were confident that they had cracked the problem of unemployment. The new problem was how to deal with the inflationary pressure resulting from continuous full employment. Very low British unemployment rates went with a slightly higher inflation rate than in Western Europe. Although the analytic debate was about the causes of inflation, for British policymakers the problem boiled down to how to reduce inflationary pressure on the balance of payments. Cashable sterling debts accrued in wartime made it important to maintain 'confidence in sterling', i.e. the assurance that the pound would not be devalued against other currencies. Confidence in the pound required keeping total demand in the economy equal to what the economy could supply for domestic consumption and exports. This suggested willingness to run the economy at a somewhat higher rate of unemployment.

This was the argument of the 'excess demand' school. Excess demand for goods and services led to balance of payments deficits. The periodic 'stops' needed to protect sterling slowed down investment. To avoid 'stop-go' the economy should be run at a 'lower pressure of demand'. This implied either higher interest rates to restrain private demand, or a lower level of public spending.

In 1958 A. V. Phillips published an influential article that claimed to demonstrate an inverse historical correlation between the unemployment rate and the rate of money-wage increases.[17] Since money-wage movements were fairly closely correlated with price movements, the

'Phillips Curve' implied that price stability was to be had for an increase in unemployment at some way beyond what had been recently experienced, but way short of the depression level: say, 2.5–3 per cent (see Appendix 7.2, p. 205).

Those who wanted to reduce the pressure of demand turned naturally to monetary policy, because, in practice, reversing the fiscal engines was politically costly: taxes, once lowered, could not readily be raised; capital programmes could not be turned on and off like a tap. But this meant overriding Keynes's own veto on the use of interest rates as an anti-boom measure. Keynesian policymakers started talking about the need for a 'fiscal–monetary mix'.

Raising Bank Rate was the traditional Bank of England response to a loss of gold. Bank Rate was put up from 2 per cent to 4 per cent between 1951 and 1952 to deal with a balance of payments crisis, its first rise (the brief spike in 1939 excepted) since 1932. Thereafter Bank Rate reverted to its first 'Cunliffe' function (see pp. 54–5 above) of managing speculative capital movements.

The theory that investment was relatively insensitive to changes in interest rates was tested in the early 1950s, with inconclusive results. In response to the sterling crisis of 1951, the Treasury imposed direct controls on imports and fixed investment, partly aimed at slowing down the accumulation of stocks. Bank Rate was raised to 4 per cent in February 1952. At the same time, there was a recession in the clothing and textile industry, caused by a fall in consumer demand, which led to a fall in stock-building in these industries. Between 1951 and 1952, the budget swung from deficit into surplus. Which of the three factors produced it: higher Bank Rate, import restrictions, or a drop in consumer spending? The Treasury concluded that the monetary contribution was slight and indirect. The reduction in bank advances was the result of a decline in the demand for finance, not a reduction in its supply. The Bank of England responded that its 'primary concern with monetary policy is the effect on sentiment, and not in terms of a logical chain of cause and effect'. By reducing fears of inflation, the rise in Bank Rate had removed the incentive to accumulate stocks beyond the working minimum. The Bank's view was rejected. The Treasury concluded that raising Bank Rate was ineffectual in controlling credit creation: the only way to control credit creation was by quantitative restrictions. Unexplored in this assessment was the question of the Treasury's timing of its own measures. If private demand was already falling, the Treasury's measures would have been strongly pro-cyclical. Such were the snares of 'fine tuning'.[18]

Although monetary policy was rejected as a cyclical balancer, a division of labour between monetary and fiscal policy evolved. Monetary policy was to be used to maintain external balance in the short-run, and fiscal policy, supported by monetary policy, to maintain overall balance in the medium-run. In the USA, too, the Fed abandoned its policy of supporting government debt at 2.5 per cent in 1951. So, hesitantly at first, monetary policy re-emerged as an active tool for short-term economic management. This was the path which led eventually to the policy orthodoxy of the 1990s and 2000s.

However, there was no more agreement than before on how monetary policy worked. What was the transmission mechanism from money to prices?

The older academic view, derived from the Quantity Theory of Money, was that there existed a stable relationship between the quantity of money and nominal income, such that action by authorities on the cash base led to a predictable multiple expansion or contraction of bank deposits (the so-called money multiplier). But the authorities were not persuaded that such a relationship existed. The Bank of England stuck to its pre-war view that 'a change in the supply of money is by no means rigidly associated with a similar change in the amount of spending . . . we cannot say in advance what result a particular change will have'.[19] This was because of uncertainty about the effects of interest rate changes on velocity: the legacy of Keynes's liquidity-preference theory of the rate of interest. Scepticism about the efficacy of monetary policy was expressed by the influential Radcliffe Report of 1959, which echoed the prevailing sentiment that 'monetary policy had little to do with inflation, and was largely ineffective as an instrument of demand management'.[20] The Radcliffe Report reaffirmed the subordination of monetary policy: bank rate changes were to be made at the explicit directive of the Chancellor of the day. But the Bank of England got new powers to supervise the clearing banks.

The 'excess demand' explanation of inflation was challenged by the 'cost-push' school. Most British Keynesians rejected the analytical relevance of 'Phillips Curve' Keynesianism, pointing out that Phillips's data mostly preceded the existence of a full employment guarantee by the state: Victorian domestic servants, agricultural workers and casual labourers did not strike for higher wages. In the new situation, trade unions could push for higher wages without the risk of their members becoming unemployed. A modest check to demand would not stop inflation, since there was no trade-off between inflation and unemployment to be had short of abandoning the full employment commitment. The only policy that would simultaneously maintain full employment and keep prices stable was control over costs.[21]

The solution which seemed most congruent with the Keynesian philosophy of social compromise was a compact between government, capital and labour. American analysts talked about a convergence between the interests of Big Government, Big Business and Big Labour. Government would guarantee full employment; employers and unions would jointly restrain the rise in costs. Some degree of capital–labour co-operation was achieved in all the Western democracies: in the USA the 1950 Detroit treaty between General Motors and the United Auto Workers linked wage increases to increases in productivity and the cost of living index. In Germany, wages for the whole economy were set by national employer–union bargains.

In Britain it was far more difficult to achieve such deals, because of the adversarial system of industrial relations and the fragmented nature of trade unions. Loath to provoke unemployment by too vigorous a use of interest rate policy, Conservative governments in the UK embarked on the wearisome road of trying to control costs. Exhortations to 'pay restraint' started to buttress policies of demand restraint. But, for any Conservative government, coming to an understanding with the trade unions on wages was very difficult because the unions were so tightly bound to the Labour Party. In addition, union leaderships themselves could not deliver any such deal because of the power of shop stewards, the elected workers' representatives in plants and factories. In Britain cost control proper, popularly known as 'incomes policy', started in 1964. At first voluntary, it became a legislated six-month wage freeze in 1966. The alternative, which did not seem feasible until the late 1970s, was to reduce the unemployment costs of deflation by busting the unions.

Although these debates inflamed the academic journals, inflationary pressure in fact remained extremely subdued in the 1950s, and this continued into the mid-1960s, despite the very low levels of unemployment. The decisive constraint on inflation was the exchange rate. As long as Britain was committed to maintaining the dollar–sterling exchange rate established in 1949, domestic inflation could not take off. The low output cost of maintaining the fixed sterling peg was the result of a combination of a private investment boom, the falling cost of foodstuffs and raw materials (reflected in an improvement in the terms of trade), and the relatively modest character of 'wage push' by the unions. As a result, UK inflation averaged just over 4 per cent a year in the 1950s and 1960s, within the comfort zone of central banks, bond markets and Keynesian economists, though still somewhat higher than that of the country's competitors. The US rate of inflation was just above 2 per cent per year.

III. GROWTH KEYNESIANISM: 1960–70

The achievement of full employment in the 1960s shifted the attention of Keynesian economists from the task of maximizing employment to the task of maximizing growth. Growth Keynesianism started out as an Anglo-American phenomenon. This was because the UK and the USA were the slowest growing of the major industrial economies.

Growth Keynesianism was backed by exuberant self-confidence. In 1955, Paul Samuelson – the most arrogant and clever of the American Keynesians and author of the best-selling textbook *Economics*, which defined what economics was for generations of students – assured the Joint Committee on the Economic Report of the President that 'with proper fiscal and monetary policies, our economy can have full employment and whatever rate of capital formation and growth it wants'. He added, for good measure, that the government 'can accomplish all this compatibly with the degree of income-redistributing taxation it ethically desires'.[22] The economists had the tools. It was only necessary to get governments to use them. With the political left coming to power in the 1960s, the Keynesian economists found governments ready to act on their precepts. An OECD Report of 1965 noted that 'it did indeed seem that the Keynesian "New Economics" was making it possible to achieve sustained non-inflationary growth at a high level of capacity utilisation throughout the Western world'.[23]

In Britain the chosen comparators were the exceptionally fast-growing continental economies of Western Europe. In the United States it was – incredible as it now seems – the Soviet Union which posed the challenge, especially in the fields of aerospace and defence, the Russians having launched their first Sputnik satellite in 1957, with loud claims of being about to 'bury' the capitalist West economically. In fact, the Soviet growth rates were also high during the 'golden age'. There was talk of 'secular stagnation', never far from the surface of American discussions. Germany, whose growth record was exemplary, also succumbed to the fear of slow growth, following its first recession in 1965. By that time there was a general feeling that the capitalist world needed a Keynesian boost.

The analysis was deceptively simple. Managing the cycle alone would not enlarge industrial capacity sufficiently to lower unit labour costs. Thus faster growth was the key to lower inflation, and would also provide resources for increased welfare, and (in the US) defence, spending.

This analysis coincided with increased political pressure for public spending. By the 1960s, most Western governments were spending up to 40 per cent of their national income. The Keynesian state was morphing into the social democratic state. There was no intrinsic economic connection between the two, but Keynesians tended to be social democrats and thus predisposed to use public spending both to ensure sufficient aggregate demand and to redistribute wealth and income to the poor. Governments were also faced with what has been called 'the entitlements revolution', as the claim for economic rights spread to women and excluded groups. In the USA, where federal spending was a smaller fraction of GDP than central government spending in Europe, the 1960s saw the rise of Martin Luther King and the Civil Rights movement.

The growth of the state made it harder to keep the government's budget in balance, because the demand for increased social spending was unmatched by a corresponding willingness to pay higher taxes.

Faster economic growth offered a way of producing extra revenues to square the circle. As the British Labour Party's election manifesto of 1964 declared: 'Economic growth sets the pace at which Labour can build the fair and just society we want to see.'[24]

The twin commitments to full employment and the sterling–dollar exchange rate had entailed 'stop-go': spurts of growth were followed by 'stops' whenever demand expansion threatened the sterling–dollar exchange rate. Governments eventually decided that breaking out of 'stop-go' required that demand-management be set in the context of a medium-term plan for growth, the model being the French system of 'indicative planning'. Indicative planning started in the last three years of Conservative rule (1961–4), with a targeted real annual growth rate of 4 per cent (as opposed to the 2.8 per cent average of the 1950s). This was confirmed by the more ambitious National Plan produced by the new Labour government in 1965, which projected a 25 per cent increase in national output over six years.[25] A parallel Prices and Incomes policy was put in place to restrain costs. The fiscal counterpart of the strategy was Conservative Chancellor Reginald Maudling's 'dash for growth', a planned increase in public spending of 7.5 per cent between 1963 and 1964. (Public Sector Net Borrowing went up from 4.96 per cent of GDP in 1962 to 8.53 per cent in 1965.) The belief – more accurately, hope – was that rapid output expansion would cause enough productivity growth and *ex ante* saving to avoid inflation and deterioration in the balance of payments.

A basic weakness in the Keynesian mindset was the assumption that any structural problems faced by an economy would yield automatically to faster demand expansion. Nicholas Kaldor, Labour's chief economic adviser, and the cleverest as well as the most inventive of the British Keynesians, realized this was not so. He understood that something was going wrong on the supply-side of the British economy. His more subtle analysis suggested a growth strategy with combined supply-side and demand-side features. Devaluation of the pound would not produce the required increase in exports without a shift from services to manufacturing. Basing himself on Verdoorn's law, Kaldor argued that economies of scale caused output in manufacturing to rise faster than employment, raising labour productivity as markets expanded and thus creating a virtuous circle of rising productivity and expanding exports.[26] Britain, he said, was suffering from 'premature senility': the comparatively early contraction of its agriculture had robbed it of the surplus labour supplies which its competitors had available to expand their manufacturing capacity. So what was required was a shift of workers from services to manufacturing industry. Kaldor persuaded the Labour government to introduce a Selective Employment tax in 1966. This was a poll tax on all employment, part of which would be rebated to manufacturing businesses. The tax would have the double effect of shifting labour from services to manufacturing and, by limiting domestic consumption, from domestic production to exports. If it were true that productivity growth was a function of investment in manufacturing, a planned expansion of manufacturing output would carry few inflationary risks, especially if an incomes policy were used to restrain wage costs.

American Democrats were also excited by the thought of engineering economic growth. They attacked the Republican Eisenhower administrations of the 1950s for attaching too much importance to balancing the budget. Eisenhower had allowed the surplus on the full employment budget to creep up, and with it American unemployment, which reached 7 per cent by the end of the 1950s.

In 1960 the President's Council of Economic Advisers estimated that the economy was using only 90 per cent of its potential output, because of 'fiscal drag'. The policy of setting tax rates and spending totals to balance the budget at a high level of employment, and leaving them there, was not enough, because if tax rates were left unchanged, the full employment surplus automatically expanded with the growth of the economy, making the actual budget increasingly deflationary. By 1960 the estimated full employment surplus had risen to $12 billion through what Lester Thurow called 'passive fiscal policies'.

Much the same conclusion was drawn by 'the new stagnation' theorists. They were impressed by the fact that the upswing of 1958–60 had soon petered out. Secular stagnation was an old American obsession. The stagnationists claimed that what had made American capitalism so dynamic was its expanding frontier. With the 'closing of the frontier' at home, and the exclusion of American exports from communist China, this dynamism was exhausted: a new frontier had to be created by state spending. Statistical series showed a widening gap between actual and potential output after 1955. So a big tax cut and/or expenditure increase was needed to reduce the full employment budget surplus. The victory of the Democrat John F. Kennedy in the 1960 presidential election offered a chance to try out the new strategy.[27]

However, the high policy expectations of the growth Keynesians were soon to be disappointed.

In Britain, the Labour government of Harold Wilson (1964–70) failed to develop a balance of payments strategy consistent with its growth targets. Sterling should have been devalued when the government came to power, as Maudling's 'dash for growth' had led to an unprecedented balance of payments deficit of £800 million. But the incoming Labour government rejected this course, because it feared the discredit of a devaluation. So the 'go' policy was continued until a growing balance of payments deficit forced another 'stop' in July 1966, accompanied by a year's wage freeze. These July measures failed to restore confidence, however; withdrawals of sterling continued, and the pound had to be devalued by 14.3 per cent in November 1967. Much more savage cuts were enacted by the new Chancellor, Roy Jenkins, in 1968, who achieved an overall budget surplus (in both current and capital spending) for the first time since the war. However, the ending of the period of 'severe restraint' on incomes led to a wage explosion in 1968, which sent the inflation rate up from 5 to 8 per cent, and largely undid the effects of fiscal austerity. 'Stop-go' was followed after 1966 by a more or less continuous 'stop' until 1970. The prolonged slowdown of the late 1960s destroyed the government's growth strategy. The average rate of growth over the period 1964–70 was actually lower than it had been during the Conservatives' 'thirteen wasted years'. More ominously, the 'stop' of 1966 inaugurated the era of 'stagflation', the simultaneous growth of unemployment and inflation, which was soon to discredit the whole theory of demand management.

The American trajectory was different, though it ended in the same place. The expenditure increases of $17 billion between 1960 and 1962 (mostly on military and aerospace spending) reduced the full employment surplus from $12 billion to $7 billion. Unemployment fell to 5.5 per cent and output rose by 6.5 per cent. But the full employment surplus then started to rise again, suggesting that more radical therapy was needed. The revolutionary principle behind President Kennedy's $13 billion tax cut of 1963 (enacted the following year, after his assassination) was that taxes were to be cut when the economy was well on the way to recovery, and the actual budget was in deficit. There were further tax cuts and expenditure increases in 1965 (the latter to finance 'guns and butter': rising military expenditure caused by the Vietnam War and Lyndon Johnson's 'Great Society' programme). Only in the 1960s then, in Tobin's judgement, did 'the view of the economic mechanism commonly accepted by men of affairs' finally move into line with the 'models' that economists had long worked with; only then were the 'phobias about public spending, budget deficits, and internal public debt . . . largely overcome or forgotten'.[28]

At first everything went according to the script. Fuelled by rising public spending and tax cuts, the US economy entered a long boom that lasted until 1969. In 1966, unemployment dipped below 4 per cent, then reckoned as full employment. However, inflation started to pick up, from 2 per cent in the early 1960s to 5.5 per cent in 1969. The Administration did not seek a temporary tax surcharge until 1967, and it was not enacted until June 1968. In 1971, following a haemorrhage of gold, President Nixon devalued the dollar and imposed wage, price and import controls.

In other industrial countries, fiscal Keynesianism was adopted as a growth strategy in the 1960s in face of the perceived exhaustion of opportunities for 'catch-up'. Further impetus was given by the establishment of the customs union of the European Economic Community (EEC) in 1958, which made illegal the protectionist measures which had shielded domestic industries from competition. In Germany, Ludwig Erhard and his state secretary Alfred Müller-Armack enacted a Growth and Stability Law in 1963, with a commitment to high employment. The growing worry about the end of growth was seemingly confirmed in 1965, when the German economy experienced its first post-war recession. A new Stabilization and Growth Law of 1967, based on the views of the Social Democrat Karl Schiller, mandated the Federal Government to establish quantitative targets for prices, employment, growth and the balance of payments. The operational aim was a budget balance over the cycle, in which surpluses accumulated in good years were disbursed in downturns. A major expansionary budget in

1967, Germany's first recourse to deficit financing, created an unprecedented boom in 1968–70. However, inflation rose at the end of the 1960s, largely through the inflow of American dollars. With the devaluation of the dollar in 1971, the Bundesbank, which had never accepted the Keynesian prescription, tightened monetary policy, bringing stagflation to Germany. The briefness of the German flirtation with Keynesianism ensured that its own model of 'Rhenish capitalism' survived the neo-liberal reaction of the 1980s.

IV. REASONS FOR THE STRENGTH OF THE BOOM

Figure 12, which includes average growth rates across the UK, the USA, France, Germany and Japan, shows that the period running from 1950 to 1975 was a golden age for the global capitalist economy, with unprecedented growth in living standards, low unemployment and reduced volatility. This compares very favourably with both the pre-war period and the subsequent years of 'the Great Moderation'.

It is reasonable to ask whether it was Keynesian policy which made the 1950s and 1960s 'golden'. Was it a demand-led or a supply-led boom? James Tobin has no doubt it was because 'virtually all advanced

Figure 12. GDP per capita growth in interwar years, Keynesian Age and post–1975[29]

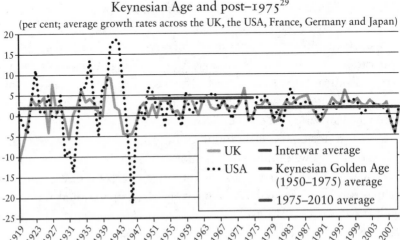

(per cent; average growth rates across the UK, the USA, France, Germany and Japan)

democratic capitalist societies adopted, in varying degrees, Keynesian strategies of demand-management'.[30] The alternative explanation is that the global economy was experiencing extraordinarily favourable conditions of supply.

In an influential article of 1968 entitled 'Why has Britain had Full Employment since the War?', Robin Matthews answered that it was not because of 'Keynesian' fiscal deficits, but because of the private sector investment boom. The rate of capital accumulation and technical change after 1948 was much higher than in the forty preceding years. He pointed out that 'throughout the post-war period the Government, so far from injecting demand into the system, has persistently had a large current account surplus . . . Fiscal policy as such therefore appears on the face of it to have been . . . quite strongly deflationary'[31] – and, by implication, non-Keynesian.

The weakness of this argument is that it uses current spending as a test of the impact of Keynesian policy, whereas the total impact of the budget on the economy should be measured by the combined current and capital spending balance sheet. Whereas the current spending budget remained in surplus, with revenues exceeding expenditure, the public sector had a financial deficit throughout the Keynesian period. If the two are combined, the result is a small budget deficit throughout.

Figure 13 shows the British government budgets to be either in almost continuous surplus or in almost continuous deficit during the Keynesian 'golden age'. Which it was depends entirely on whether capital spending is included in, or excluded from, the budget accounts.

Even for those who believed in distinguishing current and capital spending in theory, separating them out in the national accounts proved very tricky. In old Treasury jargon, current expenses were recorded 'above the line' and capital expenses 'below the line'. In 1945, Keynes himself had remarked that 'the present criterion leads to meaningless anomalies'. A capital contribution to school buildings was 'above' in the Exchequer accounts and therefore paid for out of revenue, and 'below' in the local authority accounts and paid for out of loans.[32]

Instead of trying to clear up the anomalies, the drastic decision was taken in 1968 to substitute a new measure, the Public Sector Borrowing Requirement or PSBR, made up of the deficits of central and local

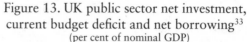

Figure 13. UK public sector net investment,
current budget deficit and net borrowing[33]
(per cent of nominal GDP)

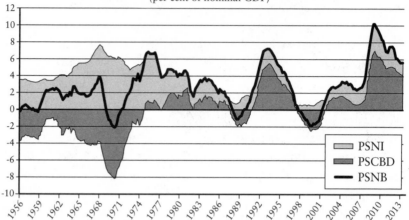

government plus those of the nationalized industries, as the correct measure of fiscal sustainability. The focus on a single deficit number would later play into the hands of those who regarded all deficits as bad.

In general public finances were well controlled in the Keynesian era. PSBR fell from an average of 7.5 per cent of GDP (1952–9) to 6.6 per cent (1960–69). The national debt fell from 150 per cent to 50 per cent of GDP over the period.

By the 1960s the state was spending close to 40 per cent of national income. It was what Keynes called the 'semi-socialised' character of the new economy, represented by the enlarged public sector, which brought stability to the economy, despite the erratic character of actual fiscal policy.

European economies and Japan had unusually high rates of economic growth in the 1950s because they were able to exploit the 'advantages of backwardness'. The main problem for countries such as Germany, Japan and Italy was shortage of supply, not of demand, much of their capital equipment having been destroyed in the war. This gave them a chance to modernize their industrial plant; the Federal Republic of Germany also benefitted from the skills and hard work of millions of immigrants, mostly from its severed eastern territories. The problems facing these countries did not demand Keynesian solutions. Restoring and modernizing war-damaged supply to feed hungry populations set

Figure 14. UK public spending and tax revenue[34]
(per cent of GDP)

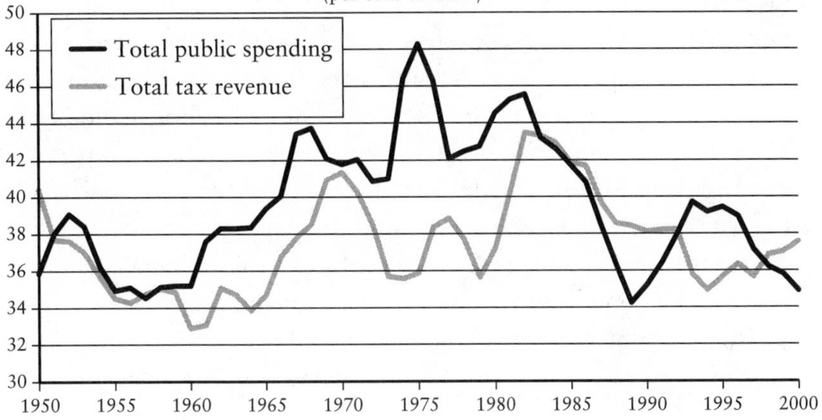

up a huge demand for investment, which needed orderly conditions but no artificial boosting: as Konrad Zweig noted, for Germany 'a second industrial revolution had to start afresh to rebuild the country'.[35]

After the war, writes Moses Abramovitz,

> the countries of the industrialized 'West' were able to bring into production a large backlog of unexploited technology. The principal part of this backlog is deemed to have consisted of methods of production and of industrial and commercial organization already in use in the United States at the end of the war, but not yet employed in the other countries of the West.[36]

It was through 'catch-up' that countries like Germany, Japan and Italy developed such a formidable exporting capacity in steel, machinery, ships, motor cars, chemicals and other commodities. The combined scarcity and opportunities for technological catch-up gave capital a high marginal productivity, leading to high private investment demand. A high rate of productivity growth allowed a sufficient rise in real incomes to satisfy workers' aspirations while keeping unit costs fairly stable. This was true of all the fast-growing industrial nations. However, as the economic capacities of follower countries (in Europe and Japan) converged on the leader (the USA), opportunities for productivity catch-up were bound to wane.

The exploitation of potential for catch-up depends on such factors as opportunities for diffusion of technology, social capacity, industrial adaptability and business confidence. The United States already had a big technological lead in 1918. But in the interwar years, European catch-up was frustrated by the years of disturbed political and financial conditions which followed the conflict, by the uneven impacts of the Great Depression, and by the shrinking of international trade. After 1945, 'the three elements required for rapid growth by catching up came together . . . large technological gaps; enlarged social competence . . . and conditions favoring rapid realization of potential'.[37] Of the last, Abramovitz writes there was on this occasion

> a strong reaction to the experience of defeat in war, and a chance for political reconstruction. The postwar political and economic reorganization and reform weakened the power of monopolistic groupings, brought new men to the fore, and focused the attention of governments on the tasks of recovery . . . The facilities for the diffusion of technology improved. International markets were opened. Large labor reserves in home agriculture and immigration from Southern and Eastern Europe provided a flexible and mobile labor supply. Government support, technological opportunity, and an environment of stable international money favored heavy and sustained capital investment. The outcome was the great speed and strength of the post-war catch up process.[38]

We should bear in mind, also, that increased government spending may have expansionary effects without any specific Keynesian theory or policy being involved. The classic cases are wars and arms races. It is difficult in the so-called Keynesian age to distinguish Cold War spending from Keynesian spending.

To what extent were the domestic conditions which facilitated catch-up put in place by the Keynesian revolution? Apparently, not much. To be sure, governments produced and consumed a larger share of GDP than before the war, and this contributed to stability. But this was because of the extensive post-war nationalizations and expansion of social services. Neither had an explicit warrant in Keynesian theory; neither was undertaken for Keynesians reasons. Yet, as John Hicks put it in 1974:

The combination of more rapid technical progress (surely a fact) with the socialist tendencies which increased demand for collective goods (surely also a fact) could have produced such a boom without the added stimulus of Keynesian policies. It is still unclear how much is to be attributed to the one and how much to the other.[39]

The post-war trading and monetary regimes undoubtedly facilitated the diffusion of best-practice technology. Keynes's handiwork can be found in the setting up of both, but the ideas that inspired them – trade liberalization, currency convertibility at fixed exchange rates – were of ancient provenance. What was intended to be restored was the nineteenth-century free trade/gold standard system, improved by experience of the interwar years. This reflected the American conviction that the troubles of that period had been brought about by trade and currency wars. Keynes influenced Harry Dexter White, the architect of the Bretton Woods system, but there were more parochial influences.

Keynes's own specific idea – 'the doctrine of creditor adjustment' (pp. 127–8) – was not accepted at Bretton Woods. This meant that the 1944 Agreement provided no mechanism for dealing with the 'dollar gap' that resulted from a quasi-permanent US current account surplus. In the 1920s, America's export surplus had been a deflationary drag on the world economy. In the 1950s the surplus was gradually whittled away, turning negative by the end of the decade. This was partly due to the renewed competitiveness of the continental European (and Japanese) economies, helped by a transfer of technology through American investment, and by the US commitment to keep Western Europe and Japan free from communism. This led the USA to acquiesce in the large sterling, franc and deutschmark devaluations against the dollar in 1949; it led to the huge outflow of American dollars on government account (Marshall Aid, military spending in Europe), later supplemented by large private outflows; and it led the United States to promote a European Payments Union, and allow the Union to discriminate against American goods, while also giving Japan privileged entry to the US market. The trend in the balance of payments in turn enabled exchange rates to be gradually stabilized and currencies to become convertible. This promoted trade liberalization, which in turn fuelled economic growth. By the end of the 1960s America's current account surplus had turned into a deficit.

America's role in the first phase of the golden age was not unfairly summed up by the banker Russell Leffingwell in 1960:

> Wisely we undertook to set the world to rights. We gave money and know-how to our foreign friends, we made fixed foreign investments, and we policed the world against the Russian and Communist Chinese with foreign bases and foreign based troops and ships and planes. All this involved spending immense sums of dollars abroad.
>
> We and our friends abroad had been so obsessed by the thought of the ... dollar gap ... that until recently few noticed that the dollar shortage had disappeared and a dollar glut had taken its place ... Our favorable trade balance has dwindled to little or nothing.
>
> We are still spending abroad billions more than our income from abroad, and the resulting deficit is reflected in our loss of gold and increased short-term debt to abroad ... For the first time in more than a quarter of a century we are being subjected, willy nilly, to the disciplines of the gold standard.[40]

In fact the United States continued to 'live beyond its means' right up to the collapse of the gold–exchange standard in 1971 and beyond, by inducing other countries to accept US debt. This debt, in turn, became the major source of the expansion of global aggregate demand.

In Nicholas Kaldor's summary:

> ... the continued excess of dollar outlays over receipts provided the rest of the world with a steady increase in international purchasing power ... As a result world production, and particularly world industrial production, grew at a pace and with a continuity never before experienced in human history. If it had not been for the growth of world income generated by the continued rise in net dollar outlays by the United States, Germany, Japan, Italy and dozens of smaller countries could never have experienced the fast growth of production, employment and real income which the (much faster) rates of growth of their exports made possible.[41]

It's not surprising that most countries could run budget surpluses in the Keynesian heyday.

Is there any influence of Keynes on all this? These American policies, we may say, had Keynesian effects, but they were not undertaken
for Keynesian reasons. However, the influence of Keynes cannot be
so easily discounted. The economies that maintained full employment during the golden age were not the limited state economies he
had analysed in the 1930s. The role of policy was much larger,
whether or not undertaken for 'Keynesian' reasons. At the very least
financial obstacles to the pursuit of demand-expanding policies had
been seriously weakened. And the belief that the government could
and would prevent depression was an independent source of investment confidence. One has only to think of the British Treasury's
resistance to rearmament in the 1930s, for *financial* reasons, to realize how far analysis had shifted.

However, with the good came the bad. The Belgian-American
economist Robert Triffin identified his 'Triffin paradox' in 1960.[42] In a
gold–exchange-rate system, a growing world economy needed continuous growth in reserves which only dollars could provide; but in
exporting more dollars than it was receiving the US government was
undermining confidence in the dollar as a reserve currency. The unfolding of this 'paradox' might have been postponed had America not got
involved in the Vietnam War. But vast military spending overseas,
coming on top of President Johnson's 'Great Society' policy, made the
fixed exchange-rate system unviable. Once inflationary expectations
got built into the global system, fiscal policy was disabled. Raising
taxes could no longer be used to fight inflation, since labour unions
would ask for higher wages to compensate for reductions in take-home
pay; lowering taxes to stimulate demand would only ratchet up prices.

The basic question is unresolved. The Keynesian era did see a gradual build-up in inflationary pressure and this was caused by
government policies adding to already buoyant private sector demand.
This was due partly to over-anxiety to avoid a repeat of the Great
Depression, but also to political pressures on the budget which had
nothing to do with Keynesian analysis. With notable exceptions,
Keynesians were also indifferent to policies to improve the supply-
side of the economy. We should note too that there was nothing in
Keynesian theory itself which mandated a particular rate of unemployment. Against this, the determination of governments to keep the

boom going gave the advanced world twenty-five continuous years of unprecedented real growth, which also pulled up the real incomes of much of the developing world. Anti-Keynesians who go on about inflation seem entirely oblivious to the gains in welfare achieved in this period. But to them the microbe of inflation has always been a greater evil than the scourge of unemployment.

V. STAGFLATION KEYNESIANISM: 1970–76

The Keynesian theory of economic policy was destroyed by the stagflation of the 1970s – simultaneously rising inflation and unemployment. The Keynesian promise had been to minimize unemployment without igniting inflation or resorting to oppressive controls. When it failed to deliver on both, it became politically useless.

Stagflation was entirely unexpected by the Keynesian establishment of the day, the top officials in finance ministries and central banks, their political masters, and the academic economists advising them. Accustomed as they were to the world of Bretton Woods and the stable Phillips Curve, they believed that governments were tooled up to keep the business cycle within narrow limits, even in the face of serious 'shocks'. In the 1970s the tools stopped working. Richard Nixon's 1971 confession – 'I am now a Keynesian in economics' – was the last expression of Keynesian faith by a national leader.

But who killed Cock Robin? Keynesian policy had not been needed except as a background factor sustaining the private sector boom of the 1950s. One could argue that it was the attempt to turn it into a growth policy in the 1960s which first caused it to misfire. The political logic seemed compelling: a slowdown in growth was bound to endanger the fragile social compromises of the 'golden age' – notably full employment and expanding social provision at moderate cost. But the attempt to turn Keynesianism into a growth engine put far bigger demands on economic forecasting than the state of knowledge justified.

For the United States, which set the economic conditions for most of the non-communist world, faster growth was also required for

Cold War purposes. There was always a nexus between Keynesian logic and military logic, so it is not surprising that a combination of fears of a growth slowdown, Great Society programmes and the Vietnam War should produce excess demand conditions in the mid-1960s; or that these should spill over, via the growth of the US trade deficit, into the rest of the OECD world. It was also inevitable that four years of excess demand (1965–9), as indicated by a positive GNP gap (actual output running ahead of potential output), should lead to rising inflation; and that subsequent attempts to reduce inflation would carry far heavier employment and output costs than in the days of the reliable Phillips Curve.

The misery or 'discomfort' index (the sum of unemployment and inflation) chronicled the deteriorating macroeconomic position (Figure 15).[43]

It now appeared that each economic expansion increased inflation more than output; and each economic contraction reduced output more than inflation. With his piercing anti-statist antennae, Milton Friedman had already sensed, in 1968, that the 'Curve' was playing up and had his theoretical explanation ready: the persistent attempt of the Keynesian establishment to hold unemployment below its 'natural' rate.

The dismal sequence is summarized in the OECD Report 'Towards Full Employment and Price Stability' (1977), its title reflecting a

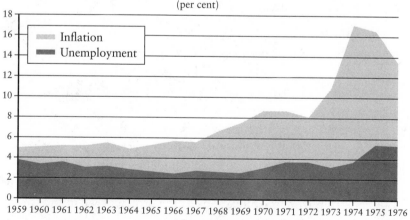

Figure 15. The discomfort index in the OECD
(per cent)

by-now vestigial Keynesian commitment. The authors' narrative is divided into the following periods:

Onset: 1965–9

Excess demand in the USA. Failure to raise taxes to finance the government's spending programmes – notably for Johnson's Great Society programmes and the war in Vietnam – 'provides one of the most striking examples of the difficulties encountered when the needs of demand management conflict with perceived requirements of social policy or "political necessity"'.[44] Excess demand led to rising inflation in the USA from 1967 onwards, which spilled over into the rest of the developed world through the growing deficit in the US current account. The US, that is, exported its own 'excess demand' to Europe. At the same time, attempts to control costs by means of prices and incomes policies broke down. In Europe, price inflation accelerated following a series of wage explosions and labour-market disruptions in 1968. (This year, it should be remembered, was the peak year of the university campus revolts in both the USA and Western Europe: in Paris, mass student demonstrations and occupations came within a whisker of overthrowing de Gaulle's government.)

Deterioration: 1969–73

These years can be divided as follows:

1. *The Mild Recession of 1970–71*
   Modestly restrictive policies in 1968–9, designed to reverse the rise of inflation, produced a mild recession in 1970–71 on both sides of the Atlantic, which failed to eliminate the higher inflation but nearly doubled the rate of unemployment.
2. *The Breakdown of Bretton Woods, 1971*
   The rise in unemployment, and looming elections in a number of OECD countries, prompted a simultaneous shift to expansionary policy in the early 1970s. The Bretton Woods system was already under strain from the late 1960s as the growing size of the United States payments deficits 'effectively removed the balance-of-

payments constraints in other OECD countries, and facilitated a massive expansion of money supplies'.[45] However, the Triffin paradox now came into play. The drain of dollars from the Fed drained confidence in America's commitment to maintain the dollar–gold peg. The reduction in US interest rates in late 1970 brought about a massive flight from the dollar. Official settlement deficits trebled between 1970 and 1971. In August 1971, Nixon suspended the dollar's convertibility into gold and imposed a 10 per cent import surcharge. Attempts to restore the fixed exchange rates (the Smithsonian parities) between 1971 and 1973 broke down, with generalized floating taking its place. The OECD Report authors believe that the elimination of the balance of payments discipline on domestic monetary policy was a 'significant factor' in explaining the explosive character of the subsequent boom, and especially its *monetary* character.

3. *The Boom Gets Out of Hand, 1972–3*

The boom was led by monetary expansion as short-term interest rates tumbled and real long-term interest rates for borrowers turned negative. Both narrow and broad money growth accelerated in 1971–2. Fiscal expansion reinforced the monetary boost, especially in the UK. Between the last half of 1972 and the first half of 1973 the world experienced the fastest upswing since the 1950s. OECD GNP rose by 7.5 per cent and industrial production by 10 per cent. Inflation accelerated. More than half the acceleration could be attributed to the rise in food prices, and speculation in stocks. As the OECD Report tells it, it was the over-rapid increase in demand which drove up the 'prices of food, raw materials and industrial products'. Induced wage rises added a wage-price spiral to the initial inflation.[46] The key point, though, is that while the monetary and fiscal expansion raised the inflation rate to 7.5 per cent, unemployment barely shifted. Once more the engines were put into reverse. Short-term interest rates rose from an average of 4 per cent early in 1972 to 10 per cent in mid-1973. Fiscal policy tightened. Growth in GNP slowed from 8 per cent in the first half of 1973 to 3 per cent in the second half. 'In general the prospects as seen in the latter part of 1973 were for a moderate policy-induced cooling-off period, with some modest reduction of inflation – in other words, a repeat performance, at higher rates of inflation, of the 1969–71 episode.[47]

Oil Price Shock, Inflation and Recession: 1973–5

The quadrupling of oil prices in 1973–4 had a shattering psychological impact on an already disordered global economy, magnifying first inflation and then recession in the industrial world. The rise in the price of imported energy, plus the induced increases in the price of domestically produced energy, increased the inflation rate to 15 per cent in the spring of 1974. Attempts to restore real wages in the face of the sudden price hike set in motion further rounds of the wage-price spiral, with governments expanding demand in an effort to avoid an even more serious recession. The rise in the cost of major input prices, unaccompanied by falls in real wages, reduced profitability. In 1975, inflation peaked at 30 per cent in Japan and at 25 per cent in the UK. The combined current account of OECD countries moved from a small surplus in 1973 to a deficit of $33 billion in 1974.

The oil shock had a contractionary effect on OECD economies in 1974–5, which this time governments made little attempt to offset. Between July 1974 and April 1975 industrial production fell by 10 per cent, with big falls in the prices of industrial materials, commodities and food. Unemployment rose from 8 million to 15 million – up to 5.5 per cent, though this understates the extent of the problem since much of the adjustment to lower labour demand took the form of under-employment, and the net return of migrant labour in Europe. 'The simultaneous lagged effects of restrictive policies and the external shock of the oil price increase, both acting concurrently in nearly all countries, interacting with – and reinforcing – progressive loss of confidence on the part of both business and consumers made the recession deeper and steeper than originally expected.' A recovery described as 'fragile' started in 1975.[48]

The OECD Report is probably right to see excess demand in the United States as the trigger which set off the whole disastrous train of monetary events, leading to the breakdown of the Bretton Woods system in 1971. To what extent the subsequent supply-side shocks – the commodity and wage-price explosions culminating in the quadrupling of oil prices in 1973–4 – were independent causes or induced effects of the previous demand inflation is not easily established. The common-sense conclusion is that, while individual hits could have been offset, it was the malign conjuncture which proved uncontrollable by even the most sophisticated policymakers. There was a structural break between 1968 and 1975 with which Keynesian policy could not deal.

If Keynesian policy was only one element in the boom of the 1950s and 1960s, it is illogical to blame it for the collapse of the boom in the 1970s. Where Keynesian policymakers can be faulted, however, is for their inattention to supply-side questions. By the 1970s they had come to put their whole faith in incomes policies to restrain wage push by organized labour. This restraint was not forthcoming, except in countries such as Germany, with its specific 'co-ordinated' wage-bargaining structure. However, this failure does not vindicate the pre-Keynesian view that 'free competition' was enough to secure full employment without inflation. Policies to reverse inflation after its explosion in the 1970s were inevitable. They need not have involved the repudiation of the Keynesian revolution.

VI. GREAT BRITAIN: THE END OF THE KEYNESIAN ROAD

It ended where it had started, in Britain. Edward Heath, the Conservative Prime Minister who took office in 1970, believed in tight money, not incomes policy, to control inflation. But when British unemployment reached the 'magic' figure of 1 million – 3 per cent of the workforce – at the end of 1970, the economy was reflated in a series of steps between 1971 and 1972, known as the 'Barber boom' after the Chancellor of the Exchequer, Anthony Barber. The boom expanded the fiscal deficit from zero in 1970 to £4 billion, cutting unemployment in half by December 1973, but doubling the inflation rate from 6.2 to 13.5 per cent. Attributing the price explosion to inflationary wage settlements – the government had been forced to concede a 27 per cent rise to the coalminers in February 1972 – Heath responded in September 1972 with a statutory (compulsory) incomes policy. He tried to win trade union support for this by increasing social security payments, subsidizing rents and nationalized industry prices, bailing out 'lame duck' businesses and then, disastrously, indexing wage increases to the cost of living, which he expected to start falling. But these spectacular U-turns brought no relief from rising inflation and growing industrial disorder as the unions fought his pay policy. Heath's government was brought down in February 1974, when he asked the electorate 'Who Governs Britain?' at the precise moment when it was perfectly clear that it was not him.

Later analysis of the causes of the inflationary upsurge concentrated on the explosion of credit from 1972, which, coincidentally with the start of the fiscal expansion, and the breakdown of the fixed exchange-rate system, was causing a rapid increase in the velocity of circulation. Its background was the perceived ineffectiveness of central bank lending ceilings applied to the cartel of retail banks in the face of the growth of the unregulated banking sector. By the late 1960s, foreign banks, fringe banks and hire purchase houses had begun lending aggressively, bypassing the Bank of England's ceilings. The Competition and Credit Control Act of 1971 abolished quantitative controls in favour of sole reliance on interest rates, which, it was believed – or hoped – would regulate the volume of credit as a whole. Charles Goodhart, one of the authors of the policy, has recalled the reasoning at the time: 'If there was no effect on M3 [broad money] of putting on ceilings, why should there be an effect in removing them? The effect, it was suggested, would be more on the asset composition of portfolios, than on the overall aggregate.'[49] This proved wrong. M3 rose by 28 per cent in 1973, far exceeding forecasts based on previous experience of fiscal expansions. Goodhart attributes this mainly to the government's refusal to sanction an increase in interest rates at a time when Heath was trying to win employers' assent to a price freeze. But the previous relationship between the demand for real cash balances and interest rates also broke down. With the interest rate weapon seemingly disabled, the Bank restored quantitative control of credit in 1973 by imposing the so-called 'Corset', which penalized the banks for bidding for extra funds.

The Keynesians had no compelling theoretical story to explain this disastrous concatenation of events. Loath to give up the full employment commitment, they argued that the problem was social: the breakdown of the contract between employers and unions. Since it was indisputable that both the Phillips Curve and the incomes policy versions of Keynesianism had collapsed, there was both a narrative and a policy vacuum.

In the 1970s, the 'ungovernability' thesis was much invoked to explain the collapse of the Keynesian social compromise. The economist Thomas Balogh got to the heart of the problem when he wrote in 1972:

> Full employment fundamentally altered the relative power of classes but without any change in class stratification. If there is no industrial reserve army, the power and privilege of the employer is weakened. Suddenly an overwhelming increase in bargaining strength is conferred to the unions. At first the system works not too badly but after a short time the change in the balance of power, since it is unaccompanied by a change in social attitudes and institutions, leads to inflation and through inflation and lack of business confidence to political unrest. This is the direct consequence of the increase in concentration of economic power on both sides when combined with full employment. The outcome of collective bargaining is then no longer determined or limited by the real resources of the community.[50]

The crux of the matter was 'the real resources of the community'. The premise of the growth Keynesians was that without a 'healthy rate of economic growth' the struggle for relative shares of the national income would bring inflationary pressure, requiring the imposition of much stronger control measures than 'voluntary' restraints. Once growth slowed down in the 1970s, inflation took off. Barring a dramatic shift to the left, there was no alternative but to recreate the 'reserve army of the unemployed' and, concomitantly, to destroy one of the two pillars of concentrated economic power, the trade union movement.

In 1976, the Labour Prime Minister James Callaghan told a startled Party conference:

> We used to think that you could spend your way out of a recession, and increase employment by cutting taxes and boosting Government

spending. I tell you in all candour that that option no longer exists, and that in so far as it ever did exist, it only worked on each occasion since the war by injecting a bigger dose of inflation into the economy, followed by a higher level of unemployment as the next step. Higher inflation followed by higher unemployment . . . That is the history of the last twenty years.[51]

That the worsening economic performance of the period 1968–75 was due to a conjuncture of 'shocks' that would have tested any policy regime which encountered them was ignored. A new story had taken hold. And the narrator was Milton Friedman.[52]

7

The Theory and Practice
of Monetarism

'Had Keynes begun his first few chapters with the simple statement that he found it realistic to assume that modern capitalistic societies had money wage rates that were sticky and resistant to downward movements, most of his insights would have remained just as valid . . .'

P. Samuelson, 1963[1]

'. . . expectations, since they are informed predictions of future events are essentially the same as the predictions of the relevant economic theory.'

J. F. Muth, 1961[2]

By the mid-1970s the Keynesian episode was over, though some fragments were rescued from the wreck. In the following years, economics reverted to its pre-Keynesian origins. 'Everything that Keynesians took as policy targets', writes Orsola Constantini, 'were now taken to be necessary characteristics of a well-organized economic system.'[3]

Why did this unravelling happen? The accepted answer is that the reaction against Keynesianism was triggered by the failures of Keynesian policy in the 1970s, in particular to control the inflation produced by its commitment to full employment. But in fact the reaction against Keynesianism had been biding its time for many years among those economists who had never accepted Keynes's theory and had acquiesced only reluctantly in Keynesian policy. It can be traced back to the compromise that had launched the Keynesian revolution.

I. KEYNES AND THE CLASSICS

In the neo-classical economic models, full employment was assured by wage and price flexibility. Economists even before Keynes had recognized that these mechanisms were partially inoperative, because 'frictions' – business and union monopolies, fixed wage contracts, unemployment benefits and other government interferences – impeded them. Hence some 'classical' economists were willing to support public works, or countercyclical policy, to maintain employment, while preserving models of the economy that assumed full market adjustment.

Keynes produced a model which had nothing to do with the existence of such institutional obstacles to wage and price adjustment. What he aimed to show was that, even without these frictions, a market economy would not be optimally self-adjusting. There was no 'automatic tendency' for the rate of interest to fall sufficiently to employ all intended saving, nor for real wages to fall sufficiently to employ all those looking for work. Whether or not equilibrium or market-clearing prices for saving or work existed, they were not known, or knowable, to those whose decisions determined prices in the market. In a competitive market system, uncertainty attaching to such prices was inherent and ineradicable.

The counterattack started not with a rejection of Keynesian policy prescriptions, but with an assault on Keynes's theory. In essence, the non-Keynesians invented new arguments to show why flexible money-wages would always maintain full employment.[4] Since, unfortunately, wages were not flexible, Keynesian policy could be justified on political, efficiency and, perhaps, human grounds. One had only to assert that, with (unexplained) time-lags in the price-adjustment process, any policy which averted a slump was good. This was the essence of the truce between Keynes and the Classics. They carried off the theoretical honours, he won the policy war.[5]

II. THE NEO-CLASSICAL SYNTHESIS

The origins of the attempt at synthesis can be traced back to the Oxford meeting of the Econometric Society in September 1936, which started the mathematicization of Keynes's *General Theory*. At this meeting, John Hicks presented his 'classroom gadget' – the IS/LM (investment-savings, liquidity-money) model – which he published in the June 1937 issue of *Econometrica*.[6] Hicks reduced the *General Theory* to a multi-equational system that yielded a Walrasian full employment solution in the absence of restrictions on the movement of interest rates and wages (the neo-classical case) or a quantity-adjusted equilibrium if wages and interest rates were fixed (the Keynesian case). He did not say which was more likely.

The IS/LM apparatus was not a theory, it just provided different ways of arranging possibilities. In Hicks's own view, which came to be widely accepted, Keynes's 'general' theory was a 'special' case of the more general neo-classical theory, with restrictions imposed on the movement of wages and interest rates. Given such price 'stickiness', choice of policy instrument depended on the slope of the schedules: Keynesians emphasized situations where monetary policy is *relatively* ineffective, because of liquidity preference, and investment is *relatively* unresponsive to changes in interest rates. They preferred fiscal to monetary policy because it acted directly on the components of demand.

Alan Coddington calls the IS/LM model 'an analytical receptacle of quite astonishing versatility and resilience within which even the antagonists in protracted controversies have been able to find a common framework for their disputes'.[7] According to Warren Young it became 'the conceptual manifestation of the quest for continuity and certainty', providing the authorized means for economics students to digest the *General Theory*.[8] It is through this mathematically elegant paradigm, reduced to a famous diagram, that those developing and applying Keynes's ideas were led to understand them. (For the IS/LM diagram and explanation, see Appendix 7.1, p. 203.)

By the 1950s, Paul Samuelson had written that economists had 'worked toward a synthesis of whatever is valuable in older economics and in modern theories of income determination. The result might be called neo-classical economics and is accepted in its broad outlines by all but about 5 per cent of extreme left wing and right wing writers.'[9]

The neo-classical synthesis was predicated on two contradictory beliefs: belief in the optimizing agent, and belief in wage and price rigidities. The former preserved the neo-classical structure of micro-economics, while the latter provided the rationale for interventionist policies to offset collapses in investment. There was now a logical gap between microeconomics and macroeconomics, since wage stickiness and the resulting persistent unemployment is inconsistent with individual optimizing behaviour. Keynes had set out to fill logical gaps in the classical theory. Classical economists now started to complain that Keynesian models were not properly grounded in microeconomics: they lacked incentives like market prices to push the human puppets this way and that; labour supply was assumed to be fixed; household savings were assumed to be dependent only on current income; business investment was deemed to depend on expected sales rather than on profitability. It was a 'demand-determined' world view, which left hardly any scope for supply adjustments. None of this mattered much against the background of the huge demand-deficiency of the 1930s. It became much more important in the high employment economy of the postwar years.

III. THE EMERGENCE OF THE COUNTER-ORTHODOXY

The revolt against the Keynesian policy orthodoxy is popularly, and rightly, associated with the Chicago economist Milton Friedman. However, Friedman built on an undercurrent of dissatisfaction with the Keynesian approach to economic policy which had started long before Keynesian policy failures gave it political voice.

The origins of an organized 'counter-orthodoxy' – the intellectual and political reaction to the post-war consensus – can be traced back to the 1938 'Colloque Walter Lippmann', a conference arranged by the French philosopher Louis Rougier to discuss Lippmann's 1937 book An Enquiry into the Principles of the Good Society. It was at the colloquium that the German economist Alexander Rüstow coined the term 'neo-liberalism' to describe the intellectual movement that sought to reboot the 'classical' liberalism of the pre-Great Depression era, and which had begun with debates in the universities of Vienna, Freiburg and Paris and the LSE. The neo-liberal target was totalitarianism, as manifested in National Socialism and Bolshevism. Keynes should have been an ally of these neo-liberals, but the large dose of interventionism he deemed necessary to support a market economy led them to view Keynesianism in effect, if not in intention, as an ally or at least a stalking horse for the totalitarianism they were fighting. The neo-liberal solution to the ills of laissez-faire was not to insert government, but to embed the market economy in a constitutional, rule-bound order (hence the German *Ordoliberalismus*) which guaranteed free competition and denied the state discretionary power to modify market processes. A social safety net should be provided 'outside the market' for victims of economic or personal misfortune.

Keynes's relationship to this defence of classical economics comes out very clearly in his response to Hayek's *Road to Serfdom* (1944). Hayek's argument, in a nutshell, was that 'once the free working of the market is impeded beyond a certain degree, the planner will be forced to extend his controls until they become all-comprehensive'. Hayek did not attack Keynes by name. But he certainly had him in his sights as the intellectual leader of those who 'believe that real success [in combating economic fluctuations] can be expected only from public works undertaken on a very large scale'. Hayek did not accuse such economists of the coercive intent of the totalitarians. But he argued that if governments were determined not to allow unemployment at any price and not to use coercion, the result would be increasing misallocation of resources and rising inflation. He warned that 'we shall have carefully to watch our step if we are to avoid making all economic activity progressively more dependent on the direction and volume of government expenditure'.[10]

Keynes responded to Hayek in a letter of 28 June 1944. He congratulated him on having written 'a grand book ... morally and philosophically I find myself in agreement with virtually the whole of it; and not only in agreement, but in a deeply moved agreement'. However, he had three objections. First, you admit . . . that it is a question of knowing where to draw the line. You agree that . . . the logical extreme [of laissez-faire] is not possible . . . But as soon as you admit [this] you are done for . . . since you are trying to persuade us that so soon as one moves an inch in the planned direction you are necessarily launched on the slippery path which will lead you in due course over the precipice.

Secondly, Keynes rejected, on prudential grounds, Hayek's belief that depressions had to be allowed to run their course. This, he said, 'would only lead in practice to disillusion with the results of your philosophy'. In effect, Keynes accused Hayek of putting economic ideology ahead of statecraft. It was Hayek's policy, not Keynes's, which endangered liberalism, by threatening to provoke revolution.

Thirdly, Keynes denied that the totalitarian slide would occur in societies with robust traditions of freedom and democracy. 'Dangerous acts can be done safely in a community which thinks and feels rightly, which would be the way to hell if they were executed by those who think and feel wrongly.'[11] This is a strong, but static dictum. What it ignores is Hayek's claim that the stock of 'right feeling' can be depleted by government policy: it is not independent of the acts being done. It then becomes a matter of judgement as to which set of economic and social practices is most likely to preserve the moral values that Hayek and Keynes shared.

The debate, as we can see, was about a fundamental question: was Keynesianism (and, more broadly, social democracy) an antidote to totalitarianism or the thin end of the wedge? Here one can say that Keynes won the major argument, but lost the minor one. Keynesianism as a policy nowhere led to serfdom, but it did lead to inflation.

IV. MONETARISM

The Road to Serfdom was the inspiration for the Mont Pelerin Society founded by Hayek in 1947. An early member of the society was Milton Friedman. Friedman was not in the business of synthesis, but of counter-revolution. He attacked Keynes's doctrines in order to demonstrate the futility of Keynesian policies. He recalled that:

During my whole career, I have considered myself somewhat of a schizophrenic ... On the one hand, I was interested in science qua science, and I have tried – successfully I hope – not to let my ideological viewpoints contaminate my scientific work. On the other, I felt deeply concerned with the course of events and I wanted to influence them so as to enhance human freedom. Luckily, these two aspects of my interests appeared to me as perfectly compatible.[12]

This is disingenuous. The motivation for his work was thoroughly political. Friedman restated neo-classical economics in order to expel the expanded Keynesian state from the economy. Shrinking the state was the scarcely avowed aim of his economics.

Friedman believed that market incentives were normally effective. This meant that economies were normally stable at what he called their 'natural' or 'equilibrium' rate of unemployment. Government interference in the structure of market incentives was the chief cause of their rocking motion. In their efforts to minimize unemployment – in Friedman's terms, to reduce it below its 'natural rate' – Keynesian governments pumped too much money into the economy, feeding misperceptions about prices, which fed inflation. They then tried, somewhat ineffectually, to stop the inflation by incomes policy, which destroyed price-adjustment mechanisms in the labour market. Governments should therefore be tied down like Gulliver, to rules that severely limited their discretion to expand the money supply at will. This was very much in line with Hayek, and can be traced back to Ricardo.

Friedman stuck firmly to the neo-classical micro-foundations. These showed that persistent mass unemployment was impossible. He went beyond the neo-classical synthesizers by claiming that inflexible price behaviour was not a sociological datum, but was caused by government interference with the working of the credit and labour markets. He thus had his own explanation for the otherwise unexplained lags in the price-adjustment mechanism. Technically, Friedmanism was an attempt to reunify orthodox microeconomics and the new macroeconomics by emasculating macro-policy to the barest minimum.

Friedman's monetarism harked back to the golden age of the Quantity Theory of Money, which had inspired the efforts of the monetary reformers of the 1920s, including Keynes himself. The economy would not normally misbehave – or seriously misbehave – if money was kept 'in order'. To put it another way, if the quantity of money was right, there would be the right amount of spending. The success of governments in disturbing the economy for political ends showed the power of money; now that power had to be harnessed by an independent central bank to prevent it from disturbing the economy.

Friedman developed and broadened his onslaught on Keynesian doctrines through a sequence of interrelated arguments running from the 1950s to the late 1960s. By 1968 his artillery was fully assembled. He won a Nobel Prize in 1976 for his achievement in the 'field of consumption analysis, monetary history and theory, and stabilization policy'. The effect of his attack was to destroy most of the Keynesian case for demand-management.

His 'permanent income hypothesis' (1957) was part of his claim that market economies were normally self-adjusting to full employment. Keynes's consumption function made spending depend on current income only. This meant that temporary shocks exert a strong influence on aggregate demand. In Friedman's view, this exaggerated the effects of fluctuations in demand. He modelled rational, forward-looking individuals as smoothing their consumption over their expected permanent (lifetime) income.[13] This had the consequence that, in a downturn, spending fell less than current income: expecting their incomes to fall only temporarily, people would use up their savings or borrow on the strength of their 'normal' earnings, expecting to rebuild their savings or pay back their debt when 'normal' times returned. There was correspondingly less need for the government to increase the budget deficit or (say) redistribute income to those with a higher propensity to consume. Spending out of permanent income kept the economy nearer full employment.[14]

At the heart of Friedman's monetary theory was his restatement of the Quantity Theory of Money (1956):[15]

$$PQ = f(M)$$
$$P = g(M)$$

where P is the price level, Q is output, f is a function of money in the short-term, and g a function of it in the long-term. In the short-term, changes in money can affect output, but ultimately a change in the quantity of money will lead to a proportional change in the price level.

Friedman took the strategic decision to base his case on what he called 'the stable demand function for money'. This meant denying the existence of Keynes's 'speculative demand for money'. Friedman claimed that Keynes's restriction of portfolio choice to money and bonds was unjustified. Portfolio choice was a choice between money and *all* utility-yielding forms of wealth, not just bonds. Because there was an opportunity cost to holding money (it yielded no interest), cash balances would always be kept at a minimum. People would use any surplus cash they had to buy shares in companies or real estate. The extended theory of portfolio choice thus confirms the assumption of the 'simple theory' that, faced with a surplus or deficit of money, people would aim to restore their real balances by increasing or reducing their spending. This restores the money multiplier and the link between money and prices.

In two gigantic books, *Monetary History of the United States, 1867–1960* (1963)[16] and *Monetary Trends in the United States and in the United Kingdom* (1982),[17] Friedman and Anna Schwartz attempted to verify Friedman's restatement of the QTM empirically. Their double conclusion was that the velocity of circulation – the speed with which a unit of money changed hands – remained remarkably constant across cycles, and that in all cases of cyclical fluctuations the change in the broad money stock preceded the change in money incomes. The econometrics, and consequently the conclusions, of Friedman and Schwartz were heavily criticized by Hendry and Ericsson.[18] Inevitably, the empirical examination was inconclusive: it always is. Friedman was not unduly worried.[19] Like Keynes, he understood that the best economics could do was to wring 'reasonable conjectures from refractory and inaccurate evidence'.[20]

The Friedman–Schwartz view that the Great Depression of 1929–32 was caused by the failure of the Fed to prevent the collapse of the money supply has become orthodox. It influenced Ben Bernanke, Chairman of the Federal Reserve Board from 2006 to 2014, and the policy of quantitative easing adopted to meet the 2008–9 recession. In addition, just as the depression was caused by the central bank printing too little money, so inflation was due to the central bank printing too much money: '*inflation is always and everywhere a monetary phenomenon* in the sense that it is and can be produced only by a more rapid increase in the quantity of money than in output'.[21]

Next in Friedman's line of fire was the Keynesian stabilization theory. This was demolished by replacing Keynes's 'uncertain expectations' by 'adaptive expectations'. Adaptive expectations postulates that people learn from experience; namely, they learn that monetary expansion leads to inflation. This means that monetary policy cannot peg either interest rates or the rate of unemployment for more than very limited periods.

Regarding the first, Friedman maintained:

> let the higher rate of monetary growth produce rising prices, and let the public come to expect that prices will continue to rise. Borrowers will then be willing to pay and lenders will then demand higher interest rates ... every attempt to keep interest rates at a low level has forced the monetary authority to engage in successively larger and larger open market purchases.[22]

In his Presidential Address to the American Economic Association, entitled 'The Role of Monetary Policy' (1968), Friedman mounted a frontal assault on the Keynesian Phillips Curve, the view that there existed a stable trade-off between inflation and unemployment.[23] We have seen that, as an empirical hypothesis, the Phillips Curve started to collapse towards the end of the 1960s, as the 'trade-off' worsened, producing simultaneously rising inflation and unemployment. The key mistake of the Keynesians, said Friedman, was that they assumed that wage bargainers had fixed price expectations (appropriate perhaps for the nineteenth-century world of long-run price stability, but obsolete for inflationary times). This inevitably led to the conflation of the short-run effects of monetary policy with the long-run. Lower unemployment could only be obtained if wage inflation lagged behind the actual inflation rate. However, pronounced inertia in face of continuous experience is contrary to the microeconomic theory of optimization. Rather, it was reasonable to assume that people adapted their behaviour to the experience of inflation.

Thus, if the government, in order to reduce unemployment, causes aggregate demand (or, in Friedman's terms, the money supply) to grow faster than the economy's productive capacity, the first effect will be to stimulate the economy; but the ultimate result will be to raise prices with no effect on employment or output. This is because workers will initially accept additional employment at the higher nominal wage brought about by the stimulus, without realizing that firms will in turn raise their prices, eroding workers' gains in real-wage terms and thus reducing their willingness to work back to the level it had been before. People base their inflation expectations on inflation in the previous period. As a result, the inflation caused by the government's stimulus becomes 'built in' to workers' expectations. (See Appendix 7.2, p. 205, for a more thorough account of adaptive expectations and Friedman's expectations-augmented Phillips Curve.) In all this, Friedman was simply echoing David Hume two centuries previously. Employment can be increased by monetary means only if increased inflation is unanticipated. But workers cannot be fooled for ever.

In developing this argument, Friedman introduced the idea of a unique 'natural' or 'equilibrium' rate of unemployment, which he defined as that rate which is consistent with stable prices (economists started talking about the 'non-accelerating inflation rate of unemployment', or NAIRU). This embodies 'the actual structural characteristics of the labour and commodity markets, including market imperfections, stochastic variability in demands and supplies, the cost of gathering information about job vacancies and labour availabilities, the costs of mobility, and so on'.[24] Since the natural rate of unemployment is unknowable, it seemed reasonable to say it is the rate which establishes itself in the absence of unforeseen shocks, of which the chief is erratic monetary policy. If the equilibrium rate of unemployment is socially unacceptable, the remedy is not to inflate the money supply, but to undertake structural reforms to reduce 'market imperfections'. As we can see, what was being reinstated was the neo-classical idea that an unimpeded market always produces a Walrasian full employment equilibrium. Friedman would provide the theoretical rationale for the 'supply-side' policies of Thatcher and Reagan in the 1980s and the 'structural adjustment' policies later advocated by the IMF as a condition for loans to needy countries.

Although monetary policy (and, even more so, fiscal policy, which operates with 'long and variable lags') is ruled out as a short-term regulator of business activity, monetary policy comes into its own as a stabilizer of prices. To combat inflation, governments should limit the rate of money growth to the rate of productivity growth. The sole object of monetary policy should be price stability, or at least a constant inflation rate. This was not to be done by discretionary monetary policy, which gave rise to 'money illusion', but by adopting a money rule such as that the money stock would increase at fixed rate, *k* per cent each year, this corresponding to the trend growth rate. The money rule would be set independently of the business cycle, but it would keep the economy 'growing to trend'. If such a rule were to be adopted, fixed exchange rates would have to be jettisoned. Only a floating, market-determined, exchange rate would secure the necessary autonomy of monetary policy.

Thus, Friedman explains how the 'first and most important lesson that history teaches about what monetary policy can do ... is that monetary policy can prevent money itself from being a major source of economic disturbance'. 'There is ... a positive and important task for the monetary authority ... to use its own powers so as to keep the machine in good working order.' Monetary policy should

> provide a stable background for the economy – keep the machine well oiled ... Our economic system will work best when producers and consumers, employers and employees, can proceed with full confidence that the average level of prices will behave in a known way in the future – preferably that it will be highly stable.[25]

Friedman's work clearly had huge anti-Keynesian policy implications. The four main ones are as follows:

1. Friedman restated the Quantity Theory of Money, the theory that prices (or nominal incomes) change proportionally with the quantity of money.
2. As a result of this, macro-policy can influence nominal, but not real, variables; i.e., the price level, but not the employment or output level.
3. Friedman argued that inflation was always and only a monetary phenomenon. It was the total money supply in the economy which determined the general price level; cost pressures were not

independent sources of inflation, they had to be validated by an accommodating monetary policy in order to get away with a mark-up-based price-determination strategy.

4. Friedman's permanent income hypothesis suggested that it is households' average long-run income (permanent income) that is likely to determine total demand for consumer spending, rather than fluctuations in their current disposable income as suggested by the Keynesian consumption function.

As is clearer in retrospect, Friedman exploited to the full the paradox of government. The Keynesian revolution introduced the state as the stabilizer of a volatile system. How ironic, Friedman said, that the state should be the main destabilizer of the system![26] The ills which Friedman diagnosed were the result of state interference with natural market forces: the lesson first preached by economists in the eighteenth century.

At the time, many saw Friedman's achievement as a vindication of the progressive nature of economics. His model had enabled him to predict stagflation, leaving the Keynesians flat-footed. The holes in his intellectual clothes became apparent only later. His 'permanent income' consumption function assumed that, as well as being improbably far-sighted, consumers had adequate savings and access to credit to cushion their consumption in downturns. His attack on Keynes's speculative demand for money failed to recognize the role of money as a store of value. His restatement of the Quantity Theory of Money, despite its 'proofs', by no means disposed of the problem of causation which had dogged it since its inception. He assumed, rather than proved, that monetary policy alone could have prevented the Great Depression. His adaptive expectations theory failed to explain the acceleration in the rate of inflation between 1968 and 1974.

In essence, his restatement of the QTM, while more qualified than what he called 'the simple theory', reproduced its three main weaknesses: belief in the exogeneity of money; belief in a stable demand for money; and belief in the independence of monetary and real events. These were all to be tested to destruction when monetarism moved from the drawing board to policy.

Friedman's weaknesses were overlooked because his theory served

an ideological purpose. First, and foremost, it indicated that the inflation problem could be overcome without resort to controls over
wages, prices and profits, and the implications of such controls for a
free economy.[27] Control of the money supply left the price system
free. It just needed some experts in central banks with the right model
of the economy.

Secondly, monetarism suggested a political economy argument for
cutting down state spending. Keeping money well behaved would be
easier the smaller the share of state spending in national income,
because the more of national income that governments spent, the more
likely they were to resort to financing their spending by printing
money. The political right latched on to Friedman as a way of attack-
ing the growing role of the state. Monetarism was to become the way
to link popular dissatisfaction with high taxation, and the suspicion
that the welfare state was being abused by 'scroungers', with the
other great source of anxiety, inflation.[28]

Friedman's wit and eloquence would never have overcome Samuelson's self-assurance had not events conspired in his favour. It was the
emergence and persistence of stagflation that turned conjecture into
explanation, and explanation into experiment. Monetarism became
fashionable because it was not the incumbent philosophy in a time of
crisis; it had been exhaustively promoted by the neo-liberal think-
tank complex and its influential supporters in and out of government;
and its theory seemed to make sense of stagflation.

V. THE MONETARIST EXPERIMENT: 1976-85

With inflation running at over 10 per cent in the developed world by the
late 1970s, monetarism moved swiftly from the drawing board to active
service. Following the breakdown of the Bretton Woods system of fixed
exchange rates in 1971-3, governments gave up interest rate targeting
and credit controls and 'chose to guide [their] policy for the economy as
a whole by the behaviour of the quantity of money and by nothing
else'.[29] Unfortunately money refused to behave in the way Friedman
said it should. 'By the start of the 1990s economic policy had gone back

to being guided by a range of indicators; and if central banks were given clear instructions they were in terms of inflation rather than money supply targets.'[30] Short-term interest rates were the main inflation (or more broadly, aggregate demand) control mechanism: a monetary rather than fiscal version of Keynesian demand-management.[31]

Tim Congdon has usefully distinguished between American-style and British-style monetarism as it was tried out in the 1980s. Friedman believed that the monetary base – notes, coins and the cash reserves of commercial banks – was the best indicator of future changes in the total money stock, and consequently of the future rate of price increases. Total money stock included bank deposits. Empirical studies were held to demonstrate a 'reasonably stable ratio between reserves to deposits over the long-run'[32] (the money multiplier in a fractional reserve banking system). Since the quantity of cash was fully under central bank control, it was argued that 'changes in the quantity of cash, reflecting central bank operations' determined the level of bank deposits and, hence, of the money supply'.[33] This is a straightforward QTM argument, exactly the same as Keynes's in 1923. By varying the supply of bank reserves, the central bank can determine the total quantity of money in the economy and, therefore, the long-run price level.

The relationship between British-style monetarism and the QTM is less clear. British monetarism concentrated on the direct control of credit ('broad money') through short-term interest rates. With high inflation, real interest rates were negative. In the British view it was government borrowing to reduce unemployment which fuelled inflation, and therefore the deficit which government borrowing caused had to be eliminated. By 1974, Public Sector Net Borrowing stood at 9.6 per cent of GDP. Nigel Lawson, Chancellor of the Exchequer in 1983–9, promised in 1978 to 'restore budget balance discipline' as part of monetary control.

The two different versions of monetarism were tried out between 1979 and the early 1980s in the USA and Britain respectively, with pretty disastrous consequences. In 1979, Paul Volcker, the new Chairman of the US Federal Reserve Board, faced with an upsurge in inflation, switched Fed policy from targeting interest rates to targeting money. The Federal Open Market Committee (FOMC) 'would seek to hold increases in the monetary base ... to amounts just sufficient to meet monetary targets . . . recognising that such a procedure could result in wider fluctuations in the shortest term money market rates'.[34] The Fed would sell government securities in the bond market. This would reduce the cash reserves of commercial banks, forcing them to raise interest rates. Influenced by the newly fashionable theory of rational expectation (see below, p. 194), Volcker hoped that this open-market policy would reduce inflationary expectations sufficiently to allow a rapid fall in the long-term bond rate, thus avoiding, or at least mitigating, the employment and output costs of bringing down the inflation rate.

It did not turn out like this. Inflation fell from 11 per cent to 4 per cent between 1979 and 1982, but at the cost of the worst recession since the Great Depression of the 1930s. Short-term interest rates shot up to 21 per cent, ruining not only many American businesses, but also developing countries, which now had to refinance their borrowed petro-dollars at a much higher rate of interest. Inflationary expectations, as measured by bond rates, remained above monetarist forecasts for much longer than Volcker had expected. In 1982, monetarism American-style was abandoned, but Volcker was hailed as the man who had broken the back of American inflation. Unemployment came down from 11 per cent in 1982 to 5 per cent in 1990. Ironically, the worst effects of the Volcker recession were offset by the huge budget deficits Ronald Reagan ran to finance his arms build-up against the Soviet Union.

The British experiment with broad money monetarism, which ran from 1980 to 1984, fared little better than the narrow money monetarism of the US. In the budget of 1980, Chancellor Geoffrey Howe presented the medium-term financial strategy (MTFS), which called for a phased reduction in the growth of the money stock, to be made possible by a phased reduction in the public sector borrowing as a share of GDP. The government expected that the announcement of the monetary targets would lower the inflationary expectations of wage-bargainers, enabling prices to come down with only a moderate increase in unemployment. It did not work this way. With the failure of the money supply figures to behave as required, Thatcher and Howe resorted to monetary and fiscal shock therapy. A bank rate of 17 per cent drove up the exchange rate, already strengthened by North Sea oil revenues. Superimposed on this was a savagely deflationary budget in 1981, which took £4 billion out of the economy when unemployment was already rising – the first time since 1931 when, with output rapidly falling, budgetary policy was tightened. Its message was clear: Keynesianism would not be reactivated, whatever the unemployment cost. This cost was heavy. Between 1980 and 1982 unemployment rose from 5 per cent to 10 per cent, as bad as in the 1920s, and went on creeping up until 1986, hitting 3 million. In a letter to *The Times* of 30 March 1981, 364 economists, including the future Governor of the Bank of England, Mervyn King, predicted that government policy would 'deepen the depression, erode the industrial base of our economy and threaten its social and political stability'. However, almost before the ink was dry on the letter, economic recovery started, with output growing by 3.3 per cent a year on average over the following six years. At the same time, inflation fell from 17.8 to 4.3 per cent. A fall in short-term interest rates to 5 per cent by mid-1980s led to a housing boom.

In both cases, the strategy of credible gradual disinflation broke down, with inflation being reversed by shock therapy which imposed a huge cost on output and employment. Analysts pointed to the instability of the demand for money. Both the 1970s and 1980s saw continued enormous swings in velocity, which made money growth a poor predictor of future prices and income. Charles Goodhart enunciated his famous 'law' that any established relationship between money and prices breaks down as soon as the attempt is made to exploit it for control purposes. But the flaw lay with the new monetary theory itself: there was never sufficient belief in the pronouncements of the monetary authorities to make disinflation a relatively painless exercise. In an interesting retrospective piece, David Laidler partly retracts his earlier support for the medium-term financial strategy. He argues that when transitioning to a lower average rate of inflation and nominal interest rates, the demand for money will rise (the inflation tax on holding money is lower), so money growth should be slowed more gradually. In his view, the failure to recognize this was responsible for the depth of the 1980s recession.[35] By contrast, Patrick Minford argues that the gradual disinflation policy would have been too slow to be credible: it was the 'sharp monetary squeeze' (i.e. on 'narrow' money) imposed by the government in 1980 and 1981 which broke the back of inflation.[36]

The policy failures of monetarism led the Fed and the Bank of England to abandon the attempt directly to control monetary aggregates. Inflation targeting became the default position. Its great advantage was that it bypassed the interminable debates about whether money was exogenous or endogenous, whether one should try to control narrow money or broad money, what the transmission mechanism was from money to prices, etc. All one had to do was deploy old-fashioned bank rate policy plus new-fangled management of expectations. In 1993, Alan Greenspan, Volcker's successor as Fed Chairman, announced that all monetary targets were to be dropped. The Fed then used open-market operations to influence the federal funds rate, announcing a desired target for inflation and instituting rule-type behaviours to provide consistent signals to markets. (This became standard practice until 2012, when it adopted an explicit inflation target under Ben Bernanke.)[37] The European Central Bank, established in 1997, was also given an inflation target, to be achieved by varying short-term interest rates. In Britain, targeting of money was discontinued in 1985. The British government briefly sought to discipline its unruly economy, first by shadowing the deutschmark, then by making sterling a member of the European Monetary System, but after a speculative attack on the over-valued pound forced it out of the Exchange Rate Mechanism in 1992, it followed the American lead. Initially, the inflation target was set in the range of 1–4 per cent. In 1997, the incoming Labour government, fearing that this was too loose to anchor inflationary expectations properly, especially as politicians still controlled interest rate setting, transferred control of monetary policy to the Bank of England, giving it a 2.5 per cent Retail Price Index inflation target (later reduced to the 2 per cent Consumer Price Index target we have today).

The monetarist experiment was over. What survived were the two main reasons for setting up independent central banks: to get as much economic policy as possible out of the hands of vote-seeking politicians, and to find an effective way of controlling inflation. These coalesced in the idea that interest rate policy should be taken out of the hands of governments. By 2005, thirty 'independent' central banks, led by New Zealand's, were 'targeting' inflation. (The New Zealand plan had been to tie the salary of the central bank's governor, Donald Brash, to the bank's inflation performance, but this proved impracticable.)

Figure 16 shows the start of money targeting in the UK in 1976. Inflation remained high and variable: it averaged over 12 per cent a year in the 1970s and nearly 6 per cent a year in the 1980s. The inflation record improved dramatically when inflation targeting was announced in 1992. The same pattern was seen the world over.

Was it inflation targeting that 'conquered' inflation? Much depends on the weight one attaches to the fluctuating price of energy over the period 1973 to 1983.

Figure 16. UK monetary policy and inflation[38]
(RPI up to 1987, CPI from 1988)

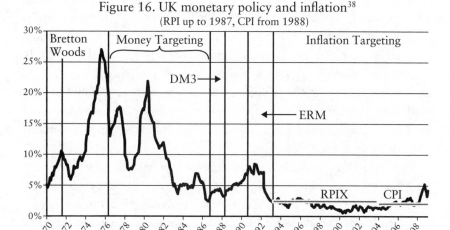

Figure 17. Oil prices and UK CPI inflation[39]

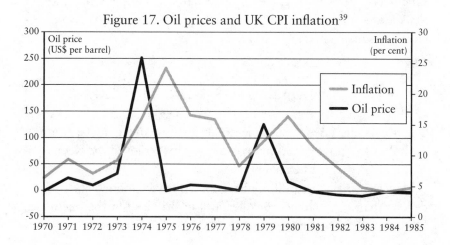

The two large spikes in oil prices in 1973–4 and 1980–82 were followed by peaks of inflation. The fall in the oil price in the mid-1970s and the early 1980s were followed closely by falls in the inflation rate. Again we have a correlation, but the causal direction is debatable. In consequence, the question of how big an influence monetary policy has on the inflation rate is no further to being decisively answered now than it was when economists and bankers debated the causes of inflation during the Napoleonic wars.

The fact that inflation in industrial countries came down worldwide in the 1990s, irrespective of the type of counterinflation policy chosen, and has never again reached the heights of the 1970s, strongly suggests that changes in the structure of the world economy, rather than deliberate changes in policy, played the key part in the result. If there is no inflationary pressure it is child's play for a central banker to keep inflation low. On the other hand, if there is a tendency towards deflation, there is little monetary policy can do on its own to reverse it. This lesson had to be learned all over again in the years following the collapse of 2008–9.

The interesting question is whether inflation could have been brought down at lower cost in unemployment. The answer is surely yes, with a better mix of policies than were politically available in countries like Britain, one of the worst hit by both inflation and unemployment. As the Treasury had pointed out in 1944, and as Kaldor had realized in the 1960s, continuous full employment required the right allocation of supply as well as the right level of demand. The simple inversion of Say's Law – 'demand creates its own supply' – proved to be as insufficient as its original.

VI. MONETARISM'S FISCAL LEGACY

The fiscal consequence of monetarism was to remove the budget as a tool of short-run demand-management. This removed the Keynesian rationale for budget deficits.

However, the Reagan Administration was much more relaxed about deficits than its Thatcherite colleagues in Britain. On the one hand, following the Friedman doctrine, the US Treasury saw no causal

Figure 18. The Laffer curve

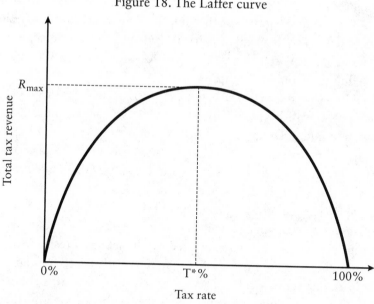

connection between public deficits and inflation. The second reason was much more important: Reagan had been elected on a programme of cutting taxes and increasing defence spending. The enactment of both, together with the Volcker recession, caused the deficit to rise from 2.8 per cent of GDP in 1980 to 6.3 per cent in 1983. The tax cuts and increased military spending amounted to a big Keynesian demand boost. But in the post-Keynesian world this 'Keynesian effect' could not be acknowledged. Instead, the large deficits were justified on 'supply-side' grounds.

The famous Laffer curve, supposedly drawn on a napkin by the economist Arthur Laffer at a boozy dinner in 1974, suggested that tax reductions would have positive supply-side effects. The logic was simple. Government revenue must be zero at a tax rate of 0 per cent, and also at a rate of 100 per cent, since no one would then bother to work. There must, however, be an intermediate rate at which revenue is maximized. The supply-siders' big idea was that, within a range, if taxes are reduced, people will work harder, productivity will go up, and the economy will grow faster. That people might choose to cash in their higher post-tax incomes in the form of leisure, or work harder to maintain their accustomed living standards if their taxes went up, was alien to the mentality of the supply-side enthusiasts. Their simplistic story, devoid of any empirical evidence, fed the illusion that tax cuts would be self-financing.[40] We see the same story being re-enacted under Donald Trump.

The British Treasury never bought into Laffer-type arguments; additionally, British anti-inflationary policy was much more closely linked to public spending cuts. Geoffrey Howe's 1981 budget marked the arrival in Britain of what later became known as 'expansionary fiscal contraction'. This claims that fiscal consolidation, while bearing down on inflation, will produce recovery by lowering interest rates and improving the profit expectations of the private sector. The roots of this *über*-Austrian idea lay in Italy – at the School of Economics at Bocconi University of Milan founded by the former President of the Italian Republic Luigi Einaudi. Einaudi, who had argued for constitutional rules banning fiscal deficits, came to influence a large cohort of Bocconi students who, in turn, rose to the heights of the global economics profession: Alberto Alesina, Silvia Ardagna, Guido Tabellini and Roberto Perotti.[41] Thirty years after Howe's 1981 budget, the works of these Bocconi School economists provided the academic justification for the sweeping austerity measures adopted by European governments after the collapse of 2008–9.

In Britain, Nigel Lawson, Howe's successor as Chancellor from 1983 to 1989, was the intellectual force behind the destruction of the last vestiges of the Keynesian fiscal constitution. In 1980, he wrote that 'Monetarism, after all, is really rather obvious. It is Keynesianism, which seems to stand everything on its head, which is the difficult and esoteric doctrine.'[42] One of the assumptions of the old QTM inherited by the new monetarism was that, with stable prices, the real economy would be cyclically stable at its 'natural' rate of unemployment. In his Mais Lecture of 1984, Nigel Lawson said: 'It is the conquest of inflation, and not the pursuit of growth and employment, which . . . should be the objective of macroeconomic policy. And it is the creation of conditions conducive to growth and employment, and not the suppression of [inflation] which . . . should be the objective of microeconomic policy.' Reduction in the 'natural' rate of unemployment required not boosting demand, but labour market reforms to boost supply.[43]

Like the Victorians, Lawson believed in annually balanced budgets. He rejected the idea of a capital budget financed by borrowing, or indeed any relevant distinction between capital and current budgeting. In his memoirs published in 1992, Lawson writes:

> Behind this criticism [that his Treasury had conflated current and capital expenditure] is a lingering belief that capital spending is either superior to current spending, or at least safer to finance from borrowing. This really will not do. The current/capital distinction does not have the same meaning in the public as in the private sector.[44]

Hence his objective was zero borrowing.[45] A large part of the capital budget was abolished by privatizing state assets. In addition, employment subsidies were ended. Between the 1960s and 1980s, public investment fell from 7 per cent to below 1 per cent of GDP, where it remained for most of the 1990s. There was an attempt to rein in social spending. In 1988, in the wake of a boom and large-scale privatizations, Lawson declared that 'in this Budget, I have reaffirmed the prudent policies which have brought us unprecedented economic strength ... I have balanced the Budget.'[46] He not only balanced his budget, he was able to cut taxes and repay debt: the epitome of a successful Victorian Chancellor. But this was a unique achievement in eighteen years of Conservative rule, and was not repeated for another ten years.

The effect of the Lawson counterrevolution was to denude fiscal policy of macroeconomic significance. Macroeconomic stabilization was left to monetary policy just as it had been at the beginning of the century. In order to meet its money supply and, later, inflation targets, the central bank had to tighten monetary policy if the government expanded its deficit. This robbed the latter of any short-term stimulative effect. Only a year after the triumphant 1988 budget, however, the Conservatives had to soften their tough year-on-year balancing objective. As the Lawson boom ended in bust, and with it a big increase in the budget deficit, the aim switched to 'balancing the budget over the medium term'. We have reached the era of Gordon Brown and his fiscal rules.

VII. FROM FRIEDMAN TO THE NEW CONSENSUS: 1985–2008

Friedmanism was just the start of a wholesale unravelling of the Keynesian system of thought. Monetarism was soon refined by the 'rational expectations hypothesis' (REH). The REH was the analytic core of what came to be called 'the new classical macroeconomics'. This built on the deceptively simple, common-sense idea, shared by Keynes and Friedman, that people's beliefs about the world influence their behaviour. It was economists' task to provide economic agents with true beliefs – true models of the economy – to help them make the best of their situation. Keynes wrote the *General Theory* to refute the Treasury View; Friedman restated the Quantity Theory of Money to falsify the Keynesian view. Both 'models' of reality were intended to change people's beliefs about how economies worked and therefore their expectations concerning the effects of policy. Now it was the turn of Robert Lucas, a former student, then colleague, of Friedman's at Chicago University. Lucas brought rational expectations into macroeconomics in 1972. He was a logical extremist. His aim was remove what he saw as a conceptual flaw – though others might see it as a lingering sense of realism – in Friedman's theory of adaptive expectations.[47]

Lucas accepted Friedman's argument that policymakers' attempt to exploit the Phillips Curve trade-off between inflation and unemployment caused the trade-off to disappear. This is because it led to changes in the behaviour of the relevant economic agents. Friedman has agents learning from, and adapting their behaviour to, changing market signals, but with an inevitable lag because it takes time to change expectations and the contracts based on them. Lucas simply abolished the lag. Rational agents should be able to process all available information efficiently in forming expectations. The Phillips Curve is vertical in the short-run as well as in the long-run, as agents instantaneously adapt their expectations in accordance with 'the model'.

Lucas carried this thought to its logical conclusion, by arguing that all policy conclusions drawn from large-scale econometric models of the type favoured by Keynesians were useless for forecasting purposes, because economic time-series are non-linear.[48] Persistent attempts to exploit correlations for control purposes lead to behavioural changes. This was an attack on the very idea of macroeconomic *policy*: optimization by individuals should be the only theoretical foundation for macroeconomic models; and transparent rules the only foundation for economic policy. This second formula sought to return monetary policy to the rule-bound era of the gold standard. It was only if monetary policy was completely predictable that it would have no real effects. (See Appendix 7.2, p. 205, for a more detailed account of rational expectations theory.)

The rational expectations revolution led to Real Business Cycle (RBC) theory. RBC theory accepted that economic fluctuations can be caused by supply (for example, technological) shocks as well as monetary shocks, but sought to incorporate short-run dynamics into a properly micro-founded inter-temporal general equilibrium framework. Business fluctuations were the 'efficient' results of optimizing agents responding to supply-side 'shocks'. The general purport of this class of models was that economies are always at full employment, since fluctuations in output are fluctuations in Friedman's equilibrium rate of unemployment, not deviations from it.[49] Of course, there may be unemployment, but this is voluntary. The *reductio ad absurdum* of this view was that an economy experiencing 50 per cent unemployment could be at full employment! Lucas is a good example of the flaw which Keynes detected in Hayek: 'how, starting with a mistake, a remorseless logician can end in Bedlam'.[50] The mistake was the theory of rational expectations itself. By 2003, Lucas was confidently claiming that 'the central problem of depression-prevention has been solved for all practical purposes', which invites the retort that one can always prevent depression by denying its existence.[51]

The idea that fully rational and informed agents were choosing to remain unemployed for year after year was too much for all converts to the REH. The long stagnation of the 1980s led to 'New Keynesianism', the attempt to incorporate 'Keynesian' features into micro-founded models by reviving the old idea that 'frictions' of various kinds can cause deviations from an optimal level of output.

New Keynesians were able to explain sticky prices in a rational expectations framework. With imperfect information and imperfect competition, firms and job-seekers may reach inferior bargaining outcomes. The so-called Dynamic Stochastic General Equilibrium (DSGE) models of the 1990s embedded into the REH and RBC structure a number of nominal rigidities and market imperfections.[52] Most common were price and wage rigidities and various forms of consumer myopia. These allowed for temporary demand shortages, on which central bank policy could have a significant short-run impact. This was the basis of the 'New Consensus'. New Keynesians accepted that there was no long-run trade-off between price stability and employment, but claimed that government could influence employment in the short-run.

There has been a further softening of the hard edge of the REH. The earliest versions equated rationality with prodigious capacity to acquire and process information. Behavioural economists pointed out that this was not a necessary condition of rational behaviour. Faced with 'cognitive overload' people rely on mental short-cuts, or heuristics (rules of thumb). Examples include anchoring (relying on the first piece of information), availability (prominent examples), and familiarity (extrapolating from past situations). These were reasonable ways of forming expectations. 'Nudging' expectations in the desired direction became the chief instrument in the central banks' tool kit. Simon Wren Lewis put a New Keynesian gloss on this policy procedure, arguing that 'implicit or explicit inflation targeting by independent central banks ... reflected an understanding of the importance of rational expectations. If a central bank had a clear inflation objective, and established a reputation in achieving it, that would anchor expectations and reduce the impact of shocks on the macroeconomy.'[53]

How far it makes sense to think of heuristics as reasonable abbreviations of all available information is doubtful. There is more than a whiff of magical thinking involved in the belief that thoughts by themselves can bring about desired effects in the real world. Keynes, too, believed that in face of uncertainty people fell back on 'conventions' or 'rules of thumb'. But he did not believe that these were, in general, short-cuts to calculation, because he thought that in many situations no calculation was possible. He thought that an economy built on pretence to knowledge was liable to sudden collapses when the pretence was exposed; and confidence, once deceived, could not readily be restored.

In accepting the REH and RBC theory as the framework for macroeconomic analysis, the New Keynesians surrendered Keynes's own emphasis on uncertainty – there was no uncertainty in these models, only contingently imperfect information within known probability distributions – for precious policy space. The assumption that markets take time to clear justified limited government intervention, since it meant that the actual rate of unemployment can remain above its equilibrium rate for some time. This was contrary to Keynes who argued that there is no 'natural' rate of unemployment in a monetary economy.

The theoretical compromise between the New Classical and New Keynesian economists influenced central bank policy. Thus, though the mainstream *policy* models from the 1980s onwards assumed rational expectations, they also allowed some degree of wage and price stickiness, and that meant there was still a short-term trade-off between inflation and output facing policymakers. In practice, the pre-crash central bank models of the 2000s were a compromise between adaptive and rational expectations. Rational expectations chiefly came to influence policy in the form of automatic 'reaction rules' to anchor expectations; adaptive expectations in making the inflation rate a medium-term target.[54] This was a pragmatic compromise, leaving room for attention to output: the rules, in economics-speak, were 'state contingent'.

Congdon has called this control system 'output-gap monetarism';[55] or one could call it 'constrained discretion'. The crucial point, though, is that the policy space was much too small. It failed to take into account the possibility of a large-scale collapse of the financial system.

Adjustment to 'real' shocks was increasingly sought, not in macropolicy, but in varieties of supply-side policies designed to improve the working of markets. As Stedman Jones notes for Britain:

> The major differences, and the real departure in economic terms, between the Callaghan government and the Conservatives lay in [the latter's] radicalization of microeconomic policy through various market-based supply-side reforms and their importation of market mechanisms into public service provision, something the Labour Party continued and deepened after 1997.[56]

The new orthodoxy's structural reform ideas spread across the world in the form of the 'Washington consensus' that, through the IMF and the World Bank, made the receipt of financial support conditional on the deregulation of financial sectors, the privatization of state-owned enterprises, the liberalization of markets and fiscal discipline.

The revolution in theory initiated by Friedman and Lucas ran in parallel with another theoretical enterprise particularly relevant to policy, known as the 'economics of politics'. Its main thrust was to emphasize the importance of the private incentives facing politicians and bureaucrats. The Keynesian-social democratic state was modelled as a private interest masquerading as guardian of the public interest. This was back to Adam Smith. Democracy, in theory a check on political choice, was misguided, easily manipulable and incoherent. (Voters wanted more welfare, but were not prepared to pay higher taxes.)

James Buchanan's 'public choice' theory undermined the 'benevolent despot' view of government that had implicitly underpinned much Keynesian advocacy of state intervention. Politicians, said the public choice school, were more interested in maximizing votes than stabilizing economies. By 1976, Assar Lindbeck was writing that

> a pessimist, or a cynic might . . . be tempted to say that the most severe difficulties of economic policy are embedded in the political rather than in the economic system . . . Consequently, the best thing to do would be to avoid discretionary policies altogether, rather than trying to make the interventions more sophisticated.[57]

The theory of 'government failure' thus provided a powerful argument for a limited state, in which politicians were restrained by fiscal rules, and policy placed in the hands of independent central banks. It shaped the European institutions adopted by the 1992 Maastricht Treaty, with control of inflation assigned to an independent European Central Bank, and a 'Stability and Growth Pact' to set a cap on government deficits.

Finally, and less directly, analysis of economic growth by historians such as Douglass North emphasized the importance of the right individual incentives for economic development, including private property rights and moral codes. This insight started to yield very different policy prescriptions from the concentration on boosting aggregate saving and investment totals fashionable in the heyday of Keynesian development economics. The shift was quite quick. Walt Rostow's *The Stages of Economic Growth* (1961), the bible of 1960s' 'growthmanship', and North and Thomas's 'An Economic Theory of Growth in the Western World' (1970) already inhabited different mental universes.[58]

Public choice theory is simply rational expectations theory applied to government. It takes from REH the methodology of modelling public policies as the solution to individual maximization problems.[59] In doing so, it revives the original inspiration of scientific economics, which juxtaposed the efficiency of markets with the corruption of the Prince.

The main features of what Michael Woodford called the 'new synthesis' were as follows:

1. Economists accept the crucial importance of expectations in determining the impact of alternative policies. This is a legacy of Keynes. But Keynes's distinction between uncertainty and risk was abolished. Uncertain expectations can be reduced to rational expectations, based on the presumption that current probability distributions are valid for an indefinite future. Equipped with constantly updated information, economic agents adjust instantly and efficiently to all external shocks. The New Keynesian economists inhabited this same universe of rational expectations, but, by 'relaxing the assumptions', they allowed for sluggish adjustment to shocks. Keynes's insights into the psychology of financial markets, the instability of investment, and the role of money as a store of value were irrelevant.

2. While the simple aggregate equations of Keynes's macroeconomic model (IS/LM) continued to be taught, there was a return to neo-classical standards of method. No longer was it considered acceptable to posit ad hoc supply and demand functions. Macroeconomics should best be seen as an application of microeconomics, in the sense that macroeconomic models *should* be based on optimization by firms and individuals. This is contrary to Keynes, who believed that individual behaviour is shaped by aggregate psychological and social data.

3. Mainstream economics is now based on supply not demand. It reasserted a version of Say's Law. Thus both the New Classicals and the New Keynesians believed that the long-run growth of real GDP depends on an increase in the supply of factor inputs and technological progress. Technological progress is assumed to be independent of the demand for technology. Further, many economists only accepted sticky contracts as contingent, not inescapable. The 'supply side' school of economics, by aiming to remove market imperfections, looked forward to a world of complete markets and instantly renegotiable contracts. Deregulation of financial markets, a key element in this agenda, proved to be its Achilles heel.

4. Following Friedman, mainstream economics reasserted the primacy of monetary policy. The disinflation of the 1980s and 1990s proved beyond doubt, they claimed, that central banks could control inflation. Provided money is kept 'in order', economies would stick to their long-run equilibrium growth path. This view reasserted the optimism of the monetary reformers of the 1920s, who sought in monetary policy a therapy for the fluctuations of capitalist market economies.

5. In modelling economies, New Classical economists were not fazed by the unrealism of their assumptions; indeed, they regarded this as a strength of their models. The important thing was that their models should be logically coherent. This was contrary to Keynes, who insisted on realism of assumptions. Nevertheless, the new synthesis insisted that policy should be based on econometrically valid structural models. Hence the many attempts, by methods of 'simulation', to discover fits between model predictions and aggregate time series.

6. In contrast to the Keynesian consensus during the 'golden age', it was widely thought that governments should not now try to 'fine tune' economies. Instead, stabilization policy should merely aim to assist, or give time for, the market's self-correcting capabilities, chiefly by keeping prices stable and relying on automatic fiscal stabilizers.

7. Whereas in the 1950s and 1960s stabilization was seen mainly as a control theory problem, it now took into account strategic

interaction between authorities and agents whose expectations the authorities needed to 'manage' by means of clear rules. This follows the normative prescription that governments should aim to provide agents with a consistent model of the economy.[60]

The cumulative effect of these theoretical developments was to narrow the scope of macroeconomic policy and change its explicit aim. Provided money was 'controlled', economies would be stable, for reasons given by Wicksell – but denied by Keynes – namely, that there existed a 'natural' rate of interest that balanced the saving decisions of consumers and the investment decisions of producers. Thus a monetary policy which was confidently expected to keep a low, constant inflation rate – that is, would prevent money from deceiving market participants about the real value of their contracts – was the key and, in effect, the only requirement for maintenance of an optimum equilibrium.

With acceptance of the 'natural rate' doctrine, much of macro-policy's early unemployment-reducing function was assigned to micro-policy or 'structural' reforms aimed at galvanizing individual incentives to wealth production. This in turn tended to re-establish the so-called classical dichotomy between money and the 'real world', and amounted to the theoretical abolition of the Keynesian revolution. Differences between the New Classicals and New Keynesians certainly remained, but they were political rather than theoretical.

VIII. CONCLUSION

The way in which Keynes's *General Theory* was transmuted into the New Classical–New Keynesian synthesis illustrates why there have been so few, if any, paradigm shifts in economics comparable to the overthrow of Ptolemaic by Copernican astronomy. Scientific economics is essentially a synthesizing discipline. It hoards its accumulated knowledge, spewing out any that is obviously inconsistent with it, and assimilating innovations too important to be ignored. The cases we have considered exhibit a common pattern: the pure essence of the theory is diluted for policy purposes, leaving the core theoretical structure intact. In the 1940s and 1950s Keynesian policy was grafted on to neo-classical theory. In the 1980s and 1990s, New Keynesian policy was grafted on to New Classical theory. What has remained intact throughout is the theory of the optimizing agent. Indeed he/she has now been equipped with rational expectations, further narrowing the Keynesian policy space allowed by the earlier generation of synthesizers.

One cannot survey the story of the unravelling of the Keynesian revolution without being struck by the close link between economic theory and political ideology. The Keynesian revolution created a space for government intervention in the economy. The reaction against it consisted first in minimizing the theoretical justification for that space, then in emphasizing the flaws in Keynesian policy, and finally in trying to abolish the space altogether. Despite the flaws in Keynes's own theory, and the even greater ones in those of Keynesian economists of the Samuelson generation, one cannot avoid the strong impression that the whole unravelling was driven by ideological hostility to government per se, which, as we have seen, has its roots in the original mindset of economics: a return to the roots after a long deviation.

The period of the Great Moderation, which supposedly ran from the early 1990s, when the transition to the new regime was accomplished, to the onset of the crisis in 2008, was believed to vindicate the new system of macro-management. Disconfirming events like the East Asian financial crisis of 1997–8, and the collapse of the dotcom bubble in 2001, were regarded as 'teething problems', which would be overcome by a continually updated learning process, making financial markets ever more efficient. True, the average OECD rate of unemployment in the new 'normal' was more than double what it had been in the 'old' normal (7 per cent between 1992 and 2007, as opposed to 3 per cent between 1959 and 1975), but this was seen as a legacy of bad labour-market practices which would soon yield to further labour-market reforms. By 2006, it was confidently believed that efficient markets were close to being fully established. Almost no one expected things to go seriously wrong.

As Robert Lucas remarked in 1980: 'At research seminars, people don't take Keynesian theorising seriously any more – the audience starts to whisper and giggle to one another.'[61] But these giggling economics students became architects of the policy that led to the great crash of 2008.

APPENDIX 7.1: IS/LM, THE KEYNESIAN TEACHING TOOL

The IS curve shows the locus of combinations of interest rates and output such that savings and investment are in equilibrium. It is downward sloping because, as interest rates fall, investment becomes more attractive. This increases output, and some of this output will be saved, generating a new investment-savings equilibrium at a lower interest rate.

The LM curve shows the locus of combinations of interest rates and output such that the market for money is in equilibrium, i.e. the demand for money equals the supply of money. As output increases

Figure 19. IS-LM model
(Investment-Saving–Liquidity-Money)

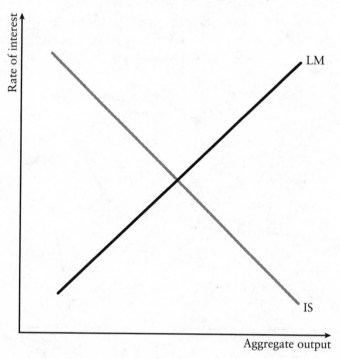

on the horizontal axis, the demand for money increases. In order for the money market to remain in equilibrium, the price of money (i.e. the interest rate) has to increase in order for supply to meet demand. This is why the curve slopes upwards.

The intersection of these curves shows the unique, equilibrium level of income and interest rates for a given quantity of money, when the markets for both goods/services and money are in balance.

The IS/LM diagrams in Figure 20 show the Keynesian (left-hand graph) and the neo-classical (right-hand graph) views of the economy. In the Keynesian account, investment is insensitive to changes in the interest rate, instead being determined by confidence, and money demand is very variable, implying a steep IS curve and a shallow LM curve. In the neo-classical account, investment is very sensitive to changes in the interest rate, whereas money demand is relatively stable, giving us the converse slopes.

Expansionary fiscal policy is shown by a rightwards shift in the IS curve, whereas an expansion in the money supply is shown by a rightwards shift in the LM curve, reflecting the difference between interaction in money and goods/services markets. As we can see, a rightwards shift in the IS curve will restore large amounts of output in the Keynesian case, but will have limited impact in the neo-classical case. The reverse is true for shifts in the LM curve.

Figure 20. Keynesian and neo-classical views
of the economy

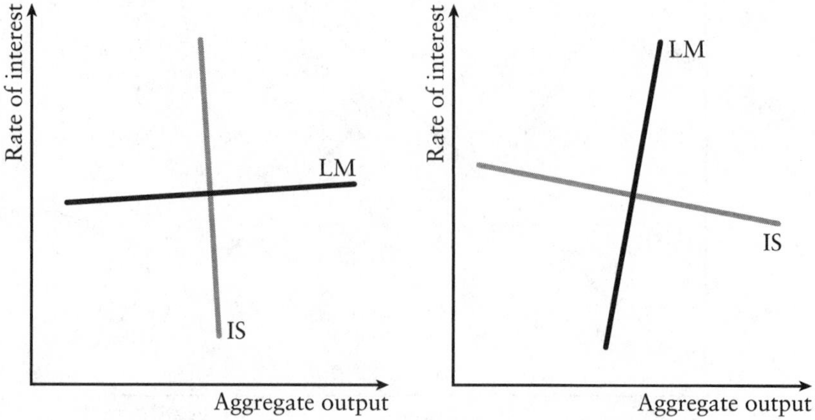

APPENDIX 7.2: THE MODELLING OF EXPECTATIONS

The Keynesian Phillips Curve

Friedman's Adaptive Expectations

The Philips Curve failed altogether to distinguish between nominal wages and real wages. In the Phillips Curve world, all agents anticipated that nominal prices would be stable, whatever happened to actual prices and wages. Take the following simple version of adaptive expectations:

$$E_t[P_{t+1}] = E_{t-1}[[P_t]] + \lambda(P_t - E_{t-1}[P_t]); 0 < \lambda < 1$$

Figure 21. The Phillips Curve, 1948–1957[62]

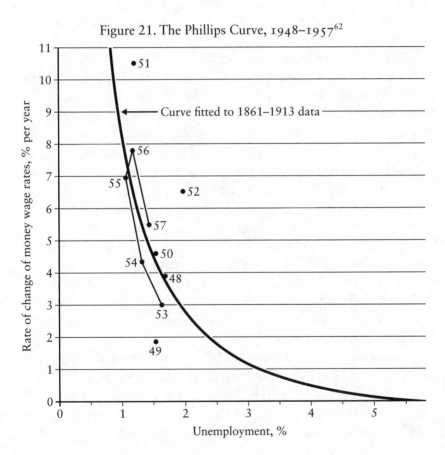

This says that agents learn from their past mistakes: $E_t[P_{t+1}]$ shows people's current expectations (in period t) for inflation in the next period $(t+1)$; inflation in the current period is shown by P_t; and $E_{t-1}[P_t]$ is what people expected current inflation to be in the last period $(t-1)$.

So current expectations of future inflation reflect past expectations and an 'error-adjustment' term, in which current expectations are raised (or lowered) according to the gap between actual inflation and previous expectations. The higher λ is, the more people take their previous mistakes into account.

It should be clear that the implication of adaptive expectations is that the economy can be stimulated only in the short-run, or sometimes only in the very short-run. Monetary policy essentially can stimulate the economy – by lowering interest rates or pushing the unemployment rate below its 'natural' rate – only in the time that it takes for people's expectations to adjust. The temporary trade-off comes from *unanticipated* inflation.

This can also be seen in terms of the 'money illusion' which stimulates the economy through making people want to spend more, but that only works in the short-run. Under the money illusion, people feel richer when, for example, the monetary authority pumps extra money into the economy, but this is only because they fail to realize that prices will rise proportionately. People are essentially taking changes in nominal variables (the money supply) as real, although purchasing power has stayed constant. The money illusion disappears in the medium- to long-run as agents adjust their expectations in response to observing increases in price.

All of this is to say that one cannot profit from the inflation–output trade-off shown by the original Phillips Curve in the medium–long-run, as the Curve itself shifts due to the level of inflation rising and people adjusting their expectations upward.

Friedman's theory of adaptive expectations gives the 'expectations-augmented Phillips Curve' (Figure 22).

The economy starts at point A, at the natural rate of unemployment (see below) where demand is equal to the economy's productive capacity. The government sees that it is on a given short-run Phillips Curve (SRPC1) and wants to take advantage of its inflation–unemployment trade-off, so it stimulates the economy to reduce unemployment to rate

Figure 22. Expectations-augmented Phillips Curve

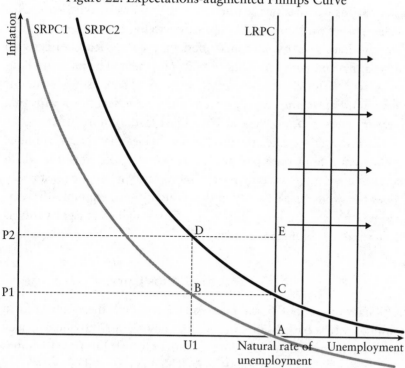

U1. At this level of unemployment, workers demand higher wages and this pushes general price inflation up to rate P1. In the short-run, the economy is at point B.

Workers realize that this price rise has eroded their wage increase in real terms, and so labour supply falls, bringing employment and output back to their 'natural' rates. But now, given adaptive expectations, agents expect inflation of P1, and this becomes built into their wage demands. The economy thus moves to point C. The short-run Phillips Curve has shifted outwards, to SRPC2, reflecting a worsening of the inflation–output trade-off.* If the government tries a similar tactic again, the

---

* On Friedman's account, short-run Phillips Curves are indexed by the inflation expectations of agents at the natural rate of unemployment. On SPRC1, for example, inflation is expected to be 0 at the natural rate, whereas agents expect inflation of rate P1 on SRPC2.

economy will move to point D and then E in the same fashion, but at a faster pace as workers have learned from their previous experience. This further pushes the short-run Phillips Curve to the right.

In the long-run, expansionist monetary policy leads directly to higher inflation, with no effect on unemployment. The long-run Phillips Curve (LRPC) is completely vertical. There is no trade-off between inflation and employment at all. In practice, this means that intervention is undesirable as it would just lead to more inflation.

Thus Friedman restated the pre-Keynesian idea that there is a unique equilibrium rate of unemployment, the 'natural' rate, towards which the economy always reverts. Furthermore, insofar as price instability erodes the productive capacity of the economy – for example, decreasing investment – the long-run Phillips Curve will shift rightwards as the natural rate of unemployment rises.

Lucas's Vertical Phillips Curve

'Rational expectations' first appeared in the economic theory literature in a famous article by J. Muth in 1961, but only filtered through to policy discussion in the early 1970s with the work of Robert Lucas and Thomas Sargent on business cycles, and Eugene Fama on financial markets.

As defined by Haberler, rational expectations is the 'radical wing of monetarism . . . best known for the startling policy conclusions . . . that macroeconomic policies, both monetary and fiscal, are ineffective, even in the short-run',[63] because agents adapt their expectations immediately.

Thus the rational expectations revolution started with a critique of adaptive expectations. Friedman's theory of adaptive expectations relied on the gradual adjustment of expectations to the experienced behaviour of a variable, so there is an exploitable trade-off between employment and inflation in the short-run. According to Lucas, however, agents will adjust their expectations immediately. This is because our knowledge includes not just what we have experienced, but current pronouncements of public authorities and theoretical knowledge of aggregate relationships too. Indeed, the rational expectations hypothesis (REH) says that agents optimally utilize all available information about the economy and policy to construct their expectations.

For instance, if the Minister of Finance announces that he will increase the money supply by 10 per cent a year to stimulate employment, knowledge of the model of the economy and of the QTM, in particular, tells us that prices will increase proportionately. So it makes sense to expect inflation to be 10 per cent a year. You do not have to wait for prices to start increasing to revise your expectations. In other words, it is rational to expect inflation to be 10 per cent a year; this is the theory of rational expectations. In this example, rational expectations is defined as belief in the QTM. Adaptive behaviour is a description of irrational behaviour, if agents know what to expect already but do not change their behaviour.

In other instances, agents adjust their expectations through repeated application of Bayes's theorem, a method of statistical inference:

$$P(A \mid B) = \frac{P(B \mid A)\,P(A)}{P(B)}$$

For instance, suppose that agents are uncertain about other agents' risk aversion. Then it is assumed that they still 'understand what is happening well enough to form rational expectations based on their prior probability assessments of the things they are uncertain about, and the information they observe as time progresses'.[64] In applying Bayes's law, agents turn their subjective bets into objective probability distributions.

Agents are able to learn and adjust their expectations so quickly and efficiently that the REH implies that outcomes will not differ systematically from what people expect them to be. If we take the price level P, for instance, we can write:

$$P = E[P] + \epsilon$$

Here, $E[P]$ is the rational expectation of the price level based on all up-to-date information; ϵ is the error term, which has an expected value of zero, and is independent of expectations. This says that the price level will differ from the expectation only if there is a surprise. *Ex ante*, the price anticipated is equal to the expectation.

Rational expectations does not imply that agents never make mistakes; agents may make mistakes on occasion. But these mistakes are only random, so each agent is correct on average over time, and at each point in time the aggregate decisions of a large pool of agents are rational. In technical terms, Lucas defined expectations as the mean of a distribution of a random variable. As the number of observations increases, the distribution resembles a bell curve or a 'normal distribution', and the expectation coincides with the peak of the curve, or, in more ordinary parlance, the average of the observations. Similarly, the errors or random events causing these errors adhere to the bell-shaped distribution, but their mean/expectation is zero.

Essentially, Friedman's distinction between a Keynesian short-run, in which agents can be fooled, and a classical long-run, in which they know what to expect, disappears. Policy can influence real variables only by using information not known to the public, otherwise it would be fully anticipated and incorporated into expectations. The Phillips Curve is vertical in the long-run and in the short-run, which rules out any fiscal or monetary intervention designed to improve an existing equilibrium. The reason is that 'money illusion' never develops. Agents adjust their inflation expectations immediately. So there is not even a brief interval of higher employment that would come about from getting people to spend more.

Mathematically, rational expectations theory yields many benefits, including the use of the 'representative agent' which greatly simplifies calculations. That is, once you assume that agents are rational and equipped with the same information and preferences, you can treat

Figure 23. The Sargent-Lucas Phillips Curve

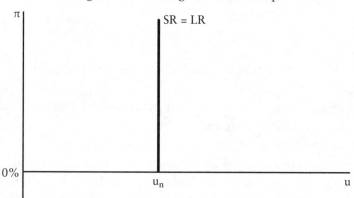

the economy as the outcome of the decisions of only one individual, the 'representative agent'. Agents who are identical in terms of their rationality, information sets and preferences will take identical decisions; so analysing their decisions as a group is equivalent to analysing their independent decisions. Therefore, mathematically, instead of maximizing the sum of utility functions, you just have to maximize one utility function. As Thomas Sargent quipped: 'All agents inside the model, the econometrician, and God share the same model.'[65]

Dynamic Stochastic General Equilibrium models (DSGE)

Like rational expectations, DSGE modelling takes root in New Classical economics, where the works of Lucas (1975), Kydland and Prescott (1982), and Long and Plosser (1983) were most prominent. The earlier DSGE models were pure Real Business Cycle (RBC) models, i.e. models that attempted to explain business cycles in terms of real productivity or consumption shocks, abstracting from money.

The logic behind RBC models is clear. If money cannot affect real variables (because of QTM and rational expectations), the source of any disturbance to the real economy must be non-monetary; that is, business fluctuations must be caused by 'real' unanticipated shocks. (Notice the use of the word 'shock'.) These shocks make the economy dynamic and stochastic. For instance, unemployment is explained in these models by rational adjustments by workers of their work/leisure trade-off to shifts in productivity.

DSGE models have explicit micro-foundations. Agents are continuously re-optimizing their utility functions, and as a result, economies in DSGE models are always in some form of equilibrium whether in the short-run or long-run. The economy always starts from an equilibrium position, and when there is a shock, it immediately jumps on to an equilibrium 'time path' – the 'saddle path'. Michael Wickens explains how 'the short-run equilibrium of the economy may differ from its long-run equilibrium but, if stable, the short-run equilibrium will be changing through time and will over time approach the long-run equilibrium'.[66] This is the role of the saddle path. Translated into English, the economy's movements are optimal responses to shocks. Market fluctuations do not reflect market failures, and government intervention can only make things worse. The economy is 'self-healing'. In technical terms, 'the implication of real-business-cycle models, in their strongest form, is that observed aggregate output movements represent the time-varying Pareto optimum'.[67]

The New Keynesians preserved the basic framework of the New Classical RBC/DSGE models, but added 'market frictions', like monopolistic competition and nominal rigidities, to make the models more applicable to the real world.[68]

APPENDIX 7.3: THE CENTRAL BANK REACTION FUNCTION

Pre-crash central bank policy combined New Classical and New Keynesian models. In New Keynesian models, monetary policy still plays a stabilizing role, 'imperfections' recreating a space between the short- and long-run. 'If a central bank had a clear inflation objective, and established a reputation in achieving it, that would anchor expectations and reduce the impact of shocks on the macroeconomy.'[69]

To illustrate how central banks decided on policy in the pre-crash years, we can use a brief, simplified version of the model used in Woodford's *Interest and Prices*.[70] The model consists of three parts:

1. *An expectational IS equation* relating current output positively to expected future output and negatively to the real interest rate; if GDP growth is expected to be strong and interest rates to be low, then output will be high.
2. *A New Keynesian Phillips Curve*, linking current inflation to expected future inflation and the output gap. If inflation in the future is expected to be high, then (for example) workers will demand increases in nominal wages, pushing up current inflation. The amount of slack/overheating in the economy will also determine inflation in that period.
3. *A monetary rule*, which attempts to describe a central bank's decision procedure. The idea is that the bank chooses an interest rate

which minimizes the size of the output gap – determined by 1. – and deviations from the target rate of inflation – determined by 2.

A common monetary rule used to capture the behaviour of central banks is the Taylor Rule,[71] which tries to show how central banks respond (or ought to respond) to developments in inflation and output:

$$i - \pi = r^* + \alpha\left(\pi + \pi^*\right) - \beta(y)$$

Here, i is the (nominal) central bank policy rate; π is current inflation; r^* is the (real) 'natural rate of interest'; $(\pi - \pi^*)$ is the gap between current inflation and the inflation target; y is the output gap.

Recall that a real interest rate is just the nominal rate minus inflation. The rule thus shows that central banks should move the real policy rate away from the 'natural' rate whenever inflation and/or output deviate from their targets in order to stabilize the economy. Coefficients α and β show the relative aversion of the central bank to inflation and output gaps. If β is 0, for example, then the central bank cares only about inflation.

PART THREE

Macroeconomics in the Crash and After, 2007–

The years running from the early 1990s to 2007 (or, seemingly, from the mid-1980s in the US) are known as the Great Moderation. This was a period of exceptional stability in world economic affairs. Between 1992 and 2007 inflation in the advanced economies averaged 2.3 per cent; economic growth 2.8 per cent.[1] Many attributed this success to the creation of independent central banks with a mandate to target inflation. With money at last expected to be 'kept in order' by independent central bankers, and governments expected to balance their budgets, the market economy was behaving as most economists said it should. The era of 'boom and bust' was over, declared Britain's Chancellor of the Exchequer, Gordon Brown.

Figure 24. Output growth in the advanced economies during the Great Moderation[2]
(per cent growth of real GDP)

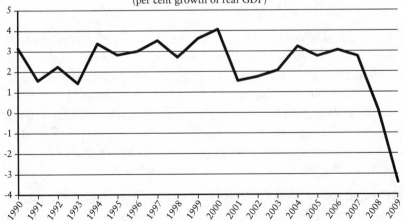

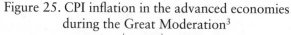

Figure 25. CPI inflation in the advanced economies
during the Great Moderation[3]
(per cent)

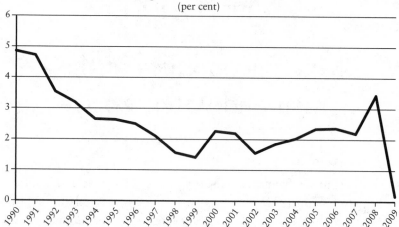

The euphoria of the pre-crash years was by no one better pre-visioned than Hyman Minsky:

> Success breeds disregard of the possibility of failure. The absence of serious financial difficulties over a substantial period leads to a euphoric economy in which short-term financing of long-term positions becomes the normal way of life. As the previous financial crisis recedes in time, it is quite natural for central bankers, government officials, bankers, businessmen and even economists to believe that a new era has arrived.[4]

The 'surprise' global economic collapse of 2008–9, the worst since the Great Depression of 1929–32, shattered the glass. It forced activist – that is, discretionary – responses from governments that were partly experimental, but that also involved using old tools which had become rusty through neglect. These emergency measures prevented the collapse from becoming another Great Depression. But they failed to produce complete recovery, and they left macroeconomic policy in a mess.

We can identify five distinct stages of the crisis:

1. The collapse of the American sub-prime mortgage market in August 2007. This activated central banks' role as lenders of last resort.

2. The escalation of the financial crisis with the collapse and rescue of the major US investment bank Bear Stearns in March 2008. The confidence among banks in the quality of each others' assets deteriorated markedly after this, leading to reduced interbank lending and much greater use of available central bank credit lines. The Fed became a global 'lender of last resort', making credit swaps available to fourteen central banks. There was no fiscal response to the first two phases.

3. The collapse and non-rescue of the investment bank Lehman Brothers during the weekend of 13–14 September 2008, which started the third and most acute phase of the financial and economic crisis. A week of total credit paralysis followed, with the payments systems everywhere endangered. Many banks in the USA, UK, Europe and elsewhere went bankrupt and had to be rescued. (Of 101 banks with balance sheets of over $100 billion in 2006, half failed.) Between September and December 2008, the Federal Reserve and the European Central Bank made available €2 trillion of credit to banks at 1 per cent interest, and started buying government and commercial debt on a small scale. In the fourth quarter of 2008 and first quarter of 2009, GDP in industrial nations fell at an annualized rate of 7–8 per cent. GDP growth slowed down in China and Asia, the main transmitters of the crisis to the developing world being the collapse in their terms of trade (including commodity prices) and paralysis of private capital markets. With an 8 per cent GDP drop, Russia experienced the fastest and steepest collapse in the G20 world.

4. Unlike in 1929–30, the economic collapse produced energetic government responses. Governments strengthened deposit insurance, recapitalized and nationalized banks with public funds, and bought toxic assets. In September 2008 the US government nationalized the insolvent mortgage lenders Fanny Mae and Freddie Mac, transferring their $5 trillion of debt to the taxpayer. US Treasury Secretary Henry Paulson announced a $700 billion bailout plan (the Trouble Asset Relief Program) to buy up distressed bank assets; the Icelandic, Benelux and German governments also bailed out parts of their banking systems.[5] In October 2008, the G20 committed its members to co-ordinated

interest rate cuts and bank recapitalizations. Substantial discretionary fiscal responses included €200 billion from the EU (mainly Germany), $298 billion from Japan, $586 billion from China and $800 billion from the USA. China's stimulus amounted to 12.7 per cent of its 2008 GDP, the US's 6 per cent. 'Cash for clunkers' was an imaginative early fiscal initiative. The consensus is that the initial response, running from autumn 2008 to spring 2009, stopped the slide into another Great Depression. The 'green shoots' of recovery started in the second quarter of 2009. Output fall slowed, risk premia fell, and stock and bond markets recovered. Led by China, Germany and Japan, economic recovery spread to the USA, the UK and the Eurozone in the second half of 2009.

Recovering is not the same as recovery. From medicine we can borrow the idea of an 'acute' phase. In the acute phase, all the main 'health' indicators are downwards. The collapse then stops and recovery starts. In a serious illness you can take yourself to be fully recovered if you get back to where you were before. In the same way, 'full health' can be said to be when the economy recovers its pre-crisis peak. But perhaps you were overdoing it before, which is why you got ill. And the same is true with economies. They may have been growing above trend pre-crash.

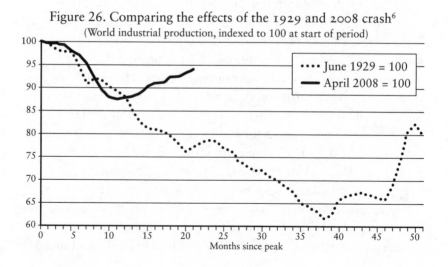

Figure 26. Comparing the effects of the 1929 and 2008 crash[6]
(World industrial production, indexed to 100 at start of period)

•••• June 1929 = 100
—— April 2008 = 100

Months since peak

So getting back to their pre-crash peak may be overdoing it again. This would be true of a recovery based on re-igniting the housing bubble.

Speed and strength of recovery varies not just from depression to depression, but from region to region. There can be a period of 'crawling along the bottom', or anaemic growth, or very strong (above-trend) recovery. A stylized representation of recovery from 2008–9 would look like this: Asia V-shaped; US U-shaped; Europe a combination of L-shaped (flat-lining) and W (double-dip).

5. Once the corner had been turned, the narrative of the Great Recession changed drastically. The banking crisis turned into a fiscal crisis, and the public debt problem took centre stage. It was at this point that the arguments for austerity began to gain traction. Austerity policies aimed to restore fiscal balances. The restoration of fiscal balance was seen as the necessary condition for recovery of private sector confidence, and hence investment and economic growth. As government tightened the fiscal screws, economic growth fizzled out, coincidentally or not.

Government success in averting another Great Depression has given rise to a piece of mythology: the world economy was saved by the central banks. Typical is the following by Chris Giles of the *Financial Times*: 'They saved the global economy from the financial crisis.'[7] This is sloppy journalism. It ignores the fact that the proportion of GDP spent by governments was twice as large as in 1929–30, so the automatic stabilizers were much larger. More importantly, it ignores the large *discretionary* fiscal stimulus in the first six months of the slump. Recapitalizing banks was a fiscal operation, involving governments raising vast sums in the bond markets. It was governments, not central banks, learning from Keynes, not from Milton Friedman, that prevented a slide into another Great Depression, just as it was governments gripped by deficit panic that aborted recovery after 2010.

The communiqué of the September 2009 G20 summit in Pittsburgh read:

Our national commitments to restore growth resulted in the largest and most coordinated fiscal and monetary stimulus ever undertaken. We acted together to increase dramatically the resources necessary to stop the crisis from spreading around the world ... The process of recovery and repair remains incomplete ... The conditions for a recovery of private demand are not yet fully in place. We cannot rest until the global economy is restored to full health, and hard-working families the world over can find decent jobs ... We will avoid any premature withdrawal of stimulus. At the same time, we will prepare our exit strategies and, when the time is right, withdraw our extraordinary policy support in a cooperative and coordinated way, maintaining our commitment to fiscal responsibility.[8]

The G20 communiqués of this period, mainly crafted by Gordon Brown, could have been important milestones in the development of global economic government. However, while Brown was engaged in 'saving the world', his domestic political base was crumbling, and in May 2010 he lost the British general election. The next two chapters will tell of the 'premature withdrawal' of fiscal stimulus, tasking only a much weaker monetary stimulus with restoring the global economy to 'full health'.

8

The Disablement of Fiscal Policy

'Now this deficit didn't suddenly appear purely as a result of the global financial crisis. It was driven by persistent, reckless and completely unaffordable government spending and borrowing over many years.'

David Cameron, March 2013[1]

I. THE FISCAL CRISIS OF THE STATE

The 'austere' fiscal response to the Great Recession is part of the story of the disablement of fiscal policy since the end of the 1970s. With the overthrow of the Keynesian revolution, the government's budget was retired as an instrument of short-run demand management. This task was left to monetary policy.

The UK is a good example of the snares of pre-crash fiscal orthodoxy. Gordon Brown's 'golden rule', announced in 1997, was that 'over the economic cycle, we will borrow only to invest and not to fund current spending'. To this was added a 'sustainable investment' rule: 'public sector net debt as a proportion of GDP will be held over the economic cycle at a stable and prudent level'.[2] This was understood to be under 40 per cent. These rules helpfully distinguished between current and capital spending. Budget balance was defined as a zero deficit on current account, and net capital spending equal to the economy's growth rate, over an economic cycle of between five and eight years, or about 2 per cent. The purpose of the Brown constitution was to create a bit more policy space for New Keynesian fiscal policy, against a background of relentless hostility to public expenditure. However, the constitution shared the general presumption of the day that, with price stability secured by monetary policy, the economy would be cyclically stable at its natural rate of unemployment. Lowering the natural rate of unemployment was the task of supply-side policy, much as Nigel Lawson had said in his Mais Lecture of 1984, though Labour put its emphasis on government training and work programmes to improve employability.

Gordon Brown was not an imprudent Chancellor. Between 1997–8 and 2006–7, the current account balance averaged 0.1%. Over the same period public sector net borrowing averaged 1.6%. With economic growth averaging 2.8% over the period, the national debt fell from 43.35% of GDP to 36.6%. Unemployment fell from 7% to 5%. Inflation averaged a little over 2% a year. This was a record of successful economic management. Brown could, and did, claim he had stuck to his fiscal rules.[3]

However, Brown's claim was less robust than it seemed. First, the successful pre-crash current account outcome was achieved by redefining when cycles started and ended, and balancing early surpluses against later deficits. By 2006–7, with the current spending budget in deficit, maintaining the golden rule over the next cycle would have been 'challenging'. Secondly, capital budget probity was being flattered by extensive use of the Private Finance Initiative (PFI) to build hospitals, schools and some expensive transport projects. PFI replaced spending financed by public debt with spending undertaken by private firms for which they were repaid by leasing agreements over periods of up to thirty years. It added nothing to the public debt, but gave rise to a higher stream of recurrent costs over the life of the asset than ordinary public procurement would have done. Its use allowed Brown to get a lot of capital spending 'off budget' and stick within the 'prudent' debt/GDP limit of 40 per cent.

The issue for macroeconomic policy is not whether PFI was a sleight of hand, but whether the investment it made possible would have taken place in its absence. A Keynesian would argue that, *given the state of public opinion*, PFI was the only way open to the government to drag private investment up to the level of full employment saving. It did this by converting uncertain into certain expectations for a large class of investments. In the absence of PFI, unemployment would have been higher and growth slower. PFI was as Keynesian as it was possible to be in a non-Keynesian world. The unfortunate

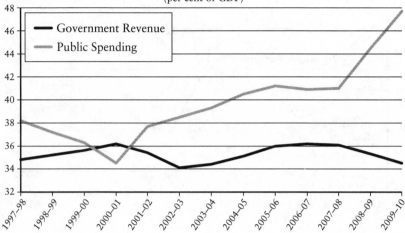

Figure 27. UK tax revenue and spending[4]
(per cent of GDP)

effect of the deception, though, was to disguise the extent to which government procurement policy was actually propping up the British economy.

The economic downturn of 2008–9 caused a large deterioration in government fiscal positions and a rise in public debt to GDP ratios.

Advanced country governments acquired large deficits willy-nilly, as their revenues shrank and their spending on unemployment benefits rose. But there were also substantial discretionary responses: in Britain these included a temporary cut in VAT from 17.5 per cent to 15 per cent and accelerated capital spending. Rescuing the banks involved governments raising hundreds of billions in the bond markets, causing deficits to balloon: the rescue of the Royal Bank of Scotland alone cost £46 billion. Rescue operations included the co-ordinated $1 trillion stimulus measures agreed by the G20 in London in April 2009, with the British Prime Minister Gordon Brown taking the lead.[5]

The acute phase of the *world* crisis was over by the third quarter of 2009; however, a secondary Eurozone crisis was superimposed on the original one in 2010–11. Given the pre-crash orthodoxy, and a widespread misunderstanding of the public financing problem, it is not surprising that the fiscal brakes were slammed on. The fact that 'Keynesian measures' had averted a politically life-threatening collapse of the world economy was considered much less important than

Figure 28. Government budget deficits[6]
(per cent of GDP)

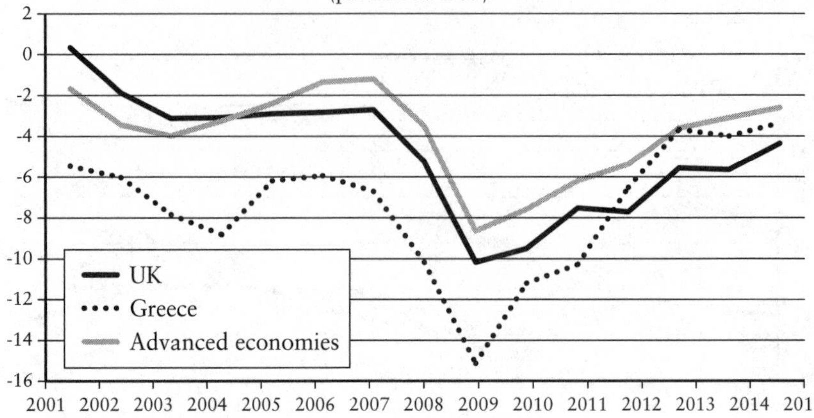

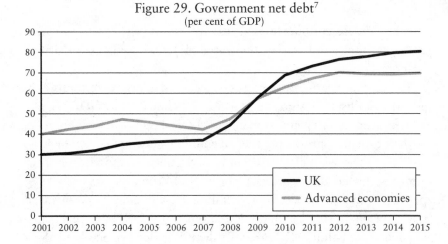

Figure 29. Government net debt[7]
(per cent of GDP)

the unbalanced budgets governments were left with. Gordon Brown refused to be 'another Philip Snowden' (for the original one, see pp. 112–13). The trouble, explained his Chancellor, Alistair Darling, was the 'Taliban wing' of the Treasury who thought Snowden was right.[8]

The global turning point can be dated from the meeting of the G7's finance ministers at Iqaluit in Canada in February 2010, which, dominated by the Greek crisis, committed governments to slashing deficits.[9] Orthodox economists argued that cutting public spending would boost output by reducing borrowing costs and increasing confidence.

In a pallid echo of Keynes's 'paradox of thrift', the larger G20 acknowledged, in a declaration following its 2010 Toronto summit, that 'synchronised financial adjustment [i.e. if all governments tried to reduce their deficits simultaneously] across several major economies could adversely impact the recovery',[10] but only President Obama stood out against the stampede towards what Germany's Finance Minister Wolfgang Schäuble approvingly dubbed 'expansionary fiscal consolidation'. Obama was supported by economists Paul Krugman, Joseph Stiglitz, Robert Shiller, Larry Summers, Nouriel Roubini and Brad DeLong. But 'expansionary fiscal consolidation' became the consensual view of Europe's finance ministers.[11] The majority of financial economists supinely followed the lead of the consolidators. Of the UK's top economic journalists, Martin Wolf and Samuel Brittan of the *Financial Times* and Larry Elliott of the *Guardian* were lonely dissenters. This was at a time when global output was still 5 per cent below what it had been pre-crash.[12] The British economics profession was largely silent.

This change of gear presumed that the recovery from the slump that had started in the third quarter of 2009 had gained strong *independent* momentum, and that fiscal consolidation was needed to maintain this momentum. In practice the shift to austerity in the UK and the Eurozone was followed by a marked slowdown in recovery, so much so that by mid-2010 most commentators were predicting a 'double-dip' recession or an L-shaped recovery. The truth was that the economies of the world were on life-support, and governments were switching the machines off.

II. THE BRITISH DEBATE

Contrary to David Cameron's rhetoric, UK public finances before the crash were not out of line with major comparators (see Figures 28 and 29). The real deterioration in the UK government's position, as for all governments, took place because of the slump, the British economy contracting by about 7 per cent between the second quarter of 2008 and the third quarter of 2009.

Labour's Chancellor of the Exchequer Alistair Darling announced a 'fiscal consolidation plan' in his pre-budget statement of autumn 2009. This committed the government to reducing the budget deficit, then projected to be 12.6 per cent of GDP in 2009–10, to 5.5 per cent by 2013–14, and to have net debt falling as a percentage of GDP by 2015–16.

Two letters that appeared in the British press early in 2010 give the flavour of the British debate. Twenty economists, headed by Tim Besley, wrote a letter to the *Sunday Times* on 4 February 2010, arguing that a faster pace for deficit reduction, especially on the spending side, was needed to sustain the recovery and restore confidence. Marcus Miller and Robert Skidelsky fronted a reply in the *Financial Times* on 18 February, arguing that the 'timing of the measures should depend on the strength of the recovery'. Each letter got the support of a Nobel Prize-winner. The war of the economists had resumed. It has continued ever since.

Martin Wolf explained the state of opinion in mid-2010. The cutters emphasized that world economic recovery had been stronger than expected, that government deficits 'crowd out' private spending, and (if they were Austrian economists) that a deep slump was needed to purge past excesses. More moderate cutters argued that cutting the deficit would avoid a spike in borrowing costs, pointing to the peaking of Greek government debt at 12 per cent. Should fiscal tightening lead to the weakening of the recovery, monetary expansion (quantitative easing) was always available to offset it. The postponers emphasized the fragility of the recovery, its dependence on fiscal stimuli, and the existence of huge private sector surpluses. Wolf agreed with the postponers. 'If anything, further loosening is needed.'[13]

Of key importance in swinging the debate in the UK over to the fiscal consolidators' side was the political narrative spun by the Conservatives. As Chancellor of the Exchequer from 1997 until 2007, Gordon Brown had imprudently made 'prudence' his watchword. The Conservatives now milked the story of Brown's fall from grace for maximum electoral impact. Reckless spending by the Labour government had not only contributed to the scale of Britain's economic collapse, but had left Britain dangerously deep in debt. The Conservative narrative also protected the City of London by blaming the crisis on Labour.

A key point in this tale spun to deceive was that a large part of the post-crash deficit was not cyclical, but 'structural'; that is, caused by government over-spending preceding and during the crash. Therefore, it was not sufficient to rely on the natural forces of recovery to eliminate the deficit: surgical operations were needed. And unless the government started on such operations immediately, belief in the government's determination to restore budget balance would wither, causing confidence to flag and recovery to falter.

The Conservatives did not actually accuse the Labour government of having caused the world slump. Their charge was that, by breaking its own fiscal rules it had deprived itself of the 'fiscal space' to respond to the crisis by weakening confidence in government's management of the public finances. A government, like any household threatened with mortgage foreclosure, should cut its spending as soon as possible: instead the Labour government had increased its spending. The government was unable to make a successful defence of its record and, in the general election of May 2010, lost power to a largely Conservative Coalition government, headed by Cameron. George Osborne became Chancellor of the Exchequer. In October 2008, Osborne had denounced the growing public deficit as a 'cruise missile' aimed at the heart of the British economy. As Chancellor, he was so vociferous about the dire straits to which Labour had reduced the public finances that people wondered whether he was inviting speculators to do a 'bear' on Britain.[14]

Osbornism

In his first budget, in June 2010, Osborne pointed to the consequences of failure to tackle the deficit:

> Higher interest rates, more business failures, sharper rises in unemployment, and potentially even a catastrophic loss of confidence and the end of the recovery. We cannot let that happen. This Budget is needed to deal with our country's debts. This Budget is needed to give confidence to our economy. This is the unavoidable Budget.

He announced tax increases and spending cuts, which, he claimed, would reduce the budget deficit (public sector net borrowing, PSNB) in a 'single parliament', i.e. by 2015, from 11 per cent of GDP to 1 per cent. Net debt would peak at 70 per cent of GDP before falling to 67.4

per cent in 2015–16. At the same, he specifically pledged to liquidate the 'structural' or 'cyclically adjusted' deficit' (see below, p. 237), then estimated at 5.3 per cent of GDP, over the same period.* The measures he announced represented a fiscal policy tightening of 6 per cent of GDP. The Office for Budgetary Responsibility (OBR), the new Treasury watchdog he had set up, predicted that this would reduce the growth rate in the economy by only 0.4 per cent over the following two years.

Basing his policy on OBR forecasts, Osborne predicted that the British economy would grow 2.3% in 2011, 2.8% in 2012, and 2.9% in 2013.[15] The fiscal forecast thus depended on the output forecast. Actual growth turned out to be 1.5% in 2011, 1.3% in 2012, and 1.9% in 2013, and Osborne had to borrow £40 billion more in 2010–11 than he had anticipated because of the growth slowdown. In 2010, the OBR reckoned that the economy would grow by 17.2 per cent between 2010 and 2016; in fact it grew by 12.9 per cent (see p. 270). Such errors were bound to wreak havoc with the budget figures. PSNB was still over £50 billion in 2015–16: it is now expected to fall to £30 billion by 2021–2. Net debt (in November 2017) was now expected to peak at 88.8 per cent of GDP in 2017–18. Five-year targets, actual or rolling, have been abandoned. The 'structural' deficit has slowly come down, but this was because the economy eventually started growing faster than Osborne was able to cut spending. His cuts *delayed* the reduction of all the deficits, rather than expedited them.

So much for the record. Three questions may be asked. The first, and broadest, concerns the theory of fiscal policy in a slump. The second examines the confusions surrounding the notion of the 'deficit' and its financing. The third is about the effect of the slump on the long-term growth prospects of the economy.

The Theory behind Austerity

Keynesians say that national output falls when there is an excess of planned saving over planned investment. Typically the private sector

---

* Osborne left himself some room for manoeuvre by making these five-year 'rolling targets', leaving it for the OBR to judge whether he was 'on course' at the start of any five-year period.

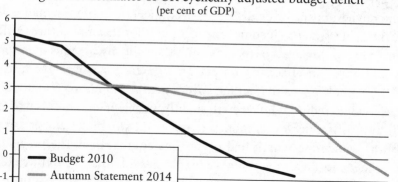

Figure 30. Estimates of UK cyclically adjusted budget deficit[16]
(per cent of GDP)

wants to save more than it wants to invest. To the extent that this creates an excess demand for bonds, the private sector's excess saving will be exactly mirrored by an increase in the public sector's 'dissaving' – more familiarly, by an increase in the budget deficit. If the government now tries to increase its own saving by cutting its spending, the result will be a fall in national income and output until the excess of saving over investment is eliminated by the community's growing impoverishment.

An identical argument can be made in terms of output and income. If output falls below trend there is an 'output gap': the economy is producing less output than it could, there is spare capacity of plant and workers. If there is an output gap, an increase in loan-financed government investment will cause a multiplied increase in output. By the same token, a reduction in the deficit (fiscal consolidation) would cause the output gap to grow – spare capacity to increase by a multiple of the reduction.

The crucial mistake in Osborne's austerity policy was to ignore the distinction between the numerator and denominator of the public debt fraction. He concentrated on cutting the numerator (the deficit) and ignored the effect of his policy on the size of the economy (the denominator).

Although Osborne no doubt had an ideological reason to slash the deficit, the technical mistake was that of his advisers. The OBR's

Fiscal and Economic Forecasts running from June 2010 largely ignore the impact of changes in government spending on national saving, investment, income and output. For example, the OBR Forecast of June 2010 (p. 33) said that the fiscal consolidation would have 'no effect' on output growth. In November 2011, the OBR acknowledged that falling government consumption and investment would reduce GDP growth slightly, but claimed that this would be 'fully offset' by looser monetary policy (p. 56). In December 2012 it was wondering why it had overestimated growth in the previous two years. Its answer was higher than expected inflation and weaker than expected investment (p. 27). By December 2013 it was admitting that 'Fiscal consolidation is highly likely to have reduced growth in recent years', other things being equal. However, with a budget deficit of 11 per cent of GDP 'other things would almost certainly not have been equal' (p. 53).

The OBR never attempted to update its pre-crash estimates of the fiscal multiplier. Its forecasting model, in other words, was a barely modified pre-crash model, in which fiscal multipliers were assumed to be close to zero because the economy was at full employment. This was despite the fact that the British economy had shrunk by almost 7 per cent between 2008 and 2009, from peak to trough of the crisis.

The OBR's understanding of the economy was boosted by three academic arguments.

The IMF and fiscal multipliers

At the end of 2008, with output still falling, IMF forecasters spoke of a multiplier of between 0.3 and 0.8. What this meant was that fiscal expansion could not help the economy; even more importantly, that fiscal contraction would do it very little harm. Nothing better illustrates the orthodox pre-crash mindset that budget operations had no effect on the real economy. In March 2009, at the depth of the crisis, IMF staff reinforced the message that it was safe to start cutting deficits by estimating negative fiscal multipliers of between 0.3 and 0.5 for tax increases, and 0.3 and 1.8 for spending cuts. By 2013, IMF economists Olivier Blanchard and Daniel Leigh admitted they had got it wrong: fiscal multipliers had been 'substantially above 1'.[17] Their review of the evidence from twenty-six countries, entombed in tortuous econometrics and technical jargon, concluded that 'the fore-casters significantly underestimated the increase in unemployment and the decline in domestic demand associated with fiscal consolida-tion'. They found an 'unexpected' output loss of 1 per cent a year 'for each 1 per cent of GDP consolidation'. Their models, they said, had let them down: 'Under rational expectations, and assuming that the forecasters used the correct model, the coefficient on the fiscal con-solidation forecast should be zero.' This was as near as their prose allowed to admitting that they had been using the wrong model. But so had every other prominent forecasting organization. They were all wrong together. On such foundations was policy built and lives blighted.[18]

The Bocconi School

In 2010, the doctrine of 'expansionary fiscal contraction'[19] swept Europe's finance ministries. Propounded by economists of the Boc-coni School in Italy, it reversed the sign of the Keynesian multiplier by claiming that fiscal consolidation would cause output to grow by increasing confidence. The boost to confidence induced by a 'credible programme of deficit reduction' would stimulate enough extra demand to more than offset any adverse effects of fiscal contraction.

In April 2010, a leading proponent of this doctrine, Alberto Ales-ina, assured European finance ministers that 'many even sharp reductions of budget deficits have been accompanied and immedi-ately followed by sustained growth rather than recessions *even in the very short run*'.[20] A key point in Alesina's presentation was that spending cuts were much more effective than tax increases. Osborne took him at his word. In his consolidation plans, tax increases played a minor role; the emphasis was on spending cuts, especially cuts to welfare and public sector employment.

Following criticism of his methodology and findings by IMF and OECD staff, Alesina became considerably more circumspect. By November 2010 he was writing: 'sometimes, not always, some fiscal adjustments based upon spending cuts are not associated with eco-nomic downturns'.[21] But the damage had been done.

Since 2011 little has been heard of 'expansionary fiscal contrac-tion'. We got the contraction, but not the expansion.

Reinhart and Rogoff and the 90 per cent barrier

Two American economists, Carmen Reinhart and Kenneth Rogoff, produced another correlation to bolster the austerity case. They attributed the 'vast range of crises' they had analysed to 'excessive debt accumulation'.[22] They noticed that, once the public debt–GDP ratio crashed through the 90 per cent barrier, 'growth rates are roughly cut in half'.[23] Early in 2013 researchers at the University of Massachusetts examined the data behind the Reinhart–Rogoff work and found that the results were partly driven by a spreadsheet error:

> More importantly, the results weren't at all robust: using standard statistical procedures rather than the rather odd approach Reinhart and Rogoff used, or adding a few more years of data, caused the 90% cliff to vanish. What was left was a modest negative correlation between debt and growth, and there was good reason to believe that in general slow growth causes high debt, not the other way around.[24]

Reinhart and Rogoff explained lamely that:

> We do not pretend to argue that growth will be normal at 89% and sub-par (about 1% lower) at 91% debt/GDP any more than a car crash is unlikely at 54mph and near certain at 56mph. However, mapping the theoretical notion of 'vulnerability regions' to bad outcomes by necessity involves defining thresholds, just as traffic signs in the US specify 55mph.[25]

It is hard to believe that even academics are so naïve as not to realize that politicians and journalists would seize on the actual speed limit rather than the 'vulnerability regions'. George Osborne said that Reinhart and Rogoff were the two economists who influenced him most.[26]

It is important to understand why these economists got things wrong. Technical mistakes in data mining there may have been, but these were trivial. The reason they were wrong was that the forecasting models they were using led them to expect the results they got: fitting the data to the model was child's play for a competent technician. These models were based on the neo-classical tool kit – rational expectations, optimizing agents, forward-looking consumers, unimpeded markets, equilibrium – which demonstrated the stability of economies at their natural rate of unemployment. The forecasters got what they expected and started scratching their heads only when real events proved them wrong.

The main features of the British Treasury's position in 2010 reflected the mainstream forecasting models of the time:

1. Based on the Bank of England's macroeconomic model, the Treasury forecast a V-shaped recovery, with economic growth bouncing back to about 3 per cent as early as 2011.[27] They discounted the possibility of an L-shaped recovery and 'underemployment equilibrium'. In short, they accepted the IMF's position on the smallness of the fiscal multipliers.

2. With a strong economic recovery, gradual deficit reduction would not be contractionary: in fact it would keep the recovery going by giving confidence that public finances were being brought under control. Repairing the damage of the Brown Chancellorship loomed larger in the Osborne–Treasury mind than repairing the damage of the slump. In any case, any minor contractionary impact of fiscal tightening could be offset by monetary (quantitative) easing. These were the essentials of Alesina's doctrine.

3. Confidence was especially important because of the worsening of the Eurozone debt crisis, especially that of Greece. So the Treasury argument was that, provided the government had a 'credible' deficit reduction plan, there would be no domestic obstacle to rapid and sustained recovery, but if it did not, it might well face a confidence-destroying fiscal crisis. In fact, Osborne argued that austerity would *generate* confidence, because it signalled the government was 'living within its means'.

To explain the nugatory fiscal multipliers estimated by the IMF and others, three familiar items from the neo-classical repertoire were trotted out.

Real crowding-out

The American economist John Cochrane wrote: 'If the government borrows a dollar from you, that is a dollar that you do not spend ... Jobs created by stimulus spending are offset by jobs lost from the decline of private spending. We can build roads instead of factories, but fiscal stimulus can't help us to build more of both.'[28] This was the replay of the Treasury View of the 1920s. In his first budget, George Osborne talked about an overblown state 'crowding out private endeavour'. Thus closely did policymaking track academic simplicities.

Ricardian equivalence: government borrowing is simply deferred taxation. Expecting to pay taxes, people would increase their savings. The increased savings would completely offset the extra government spending, leaving a multiplier of zero. Osborne actually referred to 'Ricardian equivalence' in his Mais Lecture of 2010.[29]

Financial crowding-out

The government's increasing demand for funds puts upward pressure on interest rates. The rise in interest rates will offset any stimulus afforded by the extra borrowing. This was a cogent argument for the Eurozone, where the European Central Bank was constitutionally debarred from buying government debt. However, it was untrue for the USA, the UK, China and Japan, whose central banks could be ordered or persuaded to buy gilts to offset any sign of a rise in long-term interest rates. This would enable the deficit to continue without financial crowding-out. In the extreme case (see Appendix 8.1, p. 246), the deficit can be entirely financed by advances from the central bank.

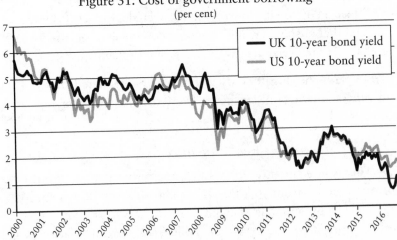

Figure 31. Cost of government borrowing
(per cent)

In practice, the UK Treasury was able to go on borrowing at very low rates of interest, mainly because the Bank of England was buying up government securities.

The confidence fairy

This was decisive for the Treasury. Greek government bond yields rose to 10 per cent in May 2010. As Besley and co. pointed out in their letter to the *Sunday Times*, the risk was that 'in the absence of a credible deficit reduction programme' there would be a 'loss of confidence in the UK's economic policy framework'. Agents with the correct model of the economy (i.e. Besley and co.'s model) would realize that a government which embarked on fiscal expansion was out of control. This would lead to a crisis of confidence, leading to an escalating cost of government debt as fear of default grew.[30]

The analogy with Greece was entirely misconceived, because the Greek government depended on the international bond markets; Britain's did not. The further assumption that bond markets had the 'correct' model of the economy is ludicrous. In April 2010, they had 'priced in' a self-sustaining recovery. By July they were 'pricing in' a double-dip recession.[31] They were the creators of the 'noise' on which their deals depended.

The Treasury's arguments were different ways of saying there was no output gap and therefore no positive multiplier. They are contemporary versions of the Treasury View which Keynes fought against in 1929–31, and which he wrote the *General Theory* to refute; modern restatements of Say's Law. Economics had come full circle.*

At the popular level, austerity policy was supported by a collection of such catchphrases as 'The gravity train had to stop' and 'You can't

---

* As far as I can tell, the idea of bringing idle resources into use by means of the balanced-budget multiplier was never considered by policymakers. The government increases its expenditures (G), balancing it by an increase in taxes (T). Since only part of the taxed money would have actually been spent, the change in consumption expenditure will be smaller than the change in taxes. Therefore the money which would have been saved by households is injected by the government into the economy, itself becoming part of the multiplier process. The multiplier is greater still in a progressive tax system, since the rich save a greater proportion of their incomes than the poor. For advocacy of this policy, see Stiglitz (2014).

spend money you haven't got', which came much more readily to mind than more sophisticated Keynesian arguments. Two exhibits from the treasury of financial folklore resonated strongly with the public.

First, was the Swabian housewife. This mythical lady made her appearance on the world stage when German Chancellor Angela Merkel praised her in 2008 for her frugality, which, she implied, should be followed by business and governments. The latest version of this prudent housewife was produced by the British Chancellor of the Exchequer Philip Hammond in his spring budget statement of March 2018: 'First you work out what you can afford. Then you decide what your priorities are. And then you allocate between them.' This is good advice for households, but nonsense for governments. With its power to raise taxes, to borrow and re-borrow, and to print money indefinitely, the government's budget constraint is much looser than that of the individual household.[32]

The second was the claim that the national debt was a 'burden on future generations'. There are two fallacies in this. First, insofar as spending is financed by bonds, not taxes, this represents an intra-generational transfer between bond-holders and taxpayers at a single point in time.[33] Secondly, if a government borrows from this generation to create assets for the use of future generations (as in the case of a long-gestating infrastructure programme) or, indeed, simply to avoid periods of 'lost growth', no net burden arises for any generation, present or future.

There was a more substantial public finance argument in favour of balancing the budget at full employment. This was that the public sector was bound to allocate capital less efficiently than the private sector. It was one thing to have the unemployed digging holes and filling them up again; another to replace private sector with public sector jobs. At full employment, efficiency issues replace demand-maintenance questions.

Having given full allowance for the attraction of orthodox rhetoric, it should not have been too difficult for competent politicians to get over the idea that 'If no one's buying cars there's no point in making them', or 'If the government borrows money to build you a house, that's a benefit both to you and your children'.

The Mythology of the Structural Deficit

With the onset of the crisis the fiscal numbers worsened dramatically. Public sector net borrowing (PSNB) in 2009–10 was projected to be 11.2 per cent of GDP. The national debt was set to rise to 65 per cent of GDP in 2009–10 and to 75 per cent in 2013–14. It was the abrupt turnabout in the fiscal position that converted the story of Gordon Brown's prudence into one of extravagance, clearing the ground for the consolidators. 'Cutting the deficit' became Osborne's obsession. But which deficit was to be cut?

The basic concept for the deficit is *public sector net borrowing*. This is the raw, unadjusted difference between government receipts and expenditure. At any given rate of taxes and spending, PSNB rises automatically in a downturn as tax revenue falls and spending on unemployment increases; and it shrinks automatically in an upturn for the reverse reason, providing economies with a 'built-in' stabilizer. It can either be a plus number (meaning the budget is in deficit), a minus number (meaning a surplus) or zero (meaning balance).

But there is also a *'structural'* or *'cyclically adjusted'* deficit: the excess of government spending (both current and capital) over 'normal' revenue – the revenue it would expect to receive if the economy were normally employed. (CAB (Cyclically Adjusted Budget Balance) = BB (Budget Balance) – CC (Cyclical Component).) The OBR explains:

> The size of the output gap . . . determines how much of the fiscal deficit at any one time is cyclical and how much is structural. In other words, how much will disappear automatically, as the recovery boosts revenues and reduces spending, and how much will be left when economic activity has returned to its full potential. The narrower the output gap, the larger the proportion of the deficit that is structural, and the less margin the Government will have against its fiscal target, which is set in structural terms.[34]

It was the 'structural' deficit, 'the sticky bit', which would remain after recovery that Osborne aimed to reduce to zero by 2015–16.

The structural deficit is a typical piece of new classical myth-making. It reflected the prevailing orthodoxy that fiscal expansion cannot *raise* the 'normal' or 'trend' rate of growth of a market economy, but it can *reduce* it, by diverting resources to the less efficient public sector. In other words, it comes out of the 'crowding-out' stable of thought. From this point of view, structural deficits are especially vicious since, unlike the automatic deficits that arise from an economic downturn, they are deliberately predatory on the private sector. But for a Keynesian this is the reverse of the truth: the 'normal' level of economic activity set up as a benchmark by the new classical economist, against which to estimate the size of the structural deficit, may be severely sub-normal in terms of an economy's productive potential; in which case the so-called 'structural' deficit is simply the deficit the government should 'normally' run to keep the economy fully employed. It is part of the state's fiscal sustainability, not a derogation from it.

In November 2008, Gordon Brown's Treasury estimated the structural budget deficit at 2.8 per cent for 2008-9. In June 2010, Osborne pledged to liquidate a structural budget deficit of 5.3 per cent for 2009-10. (See Figure 32 for IMF estimates.)

How had a cyclical downturn caused the estimate of the structural deficit to roughly double? The answer given by the Osborne Treasury was that the previous government had overestimated the 'normal'

Figure 32. Estimates of the UK structural deficit, pre- and post-crisis[35]
(per cent of GDP)

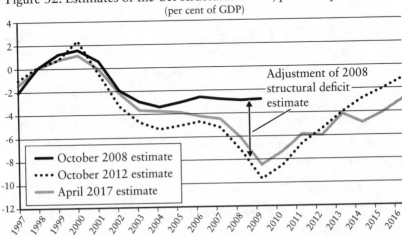

rate of growth of the British economy and therefore the revenues that would accrue from it:

> ... a property boom and unsustainable profits and remuneration in the financial sector in the pre-crisis years drove rapid growth in tax receipts. The spending plans set out in the 2007 Comprehensive Spending Review were based on these unsustainable revenue streams. As tax receipts fell away during the crisis, the public sector was revealed to be living beyond its means.[36]

There is obviously some truth in this. The British economy had been growing in a lopsided way, with the financial sector ballooning while the rest of the private economy stagnated. Labour's pact with the Mephistopheles of high finance ruined it in the end. But the tale of the structural deficit also reveals the flimsy nature of the macro-economics on which policy was – and continues to be – based.

Hysteresis

In a 1986 paper Olivier Blanchard and Larry Summers used the word *hysteresis* to describe a situation not when output falls relative to potential output, but when potential output itself falls as a result of a prolonged recession.[37] What happens is that the recession itself shrinks productive capacity: the economy's ability to produce output is impaired, on account of discouraged workers, lost skills, broken banks and missing investment in future productivity. That is, economic contraction and slow recovery can damage the supply-side of the economy, so recovery becomes a matter not of increasing demand but of rebuilding supply. In the post-recession years, the impact of hysteresis was felt not so much in the continuation of high unemployment but in the collapse of productivity, as workers were forced to move to lower productivity jobs.[38]

Marcus Miller and Katie Roberts have produced a stylized picture (Figure 33) of what may have happened in countries like the UK since 2008.

Instead of supply recovering to restore previous potential output, the economy resumes growth with a lower potential output. This matters for the structural deficit in the sense that lost productive capacity, and the concomitant reduced tax base and larger spending,

Figure 33. Hysteresis[31]

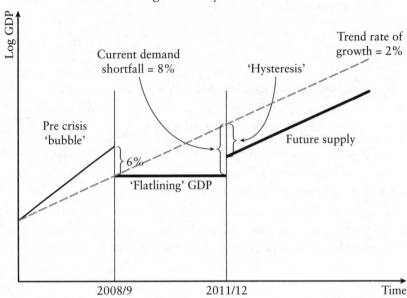

turns deficits that previously were cyclical into deficits that are structural. With fewer people paying taxes when the economy returns to growth, the cyclical deficits will persist.

Figure 34 focuses on labour supply. In the first instance, demand for labour falls as a consequence of an external shock – for instance a banking crisis, as in 2008. This shifts the labour demand curve from LD1 to LD2 with the result that employment decreases from point A to B. Over time, the skills of those who have been made redundant by the fall in demand start to depreciate. This is represented in the shift in the labour supply curve from LS1 to LS2. Even with a resurgence in demand bringing back the curve from LD2 to LD3 the depreciation of skills has left the economy at a permanently lower level of employment, D.

The implication of hysteresis is that any policy which minimizes the period of recession minimizes the loss of potential output. It is a modern answer to the Treasury View.

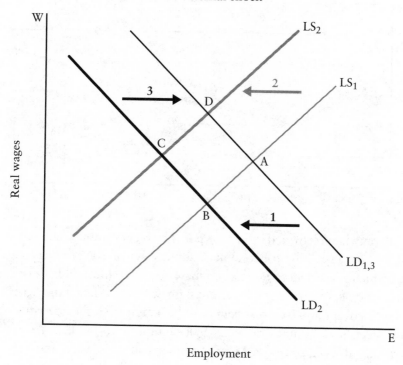

Figure 34. Adjustment of labour supply in response
to an external shock

III. AUSTERITY: A COMPARATIVE ASSESSMENT

The recovery patterns shown in Figure 35 are correlated with the intensity of austerity policies. Contrary to Alesina, the less austerity, the quicker the resumption of growth. The crucial years are 2011–12, when the US continued growing, the UK grew but at a weaker rate than the US, and the Eurozone went into a double-dip recession.

American policy was broadly Keynesian, despite anti-Keynesian rhetoric which was fiercer than anywhere else, except Germany. Fiscal austerity only really started in 2013 when Congress forced spending cuts on the Obama Administration. By then, however, the

Figure 35. Post-crash outcomes: UK, USA and Eurozone[40]
(real GDP, indexed to 100 at start of period)

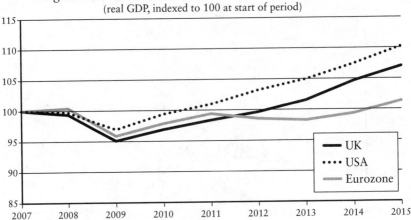

economy had recovered its lost output. The Bush Administration produced the $152 billion Economic Stimulus Act of 2008, a large part of which consisted of $600 tax rebates to low- and middle-income households. In early 2009 President Barack Obama signed the American Recovery and Reinvestment Act. This mandated the government to inject $831 billion (originally $787 billion) into the US economy over the decade 2009–19. Most of this was spent in 2009 and 2010. In July 2010, a report of the President's Council of Economic Advisers claimed that the stimulus had saved or created 2.5–3.6 million jobs, and had caused US GDP to be 2.7–3.2 per cent higher than it would have been without the stimulus. This was in line with the projections by the non-partisan Congressional Office of the Budget.[41] Fiscal expansion was accompanied by monetary easing in the form of quantitative easing (QE). The US performance was not especially robust: the proportion of working-age adults in work fell from 72 to 67 per cent, income inequality widened, productivity fell. But it was much better than in Britain and Europe. It showed that Keynesian policy worked.[42]

The Eurozone has had the worst record, partly because EU fiscal rules mandated balanced budgets, mainly because austerity was imposed on Eurozone governments as a condition of loans from the ECB and IMF. Italy, Portugal, Spain and Greece all experienced double-dip recessions. A recent study estimates that cumulative output losses due to fiscal austerity in the euro area between 2011 and 2013 range from 5.5 per cent to 8.4 per cent of GDP, depending on estimates of the multiplier.[43] Greece is the worst example; the country was set up to fail by a troika of creditors, which forced it to implement impossibly stringent austerity policies in order to receive additional loans, its GDP, in consequence, falling by 27 per cent. The euro crisis was only finally overcome in 2013–14.[44]

The UK is an intermediate case. The British government was not forced into austerity, it chose it. The main impact of austerity was felt in 2011–12. In late 2010, George Osborne was proclaiming that the economy was 'on course' and that Britain was 'on the mend'.[45] The economy promptly proceeded to flat-line for two years. Osborne later admitted that he had got himself 'into a sort of hole: shut in my room, didn't go out'.[46] The stagnation forced a rethink. The fiscal consolidation targets were pushed outward in time; further monetary measures came in the form of a second (and then third) bout of monetary easing, and the Treasury started to subsidize crippled bank lending. The economy slowly mended as the austerity was relaxed.

Jordà and Taylor presented a 'counterfactual analysis' of Coalition austerity in the UK during the Great Recession. Their analysis of what would have happened to the patient had he not taken the medicine (austerity) is shown in Figure 37.

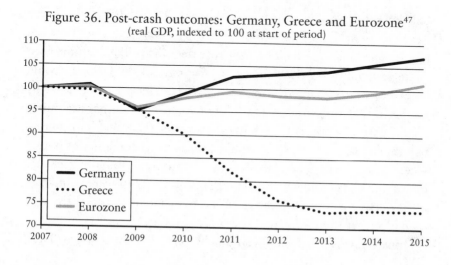

Figure 36. Post-crash outcomes: Germany, Greece and Eurozone[47]
(real GDP, indexed to 100 at start of period)

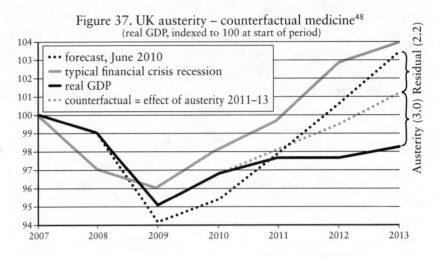

Figure 37. UK austerity – counterfactual medicine[48]
(real GDP, indexed to 100 at start of period)

Simon Wren-Lewis of Oxford University calculates the cost of austerity up to 2017 as between £4,000 and £13,000 per household.[49] As for workers, the situation was worse still. Ninety per cent of the population have not had a pay rise for ten years, and household debt is back to its pre-crash level.

IV. CONCLUSION

One might be tempted to conclude that the debate between the Keynesians and the Osbornians, like the confrontation between Keynes and Sir Richard Hopkins before the Macmillan Committee in 1930, resulted in no clear-cut victory for either side. Osborne could (and did) argue that GDP had recovered to its pre-crash level by 2013–14, that Britain now had full employment, and that the public finances were relatively sound. In other words, the Keynesian contention that, in the absence of a stimulus, the British economy was bound to remain in semi-slump, had no foundation. Automatic recovery forces and the confidence-raising effects of austerity were enough to lift the economy out of slump territory. In different words, there were no multipliers to be had from fiscal stimuli.

However, this conclusion would be wrong, for three reasons. First, it does not acknowledge that the return to growth in mid-2009 was not 'automatic', but was the result of the Keynesian measures taken in Britain and elsewhere to stimulate the economy. The reversal of these measures in Britain did not 'restore' growth; it was accompanied by a reduction in growth by an estimated 1 per cent a year between 2010 and 2015.[50]

Secondly, all competent authorities agree that fiscal contraction delayed recovery, slowed down growth and destroyed growth potential. Headline unemployment in Britain has fallen to just under 5 per cent, the lowest since 1975, but this excludes the millions of part-time workers who say they would work full-time if they could, those forced into precarious self-employment and on to zero-hour contracts, and those over-qualified for the jobs they do. The vaunted flexible labour market revealed by the recession has delivered a sizeable 'jobs gap'. If we take just two categories – those claiming unemployment benefit and those of the employed who say they would work longer hours if such work was available – about 11 per cent of the British workforce is 'under-employed'.[51] The opportunity to use available labour and cheap borrowing costs to build infrastructure was ignored: only 105,000 houses were built in Britain in 2011, the lowest number since the 1920s.

Thirdly, fiscal austerity was partly offset by monetary expansion and a fall in the sterling exchange rate. This is in line with the view that fiscal contraction in a recession need not cause a decline in aggregate demand, if there are offsetting forces of demand expansion. Still, the stagnation of 2010–12 suggests that the theory linking fiscal tightening to recovery is wrong. It was based on the careless view that a reduction in public spending is the same thing as a reduction in the deficit. But if the reduction in public spending reduces the growth rate, as is now generally acknowledged, it simultaneously reduces government revenues. This simple fact explains the disappointing progress towards deficit reduction.

In reality, the only deficits the deficit-hawks really mind about are deficits incurred to protect the poor. The wealthy have never been against tax cuts for themselves, even if this widens the deficit; and their economist friends have been busy demonstrating what wonderful multipliers are available for the economy if governments take this course. To cut the deficit for the poor and expand it for the rich – what more could one ask of government fiscal policy?[52]

APPENDIX 8.1: MONETARY FINANCING OF THE DEFICIT

A government with its own central bank does not have to raise money from the public to pay for its spending. It can simply order the central bank to print the money on its behalf. It incurs a liability to 'its' bank but not to anyone else; and its debt to its own bank never has to be paid back – a debtor's dream! To limit this unique privilege of printing money, the convention (and in some cases legal requirement) has grown up that government spending has to be covered by taxation or borrowing from the public (considered deferred taxation). 'Monetary financing' of the deficit is advocated as a 'last resort' policy only for a 'worst-case scenario', when orthodox fiscal expansion to counter a recession is disabled by fears of rising debt.[53]

Technically, the central bank credits the Treasury with, say £50 billion, or alternatively the Treasury can issue £50 billion worth of debt, which the central bank agrees to hold indefinitely, rebating any interest received to the Treasury. The advantage of such financing is that it will raise aggregate demand without enlarging the national debt – the money the government owes to its holders. (For it to have its full effect, the increase in the money supply must be seen as permanent.) But, as Adair Turner writes: '[I]t is also clear that great political risks are created if we accept that monetary finance is a feasible policy option: since once we recognise that it is feasible, and remove any legal or conventional impediments to its use, political dynamics may lead to its excessive use.' More succinctly, Ann Pettifor put it thus: 'It is the bond market that keeps governments . . . honest.'[54]

It follows that I do not agree with modern monetary theorists that, because the government creates the money it spends, it is freed from the budget constraint faced by the individual firm or household. It is, of course, true that if the government spent no money, there would be no taxes. (But then there would be no government either!) But it does not follow that the money it spends automatically returns to it as tax revenue. As Anwar Shaikh rightly notes: 'There is no such thing as a money of no escape.'[55] The value of modern monetary theory is not in trying to prove that government can issue debt without limit, but in emphasizing that the 'bonds of revenue' are far looser than the deficit hawks claim.

9

The New Monetarism

'The government's real case is that expansionary monetary policy will offset any contractionary influence of the Budget.'
Financial Times, 2010[1]

'The problem with QE is that it works in practice, but it doesn't work in theory.'
Ben Bernanke, 2014[2]

'While monetary policy . . . provided the necessary emergency medicine after the financial crash, we have to acknowledge there have been some bad side-effects. People with assets have got richer. People without them have suffered.'
Theresa May, 2016[3]

'I find it hard to reach the conclusion that, over a longer time-frame, the outcome of our policies has been – or will be – to redistribute wealth and income in an unfair or unequal way.'
Mario Draghi, 2016[4]

The withdrawal of fiscal stimulus in 2010 left only one expansionary tool – monetary stimulus. Quantitative easing (QE) – buying up government debt in order to put more money in the hands of private business – was the inferior substitute for fiscal expansion, and the offset to fiscal contraction. This is the straightforward economics of the matter. It may be that politically it was the only thing that could have been done. But no one should pretend that it was superior. The chosen vessel for watering parched economies was much more leaky than the rejected alternative.

I. PRE-CRASH MONETARY ORTHODOXY

Throughout the Keynesian ascendancy, the Bank of England had demanded that it be given 'operational independence' to prevent democratic governments from inflating the money supply. In 1998 the Bank finally got what it wanted.

The Bank of England Act mandated the Bank of England: '(a) to maintain price stability, and (b) subject to that, to support the economic policy of Her Majesty's Government, including its objectives for growth and employment'.[5] The Bank's Monetary Policy Committee (MPC) was empowered to set the level of the official interest ('base' or 'policy') rate[6] independently of Parliament, a break from post-war practice when the policy rate was determined by the government: Margaret Thatcher, for example, used to veto rises in interest rates on the ground that it would 'hurt our people'. In the new regime, the Bank would control inflation by varying Bank Rate. Inflation-targeting was from the outset 'conceived as a means by which central banks could improve the credibility and predictability of monetary policy. The overriding concern was . . . to reduce the degree of uncertainty over the price level in the long run because it is from that unpredictability that the real costs of inflation stem.'[7]

Having learned from the experience of the failed monetarist experiment of the 1980s, the Bank of England did not directly target money, yet 'for each path of the official rate given by the decisions of the MPC, there is an implied path for the monetary aggregates'.[8] Thus the monetary aggregates remained the most important indicator for monetary policy. The MPC's preferred measure for this was broad money (M4), which included bank deposits. In addition, the Bank retained its traditional role as lender of last resort, a role denied to the European Central Bank.

Bank Rate, less familiarly the 'base rate', is the interest rate or 'price' that the central bank charges for lending money to member banks. The theory is that a change in the base rate pushes the yield curve upwards or downwards. It is immediately transmitted to the inter-bank lending rate. Banks will then adjust their own lending rates, both short-term and long-term. This will affect how much income is saved and invested. In 1930 the Bank of England had denied that it had such power over commercial lending rates, and uncertainty remained about the impact of the short-rate on the long-rate.[9]

The supposed transmission mechanism from the base rate to the level of spending and prices in the economy can be summarized by Figure 38. The channels work as follows:

- *Market rates*: changes in the official rate affect the structure of market rates.
- *Asset prices*: 'Lower interest rates can boost the prices of assets such as shares and houses. Higher house prices enable existing home-owners to extend their mortgages in order to finance higher consumption. Higher share prices raise households' wealth and can increase their willingness to spend.'[10]
- *Expectations/confidence*: Changes in the policy rate influence expectations about the future course of the economy. Expectational effects are unpredictable. Take, for example, a rise in the policy rate. On the one hand, this might be taken as a sign that the central bank wishes to slow down the growth of the

Figure 38. The transmission mechanism of monetary policy[11]

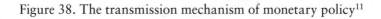
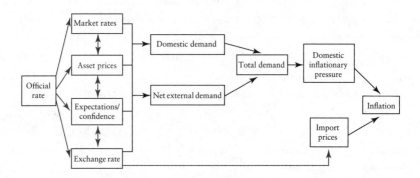

economy to stop it from 'overheating', dampening expectations of future growth. But it could also be interpreted as a sign that the economy is growing faster than the central bank had previously predicted, which might increase confidence in the economy.[12]

- *Exchange rate*: An unexpected decrease in the interest rate relative to overseas would give investors a lower return on UK assets relative to their foreign currency, tending to make sterling less attractive. That should lower the value of sterling, increasing the price of imports and lowering the price of exports. At first glance, this would appear to increase UK output, but the effects of exchange rate changes can be unpredictable. For example, if the change in export and import prices have a negligible impact on demand (in technical terms, if UK import demand and demand for exports are 'price inelastic'), then output will *fall*.*

The Bank's approach can be captured by the Taylor Rule (see Appendix 7.3): when inflation is above target, this signals that spending is growing faster than the volume of output being produced, so the Bank of England should increase the base rate to make savings more attractive relatively. Conversely, if inflation was below target, the base rate should rise.

The framework of policy was Wicksellian rather than Friedmanite: bank rate should be set to achieve the target rate of inflation. But 'flexible inflation targeting' incorporated the New Keynesian feature of allowing for (small) shocks to Wicksell's 'natural' rate. The policy framework also emphasized the importance of policy rules to anchor expectations. In normal times the Bank would 'set interest rates such that expected inflation rate in two years' time is equal to the target'. But in the face of a shock its aim should be to 'bring inflation back to target over a period of more than two years and explain carefully why the heuristic has changed'.[13] In this way the Bank could adapt its policy to changing circumstances and evolving knowledge, 'so that the policy regime as a whole is robust to changing views about how

---

* This is known as the Marshall–Lerner condition: if the sum of export and import demand elasticities is greater than 1, then a fall in the exchange rate will have a positive impact on the trade balance and increase output. Otherwise, the trade deficit will widen and output will fall.

the economy works'.[14] At least, that was the theory. The contradiction between setting a policy rule to anchor expectations, and explaining why it could not be relied on, was never resolved.

The Bank's preference as between inflation and output can be captured by the following 'loss function':[15]

$$Loss_t \equiv \left(\pi_t - \pi^*\right)^2 + \lambda\left(y_t\right)^2$$

Here π represents current inflation, π^* the inflation target, and so $\pi_t - \pi^*$ gives the gap between desired and current inflation. Similarly, y_t represents the output gap, λ is a term representing the Bank's concern with output. If $\lambda = 0$, the Bank does not care about output and will attempt to curb inflation at all costs. If λ is high, the Bank might tolerate higher inflation if this avoids a fall in output and employment. Finally, the inflation and output gap terms are squared to show that (a), deviations from target inflation and output in either direction are equally undesirable and (b), large deviations are much less desirable than smaller ones.[16]

A much-praised feature of the British arrangements was the symmetrical nature of the inflation target.[17] Policy was set to avoid the evils of both inflation and deflation. An inflation rate expected to run above target would indicate that aggregate demand was running ahead of aggregate supply; an inflation rate below target would indicate a shortage of demand relative to supply. Targeting the inflation rate was thus a way of balancing aggregate demand and supply, with the inflation target replacing the Keynesian full employment target. This reflected Milton Friedman's view that unemployment would normally be at its 'natural' rate if prices were kept constant. Varying bank rate to meet a pre-set inflation target was the monetary version of fiscal fine-tuning.

This pared-down version of macroeconomic policy rested on the view that the expectation of stable inflation (together with 'prudent' fiscal policy) would cause the real economy to be stable, barring large shocks. Certainly the Great Moderation years saw a decent correlation between growth and low inflation, in apparent vindication of central bank policy.

But whether the anti-inflation commitment was the main cause of low inflation is doubtful. There was a large downward pressure on

Figure 39. Output growth and inflation in the advanced economies during the Great Moderation[19]
(per cent)

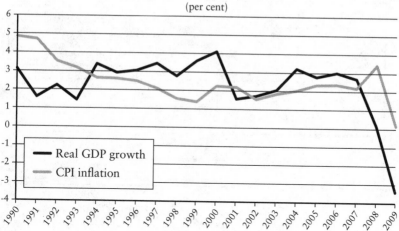

prices following the entry of hundreds of millions of low-wage workers from China, East Asia and Eastern Europe into the global labour market.[19] Mervyn King acknowledges the help from this factor when he talks about a 'nice' environment for monetary policy.[20]

But, with a rogue elephant in the corner, the whole system is liable to crash down, and this is what happened in 2008–9. The rogue was the financial sector. Deluded by their apparent success in keeping inflation low, policymakers ignored the troubles brewing in the banks. With the unexpected collapse of the financial system in 2008–9, monetary policy faced a challenge not seen since the Great Depression.

II. WHY QUANTITATIVE EASING?

The Bank of England was slow to respond to the growing signs of banking crisis. In Howard Davies's words, '[it] lectured on moral hazard, while the banking system imploded round it'. Unlike the US Federal Reserve, the European Central Bank also worried about 'imaginary inflationary dangers'.[21] But following the collapse of Lehman Brothers in September 2008 the policy rates of the main central banks were rapidly slashed towards zero.

Figure 40. Cutting interest rates: central banks' base rates[22]
(per cent)

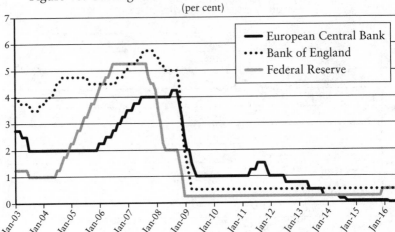

This was the traditional response. With the economy still in free fall, interest rate policy could do no more. An extra tool was needed. Alistair Darling, Britain's Chancellor of the Exchequer, announced on 18 January 2009 that the Bank of England would set up an asset purchasing facility (APF), which would be 'useful for meeting the inflation target'. Quantitative easing had arrived.

Two days later, the Governor of the Bank, Mervyn King, explained the thinking behind it:

> The disruption to the banking system has impaired the effectiveness of our conventional interest rate instrument. And with Bank Rate already at its lowest level in the Bank's history, it is sensible for the MPC to prepare for the possibility . . . that it may need to move beyond the conventional instrument of Bank Rate and consider a range of unconventional measures. They would take the form of purchases by the Bank of England of a range of financial assets in order to expand the amount of reserves held by commercial banks and to increase the availability of credit to companies. That should encourage the banking system to expand the supply of broad money by lending to the private sector and also help companies to raise finance from capital market.[23]

The theoretical case for QE was built on the idea of a liquidity trap.

Figure 41. Liquidity trap

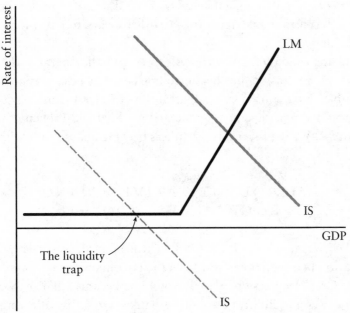

The situation which produces the 'trap' is one in which the expected rate of return on investment (Wicksell's 'natural rate of interest') is lower than the lowest rate of interest banks are willing to charge for loans. The zero bound is the limit of what interest rate *policy* can achieve to lower commercial banks' lending rate. At the zero lower bound (ZLB) the demand for money to hold becomes perfectly interest elastic (expands without limit).* This is because the sense of

---

* See Krugman (1998). While both Krugman and Keynes pointed to the existence of a liquidity trap, their ideas are subtly different. According to Paul Krugman a liquidity trap – and consequently the need for QE – occurs when 'a zero short-term interest rate isn't low enough to produce full employment' (Krugman (2014)). In Figure 41, the expected profit rate has fallen so much that only a sizeable negative nominal interest rate could restore full employment. Keynes's trap, on the other hand, arises when reductions in the bank rate cannot bring down the long-term rate of interest, because investors who expected long-term rates to rise (and therefore to make a capital loss on bonds) will sell their bonds for cash, forcing up the long-term rate. The zero bound is the limiting case, but ineffectiveness of orthodox monetary policy might occur before that limit is reached, because of uncertainty attaching to future

security from holding cash, even at zero interest, trumps the cost of forgone expected financial returns. Once the zero lower bound is attained, central banks must turn to other means to lower loan rates in the market.

QE was called *unconventional* monetary policy because the conventional pre-crash policy of controlling credit by price was no longer available. As a consequence, central banks had to gamble with the Fisher–Friedman version of monetarism which had broken down in the 1980s. Willy-nilly, central bankers became quantity theorists.

III. QUANTITATIVE EASING PROGRAMMES, 2008–16

The Fed was quickest off the mark. The need for large-scale QE was the lesson Ben Bernanke drew from the Friedman and Schwartz story of the Great Depression. Shortly before he became Chairman of the Federal Reserve Board in 2006, Bernanke wrote: 'By allowing persistent declines in the money supply and in the price level, the Federal Reserve of the late 1920s and 1930s greatly destabilized the U.S. economy.'[24] Equipped with this historical lesson, Bernanke and most other central bank governors were determined to avoid this mistake when the crisis hit in 2008. The Fed announced its first asset purchase programme in November 2008.[25] 'Extraordinary times call for extraordinary measures,' declared Bernanke.[26]

In its initial round of purchases (QE1), between November 2008 and March 2010, the Fed bought $1.25 trillion of mortgage-backed securities (MBS), $200 billion of agency debt (issued by the government-sponsored agencies Fannie Mae and Freddie Mac) and $300 billion of long-term Treasury securities, totalling 12 per cent of the US's 2009 GDP. Its second round of purchases (QE2) – $600 billion of long-term Treasury securities – ran between November 2010 and June 2011, and its third round (QE3) started in September 2012 with

---

bond yields. Either trap might justify the launch of unconventional monetary policy, but Krugman's trap became the rationale for QE, because it avoided the problem of having to model uncertainty.

monthly purchases of agency mortgage-backed securities.[27] The programmes were wound up in October 2014, by which point the Fed had accumulated an unprecedented $4.5 trillion worth of assets,[28] equivalent to just over a quarter of US GDP in 2014. In the composition of its purchases, the Fed, as we shall see, was more adventurous than its British counterpart.

In the UK, QE has come in three bites. The Bank of England injected £200 billion of electronic money into the British economy between March 2009 and January 2010 (QE1), and £175 billion between October 2011 and November 2012 (QE2 and QE3), making £375 billion in all, or 22.5 per cent of 2012 GDP. The majority of its purchases were of highly liquid gilts, though the Bank also bought a small amount of commercial paper and corporate bonds. After the Brexit vote in June 2016, the Bank of England decided to resume QE in August.

For the ECB, 'repo' operations, known as LTROs or long-term refinancing operations (designed to refinance banks), remained its main source of balance-sheet expansion until it started its asset purchase programme in 2015.[29] That is, it was bank salvage, not monetary policy. In 2012, the ECB President, Mario Draghi, promised to do 'anything it takes' to preserve the euro. This pledge, which was opposed by Jens Weidmann, President of the German Bundesbank, saved the European Monetary Union. In March 2015, the ECB started to buy €60 billion of euro-area public sector debt per month. A year later, this monthly amount was increased to €80 billion and high-grade corporate bonds became eligible for purchase. The amount dropped back down to €60 billion in April 2017, and to €30 billion in January 2018. In July 2017, the ECB held assets to the value of 40 per cent of 2016 Eurozone GDP.[30] For each of the three central banks, the scale of their balance-sheet expansion was unprecedented.[31]

Three strong arguments backed the new programmes. The first was that they were simply an extension of the 'open-market operations' technique practised by all central banks as part of their normal money-market management. Open-market operations (OMOs) were the means by which the central bank supplied the banks' *marginal* liquidity needs on a daily basis, either by buying or selling government securities or by means of 'repo' transactions, so as to keep the inter-bank lending rate close to the policy rate. However, QE was 'unconventional' in the sense that the technique had never been used outside Japan in a situation in which the *total* supply of liquidity had dried up. Nevertheless, the fiction persisted that QE did not mark a permanent expansion of the money supply, since the bonds which were bought would be sold again as soon as the economy was back to 'normal'.

The second argument was pragmatic: fiscal policy had been 'disabled' by the huge expansion of public deficits in the first six months of the crisis, and conventional monetary policy by the zero lower bound. QE was the best of a waning number of options.

The third argument was ideological. Monetary expansion was preferable to public investment, since it avoided a 'government role in the allocation of capital'.[32]

IV. HOW WAS QE MEANT TO WORK?

Tim Congdon explains the expected real balance effect by invoking Fisher's Santa Claus: agents finding themselves with excess money balances at the existing rate of inflation spend the excess by increasing their purchases. The cumulative attempt of recipients to get rid of the extra money raises all prices to a level at which the desired ratio of money-holding to expenditure has been restored. Thus a stable demand for real balances is brought into equilibrium with the increased supply of money through a rise in nominal income. How this rise will be shared between output and prices will depend on the size of the output gap.[33]

How much extra money will Santa Claus need to spray round the community to achieve a given inflation target? In the Fisher theory the answer was given by the money multiplier: the amount of new bank loans which can be created by an increase in reserves ('base money') in a fractional reserve banking system. If the reserve requirement is 10 per cent, an injection of £1,000 will enable additional loans of £900, leading to additional spending and deposit creation, with the total of new money summing to a multiple of the original injection.[34] If the money multiplier is known, then so will be the effect of any given amount of QE on nominal income (output plus prices).

However, if the money-multiplier mechanism is leaky, the amount of new money needed to raise nominal income to a desired level is unknown. For example, the excess could 'automatically be extinguished through the *repayment* of bank loans, or what comes to the same thing, through the purchase of income yielding financial assets from the banks', leaving the quantity of money (deposits) the same.[35]

Keynes had pointed out the problem when he warned in 1936 that, 'if . . . we are tempted to assert that money is the drink which stimulates the system to activity, we must remind ourselves that there may be several slips between the cup and the lip'.[36] He identified two such slips or 'leakages' from the circular flow. First, creating extra bank reserves would have no influence on spending if 'the liquidity-preferences of the public are increasing more than the quantity of money'.[37] In other words, the effect of money on prices depended on the amount spent, not on the quantity created. In his earlier *Treatise on Money* he had identified another slip. Even if demand were to be stimulated by cash injections, it might not be demand for currently produced output. Recipients of the new money might use it to buy existing assets, such as stock exchange securities or real estate or Old Masters.[38] In this event QE would have to rely on an indirect *wealth effect* on consumption to achieve its desired impact on nominal income.

It was considerations of this kind that led Keynes to conclude that the only secure way to get new money spent in a slump was for the state to spend it itself.

How did the Bank of England expect QE to work *in practice*? The answer is, it didn't quite know. Its chosen route, in the Bank's own words, was 'the creation of central bank reserves . . . by buying outright from the private sector assets that have either a longer duration and/or higher credit risk than the corresponding liability'.[39] In non-Bank speak, it would create riskless cash reserves for the banks by buying their riskier assets.

What, in the Bank's view, would this achieve? In its earliest presentations, the Bank of England specified two main transmission channels from these reserves to spending. The first was the 'portfolio substitution' channel; the second, the 'bank funding' channel. They are illustrated in Figure 42 below.

The bank funding or, more familiarly, lending channel was a

Figure 42. Four key monetary debates[40]

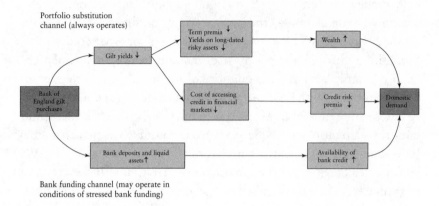

straightforward substitution for the inability of the Bank to get its base rate of interest below zero. As a result of QE, commercial banks would hold significantly higher levels of reserves. This would induce them to lower the interest rates they charged on loans. This would increase their loan portfolios. The spending of the loans would expand the economy.

In practice, the Bank of England didn't much believe in this channel, and believed in it even less after a short period of experience. Only 30 per cent of government securities were bought from banks; the rest from non-banks. The reason is understandable. Given the impairment of banks' balance sheets, and the collapse in the confidence of borrowers, there was not much hope for a rapid increase in bank lending. Therefore QE1 was explicitly designed to get round the banking system, not through it.

The Bank of England (like the Fed, but unlike the ECB) put its main hopes in portfolio rebalancing/substitution. This was to be activated by buying government bonds from private investors, like pension funds and insurance companies. As the Bank put it:

> Insofar as investors regard other assets – such as corporate bonds and equities – as closer substitutes for government bonds than money, we might expect them to re-balance their portfolio towards these assets if their money holdings are boosted by temporary bond purchases . . . This would tend to put upward pressure on the prices of those assets.[41]

Keynes had thought that if bond yields fell too low, people would prefer to hold cash than buy bonds. But the Bank reasoned that a policy aimed at reducing the excess demand for bonds would cause investors to switch not to cash but to financial assets like equities, which promised higher, if riskier, returns. The increase in the paper wealth of the new asset holders would encourage them to spend more.* In other words, the Bank, following Friedman's lead, implicitly jettisoned the speculative demand for money from Keynes's liquidity preference function. The desire for liquid assets might go up, but there would be no leakage from the circular flow of money.

As time went on, the Bank discovered extra channels. In particular, it started to attach increasing importance to the effect of its *announcements* in activating the required responses. At first it hoped to take advantage of their 'surprise' effect. When it discovered that the surprise soon wore off, it started to emphasize signalling and 'forward-guidance'. When the Bank acts, its actions give clues to what it will do in the future, and these clues are signals; 'forward-guidance' is an explicit commitment to act in a certain way under specified conditions. In its most explicit form, the forward-guidance channel works through policymakers making long-term commitments to keep interest rates exceptionally low. The policy boasts a placebo effect – self-fulfilling prophecies producing a recovery without undertaking the significant risks of expanding the central bank's balance sheet.

Hence, the commitment to continue the low bank rate and asset purchases for a definite length of time was considered crucial to achieving the hoped-for effect of the policy, i.e. raising the inflation rate. Like similar pronouncements from the Treasury concerning time-limited deficit-reduction targets, signalling and forward-guidance were attempts to boost the credibility of the policy.

In 2013, Mark Carney, the new Governor of the Bank of England, signalled the Bank's intention to keep bank rate at its then current level of 0.5 per cent until unemployment had fallen to 7 per cent.

---

* The Bank also bought a modest amount of commercial paper and corporate bonds. The reason for these interventions was to increase liquidity in the money-market. The following year, as the Bank became satisfied with the level of liquidity achieved, these assets were resold.

As the BBC explained:

The Bank can only directly control the short-term interest rate. But this rate has already been cut to the lowest level that the Bank feels comfortable with ... another way for the Bank to support the economy has been to offer this indicator, by which companies and mortgage borrowers can estimate for how long such low interest rates may be around for in terms of months or years. Forward guidance is thus a way of converting low short-term interest rates into lower long-term interest rates. The thinking is that if the High Street banks can be convinced that they will be able to borrow overnight from the Bank of England at just 0.5% for many nights – indeed many months or years – to come, then they will hopefully be willing to lend money out to the rest of us for the longer term at a commensurately lower interest rate as well.[42]

There is a trade-off between credibility and pragmatism. Bank Rate was kept at 0.5 per cent until August 2016, even though British unemployment had been below 7 per cent for the previous two years. However, commitments to keep a policy in place for a period of time cease to be credible if circumstances point to a change of policy. In October 2017 base rates started to come off the floor for the first time since the crisis began. How long it will be before they reach what is regarded as normal depends on the momentum of recovery, about which no one can be certain. However, it could be argued that the emergency short-term rate of close to zero set in the winter of 2008 is now well below the equilibrium rate for a recovered economy – its only effect being to sustain 'zombie' companies which should exit economic life.

It should be noted that the explicit purpose of the whole exercise was to *raise* inflation to its target of 2 per cent. In fact, the expectation of higher inflation was a crucial part of the mechanism for increasing spending: if households and firms expect prices to go up (or, equivalently, the real rate of interest to fall) they will increase their current purchases of goods and machinery to get them at a cheaper price. Who would not buy today, if they expect higher prices tomorrow? However, if higher prices were expected to boost investment, it was soon realized that, if this was achieved, inflation would depress consumption by increasing goods' prices. As far as increasing output was concerned, raising the rate of inflation was a double-edged sword.

V. ASSESSMENT

How does one assess the achievement of QE? As with any assessment of policy, a fundamental problem lies in the difficulty, indeed impossibility, of isolating the impact of the policy from contamination by external factors. It is relatively easy to evaluate the impact of QE on financial variables such as interest rates, bond rates, stock exchange prices, and so on. But what is the effect of such changes on real GDP? There is no particular virtue in achieving financial targets as such. It matters not whether interest rates or asset prices go up or down, except in terms of their effects on output and employment. These financial events were simply transmission mechanisms to the real economy. If they fail to transmit recovery the policy is useless.

In Figure 43, the dark grey bubbles are what the authorities wanted to achieve through QE, while the effect of the medium grey bubbles is indeterminate. What they didn't want were the light grey bubbles: for banks to sit on their reserves and not lend; and for investors to buy financial assets and not spend. There was clearly a risk of asset bubbles, but the Bank hoped that an asset boom would produce increased capital investment and consumer spending through a wealth effect. In this 2013 assessment of Britain's experience of QE there were five light grey bubbles and only three dark grey ones.

The Portfolio Rebalancing Channel

This channel was supposed to work, in the first place, by depressing the yield of gilts. This would induce holders of gilts to switch to equities: 'If QE successfully raised equity and corporate bond prices, we might expect firms to respond by making more use of capital markets to raise funds. In other words, there would be a positive effect of QE on the quantity of debt and equity raised, as well as its price.'[43]

Joyce et al. estimate that the first (£200 million) wave of the Bank

Figure 43. Good and bad outcomes of QE[44]

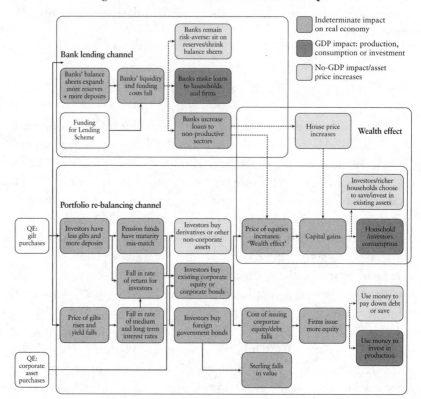

of England's asset purchases, from March 2009 to January 2010, reduced gilt yields by around 1 per cent, comparable to a 1 per cent reduction in short-term rates.[45] Meaning and Warren (2015) estimate that the total £375 billion of QE reduced yields by around 0.25 per cent through the effects of increased supply of bonds alone (i.e. excluding expectational effects).[46] This lowered borrowing costs throughout the economy. The fall in the cost of government borrowing, and interest payments on the national debt, improved the fiscal numbers, enabling budgetary policy to be somewhat looser than it would otherwise have been, given the commitment to austerity. And it lowered, at least temporarily, the cost of finance for companies, which had spiked dramatically in 2008–9.[47] External MPC member David Miles believes that 'a significant part of the fall in spreads on sterling corporate bonds is specifically linked to the Bank of England's purchases of gilts'.[48]

Over the period from 4 March 2009 to 22 January 2010, the FTSE index rose by 50 per cent. But so did the Euro Stoxx 50 and the German Dax without the benefit of QE. Even the Bank of England, hardly a disinterested observer, concedes that it 'would be heroic to attribute all of these gains to QE'.[49] Nevertheless, 'the evidence is consistent with [a portfolio rebalancing channel] effect', though it is 'impossible to know what would have happened in the absence of QE'.[50] The equity and housing markets recovered much more quickly than the rest of the economy, but there is no way of showing how much of this was due to QE.

The Bank Lending Channel

What is clearer is that QE failed to stimulate bank lending. While commercial bank reserves at the Bank of England ('narrow money') rose dramatically (from £30 billion in March 2009 to over £300 billion by the end of November 2013),[51] the annual growth rate of bank lending fell from 17.6 per cent in February 2009 to negative in September 2010 (Figure 44). Theory tells us why. The private sector was increasing its saving. Banks were less willing to lend, and firms and households to borrow. The increase in central bank cash was not nearly enough to offset the huge rise in liquidity preference. Even Mario Draghi, the President of the ECB, was forced to admit that the monetary expansion would fail to unblock the bank lending channel if 'banks . . . hold on to precautionary balances'.[52]

The consensus view is that the modest recovery in UK bank lending in 2012 was mostly due to the government subsidizing programmes like Funding for Lending and Help to Buy, which were fiscal rather than monetary policies. Funding for Lending was introduced in July 2012, and Help to Buy in April 2013. The first was 'designed to incentivise banks and building societies to boost their lending to UK households and private non-financial corporations (PNFCs) . . . by

Figure 44. Growth in UK bank (M4) lending[53]
(per cent)

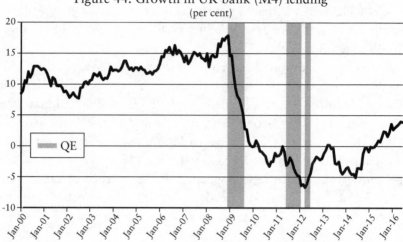

providing funding to banks and building societies . . . with both the price and quantity of funding provided linked to their performance in lending to the real economy'.[54] The second was designed to help people with as little as a 5 per cent deposit to buy a home; the government encouraged banks to approve such mortgage requests by guaranteeing the repayment of a percentage of the loan. But to this day bank lending is well below the historical average.

The failure of QE to revive bank lending has led to even more unconventional policy. In January 2017, Mario Draghi started taxing 'excess' reserves held by commercial banks at the ECB in order to encourage them to lend. There is a limit to this – commercial banks will turn to other methods of storing money if it becomes expensive to store reserves at the central bank. In early 2016, the Bavarian Banking Association recommended that its member banks start stockpiling physical cash.[55]

The dilemma is straightforward. If negative rates on central bank reserves do not feed into lending rates, they are useless; if they do, they will hit banks' profitability unless banks start charging depositors interest for holding their money in banks as well.[56] If this happens, there will be a flight into strong-boxes.[57]

The Exchange Rate Channel

The Bank supposed that part of the extra cash it pumped into the economy would be used to buy foreign securities, forcing down the exchange rate and thus enlarging export demand.

Figure 45 shows that the fall in the sterling exchange rate preceded QE; further, it only very temporarily improved the current account balance.[58]

The Signalling Channel

It is hard to gauge the impact of signalling. A number of analyses have used 'event study' methodology, inspired by the efficient market hypothesis. This asserts that market prices adjust to 'news' rather than actual events. Using this method, researchers have discovered announcement effects on bond yields, currency and equity prices.[59] But those committed to the 'surprise' theory of market behaviour are bound to conclude that central bank announcements will be subject to diminishing returns, and this seems to have been the case. Market participants, having accustomed themselves to unconventional

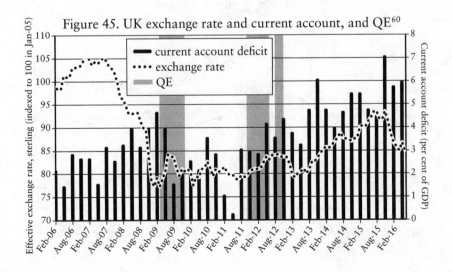

Figure 45. UK exchange rate and current account, and QE[60]

monetary policy, became increasingly acute in guessing the size and timing of the next wave. As a consequence, QE2 had much less impact than QE1. However, central banks played the strategic game. By announcing changes in the composition of purchases, like the Fed's 'Operation Twist' and the Bank of England's decision to 'increase the amount of shorter dated securities', they were able to surprise investors and continue, at least in their own view, to make impacts on yield curves.[61]

Through the four channels above, the injection of narrow money (M1) was supposed to influence the movement of broad money and, through broad money, growth in nominal GDP.

Broad Money

Broad money is largely synonymous with bank lending. As we have seen, bank reserves went up while bank lending fell. The same story can be told with broad money.

The presumed relationship between narrow money and broad money (the money multiplier) never emerged, because the decrease in velocity of circulation offset the effect of QE. 'I accept that the

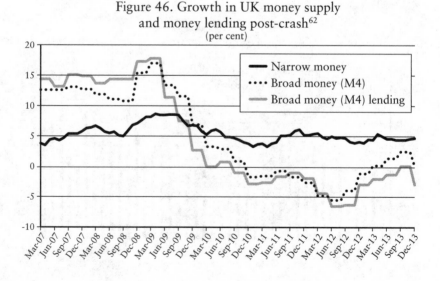

Figure 46. Growth in UK money supply
and money lending post-crash[62]
(per cent)

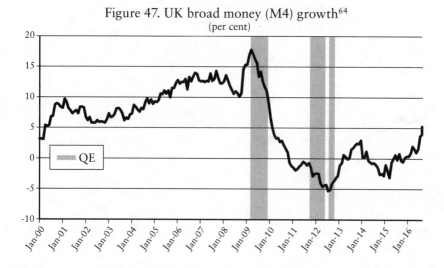

Figure 47. UK broad money (M4) growth[64]
(per cent)

growth of money in the QE period has been much lower than I had been hoping,' wrote Tim Congdon to the author. 'Nevertheless, it has stopped a much worse recession.'

Effect on Output and Unemployment

The Bank of England estimated that the level of real GDP was boosted 1.5–2 per cent by QE1.[64] There is huge uncertainty about this: we can be reasonably confident about the sign of the effect but not its magnitude. What is clear from the table overleaf is that the monetary injection over the period 2009–12 far from offset the depressing effects of fiscal policy, as the Treasury had expected.

In 2012, the Bank of England stated that: 'Without the Bank's asset purchases, most people in the United Kingdom would have been worse off ... Unemployment would have been higher. Many more companies would have gone out of business.'[65] It is impossible to say.

In a 2016 assessment, the Bank concluded that it was not asset purchases as such which boosted activity, but their effect on sentiment.[66] Keynes, too, had written that 'a monetary policy ... may prove easily successful if it appeals to public opinion as being reasonable and

Figure 48. UK output and unemployment[67]

Year	Real GDP growth (%)	Unemployment (%)
2005	3.0	4.8
2006	2.5	5.4
2007	2.4	5.3
2008	−0.5	5.7
2009	−4.2	7.6
2010	1.7	7.9
2011	1.5	8.1
2012	1.5	8.0
2013	2.1	7.6
2014	3.1	6.2
2015	2.3	5.4
2016	1.8	4.9

practicable and in the public interest, rooted in strong conviction, and promoted by an authority unlikely to be superseded'.[68]

Effect on Inflation

QE was meant to have a joint effect on prices and output, but there was considerable confusion about the relationship between the two. Was it the effect on output that was supposed to bring inflation up to target? Or was it the rise in inflation (more accurately, the expected rise in inflation) which was supposed to lift output? Targeting inflation presupposed that inflation governed output: people would spend more because they expected prices to go up. This is how the real balance effect was supposed to work. Keynesians reversed the causality: it was people spending more that caused prices to go up. Therefore the target should have been output, not inflation; and the tool fiscal policy, not monetary. The Bank's failure to boost inflation (except possibly in the first bout of QE) was due to a deficiency of aggregate spending.

Who was right? Figure 49 shows that the period 2008–16 demonstrated no better correlation between money (narrow or broad) and

Figure 49. UK CPI inflation and QE[69]
(per cent)

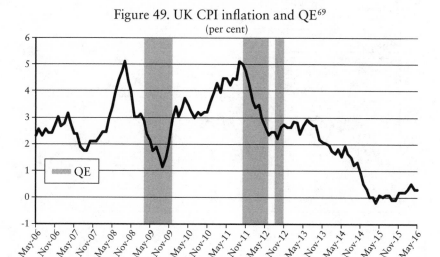

inflation than did the monetarist experiment of the 1980s. The best correlation during the Great Recession was with oil prices (Figure 50).

The Keynesian conclusion is clear. The inability of QE to get inflation up to target 'in the medium term' was due to the government's failure to get output up to trend in the short-term. This was true not just of the UK. The Bank of Japan has been using QE for nearly four years without getting inflation anywhere near its 2 per cent target. In the circumstances Governor Haruhiko Kuroda's pledge to deliberately overshoot the target in order to raise inflation expectations was somewhat lacking in credibility.

Distributional Effects

The effects of QE were supposed to be distributionally neutral. It wouldn't be true to say that savers were bound to lose and asset-holders bound to gain from QE, as many savers own pension funds. Nevertheless, the balance of gain went to the rich. The median or typical household in UK held only around £1,500 of gross assets, while the top 5 per cent of households held an average of £175,000, or around 40 per cent, of the financial assets of the household sector held outside pension funds.[70] By enriching the already wealthy, QE

Figure 50. Oil prices and UK CPI inflation[71]

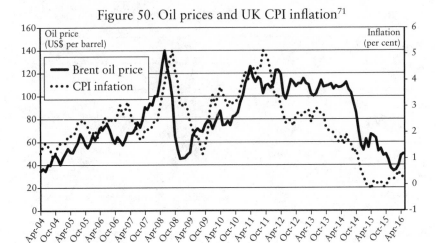

Figure 51. Distribution of UK household financial assets, 2011[72]
(sterling, thousands)

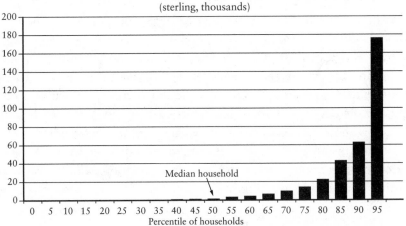

increased the well-documented concentration of private wealth in ever fewer hands. But richer households have a much lower marginal propensity to consume – that is, they spend a lower proportion of new income than poorer people. So enriching the already wealthy had a much smaller impact on overall spending than if the same amount of money had gone to lower-income groups.

This distributional effect is not a generic consequence of QE but of the way it was done. The political neutrality of the Bank was thought to be its great advantage in conducting macroeconomic policy, because it would not be tempted to direct money for political ends, i.e. to secure the re-election of the government. In a speech at the LSE in 2017, Mark Carney repeatedly claimed that the central bank was an agent of 'the people'.[73] But the chain of accountability is not clear. Theoretically, the central bank acts on a mandate from the government, which depends on renewable popular support. This larger accountability is jammed, though, because only a small group of insiders understands the technique of monetary policy. In practice, the bank's accountability is to the financial system, which means to existing asset owners.

USA and Eurozone

Let's look again at the diverging recovery rates between the UK, USA and the Eurozone. In the last chapter it was suggested that these can be correlated with the impact of fiscal policy. Can we find a similar relationship with monetary policy? Or, more plausibly, was it the combination of the two which explains the different outcomes?

There is general agreement that QE was more successful in the United States than in the UK, and less successful in the Eurozone than in either. The broad explanation for these discrepancies is that there was more 'stimulus' from *both* fiscal and monetary policy in the

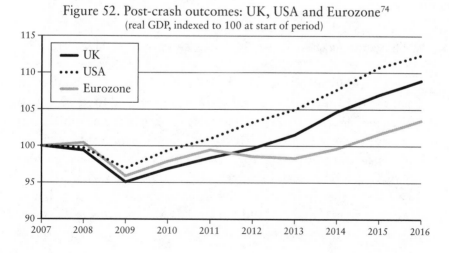

Figure 52. Post-crash outcomes: UK, USA and Eurozone[74]
(real GDP, indexed to 100 at start of period)

USA than in the UK, and more stimulus from monetary policy in the UK than in Europe.

Studies of US 'credit easing' show that it achieved a bigger 'bang per buck' than asset purchases in the UK. Whereas in the first round of QE in both countries (2008/9–10) the Fed injected only half the amount of money relative to GDP as the Bank of England (7 per cent to 14 per cent), it is estimated that the injection had double the effect on GDP (4 per cent as against 1.5–2 per cent).[75] If this is so, the probable reason is that the Fed's QE programme was overwhelmingly targeted at the most distressed parts of the financial system and purchased riskier mortgage-backed securities, whereas the Bank of England bought virtually only Treasury gilts. However, one cannot segregate this supposedly 'bigger bang per buck' from the simultaneous $800 billion fiscal stimulus enacted by President Obama in February 2009. What seems clear enough is that the US authorities, both monetary and fiscal, were together willing to take bolder action to get the US economy moving again than those in the UK and the Eurozone.

The euro was afflicted by two original sins – the disconnect between fiscal and monetary policy and its neo-liberal monetary constitution. The European Central Bank was technically debarred from buying government debt. As a result, the monetary response to the crisis can be summarized as 'too little, too late'. Its first response to the storm signals was actually to *raise* interest rates in July 2008. It was then slower than the Bank of England and the Fed to cut them as the Great Recession unfurled. Similarly, it only arrived at QE on the UK and US scale in 2015.

The consequences of the ECB's passivity before then were dire. Whereas in the UK monetary policy was used deliberately to offset the effects of fiscal austerity, in the EU there was no offsetting action from the ECB. By 2011 US real GDP had recovered to its pre-crash levels; the UK followed in 2013, but the Eurozone not until 2015, after suffering a double-dip recession. Only since 2015, with the Juncker investment programme (see above p. 257), have expansionary monetary and fiscal instruments both come into play.

Why was the ECB was so slow to act? The three central banks have somewhat different mandates but this was not decisive.[76] A more important institutional constraint was that the ECB's rules forbade it from holding more than a third of any specific bond issue, or more than a third of any one country's debt. Without a single eurobond jointly guaranteed by all members, this limitation was inevitable.

An even more important explanation is the ECB's misreading of the crisis. It saw it as temporary – in February 2008, ECB President Jean-Claude Trichet was warning of the risk of an inflationary spiral.[77] This partly reflected the theoretical framework of the day in which inflation was seen as the main obstacle to steady state, market-led economic growth. In addition, until the sovereign debt crisis hit the Eurozone in 2010, the financial impact of the US collapse was limited. But the ECB's passivity also reflected a particular historical mindset. For the ECB, heir to the Bundesbank, the supreme danger to avoid was a repetition of the hyperinflation of the early 1920s. By contrast, it was the Great Depression of 1929–32, and the need to avoid a repeat of that, which had the biggest historical impact on Ben Bernanke and other US policymakers.

Governments whose policies fail to achieve their promised results *always* claim that they were pursuing policies that would have succeeded had it not been for unexpected 'headwinds'. Thus MPC member Spencer Dale, speaking in 2012:

> Some commentators have pointed to the weakness of growth over the past couple of years as evidence that the impact [of QE] has been relatively limited. But this seems a silly argument. The scale of the headwinds affecting our economy over this period – in terms of the squeeze in households' real incomes stemming from the rise in commodity and other import prices, the fiscal consolidation, the tightening in credit conditions, and the fallout from the Eurozone crisis – has been huge. These headwinds have to be taken into account when assessing the effectiveness of the policy actions taken to offset them. There is a legitimate debate as to exactly how effective our policy actions to date have been. But I have little doubt that without them our economy would be in a far worse state today.[78]

Figure 53 below, taken from a Bank of England paper, claims to show what would have happened to broad money and output growth without QE1.

Just as economic models are provable only *ceteris paribus*, so all

Figure 53. Bank of England estimates of effect
of QE on UK growth rates[79]
(per cent changes on a year earlier)

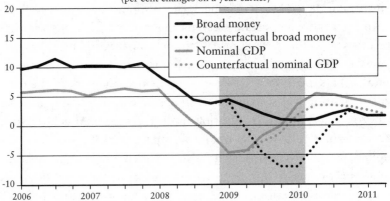

empirical assessments are relative to counterfactuals. But which headwinds to blame and which models to use depend on one's theory of the economy.

Taking his cue from the Friedman and Schwartz explanation of the Great Depression of 1929–32, Tim Congdon believes that the relative failure of QE was due to not printing enough money. 'We know', he argues, 'both that governments can print money and that economic agents have a finite demand for real money balances. We therefore believe that policy-makers can engineer whatever inflation rate they choose. The generation of inflation, and the prevention of inflation, seem extremely easy: just print the right amount of money.'[80]

In contrast, by 2014 the Bank of England had more or less given up on QE:

> the relationship between reserves and loans typically operates in the reverse way to that described in some economics textbooks. Banks first decide how much to lend depending on the profitable lending opportunities available to them – which will, crucially, depend on the interest rate set by the Bank of England. It is these lending decisions that determine how many bank deposits are created by the banking system. The amount of bank deposits in turn influences how much central bank money banks want to hold in reserve (to meet withdrawals by the public, make payments to other banks, or meet regulatory liquidity requirements), which is then, in normal times, supplied on demand by the Bank of England.[81]

Thus the Bank sought to exculpate itself both for responsibility for the crash of 2008 and for the weakness of the recovery.

VI. CONCLUSION

QE offers as good an experiment in macroeconomic policy as we are likely to get, which is not that good. Attempting an empirical assessment of its effects is bedevilled by the omnipresence of counterfactuals. We are trying to compare what happened with what might have happened had policy been different – had there been more QE, or had it been done in a different way, or had it not been done at all, or had something else been done, or had fiscal policy not been contractionary.

So the best we can do is to compare what it set out to do with the actual outcome. On this test the conclusion is reasonably clear. It promised to boost output by raising the rate of inflation, while being neutral on distribution. In fact, over five years (2011–16) it failed to get inflation up to target; it had, at best, a weak effect on output; and it was far from being distributionally neutral. After nine years of emergency money, the financial system remains as dangerously stretched as it was before the crisis, and the economy as dangerously dependent on debt.

Economic theory can help explain why.

The first generation of monetary reformers – Fisher, Wicksell, the early Keynes – believed passionately that the way to prevent booms and slumps was to keep the price level stable. The QTM seemed to give the monetary authority a scientific basis for doing this. To guarantee monetary autonomy the reformers were willing to jettison the erratic control of the gold standard. But they were no more willing than the gold enthusiasts to entrust monetary policy to governments. Monetary policy should therefore be independent both of the gold standard and of the state.

The main disputes at this stage concerned the transmission mechanism from money to prices. This harked back to still-earlier disagreements about the nature of money. Was it cash or credit? For Fisher, money was cash: control of the monetary base or 'narrow' money was key to control of prices. Since even at that time most transactions were financed by credit, there needed to be a determinate relationship between money and credit, which was found in the monetary multiplier. This depended on the existence of a 'real balance effect'. Enter Fisher's Santa Claus, sprinkling the cash equivalent of goodies round the house. Milton Friedman and the American monetarists were Fisher's heirs.

Wicksell saw money as credit, not cash. The key to control of the money supply was the control of bank credit. This could only be done by regulating the price of credit (or interest rate); the terms on which banks made loans. The early Keynes was a Wicksellian; and central bank policy in the Great Moderation of the early years of this century, with its reliance on Taylor rules, owed more to Wicksell than to Fisher or Friedman.

However, Wicksell raised a troubling problem for those who relied on monetary therapy alone to keep prices steady. As Henry Thornton had already noted, there were two interest rates needing attention, not one. The first was Bank Rate, and the structure of commercial lending rates which supposedly depended on it. The other was the 'natural', or 'equilibrium' rate, the expected real rate of return on investment. The task of the central bank was to keep the market rates equal to the natural rate.

This was the point of entry for the Keynesian revolution. Keynes came to see that the crucial element of volatility in market economies was not in fluctuations in the price level but in fluctuations in Wicksell's natural rate. So policy should be directed not to stabilizing prices, but to stabilizing investment. Fiscal policy had to be the main instrument of 'demand-management', since it was spending, not money, which needed to be managed.

The economic collapse of 2008–9 showed that monetary policy directed to the single aim of price stability was not enough either to maintain economic stability or to restore it. The economy collapsed, though the price level was stable.

QE was an attempt to apply Friedman's lesson of the Great Depression, as learned by Bernanke, to a situation where nominal interest rates had reached their zero lower bound. Preventing a collapse in the money supply was to be achieved by what was euphemistically called 'unconventional' monetary policy, but was really just a re-run of Fisher's Santa Claus. Pump enough cash into the economy and the extra spending it produced would soon lift it out of the doldrums. But this supply-side monetary therapy took no account of the collapse of investment demand. The recipients of the central bank's cash either did not spend it, or did not spend it on currently produced output, so 'broad money' – bank deposits – fell, even as narrow money (reserves) exploded. In the language of Keynes's *Treatise on Money*, the money got stuck in the 'financial circulation'. At best it achieved about 20–25 per cent of the expected output gain, but at the cost of pumping up unstable asset prices and producing a finance-led recovery.

The crisis left the relationship between fiscal and monetary policy unresolved. If push came to shove, most policymakers in 2009 would have said that fiscal consolidation would restore sufficient 'confidence' to allow monetary policy to raise the rate of inflation. In fact, confidence was not restored. This left monetary policy 'overburdened'. It was now expected to push up output as well as prices, with no more agreement than before about which pushed up what.

The best that can be said for QE is that it was a default position. Central banks were right to reduce Bank Rate to the zero bound. But the main effect of their reliance on portfolio rebalancing to boost output was to boost the portfolios of the wealthy, with minimal effects on output. One doesn't need headwinds to explain why.

APPENDIX 9.1: A NOTE ON TIM CONGDON

Professor Congdon occupies an important but lonely position in the history of monetary thought and current debates about monetary policy. He can be called a Keynesian monetarist.

He is a monetarist in that he believes that the level of (nominal) national income is *determined* by the money supply, i.e. that changes in the money supply are the primary *cause* of changes in national income. (He also adds 'and wealth' from time to time.) Further, he believes that changes in the money supply have an *equi-proportional* impact on income; if the money supply increases by 20 per cent, then income will increase by 20 per cent too.[82]

All of which is to say he believes in the Quantity Theory of Money. But he is a broad money monetarist. He believes that *broad* money (cash and bank deposits, roughly speaking) is the relevant measure of the money supply. As such, he stands in contrast to Fisher and, at some points in his career at least, Friedman, who thought that national income was determined by the amount of 'base' or narrow money in the economy (cash and central bank reserves), as these in turn determine the level of bank deposits via the 'money multiplier' effect.*

As far as policy is concerned, Congdon believes that (a) the central bank can directly control the level of broad money in the economy, and (b) that as long as money growth is kept stable by the central bank, economic disaster can be avoided. In his account, the 2008 crash was caused by a fall in the quantity of money, and if central banks had simply pumped more money into the economy, then we could have been spared the worst of the recession.

So much for Congdon the monetarist. Congdon is also a peculiar kind of Keynesian in that he takes his Keynes from Keynes's *A Treatise on Money*, not from *The General Theory*. Like Keynes, he believes in the possibility of *autonomous* collapses in the money supply (e.g. following a shock to investment), leading to falls in nominal income, but believes that these can be successfully offset by the monetary authority pumping money into the economy – if necessary without limit. Congdon's spiritual home, that is, is with Irving Fisher, Ralph Hawtrey and the monetary reformers of the 1920s who tried to use monetary policy to prevent the oscillations of the business cycle. But he condemns the Keynesian attachment to 'fiscal policy' as at best redundant, and at worst (the more general case) pernicious.

Thus Congdon rejects equally the fiscal element of the Keynesian revolution and the money-multiplier mechanism of most monetarists. So he is something of an outlier. I have benefitted enormously from my exchanges with him, as well as from his published writings, but I always end up not quite understanding why he holds the positions he does – and so passionately. So the object of this note is to ask: is his position coherent? Are his prescriptions useful?

The interrogation can be grouped into three parts: his use of evidence; the gaps in his theory; and his rejection of any sort of fiscal policy.

---

* See p. 35 for more on the distinction between broad and narrow money, and pp. 258–9 for discussion of the money multiplier.

Evidence, and the Use Thereof

Evidence is of utmost importance to Congdon. In contrast to mainstream work in economics – 'unscientific and shoddy'[83] – he believes that the monetarist approach is on the side of logic and facts, and that the evidence for his position is so 'overwhelming' that monetarism can be treated as a 'true proposition'.[84] So we might start by seeing if the evidence he presents can meet this high bar.

Congdon's central piece of confirmatory evidence is the correlation between the rates of growth in nominal income and broad money over time. In one of our (many) exchanges, Congdon wrote, 'the evidence is overwhelming – from all countries in all periods of more than a few quarters – that changes in [the money supply] and [nominal income] are related'.[85]

Could such evidence, by itself, secure the monetarist position? Surely not. Congdon's claim is that changes in the money supply *cause* changes in national income. But we know that correlation does not imply causation, and in a fiat money economy there are compelling reasons to believe that the arrow of causation can run in the opposite direction. Nearly all money in the modern economy is created by commercial banks making loans,[86] and it is plausible that banks' lending behaviour is caused by changes in the real economy.

Congdon knows this. In contrast to his statistical over-confidence, he recognizes elsewhere that 'the citing of numbers does not establish a definite causal link or prove a rigorous theory beyond contradiction'.[87] Moreover, the faith he has in his evidence is not especially consistent. Indeed, he can veer from certainty to circumspection in the space of a page. In the Introduction to his *Money in the Great Recession* (2017), underneath a figure showing the behaviour of broad money in the 2000s, Congdon writes that 'it is immediately clear that a decline in the rate of change in the quantity of money must have had a role in the Great Recession, just as it did in the Great Depression'.[88] Yet later in the very same paragraph he cautions: 'more research and analysis is needed before strong statements about causality can be ventured'![89]

Interpretation aside, what about the evidence itself? In his contribution to *Money in the Great Recession*, Bank of England economist Ryland Thomas disputes the evidential backing for monetarism. First, he notes that 'the behaviour of nominal spending in the early years of the [Great Recession of 2008–9] . . . did not conform to a simple monetarist relationship where spending follows broad money growth with a lag'.[90]

Such a finding is uncomfortable for Congdon. Nevertheless, he tries to circumvent this genre of criticism by conceding that, in the short-term, the causal link between broad money and nominal income/wealth can break down because of Keynesian-type 'animal spirits'[91] – a notion which elsewhere in the book he castigates as 'woolly', 'imprecise' and 'journalistic'.[92] Similarly, he emphasizes that changes in the money supply determine the 'equilibrium' level of nominal income and wealth, but that actual values can fluctuate around this point.[93]

Keynes's rejoinder – 'in the long-run, we are all dead' – is apposite here. How long or short is the short-run? What happens in the short-run – in a recession, for example – has an enormous impact on people's lives over a long period. Equilibrium theory is no use for analysing short-run fluctuations, since it excludes these by assumption. Yet Congdon has no qualms using the QTM to support his short-term policy prescriptions,[94] even though it is an equilibrium theory.

In fact, Thomas's statistics pose an even more fundamental problem for Congdon. Using data stretching from 1870 to 2010, Thomas notes that there is no evidence of a stable monetarist relationship 'where contractions in money lead contractions in nominal GDP . . . in many periods broad money growth appears to move contemporaneously with or even to lag nominal spending'.[95]

That is to say, changes in nominal spending have often occurred *before* changes in broad money. In contrast to Congdon's view, Thomas rightly concludes that 'the relationship between money and spending within and across business cycles [i.e. in both the short- and long-run] is complex'.[96] The evidence, then, does not prove Congdon's case, as he seems to believe. It does not disprove it either. Highly abstract theorems like the QTM are so enfiladed with *ceteris paribus* conditions that they are neither provable nor disprovable. Thus it is always possible to say that quantitative easing in the UK in 2009–10 failed to boost broad money growth to the expected extent because of a misguided simultaneous tightening of banking regulations.[97] A robust theory should not require too many qualifying conditions.

Theoretical Gaps

Congdon relies on theoretical argument – as all economists must – to support his monetarist hypothesis. Specifically, he proposes a transmission mechanism from money to nominal income/wealth based on the 'real balance effect'.[98] Congdon calls this the 'hot potato argument';[99] it is the necessary assumption on which his theory hangs.

The basic argument is that agents have a desired ratio of money to expenditure. In the event of a monetary shock – if the central bank expands the money supply, for example – then agents end up with 'too much' money relative to this ratio.[100] As a result, they increase their spending to get rid of the excess. The process continues until the excess is 'extinguished by a rise in sales [output] or prices'.[101] Which it is depends on whether there is any spare capacity in the economy, but either way nominal income increases.

The main criticism of Congdon's transmission mechanism is that it is leaky. Take the equation of exchange, the identity at the heart of the QTM:*

$$MV = PT$$

Congdon argues that purchases of securities from the *non-bank* private sector directly increases broad money (deposits), which, according to him, will lead to an equi-proportional increase in nominal income. In other words, it has no impact on velocity. But this simply ignores the leaks. I focus on three here.

Will the money be spent?

In order for the real balance effect to work, agents have to respond to an increase in their deposits by actually *spending* their extra money; if they hoard it, the transmission mechanism breaks down. In terms of the equation of exchange, an increased propensity to hoard is reflected in a fall in the velocity of circulation.

Congdon may dismiss any such increase in liquidity preference as a short-term phenomenon. But quantitative easing has further implications for the behaviour of velocity. When a central bank engages in

* See Ch. 3 for more details and explanation.

QE by buying securities and assets from private sector agents, most of it will go to the wealthy minority that owns substantial assets. The wealthy have a much smaller propensity to spend – they save a larger proportion of any increased money they get – than the poor. The consequence of such an exercise will therefore be to slow down the velocity of circulation, as a single given unit of money will change hands fewer times. The decline in velocity will at least partially offset the attempt to increase the quantity of money. The equi-proportionality condition is violated.

Similarly, the wealthy are much more likely to spend new money on buying assets and on financial speculation. Does this matter for Congdon's transmission mechanism?

What if the money is spent on assets?

In the equation of exchange, T is composed of a mix of transactions that contribute to the real economy, and other transactions, mainly financial. The evidence presented in this chapter gives us reason to believe that a disproportionate amount of QE money will be spent on financial speculation, and not in the real economy, meaning that asset prices will rise. Should we worry?

Not according to Congdon. His argument is as follows: 'a capitalist economy has a range of mechanisms by which arbitrage between different asset markets prevents prices and yields in one class moving out of line with prices and yields in another'. Further, 'over time . . . the hot potato of excess money circulates from one asset market to another and from asset markets to markets in goods and services'.[102]

This assumes a perfect fluidity in money flows between the different factors of production. There is no allowance for stickiness. Again, Keynes's reminder that 'in the long-run, we are all dead' is the right response to this line of argument.

Recent experience does not suggest that asset bubbles simply 'sort themselves out'. Undirected expansion of the money supply, even if its intention is to boost nominal output, risks fuelling the next wave of speculation (cf. the dotcom bubble). Ironically, Congdon's QE, far from restoring equilibrium nominal income, would be a source of further monetary instability.

What if the money leaks abroad?

People can get rid of their excess money by spending it on imports and the like, so that the money leaves the economy. This, though, does not obstruct the equilibrating mechanism in Congdon's eyes. When the money leaks abroad, the exchange rate goes down, which leads to currency purchases which offset the previous leak, in a replay of Hume's price–specie–flow mechanism. Ultimately, this tactic will 'work', in that the money will eventually work itself into the real economy. As Hume said, one cannot get water to flow uphill.

Flooding the economy with money hardly amounts to a scientific monetary policy. The truth is that monetarists have no idea how much money they will need to pump into an economy to lift it out of recession. There is no reason to believe that the private sector's desired holding of cash balances is independent of the business cycle. In short, there is no predictable real balance effect. And one consequence of 'feeding the hoarder' is that when the hoarder starts to spend again and velocity approaches its 'normal' level, a lot of excess money is sloshing around the economy, setting the stage for a runaway inflation.

Rejection of Fiscal Policy

'Forget about fiscal policy. It doesn't do any good to short-run economic activity . . . and may do a lot of long-run harm.'[103]

Congdon's objection to any form of fiscal policy is the hardest part of his position to understand. It is not that he objects to increased spending in a slump. Indeed, he believes that it is indispensable. Nor does he mind much whether it is the government or the central bank which 'prints' the extra money: he often uses the two terms interchangeably. It is to the *government* spending the extra money that he objects. His view is quite different from those of people such as Adair Turner, who have advocated 'monetary financing of the deficit'. Congdon's essential point is that the state should have no influence on the way the extra money is spent. Why is this?

Once again, he believes evidence is on his side. In a 'statistical appendix' to his 2011 book *Money in a Free Society*,[104] Congdon presents data from a number of countries between 1981 and 2008 which show there is no relationship between changes in governments' discretionary spending – the spending which results from cuts in taxes or deliberate boosts to spending – and changes in output gaps. Keynesian theory would suggest that an increase in fiscal deficits would cause a shrinkage in the output gap. But there is no evidence of such an effect. Therefore the Keynesian case for fiscal policy falls to the ground.

But the logic is faulty. The fact that changes in discretionary spending and output gaps are *not* correlated can be seen as evidence of the effectiveness of fiscal policy. Governments tend to respond to negative output gaps by increasing their discretionary spending – all other things being equal, then, one might expect a negative correlation between discretionary spending and budget deficits. But other things *aren't* equal; there is no overall correlation, and so the negative correlation must be being offset by a different effect. The missing link lies in the positive effect of government spending on the output gap, i.e. in the effectiveness of fiscal policy!

Empirical support in favour of fiscal policy is at least as strong as the evidence Congdon marshals against it. Countries that responded to the Great Recession with more extensive fiscal programmes performed, on the whole, better than those which didn't.

If the evidence is inconclusive, we have to turn to theory. And indeed, Congdon appears to reject fiscal policy *a priori*. He writes: 'an increase in the public debt, due to the incurrence of a public deficit, is not an increase in the nation's wealth'.[105] This is rhetoric, not science. What if the money is spent on the creation of real assets, such as railways or houses? Following Ricardo, Congdon rejects the possibility of productive state spending.

Indeed, one of the main advantages of fiscal policy is that a government *can* direct the flow of the new spending in the economy. When a recession hits, private investment spending falls far more than consumption spending, and this cannot be wholly explained as a rational response to a fall in the long-run risk-return profile of investment – 'animal spirits' must be at play. Keynes recognized this psychological aspect to investment spending. In this event, the government can use fiscal policy to maintain a 'normal' level of investment, in order to avoid the erosion of the economy's productive capacity.

Even if the government runs a deficit in order to finance its current spending, it can contribute to the wealth of the economy. This can be explained by reference to the equation of exchange. If the government borrows money from the bond markets that otherwise wouldn't have been spent, and then spends this money, the overall velocity of money increases. Nominal income increases as a result, without any prior expansion in the money supply.

Of course, if the Quantity Theory of Money were the correct theory of macro-policy, there would be no need for discretionary fiscal policy: all the stabilization needed could be done by monetary policy. But the QTM begs so many questions, and attempts to apply it encounter so many 'leaks', that dogmatic rejection of fiscal policy seems indefensible to me on scientific grounds.

At one point in *Money in the Great Recession*, Congdon writes mockingly that 'at the start of the third millennium economists sometimes pretend to be practising a "science" or at least an intellectual discipline with scientific pretensions'.[106] Mainstream economics for him hasn't been 'scientific' enough. When it comes to explaining the Great Recession, for example, the 'mainstream view ... is *untestable*, and deserves to be condemned as unscientific and shoddy'.[107]

My difficulty with Tim Congdon is that he is constantly invoking scientific 'proofs' in a field that defies scientific testing. His scientific efforts arise from a doomed attempt to 'prove' passionately held value judgements. He is a monetary reformer *because* he has an intense dislike of state intervention. As a result he dismisses any evidence that monetary policy may be ineffective and fiscal policy may be effective. Like the monetary reformers of a century ago he turns to money to ameliorate the human lot because he cannot bear to turn to the state.

10

Distribution as a
Macroeconomic Problem

I. THE INDIFFERENCE OF
MAINSTREAM THEORY TO
INEQUALITY

The effect of distribution on the performance of the economy was the main topic of classical economics. Adam Smith's *Wealth of Nations* raised the question of how the distribution of the national product between landlords, capitalists and workers determines the growth of wealth. This was taken up by Ricardo and Marx. According to these economists, the class character of distribution enlarged or restricted economic growth. For example, for Ricardo the rent of landlords was both unearned and misspent; the bigger their rent, the less would be left for capitalist accumulation, the real source of economic growth. Governments were considered to be mainly agents of the landlord class.

With the marginalist revolution of the late nineteenth century, distribution became detached from the macroeconomy, being subsumed in the discussion of allocative efficiency. Replying to Marx's charge that the capitalist exploited the worker, the American economist John Bates Clark, in his 1899 book *The Distribution of Wealth*, used a simple aggregate production function to show that, in a competitive market equilibrium, the two factors of production, capital and labour, would be paid their marginal products – that is, in proportion to their contribution to satisfying individual preferences.[1] Distribution was off the economic agenda.

Recently, discussion of distribution has centred on the fact, and meaning, of the sharp rise in inequality since the 1970s, particularly in the United States and Britain. The most notable contributions here are Thomas Piketty's *Capital in the Twenty-First Century* (2013), a documentation of long-run trends in the distribution of wealth and income in developed capitalist economies, and Walter Scheidel's *The Great Leveler* (2017).[2] Piketty's data show both a widening dispersal of incomes and a fall in labour's wage share since the 1970s and 1980s. For Scheidel, whose history of inequality stretches back to the Stone Age, inequality is humanity's natural condition, interrupted only by wars, revolution, state failure and lethal pandemics. Both attribute the 'great compression' of wealth and incomes in the middle years of the last century to the effects of the two world wars and Great Depression. What Scheidel calls 'disequalization' since 1980 is simply the resumption of normal conditions.

Neglected by contemporary economic textbooks are the macroeconomic effects of growing inequality. This was the missing dimension in the standard explanations of the recent recession. The reason is that standard growth models dismiss recessions as temporary blips on long-run trends.

The years leading up to the Great Depression of 1929–32 and the Great Recession of 2008–9 both showed a large increase in share of income going to the rich.

To what extent was disequalization a structural cause of the collapse of 2008–9? The argument is that the more unequal the distribution of wealth and income becomes, the more fragile – dependent on debt

Figure 54. Share of US income going to richest 1%[3]
(per cent)

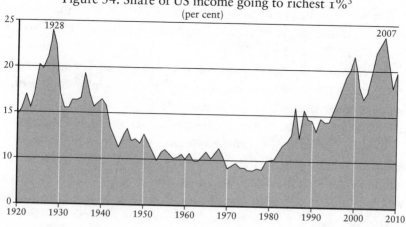

finance – will be the spending base of an economy, and therefore the more vulnerable to any collapse of confidence in the financial system. But first let us consider distribution in its microeconomic aspect.

II. THE MICROECONOMICS OF DISTRIBUTION

The key concept here is Pareto-efficiency. This is a state of optimal equilibrium, in which no one can be made better off without someone being made worse off. Pareto-efficiency is supposed to be the outcome of perfectly competitive markets. But students are also taught that there can be a range of Pareto-efficient allocations – it is Pareto-efficient, for example, for me to have 99 per cent of the income of the economy, because no one else can be made better off without me being made worse off. But there would then be no economy. Otherwise put, Pareto-efficiency leaves open the question of *distribution*: which distribution to have is a political or ethical judgement.

Economists would readily agree that redistributive policies could improve welfare if one or more of the conditions of a competitive market are not satisfied. For example, owners of monopolies could charge more for their services than they would earn in a competitive market. This would be an argument for taxing their 'rents' or breaking up their monopolies. But can redistributive policies be demonstrated to improve total utility even in the absence of such market distortions?

A heroic attempt to demonstrate just this emerged at the start of the last century. The key text was Cambridge economist A. C. Pigou's *Wealth and Welfare*.[4]

His economic agents have identical tastes, but different incomes. Pigou further assumed that the power of an additional pound or dollar to give satisfaction varies inversely to the number of pounds or dollars a person already has, a theorem known as the declining marginal utility of money. A transfer of money from the rich to the poor will thus make the rich slightly worse off, but the poor much better off. The transfer should continue until the marginal utility of money was the same for all. Perfect equality of incomes was unattainable, but the Pigou demonstration pointed the way to a much greater degree of income equalization than would be delivered by even a perfect market. The doctrine of the declining marginal utility of money became the intellectual basis of welfare economics.

This 'scientific' argument for redistribution emerged at exactly the same time as politicians were busy setting up the welfare state to stave off the threat of socialism. Marginalist economics seemed to give a scientific underpinning for policies of redistributive taxation and social insurance.

Alas, Pigou's demonstration failed. Even assuming that people had identical tastes (they all like the same things), the law of diminishing marginal utility of money is impossible to prove, because one cannot compare the marginal utility of money to a rich person with its marginal utility to a poor person in a numerical way. Economists dreamed of developing a hedonometer, described by Francis Edgeworth in 1881 as a 'psychophysical machine, continually registering the height of pleasure experienced by an individual'.[5] The only obvious field of application of such a hedonometer would be in cases of extreme sexual pleasure or fear, unsuitable as criteria for redistributive taxation.

This orthodox critique of Pigou's effort is too harsh. Granted that interpersonal comparisons of utility are rough and ready, we can and do make them. *Obviously* £100 means more to a pauper than to a millionaire; we don't need to be able to say exactly how much more in order to justify some redistribution from one to the other.

But Pigou's exercise fails to tell us how much redistribution is needed to satisfy his criterion. Attempts to secure an alternative scientific basis foundered. According to the Kaldor–Hicks criterion, a reallocation of income could be Pareto-improving if the winners would gain sufficiently to be able to compensate the losers; for example, if it made the economy grow faster. But the link between distribution and growth is too fragile to provide scientific support for redistributive taxation.

In the absence of a firm number, the hope of deriving an optimum social utility function by these routes faded. Redistribution became a political, or ethical, goal, without a secure theoretical basis in the economics of perfect competition.

Paul Samuelson summed up the position as it appeared in the 1960s:

> Under perfect competition, where all prices end up equal to all marginal costs, where all factor-prices end up equal to values of marginal products and all total costs are minimized, where the genuine desires and well-being of individuals are all represented by their marginal utilities as expressed in their dollar voting – then the resulting equilibrium has the efficiency property that 'you can't make any one man better off without hurting some other man'.[6]

Since this situation did not, in fact, hold, the case for greater equality on grounds of social justice or social cohesion was not seriously challenged in the mid-twentieth-century heyday of social democracy. But the lack of a secure economic basis for redistributive taxation was a serious weakness once the political climate shifted against progressive taxation.[7]

This happened with Reagan and Thatcher in the 1980s. Welfare spending entitlements were narrowed. Tax systems were made less progressive to 'improve the incentives' of the already rich. In the perfect markets lauded by neo-classical economists, capitalists and workers alike would be paid their economic worth. In this world, there is no rent or unearned income or free lunches. Or, rather, there was only 'rent-seeking government'.

The theoretical case against redistribution was clinched by the device of the 'representative agent'. We now have a single consumer who is paid exactly what he produces. The case for redistribution on equity grounds has disappeared. Money still has a diminishing marginal utility, but all this does is to give the representative consumer a choice between income and leisure. A clearer example of economics tracking politics would be difficult to find. By 2004, Robert Lucas could say, 'of the tendencies which are harmful to sound economics, the most seductive, and in my opinion the most poisonous, is to focus on the question of distribution'.[8]

This position has, in turn, been challenged from outside economics, by Rawlsian political theory, for example.[9] More recently, sociologists and psychologists have documented the social and psychological costs of unequal societies. Mainstream economics has been largely indifferent to such considerations.

But what about distribution as a macroeconomic question? Is there a pattern of distribution which will cause economies to be more stable, or grow faster? If so, what is it?

III. DISTRIBUTION AND THE MACROECONOMY

In the Keynesian era of the 1950s and 1960s, full employment policies and policies of greater income equality formed twin pillars of the social democratic consensus, but the dots to link them up were missing. The 'missing dots' which make distribution a macro problem are to be found in class differences in the propensity to consume. The rich save more of their incomes than the poor do.

According to the Solow growth model – the simplest in neo-classical economics – the savings ratio should make no difference to long-run output growth so long as the savings are invested. However, in Keynesian theory, market economies have no natural tendency to a full employment level of investment.

This is what gives the distributional question a macro dimension. The higher the saving ratio, the more the investment needed to maintain full employment, but the smaller the consumer market available to absorb the products of the new investment. This dilemma is at the heart of under-consumption theory.

Under-consumption theories – which might just as well be called over-saving theories – have a long lineage, starting in the early nineteenth century and featuring such names as Sismondi, Malthus, Karl Marx and Rosa Luxemburg.[10] Under-consumptionists were impressed by the fact that part of the income generated by production is saved. They then concluded (too hastily) that saving reduces aggregate demand relative to aggregate supply.

Their reasoning went something like this. Imagine an economy that uses money, in which everything produced is consumed, including machinery which wears out at a steady rate. Say's Law holds: demand equals supply.

But now suppose people decide to invest an extra 10 per cent of their earnings in new machines, rather than just replace old ones.

There will then be a simultaneous fall in demand for consumption goods and an increase in capacity to produce them. We have over-saving or over-investment in relation to demand: Say's Law is breached, a depression ensues.

Orthodox economists pointed out that this chain of reasoning neglects the fact that real incomes rise with the new investment, to enable the purchase of the enlarged flow of consumer goods. No excess stocks of capital accumulate: Say's Law holds.

The more sophisticated under-consumptionists understood that saving was not a simple subtraction from demand. They were not against saving as such, but against *over-saving*. Over-saving existed when it led to more investment in new machines than any expected demand for consumables in the future would justify. They thought this could happen when saving was divorced from the desire for more consumption goods, but was an automatic consequence of some people having too much money. The rich have more surplus income than the poor; so the more concentrated wealth became, the more over-saving, and over-investing, there would be.

By far the most influential under-consumptionist writer was the English liberal thinker J. A. Hobson (1858–1940), who can claim to have influenced both Keynes and Lenin.[11] His argument is summarized in his book *The Physiology of Industry* (1889), which he co-authored with businessman A. F. Mummery:

> Saving, while it increases the existing aggregate of Capital, simultaneously reduces the quantity of utilities and conveniences consumed; any undue exercise of this habit must, therefore, cause an accumulation of Capital in excess of that which is required for use, and this excess will exist in the form of general over-production.[12]

Hobson uses his theory to explain the business cycle. In the boom phase, the saving to income ratio rises, leading to over-saving and the collapse of the boom. As the depression deepens, the saving class reduces its saving to conserve its consumption, and the saving/income ratio falls back to a 'normal' rate, before the chronic tendency to over-save starts the whole process again.[13]

In a subsequent book, *Imperialism* (1902), Hobson applied his theory to explaining imperialism; imperialism provided a vent for surplus capital and thus a method for overcoming periodic crises of over-production.[14] Domestic under-consumption was thus the 'tap-root' of imperialism. The surplus savings which reduce consumption at home earn an income for capitalists when invested abroad. In a similar vein, the German Marxist Rosa Luxemburg thought that capitalism required external markets, such as afforded by colonies or government spending on armaments, to offset the deficiency of domestic consumption. Lenin's theory of the inevitability of wars between competing capitalist states, each seeking to export its surplus capital, derives directly from Hobson.[15]

How does Hobson explain the 'undue exercise' of the saving habit? In his books *The Problem of the Unemployed* (1896) and *The Economics of Distribution* (1900), he locates it in the class distribution of wealth and income.[16]

Hobson rejected the marginal productivity theory of rewards to the factors of production. Rather, he generalized Ricardo's theory of rent to cover the surplus of return over cost which capitalists were able to extract from the workers. This surplus was derived from their ability to monopolize the 'requisites of production', i.e. to get 'rents' or super-profits from the ownership of scarce factors of production such as land, skills, raw materials and techniques. This put them in a superior bargaining position to labour; in every market the right of the economically stronger prevailed. The more monopolized the ownership of scarce resources, the more opportunities there were to extract rent. The inequalities of wealth thus created were perpetuated and increased by inheritance. Ever alert to the existence of monopoly firms, economists were blind to the existence of monopoly conferred by ownership of the means of production.

The ownership of productive tools by the class of capitalists was at the heart of under-consumption theory. This meant that the fruits of productivity growth went unduly to the saving not the consuming class. Since Hobson assumed that savings were automatically invested, this resulted in periodic gluts of production, which led to periodic slumps. The remedy was to tax 'surplus' wealth through a graduated income tax and high death duties, and redistribute it to those with a high propensity to consume. That would end crises of over-production and the need to export surplus capital abroad.[17] Hobson attacked low wages as detrimental to both productivity and quality of life, and the high earnings of directors as vastly in excess of their economic contribution.

Hobson thus emphasized class power, but as a contingent rather than a necessary feature of a capitalist system. This was in contrast to Marx, who saw 'exploitation' of the worker – paying workers less than they produced – as necessary for profit. For Hobson, only part of profit was rent: for Marx, the whole of it. Marx's labour theory of value was an attempt to isolate that part of the price of a product which simply provided a free lunch for the owner of capital. Capitalism was driven by the quest for profit, profit derived from exploitation – extracting 'surplus value' from workers. But exploitation left workers unable to buy all they had produced. Here was capitalism's great contradiction: 'The last cause of all real crises', Marx wrote, 'always remains the poverty and restricted consumption of the masses as compared to the tendency of capitalist production to develop the productive forces.'[18] His followers regarded social democratic schemes like Hobson's for redistributing wealth within capitalism as utopian. Exploitation could be ended only by abolishing 'surplus value' – extinguishing capitalists as a class.

The Hobson–Marx under-consumption theory of capitalist crisis is at the opposite pole to the Austrian 'over-consumption' theory. According to Hayek, it is not over-saving but *under-saving* that is the problem. The crisis which produces the slump is a crisis of over-investment relative to the amount of consumption people want to postpone, financed by credit-creation by the banking system. The slump is merely the process of eliminating the 'malinvestments', those not financed by genuine savings. Slumps can be prevented by stopping banks from creating more credit than people want to save. As the following rap puts it:

> You must save to invest, don't use the printing press
> Or a bust will surely follow, an economy depressed.[19]

The Wicksellian root of this argument is clear.

Keynes was notoriously tone-deaf to Marx, but he was much more sympathetic to Hobson than to Hayek.[20] In the *General Theory* he made handsome amends for his previous neglect of Hobson, enlisting him in the 'brave army of heretics, who, following their intuitions, have preferred to see the truth obscurely and imperfectly rather than maintain error, reached indeed with clearness and consistency and by easy logic, but on hypotheses inappropriate to the facts'.[21] His criticism of Hobson was based on what he saw as a technical mistake in Hobson's reasoning: it was to suppose that

> it is a case of excessive saving causing the actual accumulation of capital in excess of what is required, which is, in fact, a secondary evil which only occurs through mistakes of foresight; whereas the primary evil is a propensity to save in conditions of full employment more than the equivalent of the capital which is required, thus preventing full employment except when there is a mistake of foresight.[22]

Hobson's problem, Keynes thought, was that he lacked an 'independent theory of the rate of interest'.[23] He assumed that changes in interest rates automatically equalized private saving and investment, giving rise, on his over-saving theory, to systemic over-investment, interrupted by crises, whereas for Keynes, the rate of interest being the price of money, not saving, the only way of eliminating the 'excess saving' at full employment was a fall in national income. Thus Hobson's was a theory of over-investment: Keynes's a theory of under-investment.

Keynes thought that the most important remedy for the unemployment of his day was to raise the rate of investment, not reduce it. This would require, in addition to public investment, keeping the long-term rate of interest permanently low, resulting in the 'euthanasia of the rentier, and, consequently, the euthanasia of the power of the capitalist to exploit the scarcity value of capital'. For 'interest today rewards no genuine sacrifice, any more than does the rent of land'.[24]

Keynes thought that the problem of securing enough investment to match full employment saving would get worse as societies got richer. The propensity to save would rise (the richer people are, the less of their income they consume) while the inducement to invest would fall as capital became more abundant. In this sense he was a long-term under-consumptionist. Once accumulation was no longer a priority, schemes for the 'higher taxation of large incomes and inheritance' would come into their own, though Keynes was doubtful about how far or fast they should go.[25] He was moderately sympathetic to the ethical case for income distribution, writing that 'there is social and psychological justification for significant inequalities of income and wealth, but not such large disparities as exist today'.[26]

Under-consumptionist theory influenced left-wing explanations of the Great Depression of the 1930s, both at the time and subsequently. The explosion of consumer credit kept consumer demand buoyant in the United States up to 1929; its withdrawal amplified the slump. Typical in its under-consumptionist reasoning is this passage from Marriner Eccles, Chairman of the US Fed from 1934 to 1948:

> A mass production economy has to be accompanied by mass consumption. Mass consumption in turn implies a distribution of wealth to provide men with buying power. Instead of achieving that kind of distribution, a giant suction pump had by 1929 drawn into a few hands an increasing proportion of currently produced wealth. This served them as capital accumulation. But by taking purchasing power out of the hands of mass consumers, the savers denied to themselves the kind of effective demand for their products that would justify a reinvestment of their capital accumulations in new plants. In consequence, as in a poker game when the chips were concentrated in fewer and fewer hands, the other fellows could stay in the game only by borrowing. When their credit ran out, the game stopped.[27]

Under-consumption also featured in Marxian explanations of the Great Depression of the 1930s. For example, James Devine argued that, in the US, stagnant wages (relative to labour productivity) meant that increases in working-class consumption could be financed only by debt. Eventually (in 1929), the over-investment boom ended, leaving unused industrial capacity and debt obligations. Once the depression occurred, recovery of private investment and consumption was blocked by falling prices, which increased the real debt burden. Trying to restore the profit rate by cutting wages only reduced prices and consumer demand further. Devine called this the under-consumption trap.[28]

IV. THE MODERN UNDER-CONSUMPTIONIST STORY

The modern under-consumptionist story starts with the big increase in inequality, noticeable in all developed countries since the 1970s.

Thomas Piketty's *Capital in the Twenty-First Century* documented in exhaustive detail the increase in inequality over the last forty years.[29] Coming on top of the crash of 2008, it rekindled interest in distributional issues in both their moral and efficiency aspects. Piketty restated the familiar social democratic charge against capitalism: that its ownership system offended the principle of distributive justice. But his analysis also led people, eager to explore causes of the Great Recession of 2008–9 deeper than the familiar tale of predatory bankers, to wonder whether the patchy and unbalanced performance of market economies in recent years was not somehow the result of growing inequality.

The fact that inequality has increased is not in dispute. Median real incomes have stagnated, or fallen, throughout the Western world even as economies have continued to grow. Egregious examples are legion. A frequently cited US statistic is that over the past two decades, the ratio of the pay of CEOs to the average pay of their workforces has increased from 20:1 in 1961 to 231:1 in 2011.[30] (For some companies, it is over 1,000:1.) Atkinson, Piketty and Saez show that inequality in the USA fell for decades after the Wall Street crash of 1929 before starting to rise again in the 1970s. Now, the top 1 per cent own over 20 per cent of US wealth. The same pattern is seen in the UK and Italy. This coincides with the transfer of wealth from the public to the private sector. Cross-country studies show that practically all the increase in advanced country wealth in the last twenty years has gone to the top 1 per cent. The rich have raced away from the poor; and the very rich have raced away from the rich.

Edward Luttwak, writing in the *Times Literary Supplement*, claims that the service economy is in fact becoming a servant economy: 'too-busy-to-live high-techies employ retinues of nannies, housekeepers, dog walkers, cat-minders, pool boys and personal shoppers'.[31] Automation of manufacturing will make more and more servants available to serve the rich.

The Gini coefficient for the UK in Figure 55 shows the spurt in inequality from 1979 to 1990. A second chart from the USA (Figure 56) shows the growing gap between mean and median income. (If only the rich are getting richer, mean incomes will rise while median incomes stagnate.)

An important reason for this divergence has been the fall in wage

Figure 55. UK Gini coefficient[32]

Figure 56. Median family income as a proportion
of mean family income, USA[33]
(per cent)

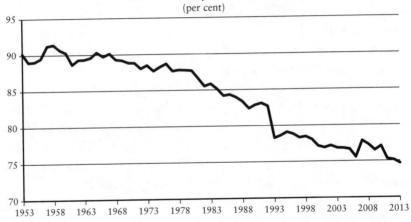

share of national income. Steady at about two-thirds for most of the post-war period, it has fallen to 55 per cent in the last two decades.

The causes of disequalization have been disputed. One of the commonest explanations is the information revolution: the technologically agile have benefitted at the expense of the rest. Another is globalization: cheap labour competition from Asian countries has driven down the median wage of Western workers. A third is the shift in the balance of power from workers to employers. All three might explain

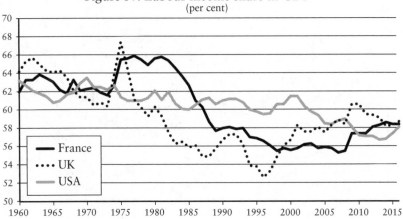

Figure 57. Labour income share in GDP[34]
(per cent)

widening inequality; only the first might plausibly explain the exorbitant gains of the top 1 per cent.

Piketty's argument is straightforward. The growing concentration of capital in fewer hands, for whatever reason, has enabled its owners to keep it relatively scarce and thus valuable. Urban real estate has taken the place of land as the main source of rent.

Piketty argues that the tendency to increased inequality, inherent in a capitalist system, was suppressed in the period between 1910 and 1960 as the two world wars and the Great Depression destroyed a mass of inherited capital, while trade-union pressure, progressive taxation and welfare prevented its reconstitution. But from the late 1970s, with the decay of these countervailing forces, the natural inequality of the system has reasserted itself, so that today it is almost as great as it was before 1914.[35]

The historical record so painstakingly dissected can be summarized by what Piketty calls the 'fundamental force of divergence', which he represents by the equation $r > g$. When the return on capital (r) continuously exceeds the growth of the economy (g), inherited wealth continues to grow faster than output and income, meaning that inequality continues to increase, since there is nothing to stop the children of today's super-salary earners become the rentiers of tomorrow. And the return to low growth, partly caused by ageing populations,

Figure 58. Share of US income going to the top[36]
(per cent)

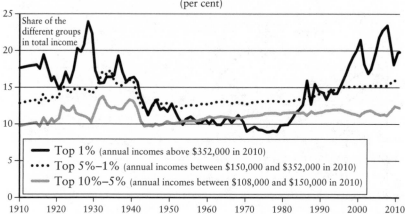

means that inequality will rise even more. Piketty predicts that growth will not exceed 1–1.5 per cent in the long-run, whereas the average return on capital will be 4–5 per cent. (This contrasts with the predictions of the American statistician Simon Kuznets, whose data – dating from 1955 – showed inequality naturally diminishing over time.)

Using large data sets, Piketty presented a U-shaped curve running from the late nineteenth century to today, with a 'compression' of inequality between 1914 and 1970.

It is a sign of the importance of Piketty's intervention that it provoked a furious debate. This has centred on his use of data and his theoretical framework. Chris Giles of the *Financial Times* led the empirical assault, asserting that the raw data used by Piketty do not show any increase in the share of wealth going to the top 1 per cent and the top 10 per cent in the UK from 1960 to 2010, rather the reverse.[37] His attempt to discredit Piketty failed, but it shows Piketty had hit a raw nerve.[38]

The second assault, on Piketty's theoretical framework, was led by left-wing economists who accused him of using a conventional marginal productivity framework to explain the returns to capital. In the words of the American economist Thomas Palley: 'Mainstream economists will assert the conventional story about the profit rate being technologically determined. However, as Piketty occasionally hints, in reality the profit rate is politically and socially determined by factors influencing the distribution of economic and political power. Growth is also influenced by policy and institutional choices.'[39]

Similarly, James Galbraith criticized Piketty's claim that the wage share in national income is technologically determined, leaving governments with scope for intervention only in the post-tax distribution of earnings. Piketty's mistake had been to treat capital as an independent 'factor of production', when a 'social' analysis of capital would have shown that its determinants included infrastructure spending, education, regulation, social insurance, globalization and much else.[40]

Orthodox theorists attribute the build-up of debt, leverage and financial fragility before the crash to 'misperceptions' by households, businesses and banks about the sustainable level of lending and borrowing. This is true, of course, but banal. One really wants to know about the source of these misconceptions. Under-consumptionist theory provides one answer: the growth of inequality. Households increase their debt because wages have fallen, but they still wish to consume as much as before. Governments encourage easy credit conditions to offset stagnant real earnings. Banks and firms become 'over-leveraged' because they exaggerate the profits they expect to make from consumers' debt-enlarged incomes. Governments borrow too much because they over-estimate the revenues they will get from over-borrowed financial systems. Thus excessive credit creation, which the Hayekians see as *the* cause of the financial collapse of 2007–9, can, on further analysis, be rooted in the stagnation or decline of consumption from earnings. 'Consumption-smoothing' – consuming expected future wealth today – is the name of the game.

A key argument in this tradition is that a balance between capital and labour existed in the Keynesian era of the 1950s to 1970s; in fact, it was what made Keynesian policy possible. Strong trade unions were able to push wages up in line with productivity; extensive government transfers kept up mass purchasing power. The commitment to full employment created a favourable climate for business investment, and hence improvements in productivity, and the state's own capital spending policies maintained a steadiness of investment across the cycle. Consumer credit was restricted. As a result, business cycles were dampened, and economies enjoyed unprecedented rates of economic growth.

However, this benign capitalist environment unravelled in the 1970s. First, wage-push by unions led to rising inflation. Attempts by governments to control inflation by prices and incomes policy broke down. With wage inflation pushing ahead of profit inflation, the only solution available under capitalism was to recreate the Marxist 'reserve army of the unemployed'. This was done through opening up domestic economies to global competition. Higher unemployment simultaneously shifted income from wages to profits and brought down inflation, but at the cost of a secular stagnation.

According to Palley, the collapse of the dotcom bubble in 2001 reflected deep-seated contradictions in the existing process of aggregate demand generation. He saw these as resulting from a deterioration in income distribution. The resulting depressive forces were held at bay for almost two decades by a range of different demand compensation mechanisms: steadily rising consumer debt, a stock market boom, and rising house prices. However, these mechanisms were now exhausted. Fiscal policy would help only temporarily unless measures were taken 'to rectify the structural imbalances at the root of the current impasse'. Without this, 'the problem of deficient demand will reassert itself, and the next time around public sector finances may not be in such a favourable position to deal with it'.[41]

Written in 2001, this was a prescient forecast of the disablement of fiscal policy following the crash of 2008. From 2001 the US housing bubble really began to inflate. The reason is clear enough: the Federal Funds Rate was kept at 1 per cent between 2001 and 2004. So borrowers with no income, no job, no assets, were enticed by very low, almost zero, introductory interest rates on an adjustable-rate mortgage, and this fuelled the growth of sub-prime mortgages. Consequently, the US homeownership rate reached almost 70 per cent in 2004. By 2006, more than a fifth of all new mortgages – some $600 million worth – were sub-prime. And a third of these sub-prime loans were for 100 per cent or more of the home value, and six times the annual earnings of the borrower. In the UK, a large housing bubble was also inflating. By the end of 2007, mortgage debt reached 132 per cent of disposable income, with overall household debt reaching 177 per cent.

In February 2008, just before the US economy collapsed, Palley wrote that 'the US economy relies upon asset price inflation and rising indebtedness to fuel growth. Therein lies a profound contradiction. On one hand, policy must fuel asset bubbles to keep the economy growing. On the other hand, such bubbles inevitably create financial crises when they eventually implode.' The need, he said, was to '[restore] the link between wages and productivity. That way, wage income, not debt and asset price inflation, can again provide the engine of demand growth.'[42]

The new under-consumptionism attaches great causal importance to the 'financialization' which serves to 'redistribute income from productive activities to non-productive finance. The rich alone are the winners in that transfer, because it involves no productive activity that might possibly "trickle down" to the rest of us.'[43] Financialization is a necessary part of the neo-liberal model, its function being to 'fuel demand growth by making ever larger amounts of credit easily available ... The old post-World War II growth model based on rising middle-class incomes has been dismantled, while the new neoliberal growth model has imploded.'[44]

V. CONCLUSION

The argument of this chapter is that distribution is a macroeconomic question, because a distribution of purchasing power heavily skewed towards the owners of capital assets creates a problem of deficient demand. The financialization of the economy increases this instability by allowing debt to replace earnings from work. Quantitative easing increases it still further by creating asset bubbles.

The problem the older generation of under-consumptionists drew attention to was the failure of real wages to keep pace with productivity. But a striking feature of the post-crash years has been the decline in productivity, as workers have moved to less productive jobs. Flexible labour markets, greatly lauded by the conventional wisdom, are bound to slow down productivity growth, because it is more efficient for employers to hire cheap labour than invest in capital, physical or human. This has been a job-rich, productivity-poor, recovery.

Moreover, the fall in worker productivity must lead to even greater income inequality, and, therefore (on the under-consumptionist argument), to even greater macroeconomic instability in future, as the economy relies even more heavily on debt.

In Keynesian terms, a situation in which the inducement to invest is falling, but income inequality is rising, is the worst possible basis for both stability and growth. This is the situation in which we find ourselves today.

I I

What Was Wrong with the Banks?

'It's not a question of one rotten apple, but a rotten barrel.'
Proverb

'It should be clear that among the causes of the recent finan-
cial crisis was an unjustified faith in rational expectations,
market efficiencies, and the techniques of modern finance.
That faith was stoked in part by the huge financial rewards
that enabled the extremes of borrowing, the economic imbal-
ances, and the pretences and assurances of the credit-rating
agencies to persist so long. A relaxed approach by regulators
and legislators reflected the new financial zeitgeist.'
Paul Volcker, 2011[1]

'The long-term is what we are going to have for lunch.'
Trader's view

'Shadow banking, financial innovation, and intensive trad-
ing among financial institutions . . . gave us the credit cycle
on steroids.'
Adair Turner, 2016[2]

The brief answer to the question posed by this chapter is that from
the 1960s onwards, governments gradually relinquished their control
over banks and put their faith in market discipline; the banks used

their new freedom to develop increasingly complex financial products to boost their profits, which they sold to non-banks and each other; these little-understood products, which were used mainly to finance real estate booms in the United States, Britain, Spain and Ireland, brought about the crash of the financial system starting in 2007, which spread to the real economy.

I. PRE-CRASH ORTHODOXY

When, as an Oxford undergraduate, I opened an account at my local Midland (now HSBC) Bank in 1958, banking was safe and boring, like my estimable bank manager.

In those far-off days banking was divided into three sectors: retail banks, which took deposits and made loans to customers or businesses; building societies, which made loans for home buying; and merchant banks, which invested their clients' money. The atmosphere of retail banking was summed up by the so-called '3-6-3' rule: take in deposits at 3 per cent, make loans at 6 per cent, and be on the golf course by 3 p.m. Mortgage lending, done by building societies, was conservative, with borrowers having to put up substantial deposits. Merchant, or investment, banks were less 'safe', but in a repressed financial system, their activity was restricted. For example, exchange rates were fixed, so speculation in foreign currencies was small; the financial system was barnacled with capital controls. With tame banking, financial crises were rare, and system-threatening ones non-existent.

From the 1960s the trend was towards freeing finance from the straitjacket which the Great Depression and Second World War had placed it in. The development of the offshore euro-dollar market was an important breach in the wall of capital controls; in the 1970s banks were given the leading role in recycling OPEC surpluses. There was a relentless rundown in both capital and reserve ratios as the appetite for borrowing and lending grew, and the perceived risks fell.

As a result of deregulation, banks became 'universal'. They were allowed to do everything: take deposits, lend to home-buyers and open investment departments. They became more concentrated, more remote from their customers. Capital was set free to roam the world. In the years of the Great Moderation, bank credit gained enormously at the expense of stock market issues as a source of business finance. Banks became part of an international financial network, holding each others' assets. And these assets became more and more complex and opaque. Financial crises became more frequent and more severe.

In Ann Pettifor's summary, orthodoxy handed two great powers to bankers:

> first, the ability to create, price and manage credit without effective supervision or regulation; second, the ability to 'manage' global financial flows . . . out of sight of the regulatory authorities. By way of this shift . . . accountable public authorities handed effective control over the economy – over employment, welfare and incomes – to remote and unaccountable financial markets.[3]

Orthodox economists provided intellectual cover for the newly dominant vested interest.

The government's role was not entirely permissive. Governments also encouraged banks to lend for political purposes. The root of the 2008–9 financial crisis lies in the American housing market and, specifically, in the government's attempts to make home ownership accessible to low-income families. Building on the Community Reinvestment Act of 1977, President Clinton, in 1994, signed the National Homeownership Strategy, intended to help

> moderate-income families who pay high rents but haven't been able to save enough for a down payment; to help lower-income, working families who are ready to assume the responsibilities of homeownership but are held back by mortgage costs that are just out of reach; [and to] help families who have historically been excluded from homeownership.[4]

The government-backed institutions Fannie Mae and Freddie Mac played a large role in promoting the 'American Dream'; over the years, they were ordered to increase the ratios of their loan portfolios in low-income areas. It was the combination of deregulation and government subsidy of bank credit to low-income households which proved toxic.

II. THEORY

Behind the deregulation of banking were three propositions in theoretical economics.

'Correct monetary policy is all that is needed to secure financial stability'

Central bank models were based on a neo-classical fantasy world, with no financial frictions or default.[5] Such a world has no need for commercial banks, and as a result central banks overlooked these earthly entities in their Platonic modelling. In the UK, for example, the Bank of England's foremost macroeconomic model between 2004 and 2010 omitted the banking system from its grouping of key economic agents.

In order to keep the main model 'as simple as possible', the Bank preferred to look at financial issues through 'separate, more specialised models'.[6] But this approach placed theoretical elegance above understanding, and left the Bank unable to identify a burgeoning financial crisis in time, with an ensuing series of inaccurate forecasts and missed targets. The UK was not unique; central banks the world

Figure 59. The Bank of England's main economic model[7]

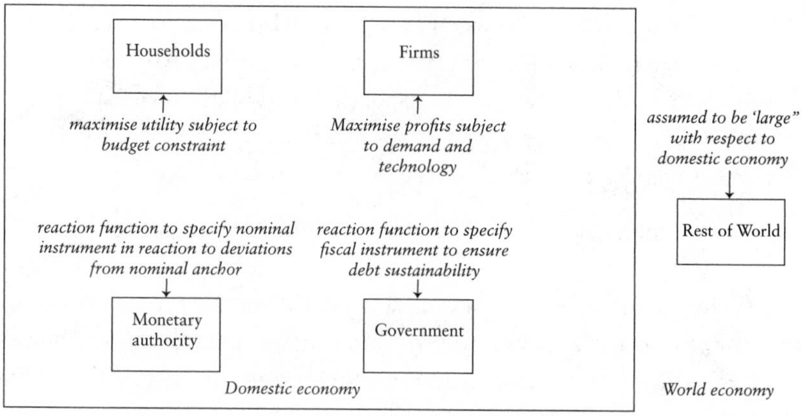

over paid scant attention to banks as a source of credit creation in their models, a fact Mervyn King has labelled 'a source of embarrassment, both intellectual and practical', for the profession.[8]

This oversight was particularly pernicious as it supported the misconception that central banks controlled the money supply. This led to a revival of the crude Quantity Theory of Money. The result was that few politicians were aware that every loan creates a deposit (money). Even bankers themselves did not fully understand their crucial role in the economy.[9]

Bad theory led to bad practice. The authors of *Where Does Money Come From?*, written precisely to clear up these muddles in money, hit the nail on the head:

> A review of the arguments at the time makes clear that the theoretical support for such deregulation was based on the unrealistic assumptions of neoclassical economics, in which banks . . . perform no unique function and are classified as mere financial intermediaries just like stockbrokers. This does not recognise their pivotal role in the economy as the creators of the money supply . . . [S]ince the 1980s, bank credit creation has decoupled from the real economy, expanding at a considerably faster rate than GDP . . . evidence that an increasing amount of bank credit creation has been channelled into financial transactions. This is unsustainable and costly to society, as it amounts to resource misallocation and sows the seeds of the next banking crisis.[10]

One hugely important macroeconomic implication arises from treating banks as mere intermediaries between savers and investors. This is that markets determine a natural rate of interest which delivers full employment – precisely the claim which Keynes set out to refute.

'Financial markets price risks correctly on average'

The efficient market hypothesis (EMH), made popular by Eugene Fama (1970, 1976) is the application of rational expectations to financial markets. The rational expectations hypothesis (REH) says that agents optimally utilize all available information about the economy and policy instantly to adjust their expectations. The implication of this is that shares are always correctly priced on average, because investors adjust their buy/sell actions instantaneously and accurately to any newly released information.

Thus, in the words of Fama, 'I take the market efficiency hypothesis to be the simple statement that security prices fully reflect all available information.'[11]

> An 'efficient' market is defined as a market where there are large numbers of rational, profit-maximizers actively competing, with each trying to predict future market values of individual securities, and where important current information is almost freely available to all participants. In an efficient market, competition among the many intelligent participants leads to a situation where, at any point in time, actual prices of individual securities already reflect the effects of information based both on events that have already occurred and on events which, as of now, the market expects to take place in the future. In other words, in an efficient market at any point in time the actual price of a security will be a good estimate of its *intrinsic value*.[12] [my italics]

There are different versions of the efficient market hypothesis. In its 'weak' form, investors make predictions about current prices using only historical information about past prices (like in adaptive expectations). In its 'semi-strong' form, investors take into account all publicly available information, including past prices. In its 'strong' or ideal form, investors take into account all information that can possibly be known, including insider information.

Several problems can be identified here. First, while it is recognized that share prices may fluctuate randomly round their 'correct' values, they will not do so permanently. If there happened to be over-valued or under-valued assets, the very action of investors trying to sell/buy them to make a profit would work as a self-correcting mechanism. This important feature of the efficient market hypothesis postulates that markets are self-correcting and thus self-regulating, with government attempts to improve on this bound to be distorting.[13] In this way, the efficient market hypothesis is essentially the modern manifestation of Adam Smith's 'invisible hand'.

There is a paradox here. On the one hand, the theory says that there is no point in trying to profit from speculation, because shares are always correctly priced and their movements cannot be predicted. But on the other hand, if investors did not try to profit, the market would not be efficient because there would be no self-correcting mechanism. There is a joke about two economists who spot a $10 bill on the ground. One stoops to pick it up, whereupon the other interjects, 'Don't. If it were really $10, it wouldn't be there anymore.' Therefore, efficient markets actually depend on participants believing that the market is inefficient and trying to outperform it.[14]

Secondly, if shares are always correctly priced, bubbles and crises cannot be generated by the market. Systematic market failure – e.g. Alan Greenspan's *ex post* explanation of the crash as 'under-pricing of risk worldwide' – cannot happen. As Eugene Fama himself put it: 'I don't know what a credit bubble means. I don't even know what a bubble means. These words have become popular. I don't think they have any meaning.'[15]

This attitude leached into policy: 'government officials, starting with Alan Greenspan, were unwilling to burst the bubble precisely because they were unwilling to even judge that it *was* a bubble'.[16] The EMH made the identification of bubbles impossible because it ruled them out *a priori*.

Thirdly, under market pressures, financial innovation would only lead to increased efficiency. There was naught to be gained from reining in the machinations of banks and financiers as they built up an increasingly complex system.

A dose of realism, or even a cursory knowledge of history, would have told these savants that markets do not work in this way.[17] Moreover, there were sound theoretical reasons to distrust an unfettered financial system. Hyman Minsky, an economist whose work was completely ignored until after the crash, argued that financial stability leads inevitably to financial fragility, as optimism turns to 'speculative euphoria' and markets become 'dominated by speculation about sentiments and movements in the market rather than about fundamental asset values'.[18]

But these arguments had no place in the neo-classical hegemony and so, despite its glaring theoretical gaps, the EMH became the intellectual underpinning of financial market deregulation.

'Mark-to-market (M2M) and value at risk (VaR) frameworks offer accurate measures of value and thus are appropriate ways of managing risk'

Mark-to-market accounting aims to estimate the 'fair value' of an asset by reference to its current market price, rather than what it cost the investor to buy. If an investor owns ten shares of a stock bought for $4 a share and that stock now trades at $6, its mark-to-market value is 50 per cent more than its book value.

But mark-to-market accountancy offers an accurate measure of value only if markets never get it wrong. In fact they often do. During a boom, confidence pushes up the market prices of stocks and other assets. The ensuing increase in reported wealth further bolsters confidence, and encourages investors to take more risks and increase their lending and speculative activities. A feedback loop develops between investors' perception of the economy and their decision-making, increasing the likelihood of a speculative bubble. Once this bursts, asset prices fall back down and investors find themselves 'over-leveraged'. Similarly, mark-to-market accounting in a bust can put undue pressure on banks, as the panic and mistrust engendered by a downturn can mean that markets undervalue perfectly healthy assets. In this way, mark-to-market accounting increases volatility by artificially enlarging and contracting balance sheets. But its doom-potential was blithely ignored.

Value at risk modelling was used by banks to assess the amount of risk they faced on their portfolios. A VaR measure takes a given portfolio, a time horizon and a probability level p, and spits out a threshold value of loss for that portfolio, representing a 'realistic' worst-case scenario. For example, if your portfolio has a one-day 1 per cent VaR of $1 million, this means that 99 per cent of the time your portfolio will not fall in value by more than $1 million over a one-day period. VaR measures were popular, as they condensed lots of risk modelling into a single, easily comprehensible figure.

VaR modelling is deeply flawed. It overlooks the worst risks by ignoring scenarios that are less likely to happen than some arbitrary threshold, lulling bankers (and regulators) into a false sense of security. As a prominent hedge-fund founder puts it: 'This is like

Figure 60. VaR modelling[19]

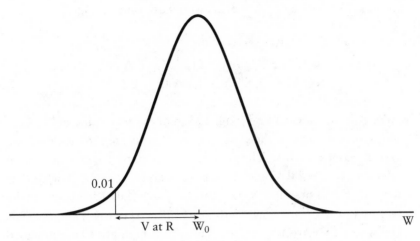

having an airbag that works all the time, except when you have a car accident.'[20] VaR measures tell you nothing about the risks beyond this threshold, which can be the difference between losing $1 million and going bankrupt. Its 'confidence intervals' are totally unwarranted.

VaR measures assume that we have the correct probabilities for all future outcomes. This is a risible assumption. In August 2007, the CFO of Goldman Sachs claimed that they were 'seeing things that were 25-standard deviation moves, several days in a row',[21] meaning that Goldman's models estimated that a single day's losses of this magnitude happened once every 1.309×10^{135} years. By way of comparison, this number is fifty-two orders of magnitude larger than the upper estimate for the number of particles in the universe.[22] Either Goldman were dreadfully unlucky, or their models were crazy.

What explains this failure? First, VaR (and other financial models) were calibrated using short-term data collected exclusively from the relatively stable period immediately before the crash, which proved useless once the boom subsided. But, more fundamentally, humans do not face a knowable distribution of probable outcomes; we face genuine, radical uncertainty, or 'unknown unknowns'. Undue faith in mathematical models, which cannot account for this sort of uncertainty, left the financial sector ignorant of the dangers it was running. The doomsday scenarios weren't doomy enough.*

III. UNDERSTANDING BANKING: SOME ESSENTIAL TERMS

Banks borrow short to lend long. This makes them vulnerable to any collapse in the value of their assets. Since banks are the lifeblood of a modern economy, their lending and borrowing have generally been subject to state regulation. Banks have been restricted in whom they can lend to and how much they can borrow. They have been legally separated by the type of assets they are allowed to own, and the type of liabilities they are allowed to incur. These regulations are designed to ensure their solvency and liquidity.

Solvency and Liquidity

A bank, like any business, is solvent when it has enough assets to cover its liabilities. If a bank's debtors start to default on their loans, the value of the bank's assets falls and threatens to make the bank insolvent. To guard against this was the purpose of capital adequacy regulations.

Liquidity, on the other hand, is the ability to meet one's short-term obligations; the bank has to have access to enough cash to pay its depositors and other creditors on demand. There has been a relentless run-down in liquidity ratios. For example, in the mid-nineteenth century banks had to hold 60 per cent cash against liabilities. This was limited to 12.5 per cent in 1981. Then it was abolished. So banks increasingly relied on borrowing to meet claims on them.

A bank can be illiquid but solvent if it owns more in assets than it owes, but has a cash-flow problem where it cannot borrow cash or sell its assets in time to meet its payment obligations. A liquidity crisis

---

* The systemic under-estimation of risk continues. The latest bank doomsday shock scenarios seriously under-estimated the exchange rate swings caused by the real-life events of Brexit and the election of Donald Trump.

is much less serious than a solvency crisis; temporary funds from the central bank can alleviate a liquidity crisis, but are of no use if the bank is insolvent.

Still, the two are somewhat related. In the period 2007–8, confusion over who was solvent and who was not meant that banks stopped lending to each other, drying up their principal source of liquidity; this led to the bank run on the UK's Northern Rock in 2007. Similarly, illiquidity can force a bank into insolvency if its financing costs exceed the interest it receives on its assets, or if it has to 'fire-sell' its assets in order to pay its debts on time.

Leverage

A bank's leverage is the ratio of its debt to its equity. It can be expressed either as a ratio of assets to capital (say, 25:1) or as the percentage of assets that are backed by capital (4 per cent). Leverage ratios are thus almost identical to capital adequacy ratios, but without the risk-weighting element, which permits banks to hold less capital for supposedly safer assets. In the run-up to the crisis, banks relied on borrowing, and not their own equity, to finance their acquisition of assets, pushing up their leverage.

Banks have an incentive to maintain as high a leverage ratio as possible. Leverage magnifies the possibility of a gain; banks can expose themselves to more risk – and thus more reward – with a smaller amount of their own capital. In the good times, banks increase their leverage as both lenders and borrowers are optimistic about their undertakings.

However, leverage also magnifies the danger of loss. If banks are leveraged at 25:1, then a fall of more than 4 per cent in the value of their assets wipes out their capital. Thus, in a downturn, if the price of an asset that is widely held by hedge funds and banks falls, the institutions' balance sheets worsen. Banks respond by selling off their assets in order to 'deleverage' themselves. This causes the price of assets to fall further, which kicks off another cycle of selling, and so on.

Immediately before the crisis, leverage (debt to equity) ratios of major banks reached over 30:1. This was by no means a historical anomaly. The difference this time was the extent of *embedded* leverage. While balance sheet leverage was comparatively low in the run-up to the crisis, even when adjusted for risk, embedded leverage was much higher. Embedded leverage measures a bank's total exposure to risk compared to its equity holdings, whether or not this risk appears on its balance sheet. It was by holding assets off their balance sheet through the use of a range of innovations that banks increased their leverage beyond the regulated limits. As we shall see in Section V, it was the massive increase in embedded leverage that brought the financial system to grief.

IV. LOOSENING THE REGULATORY NOOSE

By deregulation we mean a weakening of controls over the lending and borrowing activities of the banking system. Three important signposts on this 'deregulatory' road were:

1. The gradual dismantling of the capital controls that had limited the flow of money between countries, i.e. to whom it was possible in the world to lend money. The idea was to free up world savings so that they could be channelled to 'their most productive uses across the globe'.[23]
   Capital account liberalization was part of a broader project of financial globalization, managed by a number of international organizations with increasing power. Foremost among these was the International Monetary Fund. Dominated by the interests and free-market ideologies of rich countries, the IMF imposed a 'neo-liberal' agenda on developing countries and forced them to 'open up' their capital markets to the outside world.
   As a result, foreign money flooded into poorer countries. Though some of it financed foreign direct investment in infrastructure, much of the money took the form of speculative capital flows. These flows, otherwise known as 'hot money', allowed financiers to make short-term profits by moving capital from country to

country, but brought an unprecedented level of financial volatility to developing economies. Heeding the IMF's commandments, many countries experienced financial crises accompanied by severe downturns, most notably in East Asia and Latin America.[24] Recently, the IMF's research arm has issued a sort of a *mea culpa*, recognizing that while the 'growth benefits [of capital account liberalization] are uncertain, costs in terms of increased economic volatility and crisis frequency seem more evident'[25] and that 'full capital flow liberalization is not always an appropriate end-goal'.[26] But this came too late, and long after economists working outside the orthodox position had come to the same conclusion.

2. Controls on types of bank lending within countries were stripped away. After the Great Depression, the US Congress passed the Glass–Steagall Act in 1933,[27] which separated commercial and investment banking in order to protect key banking services (taking deposits, making everyday loans) from the risks of 'casino banking'. The Clinton Administration overturned this in 1999 with the Gramm–Leach–Bliley Act, allowing both sets of activities to be done by the same bank. In the UK, Thatcher's 'Big Bang' of the 1980s, which allowed banks into the mortgage market and commercial banks to merge with securities' houses, had similar consequences, and the model of the do-it-all, universal bank emerged. Regulatory loosening led to the loosening of moral restraints. Whereas traditional banking focused on developing long-term relationships with customers and providing them with a good service, investment banking is marked by an emphasis on short-term opportunism and risk-seeking behaviour.[28]

The effect of the deregulation of lending was to undermine the public utility aspect of banks: they became free to do whatever financial business they wanted. They grew so large that their failure would have a devastating impact on the rest of the economy. And so, when the financial sector collapsed under the weight of its own greed, governments were forced to spend billions of dollars on rescuing them. The public ended up footing the bill for a crisis that wasn't its fault. Most gallingly, banks receiving government support continued to pay out for executive bonuses, while the rest of the country put up with austerity in the name of fiscal prudence.

'Too big to fail' banks provide a textbook example of moral hazard, which arises when people take on excessive risk once they know they will not pay the price for their risk-taking if things go awry. If bankers know that the state will absorb their losses, they are free to gamble to their heart's content and are rewarded for their efforts: 'no industry has a comparable talent for privatising gains and socialising losses'.[29]

3. The weakening of capital and eligible collateral requirements for lending and borrowing. Basel I (1988) and Basel II (2003) set minimum capital requirements for making loans of different riskiness.[30] The logic seemed compelling. Suppose a bank held 10 per cent capital against its loan portfolio. A 10 per cent default on its loans would wipe out its capital. Under Basel I, internationally important banks were required to hold 8 per cent capital against all their *unsecured loans* (e.g. to small businesses), and much lower percentages for secured loans (e.g. for residential mortgages). If the risk of default on certain loans was judged to be low (as was thought to be the case for mortgage-backed securities with a AAA credit rating), they were given a 20 per cent risk-weighting; the capital banks needed to hold against these loans was only 1.6 per cent of their value (20 per cent of 8 per cent). For AAA-rated mortgage-backed securities issued by Fannie Mae and Freddie Mac (the US government-subsidized mortgage-brokers) the required capital was 2 per cent.

The perverse effects of these attempts to mitigate the riskiness of lending is easy to see. Banks came to prefer mortgage-backed securities to any others, because the risk of cluttering up their balance sheets with non-performing loans seemed so small. Credit-rating agencies gave them AAA ratings for the same reason. The underlying assumption that the risks of the various types of loans were *known* was rarely questioned.

In another key move by the US's Security and Exchange Commission at the same time, AAA-rated mortgage-backed securities were made eligible as collateral for bank borrowing. So they could be both part of the liabilities against which banks had to hold capital, and part of the capital to hold against the liabilities.

The result of these various deregulatory moves was an explosion of bank debt to finance loans to eager home-buyers tempted by nugatory interest rates and deposit requirements.

There is never a one-to-one relationship between theory and policy. Policy is an art, and an impure one at that, heavily contaminated by ideology, political beliefs and special interest lobbies. Nor was deregulation simply one-way traffic. Often it was a matter of replacing direct by indirect controls, or replacing one set of regulations by another.

Nevertheless, there is clear evidence that the financial theories described in Section II above influenced the policy of bank deregulation. The UK's Financial Services Authority was commendably honest about how the efficient market hypothesis furnished it with the following intellectual assumptions in the run-up to the crash:

- 'Market prices are good indicators of rationally evaluated economic value.'
- 'The development of securitised credit, since based on the creation of new and more liquid markets, has improved both allocative efficiency and financial stability.'
- 'The risk characteristics of financial markets can be inferred from mathematical analysis, delivering robust quantitative measures of trading risk.'
- 'Market discipline can be used as an effective tool in constraining harmful risk taking.'
- 'Financial innovation can be assumed to be beneficial since market competition would winnow out any innovations which did not deliver value added.'[31]

From these, it followed that:

- 'Markets are in general self-correcting, with market discipline a more effective tool than regulation or supervisory oversight . . .'
- 'The primary responsibility for managing risks lies with the senior management and boards of the individual firms, who are

better placed to assess business model risk than bank regulators, and who can be relied on to make appropriate decisions about the balance risk and return . . .'
- 'Customer protection is best ensured not by product regulation or direct intervention in markets, but by ensuring that wholesale markets are as unfettered and as transparent as possible.'[32]

In short, the evolution of the regulatory system created an unprecedentedly permissive environment for the financial sector. Governments put their faith in the wealth-generating power of financial innovation, and ignored the danger that their products might become too opaque to understand. The structure of these instruments became so complex that their potential for damage became unmeasurable and untraceable. If market participants cannot understand the products they are trading, this undermines the whole edifice of efficient markets. When the crisis hit, uncertainty about the value of these products and the level of entanglement between different financial institutions brought the entire sector to its knees.

V. FINANCIAL INNOVATION

The rise in embedded leverage was made possible by *securitization*.

Securitization

Securitization is the generic name for the use of financial engineering to transform illiquid assets into liquid securities. It is the process of bundling together illiquid assets such as car loans, student loans, credit card debt, mortgages and so on to form 'asset-backed securities' (ABSs) which are then sold to various investors for 'cash'. All of these assets have in common the fact that they are associated with a cash flow – borrowers have to repay the loan which backs the security to the security's buyer. The explosion of securitization was made possible by the huge increase in computing power,[33] and was a classic case of banks creating credit money out of almost nothing.

The different kinds of ABS are:

Mortgage Backed Securities (MBSs)

This is a type of asset-backed security that is secured by a collection of mortgages. It made possible the banks' 'originate and distribute' model of mortgage-lending, which played a fateful role in igniting the crisis. Instead of holding home loans on their books, banks created packages of different mortgage loans of different levels of riskiness, which were sold on to investors, often long term. Many of these securities were backed by American sub-prime mortgages – loans to high-risk borrowers.

The motivation behind pooling mortgages together was to decrease the default risk of the entire portfolio; i.e. to 'diversify' risk away and reduce the effect of 'statistical outliers'. Portfolios, as a whole, were considered to be of little risk because their returns came from a wide variety of mortgage-owners. The default by any single borrower would not have an enormous impact on the portfolio as a whole, so the dividends to the investors were assumed to be backed by stable cash flows. Thus, mortgage-backed securities were given a low risk weighting and allowed to be used as collateral, as detailed above.

However, this relied on the assumption that defaults on mortgages are not highly correlated with each other, whereas at the time there was insufficient historical data on the rate of mortgage defaults, especially on sub-prime mortgages. It turned out that mortgage defaults were highly correlated, including geographically.* So in the run-up to the crisis, the risk of MBSS was significantly under-priced.

Collateralized Debt Obligations (CDOs)

Collateralized debt obligations form a distinct but overlapping category from MBSs. CDOs can be backed by any form of debt – mortgages, corporate bonds, even other ABSs – and are split into 'tranches' of varying risk and maturity, so as to offer investors more choice. The top tranche, called the 'senior' tranche, was entitled to the first payments, although it yielded the lowest returns for the investor, due to being low risk. The bottom tranche yielded the

---

* Defaults in one area were presumed to be uncorrelated with defaults in another, which ceases to be the case in the event of a national housing market crash.

highest return, but it would only be paid what was left over from paying the other tranches.

Credit Default Swaps (CDSs)

The development of credit default swaps (CDSs) massively increased the scope and destructive power of securitization. CDSs are similar to insurance policies in that one party (the buyer) pays a regular fee to another (the seller) who will pay out in the case of the loan defaulting. As such, CDS contracts were an additional way of removing risky assets from banks' balance sheets and freeing up capital to be used elsewhere.

The key difference with a traditional insurance policy is that the buyer of a CDS does not necessarily have to hold a corresponding loan on its books, i.e. anyone can purchase a CDS, even buyers who do not hold the loan instrument. This is called a 'naked' credit default purchase. So an institution could purchase a CDS against another institution, even if it has not made a loan to it, essentially betting that it would default.

Clearly, this exacerbated the problem of moral hazard: banks were insured, so they did not have an incentive to prevent loans from defaulting. Rather, they had an incentive to lend to increasingly less creditworthy clients because these would pay high interest rates. Greek Prime Minister Papandreou compared purchases of naked CDSs to buying fire insurance on a stranger's house and hoping that it will go up flames; their purchase incentivized financial arson.

The reason is that because naked credit default swaps are 'synthetic' – meaning that there is no underlying asset on the institution's books – there is no limit to how many can be sold. In addition, these too can be securitized; e.g. the 'Abacus' CDO consisted of a portfolio of credit default swaps. As a result, in 2007, the gross value of CDSs far exceeded the 'real' value of the bonds that backed them: 'At the peak of the CDS market in mid-2007, there was at least $60 trillion of CDS outstanding . . . The underlying bonds (against whose default the CDS provided insurance or on whose default the CDS permitted bets to be taken) were a small fraction of that $60 trillion.'[34]

In other words, the majority of CDS derivatives were bought to place bets, not for insurance purposes, and this made the financial market very unstable. It is also an example of the increase in intra-financial intensity during the run-up to the crisis – the growth in trading activities between financial institutions greatly exceeded that of interaction with the real economy.

CDSs removed a large part of the risk from short-selling – betting on a stock going down in value – because they provided insurance against the bet turning out wrong. They thus encouraged speculation on the short-side. But while buying a CDS contract carried limited risk but almost unlimited profit potential, 'selling CDS offers limited profits but practically unlimited risks'.[35] In the run-up to the crisis, the banks made the crucial mistake of ruling out the possibility of the insurer having no money to pay the claims. This is what happened to the insurer AIG: it had to be bailed out for $182 billion by the Federal Reserve in 2008 due to not having enough capital to survive the wave of claims being made against it.

The fact that the insurers could themselves default meant that the banks had not effectively offloaded their risk via the use of credit default swaps.

Special Purpose Vehicles (SPVs)

Banks set up legal entities called Special Purpose Vehicles (SPVs) to hold risky assets off their balance sheets. Legally, the SPV, not the bank, was the issuer of the securities. The idea was that, once a bank transferred its risky assets to its SPV, it could effectively count them as off its balance sheet and take more risk – e.g. issue more loans – without breaching leverage rules. SPVs were what enabled banks to conceal their embedded leverage.

Asset-backed securities, including MBSs and CDOs, had to be moved off banks' balance sheets using SPVs before they could be sold to investors. SPVs then repackaged asset-backed securities into different tranches to create even more complex securities. What investors failed to notice, however, is that even the safest 'senior' tranche was not risk-free. This is because SPVs engaged in 're-securitization'. Take the example of CDOs. An SPV could take tranches from two CDOs and bundle them together to form a new CDO of CDOs. The outcome was a new financial derivative called 'CDO-squared', which held the rights to the repayments of the assets of both original CDOs. And it was possible for this CDO-squared to be combined with another CDO, which itself might have been combined with another CDO, and so on. So one could have CDOs-cubed and greater. The result was a compound embedded leverage – it became impossible to measure the risk of a given CDO and know where the risk lay.

The funding of SPVs was itself problematic. SPVs usually funded their purchases of long-term assets (loans, mortgages and so on) by issuing short- to medium-term debt in the form of 'asset-backed commercial paper' (ABCP). The ABCP was seen as low risk by investors, because it was backed by the assets held by the SPV, and so the interest rate on it was low. SPVs thus used short-term loans with low borrowing costs to purchase long-term assets with higher rates of return to make a profit. And whenever the ABCP matured, the SPV would usually issue more ABCP to 'roll over' its debts.

But this maturity mismatch meant that SPVs were very vulnerable to liquidity crises. When demand in the commercial paper market dried up in 2008 because investors lost confidence, SPVs were forced to call upon other lines of credit: namely the 'revolving credit line' set up by the parent bank. This meant that the parent bank was strained twice during the crisis: it incurred losses on its own balance sheet, and it had to pay out the losses incurred by its SPVs.

As an example of the complexity involved in analysing some CDOs, the 'Aquarius' CDO structure had a total of 180 issues behind it. Each of these issues had, on average, 6,500 loans at origination, so the Aquarius CDO had exposure to about 1.2 million loans.

Hence Warren Buffett's cry that derivatives are 'financial weapons of mass destruction'.[36] Their structure became so complex that risk became unmeasurable and untraceable. The whole financial system came to depend on the proliferation of these 'unknown unknowns'.

The Role of Credit Rating Agencies

Credit rating agencies (CRAs) became notorious for awarding AAA ratings to bank loans soon to be defaulted. Financial derivatives were given top ratings although they were far more risky than, say, German government bonds given the same endorsement. Many reasons

Figure 61. Securitization issuance trends in the UK[37]
(sterling, billions)

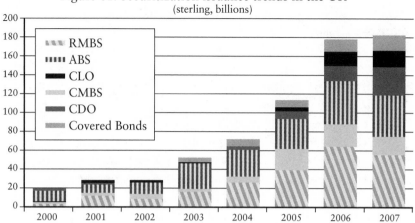

have been adduced for these false prospectuses (see Appendix 11.1). But the principal one is that the agencies were paid by the issuers of the securities (the banks), not by the investors.

These misleading ratings contributed to the crisis. The Asian Development Bank Institute explains: 'The growth of the international financial markets over the last twenty years would have been unthinkable without CRAs. Only because of the availability of clear, internationally accepted indicators of the risk of default were investors willing to invest in international securities.'[38] CDOs and other derivatives were so complex that investors essentially became overly reliant on credit rating agencies. The rating agencies also contributed to the volatility of the market by giving over-generous ratings in the upswings and overly pessimistic ones in the downswings.

Figure 61 shows the huge volume at which securities were sold in the UK, especially ABSs, MBSs (both residential and commercial), CDOs and collateralized loan obligations (CLOs).

VI. CONCLUSION

The complex web of financial instruments created during the years of the Great Moderation was supposed to immunize the self-regulating financial system from the danger of collapse. How wrong could one be! Boom and bust in real estate were central to the US sub-prime mortgage crisis of 2007, the Irish crisis of 2010 and the Spanish crisis of 2012. Major banks in Belgium, France, Germany, Ireland, the Netherlands, Switzerland and the UK all faced insolvency as the price of their mortgage-backed assets fell below the price of their liabilities.

The opaqueness of the financial tools multiplied opportunities for fraud: the doyen of financial probity, London, became the world centre of money-laundering. Crooked auditors and lawyers were employed at large salaries to hide tainted money in special accounts. Since there was no anticipation of collapse, no precautions were taken against it, or thought given to the consequences of financial collapse and bank bail-outs for the finances of governments. The huge expansion of budget deficits caused by the collapse was key to the disablement of fiscal policy we have already discussed in Chapter 8.

The main theoretical mistake behind securitization was the assumption that securities are always liquid: they can always be sold quickly and without (much) loss. This being so, securitization spreads risk round the system; the spread of risk reduces the risk faced by any individual institution; this enables them to lend more; this enables the public to get more and cheaper credit. And cheap credit, as we have seen, was the substitute for rising wages and social security.

The relationship between theory, practice and policy is a perennial issue in political economy. In the case of banking, this relationship turned toxic, as neo-classical economics, deregulation and financial 'innovation' worked together to precipitate financial crisis. The efficient market hypothesis discounted the possibility of financial crises happening. Regulators turned a blind eye to the build-up of stress in the banking system because they believed in the efficient market hypothesis. Banks used their new freedom from control to create ever-more opaque financial instruments ('securitization'). All three pledged themselves to the service of mankind.

Spiralling out of control, the financial system collapsed. Since banks are the source of the credit on which the economy depends, the economy collapsed in their wake.

APPENDIX 11.1: WHY DIDN'T CREDIT RATINGS AGENCIES DO THEIR JOB?

Credit ratings agencies were meant to provide serviceable estimates of debtor risk, but failed spectacularly in their task.

The principal reason is that they were paid by the issuers of securities (the banks) and not by investors. Banks shopped around for the best credit rating, which put CRAs under commercial pressure to rate banks' products favourably. This gave issuers undue power over their own assessments. While minimizing the risk of banking default before the crisis, the rating agencies exaggerated the risk of government default after it. They were servants of the vested interests that paid them.

Further, the market is dominated by three firms: Moody's holds 40 per cent market share, Standard & Poor's 40 per cent and Fitch 14 per cent. Barriers to entry are very large, mostly because a CRA needs to have a good reputation to succeed. So the agencies are under little pressure to rethink their methodology; more importantly, concentration creates a single mindset.

CRAs have been accused of outright 'blackmail' to solicit new business. A case in point is the scandal involving Moody's and Hannover Re, a German insurance company. Moody's provided the latter with an 'unsolicited' rating and issued it a letter saying that it 'looked forward to the day Hannover would be willing to pay'. When Hannover refused, Moody's continued providing ratings and downgraded them gradually over the years. In 2004, Moody's rated Hannover's bonds as 'junk', and this caused the firm to lose $175 million in market capitalization, despite its buoyant assessments from other agencies.[39]

Apart from the fact that they were paid by the sellers of the securities they were rating, the following technical factors contributed to the agencies' poor performance.

1. CRAs failed to acknowledge the crucial distinction between highly complex structured financial products and simpler corporate and government bonds.
2. They lacked sufficient historical data, especially relating to mortgages.

3. They under-estimated correlation in defaults. As a result, CRAs thought that securitized products (backed up by *portfolios* of loans) carried little risk, and indeed that they were less risky than these underlying loans considered individually. Many collateralized debt obligations were rated AAA when they were backed by a pool of only, say, BBB-rated loans; the strength of the CDO was supposed to come from its structure. Furthermore, the CRAs assumed a maximum 5 per cent decline in national housing prices.

4. Combined with the above, the use of normal distributions in VaR models privileged 'thin tails' (for which an extreme event is unlikely) over 'fat' ones (for which an extreme event is much more likely).

5. CRAs failed to allow for the impact of moral hazard on lending standards.

6. Giving the financial sector access to their rating methodology made it easier for issuers to 'structure to the rating'. The UK Financial Services Authority's Turner Review of 2009 says: 'the practice of making the [CRAs'] models . . . transparent to the issuing investment banks also created the danger that issuers . . . were designing specific features of the structure so that it would just meet a certain rating hurdle'.[40]

12

Global Imbalances

'In my judgment, the big challenge to monetary policy before the crisis was a serious mis-pricing in long-term interest and exchange rates and the imbalances that resulted.'

Mervyn King, 2012[1]

'If a country consumes more than it produces, it must import more than it exports. That's not a rip-off; that's arithmetic.'
George P. Shultz and Martin Feldstein, Washington Post,

5 May 2017

I. INTRODUCTION

How far did global imbalances contribute to the crisis? By global imbalances we mean persistent surpluses and deficits in countries' current accounts. A pseudo-Keynesian answer would be that the current account surpluses of China and the Middle East produced a global 'savings glut', which could only be liquidated by a decline in the world economy. But this does not explain the weakness of investment performance in the capital-importing countries. In Keynesian theory, 'excess saving' is the result of under-investment, not an independent factor. So it is the weakness in the inducement to invest which needs explaining.

The other problem with the 'global imbalances' explanation of the collapse of 2007–8 is that it is not clear how it relates to the speculative boom and bust in the housing market.

The discussion is bedevilled by tautologies and identities, so that it is difficult to work out what is causing what.

A country's balance of payments is simply that part of the national accounts that shows payments in any year to and from foreigners. Its *current account* comprises the balance of trade in physical goods and (mostly) financial services, and other income transfers; its *capital account* records exchanges of assets and liabilities.

In Hume's day, the important balance was the balance of trade; and Hume's price–specie–flow mechanism aimed to show how international trade was self-balancing through gold movements. In the nineteenth century, the purchase and sale of assets became important, but this did not change the basic story, since foreign capital investments were regarded only as deferred purchases of the capital importer's goods. Capital would flow from countries where saving was abundant and labour scarce to countries where saving was scarce and labour abundant. Capital-importing countries would repay their loans out of the increased exports the investment of the loans had made possible, eliminating the temporary imbalances. In effect, lending and borrowing capital (savings) replaced gold flows in adjusting the trade balance in the long-run.

There was also a long tradition of bankers lending money to needy foreign sovereigns: the Rothschilds, as we have seen, were international bankers, lending and borrowing across frontiers without regard to trade balances. However, standard trade theory, with its denial that money had 'motives of its own', regarded such flows as merely lubricating the real trade in goods and capital.

After the Second World War, trade was gradually liberalized, but capital flows were severely repressed. Most of these flows were political or 'official', such as Marshall Aid from the US to Europe and equivalently to Japan, and World Bank loans to developing countries. International financial flows within the banking system were minimal. Current accounts more or less balanced. The repression of capital movements brought to an end the succession of banking crises.

The unfreezing of the banking system started with the recycling of the OPEC surpluses in the 1970s. Freedom of capital movements, it was now argued, would make 'capital allocation more efficient'. Financial flows multiplied relative to trade flows: in 2011, the total exports of merchandise and commercial services increased by $21.3 trillion, while the volume of foreign exchange transactions reached $4 trillion

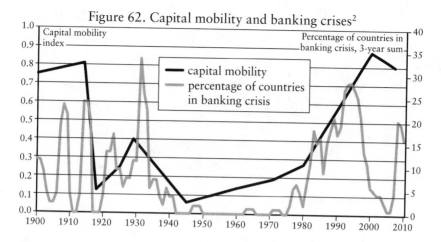

Figure 62. Capital mobility and banking crises[2]

a day. Trading in liquid assets – bank loans and equities – dwarfed direct foreign investment. An uncontrolled banking system was left free to place its bets anywhere. As long as current account deficits were being financed, no one paid any attention to them. But as John Harvey wrote: 'the driving factors of these massive financial flows [are] ... fundamentally distinct from those determining trade flows – different people, different agendas, different goals and worldviews'.[3] None of this worried the apostles of financial deregulation.

By 2007, the US was running a persistent and growing current account deficit; East Asia, especially China, but also Japan and Middle East countries (major oil exporters) were running persistent and growing current account surpluses. In Europe, Germany was running a persistent current account surplus; the peripheral Euro-zone countries were running current account deficits, especially in the five years pre-crisis. Spain's deficit, for example, grew from 4 per cent to 10 per cent of GDP in that period.

Current account imbalances might be problematic for three reasons:

1. Surplus countries might hoard their surpluses, imposing deflation and unemployment on their trading partners in a fixed exchange system (the Keynes problem).
2. Deficit countries might live 'beyond their means' if they could persuade creditors to finance their spending. But this was bound to lead to default sooner or later.

3. Deficit countries were especially vulnerable to 'capital flight' since they were more likely to default on their loans.

With capital becoming internationally mobile, the whole structure of global lending and borrowing came to depend on banks' ability to judge risks correctly across the globe. All these structural factors came into play in the run-up to the crisis and its unfolding, rendering the world economy less stable, and recovery from the slump more difficult.

II. A PRE-CRASH BIRD'S-EYE VIEW

The two graphs below show how current account imbalances built up in the years before the crisis. Figure 63 shows the growing imbalance between the USA and China. In the Eurozone, north-western Europe, led by Germany, was the main surplus area, with the Mediterranean countries running persistent deficits. (see Figure 64)

This pattern of imbalances, while somewhat worrying, was regarded as temporary. Ben Bernanke wrote: 'Fundamentally, I see no reason why the whole process [of rebalancing] should not proceed smoothly.'[4]

Martin Wolf, the respected *Financial Times* columnist, published a book in 2004 called *Why Globalization Works*. He saw globalization

Figure 63. Current account balances, pre-crash: China and USA[5]
(per cent of GDP)

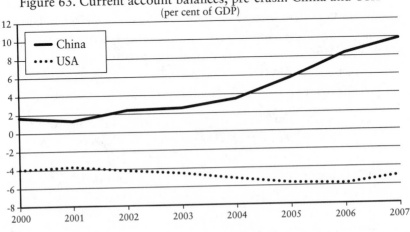

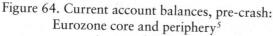

Figure 64. Current account balances, pre-crash:
Eurozone core and periphery[5]
(per cent of GDP)

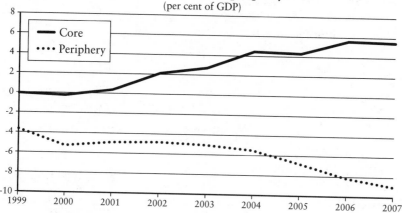

as a mighty engine for ending global poverty, and saw no problem arising from the macroeconomic imbalances that resulted from lopsided
trade. As he wrote:

> This pattern of surpluses and deficits will create difficulties only to the
> extent that the intermediation of the flows from the savings-surplus to
> the savings-deficit countries does not work smoothly. But no insuper-
> able difficulty should arise. If some people (Asians) wish to spend less
> than they earn today, then others need to be encouraged to spend more.[7]

As late as mid-2007, he thought that the possibility that 'huge calam-
ities' could be generated by world financial markets 'looks remote'.[8]
Two months later, with the onset of the banking crisis, he was having
second thoughts: 'Today's credit crisis ... is ... a symptom of an
unbalanced world economy.'[9]

III. SOME BASIC THEORY

In the standard presentation of national accounts, a country's current
account position is equal to the difference between its domestic saving and investment.

The equation for national output is:

$$Y = C + I + (X - M)$$

where Y is output, C is private and public consumption, I is private and public investment, and $(X - M)$ is exports minus imports, or the trade balance, which generally is the principal determinant of the current account balance (CAB). Therefore we can write:

$$CAB \approx (Y - C) - I$$

($\approx$ is approximately equal).

If $Y = C + I$, and S (saving) $= Y - C$, then $S = I$. Thus

$$CAB \approx S - I$$

CAB is in balance when $S = I$. An imbalance between a country's exports and imports is thus definitionally equal to the difference between its domestic saving and investment. A country with a trade surplus needs to consume more or export saving (capital); a country with a trade deficit needs to consume less or import saving (capital). Indeed, if one believes that money flows like water these adjustments are automatic.

This is the standard view. But it has been challenged by economists who treat financial flows as independent of the current account. We will take up their argument later.

IV. CURRENT ACCOUNT IMBALANCES AS A CAUSE OF MELTDOWN?

There were at least four reasons to worry about the sustainability of the current account imbalances in the pre-crash years. First, Figure 63 (p. 336) shows that in the case of China and the United States the money was *flowing the wrong way* – the phrase is 'uphill' – from a capital-poor to a capital-rich country, something Hume had denied was possible. China wasn't importing development capital from the United States to plug the deficiency in its domestic 'savings'. China was accumulating savings through its export surplus, which it was investing in US Treasury bonds. There was no net loss of money from the American economy. This allowed the Fed to keep money cheap.

Secondly, in the case of the Eurozone, finance *was* flowing the right

Figure 65. Total cross-border capital inflows[10]
(USD trillions)

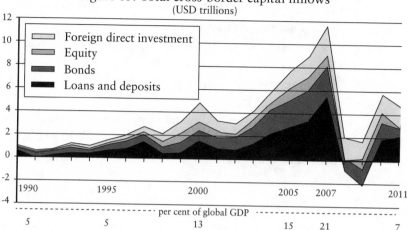

way – from capital-rich north-west Europe to the capital-poor Mediter-ranean countries plus Ireland – but it was being used partly for unproductive purposes: to finance consumption and to speculate in real estate, rather than to develop the competitive position of the borrowers. Greece was like the businessman who gets a loan from the bank to expand his business and spends it instead in riotous living. Once the real estate market collapsed, the question of ability to repay became crucial.

Thirdly, in the past, most foreign investment took the form of direct foreign investment: buying physical assets like mines or plantations or railways which are immovable. In recent times, much of it has been 'hot money', short-term loans which could be withdrawn quickly; so much so that the booms and busts caused by hot money are not 'a sideshow or a minor blemish in international capital flows; they are the main story'.[11] So financial flight was a more likely consequence of a collapse in business confidence than in the nineteenth century, though this had already started to be a problem under the restored gold standard of the 1920s.

Finally, although gold hoarding was not unknown in the nineteenth century, reserve accumulation was a more prominent feature of the pre-2007 position. This was particularly true for a handful of coun-tries in East Asia and the Middle East. Between 2003 and 2008, total international reserves (90 per cent of these being foreign exchange reserves) grew at an average rate of 17 per cent per year[12] at a time when global GDP was growing at an annual average of 5 per cent.

Under the gold standard, this accumulation of reserves would have amounted to a big increase in deflationary pressure, because these reserves would have been held in gold – buried in the vaults of the central banks. However, the pre-crash position was dominated by the 'exorbitant privilege' of the US dollar as the principal reserve currency. The fact that the reserves were held mainly in dollars allowed the US to avoid deflation, and instead run an expansionary monetary policy.* The reserve position of the dollar formed the link connecting reserve accumulation by China and expansionary monetary policy in the US.

V. SAVING GLUT VERSUS MONEY GLUT

Now consider the proposition

$$CA_A \equiv -CA_B$$

This says that country A's surplus is exactly the same as country B's deficit. But which causes which?

Country A might run a current account surplus *because* country B pays for a part of country A's goods with money rather than with goods. Country B's deficits with country A are then said to be caused by country B's spendthrift habits. Or country B might run a current account deficit because country A's policies – for example, restricting consumption or maintaining an under-valued currency – prevent country B from exporting enough to it to cover its imports from country A. Country B's deficits are then said to be caused by country A's 'saving glut'. Which is it? You can choose between China's frugality and American extravagance.

The 'saving glut' thesis was the orthodox pre-crash view. Think of the world as a single economy, in which all the saving is done in China and all the investment is done in the United States. If the Chinese want to save *ex ante* more than the Americans want to invest,

---

* Because it did not have a fixed supply of gold, the US was able to issue as many Treasury bills as it wanted.

Keynesian theory tells us that saving S and investment I are equalized *ex post* not by an an appropriate interest rate adjustment, but by a fall in global income. In these terms, the collapse of 2008 was caused by the collapse of investment in the United States, with the world economy shrinking to equalize saving and investment *ex post*.

Keynesian theory tells us why this must be the case. It is not saving which finances investment, it is bank credit. If bank credit is demanded for speculation, not investment, it has no effect in either reducing saving or increasing investment. The imbalance between the two is reduced by a fall in income. A Keynesian would say that the only way to tackle this 'structural' imbalance is by reducing the propensity to save in China and increasing the inducement to invest in the United States.

On the eve of the recession in 2007, the Chinese saved half of their incomes, but invested only 40 per cent at home, much of it in loss-making state industries. So 10 per cent was parked abroad, mostly in US Treasury bonds.

Why was China saving so much? Economist Michael Pettis offers an under-consumptionist explanation. China's high savings ratio was structurally determined by the highly unequal distribution of income and absence of a social safety net. The poverty of domestic consumption led to a business model based on export-led growth through currency under-valuation. The purchase of US Treasury bonds was part of a deliberate policy of keeping the dollar over-valued in order to help Chinese exporters. (Alternatively, one might see China's reserve accumulation as a form of precautionary saving following the East Asian financial crisis of 1997.)

On this interpretation, it was the excess of Chinese saving over its domestic investment which caused the US deficit. It was the willingness of China to finance the US deficit for its own purposes which *enabled* the American consumer to go on a spending spree. The Chinese purchase of US government securities created the conditions for a credit expansion in America, with the People's Bank of China acting as an additional source of reserves for the American banking system.

The remedy for the current account imbalance with the United States is for the Chinese to boost their domestic consumption and productive domestic investment. This requires a social safety net and banking reforms.[13]

The 'money glut' or American spendthrift explanation starts at the other end. It was American over-spending on consumption and speculation in real estate that forced the Chinese to run a surplus. The structural problem lay with the US not the Chinese economy.

The economist Raghuram Rajan has described a situation in which

> America's growing inequality and thin social safety net create tremendous political pressure to encourage easy credit and keep job creation robust, no matter what the consequences to the economy's long-term health; and where the U.S. financial sector, with its skewed incentives, is the critical but unstable link between an over-stimulated America and an underconsuming world.[14]

Alternatively, one might seek to explain the persisting American deficit in geopolitical terms: the simultaneous quest for guns and butter was part of the US commitment to policing the world without making any sacrifice in its domestic living standards to do so.[15]

The source then of America's structural deficit can be traced to the stagnation of real earnings in the United States. Easy money in the US produced no upsurge in US domestic investment. Rather, the pre-crash years saw a 'dramatic swing in corporations' use of their internal cash flow . . . from fixed investment to buy back of company stock and cash [i.e. dividends] disbursed to shareholders'.[16] As a result, cheap money hardly raised the US investment/GDP ratio. Why? American businesses could have borrowed for investment rather than speculate in property and mergers and acquisitions. Why didn't they?

One explanation is that the prospective rate of return on large classes of fixed investment acceptable to American investors had fallen below the rate of interest, low though that was. For a time ultra-low interest rates supported the construction industry and speculation in real estate. When the Federal Reserve raised the federal funds rate between 2004 and 2006, this source of activity, too, was fatally damaged. Analysts are free to apportion the blame between a dearth of investment opportunities ('secular stagnation), the quest for short-term shareholder value, and favourable tax treatment of stock-options.[17] Ironically, Chinese investors, who would have been willing to invest in the American economy long-term, were debarred from doing so on security grounds.

It should be obvious that Chinese 'over-saving' and American 'under-investment' are the same thing looked at from different theoretical perspectives; which 'caused' the other is impossible to determine empirically. Perhaps one should say that the world was kept in an unstable equilibrium by extreme saving (surplus) in China and extreme dissaving (deficit) in the US. The two extremes held the world economy together until the sub-prime crisis in the USA unwound the unstable forces.

Eurozone

The structural flaw in the EU's Single Currency Area was obvious from the start; it was a monetary union without a political union. Much of the economic growth of poorer (largely Mediterranean) members depended on continual transfers of capital from the core to the periphery. In 2009 German banks accounted for 30 per cent of the debt owed by Greece, Portugal, Ireland, Spain and Italy. When European banks were contaminated by the US-generated securitization crisis, the inter-bank lending market collapsed and the flow of private capital was reversed. Capital flight forced peripheral-country governments to borrow from the bond markets to service the debts of their domestic banks to northern European banks. As government balance sheets exploded, risk premia on government debt rose in what Paul de Grauwe has named the 'vicious circle' between bank recapitalizations and the undermining of governments' creditworthiness.[18]

In line with the saving glut thesis one can argue that German current account surpluses reflected deliberate German policy to restrain wage growth so as to improve cost competitiveness. This opened a wedge between German and peripheral Eurozone labour costs.

But lack of cost competitiveness doesn't seem to have been the main problem for the heavily indebted European countries. Rather it was that capital imports were not being used to generate sufficient foreign earnings to service and repay the loans. Instead, a debt-financed construction and consumption boom caused current account deficits to widen in Ireland, Spain, Greece and Portugal before the crisis, which required more financing. Financial flows then reversed, not because current account deficits suddenly looked worrisome, but because the collapse of the construction boom had made many borrowers in those countries insolvent. Widening current account imbalances were symptoms of the problem, not its cause.

Surveying the whole scene, it is hard to avoid the conclusion that, in the advanced world at any rate, governments had surrendered to bankers the job of keeping their economies afloat. They allowed money to be pumped from one centre to another in a widening circle of financial betting, convincing themselves that if the money wheel could be kept spinning, nothing much could go wrong with the world economy.

From this point of view, the debate between the saving and money glut theses is something of a red herring. Yes, it is quite true that China and Germany should consume more and save less; and that the United States should consume less and save more. But there is no incentive to do anything about either set of imbalances, as long as economists and policymakers believe in leaving control of financial flows to the financiers.

VI. BANKING IMBALANCES

In the nineteenth century it made sense to talk of British or French savings 'flowing abroad' to finance the capital development of their clients, because capital-rich countries like Britain and France alone had the financial markets able to mobilize money for foreign loans. It was not accidental that financial facilities were located in the country in which saving (in the sense of non-consumed income) was most plentiful. But even then there was no automatic connection between a current account surplus and foreign lending: the Rothschilds raised money from a variety of locations. The link is even weaker today, when we have a global banking system, largely detached from a specific country location, handling the money of a global elite of rich investors.

As Borio and Distayat of the Bank of International Settlements point out, a capital import is not necessarily some other country's saving. It is a credit advanced by a financial institution in one country to an investor or government in another country. The two BIS authors thus reinforce an argument central to Keynes's economics, namely, that saving is simply a decision not to consume; it is not a decision to invest. Investment is not financed by saving; it is financed by bank credit. It is financial facilities (deposits) provided by banks, not savings, which create purchasing power.[19] Such deposits can be generated anywhere, even in deficit countries. (Indeed, this was the case of the UK, which had a current account deficit with many economies in the Eurozone periphery, but which was nonetheless a major geographical source of credit.) Thus, while current account balances almost perfectly match net financial flows due to accounting identities, there is no necessary connection between gross capital flows and current account balances.

What causes the level of investment to be what it is has nothing to do with what people want to save. It depends on the ability of businessmen to finance their investments, or on the creditworthiness of borrowing governments. Where the money comes from, in a system of free capital movements, depends on where the originating banks are located. This need not be where savings (in the accounting sense of non-consumption) are most plentiful. Thus there cannot be any *direct* connection between gross capital flows and current account imbalances; and therefore between current account imbalances and the financial meltdown of 2007–8.

It wasn't the current account imbalances that were unsustainable in 2007–8; it was the balance sheets of the banks. The banks were like sovereigns allocating money, often for speculative motives, without any reference to current account positions. It was only when the banks got into trouble that the current account positions of the *countries* of destination came under critical scrutiny, with the debtor countries most exposed to capital flight.

VII. CONCLUSION

As with any dispute between debtors and creditors, apportionment of blame is, ultimately, a value judgement, which cannot be settled by accumulating facts. In both the USA and the Eurozone, the proximate cause of the banking collapse lay with the banks; at a further remove, with governments in rich countries which relied on credit expansion as the alternative to public investment and redistributive taxation; and, at a still further remove, with the economics profession that lauded diseased banking practices on the ground that they facilitated the 'efficient allocation of capital'.

The economic crisis has, in some cases at least, produced the market-led adjustment which eluded policymakers. The American trade deficit shrank from 5.8 per cent of GDP in 2006 to 2.4 per cent of GDP in 2016. China's surplus with the rest of the world contracted from a peak of 9.9 per cent of GDP in 2007 to 1.8 per cent in 2016. Germany's current account surplus with its fellow Eurozone members narrowed to just under 3 per cent of GDP in 2016 (although its overall surplus stood at a massive 8.3 per cent). In each case, the trade 'correction' has come about more through the shrinkage of consumption in the debtor countries than through an expansion of consumption in the creditor ones. Thus the 'rebalancing' that Bernanke and Wolf foresaw is taking place because of a fall in national income in the debtor countries. But, since the structural causes of the imbalances remain largely in place, any strong recovery of Western economies is bound to re-create them.

PART FOUR

A New Macroeconomics

13
Reinventing Political Economy

I. INTRODUCTION

The collapse of 2008–9 should have shifted the attention of macroeconomics from the problem of inflation in otherwise stable economies to the problem of economic, and especially financial, instability. That it has barely done so is my main excuse for writing this book.

The most important economic problems we face today stem from the wrong views about money and government. If one starts from the position that, in the absence of money, a market economy is optimally self-adjusting, then the principal, in fact only, task of *macroeconomic policy* is to ensure that money does not upset the equilibrium established in the (barter) economy. The belief that the market economy is optimally self-adjusting is usually, but not logically, connected with another: that the main source of economic disequilibrium arises from governments printing too much money. From this it follows that the task of keeping money 'in order' or, equivalently, the price level predictable, needs to be 'outsourced' to central banks equipped with inflation targets. As a corollary, governments should be bound by fiscal rules that prevent them from issuing money at will to pay for their spending. If one has the right monetary regime, supported by the right fiscal rules, the market economy will normally be stable.

The above was the dominant implicit model of political economy from the dawn of scientific economics in the eighteenth century until the collapse of the 1930s. Though actual events failed to confirm it, they were not sufficiently inconsistent with it to force a rethink of the foundations of the discipline or the principles of policy. Specifically, although crises were frequent they could be interpreted as temporary interruptions to a strongly upward momentum of economic growth. This strongly expansionist phase of capitalism ended in the 1920s, and the subsequent collapse and stagnation gave birth to the Keynesian revolution.

The Keynesian message was straightforward: if growth was to continue it was not enough to control money and keep government out of the way. The government had to be inserted into economic life as an active engineer of growth: the control of money required that it control the level of demand in the economy. After thirty years, the Keynesian system fell victim to its own success, the managed capitalism it introduced proving unable to control inflation at full employment. This reopened the road back to pre-Keynesian orthodoxy. Provided only money was kept in order by independent central banks, a lightly regulated market system could be relied on to keep economies growing steadily and stably.

The pre-crash period of the Great Moderation, running from the early 1990s, did not exactly conform to this benign prospectus: there were several financial collapses, unemployment was higher, and growth lower, than in the Keynesian age. But it did not disconfirm it sufficiently to challenge the ruling paradigm. Inflation was low and growth was reasonably stable. It was possible to believe that the era of boom and bust had come to an end.

It is impossible to regard the collapse of 2008–9 and subsequent events as merely a temporary halt on the continuing upward ascent. There is a whiff of 'secular stagnation' in the air, with a strong sense that bouts of temporary excitement will be followed by collapses. Make hay while the sun shines is what the market analysts advise us.

Despite the brittleness of the contemporary market economy, the Keynesian theory of macro-policy, which made the state responsible for managing the level and influencing the direction of total spending, has not been rehabilitated. Money and governments continue to be perceived as sources of shocks to an otherwise smoothly adjusting market system. Attacks on public deficits and debts continue to overwhelm concerns for employment, economic growth and equity.

In the last quarter of a century we have come close to creating a single world economy. Questions about the role of money and of government increasingly have to be asked and answered in a global context.

II. WHAT SHOULD GOVERNMENTS DO AND WHY?

The matters at issue can be made more precise by considering what framework of policy and institutions is needed to make market economies work acceptably well.

Terence Hutchison has helpfully classified opinions on this question as *continua* along three different curves: doctrinal, institutional and historical. Along the first curve is a range of doctrines stretching from those who assert a very smooth and rapid self-adjustment of markets up to optimal levels, to those who assert that this self-adjusting tendency is weak or non-existent.

Along the second curve views stretch from whether the framework of institutions, rules and policies needed to maintain self-adjustment is simple, natural and easy to bring about, or very complex and nearly impossible to set up. And finally, there is the historical evidence: does history show that optimal self-adjusting processes are normal or exceptional?[1]

Simplifying, if we consider just neo-classical and Keynesian economics, we find near one end of all three curves the Chicago School, and near the other end the Keynesian School.

Chicago School proponents believe that smooth and rapid self-adjustment to full employment is normal within a framework of rule-based monetary policy and 'light touch' regulation. Keynesians deny that a market system has an automatic tendency to full employment. It achieves this happy state only in 'moments of excitement'. In the Keynesian perspective, the dynamics of adjustment to 'shocks' point the economy away from, not back towards, an optimum equilibrium. Therefore, governments should actively pursue full employment policies, with such regulation of private sector activity as is necessary to bring this about.

The Austrian, Marxist and Schumpeterian schools lie at tangents to this central debate.

The Austrians believe that the information required for market self-adjustment exists only in the minds of actual market participants. This being so there is no scope even for minimal macroeconomic policy, since the central authority can never 'know better than the market'. The only alternative to market self-regulation is central planning; but this will deliver grossly inferior outcomes. No monetary policy is required if banks are subject to a 100 per cent reserve requirement. On the other hand, a well-functioning market system requires what Hayek called a 'constitution of liberty', which secures the maximum possible decentralization of market and state power, within a firm framework of law, consistently enforced. Such an equilibrium may not be 'optimal' in the neo-classical sense, but it is the best that can be done in a free society.

Both the Marxist and Schumpeterian theories are best thought of as disequilibrium theories. The key thought is from Marx's *Communist Manifesto*: under the restless dynamism of competitive capitalism, 'All that is solid melts into air, all that is holy is profaned ... '[2] According to Marx, no policies or institutions can be set up within the capitalist system to avoid recurrent and increasingly savage crises. This is because the profitability of capitalism depends on a growing reserve army of the unemployed. Equilibrium can be achieved only with the abolition of capitalism.

Schumpeterian economics likewise denies that there is either a unique full employment equilibrium or the variety of equilibria posited by Keynes. Capitalism is a dynamic disequilibrium system. There are phases and epochs, waves long and short. Keynes may have bequeathed a twenty-five-year boom, but this was just a phase of a long cycle – perhaps a Kondratiev mass production cycle. Nevertheless, there is a potential meeting between Keynes and Schumpeter, since Schumpeter, like all the earlier generation of Real Business Cycle theorists, would not have denied that stabilization policy could make the rocking less violent.

The Hutchison scheme needs one crucial modification. All the economic doctrines above presuppose the existence of some kind of state, even a minimal state. We will see that the main flaw in globalization is the attempt to integrate markets on a global scale without a state. This has rendered life in the market more insecure, more criminal and less legitimate. Markets without states are mafias.

Chicago School economics has recently been the economics 'in power'. The collapse of 2008–9 and its aftermath has been a kind of experimental test of its main theses. Do we still think of the market system as naturally stable, provided only that money is kept 'in order'? Surely not. Money *was* kept in order by the principal criterion of the time, price stability, but the economy collapsed nevertheless. Was it the vexatious interference of governments which upset the even tenor of production, trade and finance? Again, surely not. Since the 1980s there has been a big withdrawal by governments from active management and regulation. It was the deregulated global market that collapsed in 2008–9.

To be sure, one disaster should not be the test of a system's performance, any more than one aeroplane crash should discredit the theory of aerodynamics. However, the 'shock' of 2008–9 was, as we can now see, building up under the surface of a brittle prosperity, and it has left great damage in its wake from which it will take many years to recover. In other words, the question of which state of affairs is to be viewed as 'normal' – the so-called Great Moderation of the early 2000s or the ten post-cash years which followed – is still open.

These rather dry academic questions, translated into popular discourse, have become the urgent matter of contemporary politics. Since the global meltdown of 2008–9, hostility to neo-liberal statecraft has focused on globalization. Globalization has long been the picture-postcard of neo-classical economics and neo-liberal politics. In polite circles, it is still considered impious to question it. But the strains of globalization have led to an upsurge of sometimes ugly popular protest, which threatens the political legitimacy of liberal democracy.

The conclusion arising from my account seems to me inescapable. The working of the economic machine needs to be drastically improved and the rate of disruptive change slowed down to societies' (considerable) capacity for adaptation if a decent political system is to be maintained. If not, a regression to nationalism or even fascism is likely. The urgent need is to detach the championship of liberal politics from the defence of neo-liberal economics. Keynes understood that supremely well, and it is in his spirit that the following suggestions are offered.

III. A NEW MACROECONOMIC CONSTITUTION

Fiscal Theory

The essential requirement of a new macroeconomic constitution is to reverse the current balance of fiscal and monetary policy. The focus should shift from fighting inflation to fighting stagnation. This means using the budget to revive growth, and monetary policy to support fiscal policy.

Restoring Treasury control over macro-policy does not mean reverting to 'full employment' of 1950s vintage. By full employment I mean a 'socially', that is, politically and morally, acceptable level of activity. I would apply the same criterion of political and moral acceptability to inequality of wealth, earnings and incomes. Vague though these criteria are, economic policy must have some reference to what the public considers reasonable and fair if it is to escape from statistical culs-de-sac.

The narrative of 'the deficit' still dominates popular discussion. Deficits are what you always get, the orthodox story goes, when you allow politicians to 'monkey around' with money. President Donald Trump's tax cuts have been attacked by academic macroeconomists, not just for worsening inequality – a reasonable reaction – but also for increasing the deficit. Philip Hammond, Britain's Chancellor of the Exchequer, cannot invest in the social housing Britain desperately needs because it will risk his self-imposed borrowing limits.

This discussion is fundamentally unhinged. Whether the budget is balanced or unbalanced is a secondary matter. What matters is whether the economy is balanced or unbalanced at full employment, and what contribution the state budget can make to this. To offset a decline in private spending, the budget deficit has to be increased, not reduced. Instead, governments in 2009–10 set about reducing their deficits by raising taxes and cutting spending before private spending had recovered. The result has been several years of under-employment.

In the Ricardian world view, government spending is simply waste. It subtracts from productive investment, and should be limited to the few essential functions of the state. Its claim is that the private sector will provide the community with all the capital equipment it wants or needs. This is doubly false. From time to time capital may 'go to sleep', as even J. B. Say recognized. And Adam Smith himself acknowledged the need for state investment to provide public goods.

Keynesian economics built on Say's insight. Because of uncertainty, the volume of private investment will normally be less than what the public would save at full employment. Because of liquidity preference, nominal interest rates will be sticky downwards, whatever Bank Rate set by the central bank. Thus there is a permanent role for public investment to keep a growing economy at full employment. It may also be the case that public investment will need to expand to fill the growing gap between private saving and investment as economies become richer – at least to the point at which there is no further benefit to be had from adding to the community's capital equipment.

The second argument for public investment is that, owing to various 'failures', private capital markets cannot provide the community with all the capital goods it needs. This is what Adam Smith meant when he talked of investments greatly advantageous to the 'great society' which private investors lack the incentive or means to supply (see p. 82).

The public goods argument for a state investment function is that certain goods have public benefits additional to their private benefits. These external benefits cannot readily be 'internalized' by private firms because they are in essence 'free' goods, so there is no money to be made from supplying them. Public investment is justified in goods and services whose benefits to the 'great society' exceed their market value. One may think of such goods as constituting the political, legal, physical and moral infrastructure of a market economy. The state itself is the main public good. The community 'invests' in the state by paying taxes. How much tax people are willing to pay is a reasonably reliable indicator of how much they think the state is worth. Only an extreme free marketeer would claim that sufficient law and order would be provided by private protection agencies. Through its ability to tax, the state provides or supports a derivative set of public goods such as transport systems, public utilities, hospitals, schools, housing and elements of the moral, legal and religious order. Private markets would not provide enough of such goods, or in the right places, to serve the needs of the 'great society'. If capital investment were left entirely to the market it would come to an end long before its potential to raise material and spiritual well-being was exhausted.

Mariana Mazzucato (and others) have shown, correctly, that the state has played a crucial historical role in encouraging innovation.[3] To cite a particularly striking example: 'all the technologies that make the iPhone a smart phone were funded by the state, including the internet, GPS, touchscreen display and the voice-activated Siri personal assistant'.[4] State subsidy of innovation is justified because the state will be a more 'patient' investor than the private sector, more willing to gamble on an uncertain future. It is therefore a critical part of the process of capital accumulation which drives growth – a point recognized by the mercantilists, but foreign to 'scientific' economics. In analysing public investment banks, Mazzucato has suggested that they have played four different roles: as missionaries; as venture capitalists; as investors in infrastructure; and as countercyclical lenders. The latter was very clear during 2009–10 when institutions such as the Brazilian BNDES and the German KfW substituted for dried-up private bank lending.[5] The European Investment Bank has started to do the same in the European Union.

Thus, for both uncertainty and public goods reasons, Keynes in 1936 expected to see 'the State, which is in a position to calculate the marginal efficiency of capital-goods on long views and on the basis of the general social advantage, taking an ever greater responsibility for directly organising investment'.[6] However, things have gone in the opposite direction.

In the UK, public investment as a share of total investment fell from over 20 per cent in the 1950s and 1960s to about 10 per cent from the 1980s onwards, with a brief spike under Gordon Brown. Ideology has minimized the importance of market failure and magnified the importance of government failure. Even so-called serious commentators believe the state is bound to 'pick losers'. The question, of course, is not whether

Figure 66. UK public investment as a share of total investment[7]
(per cent)

government always succeeds, but whether government failure is likely to be greater or lesser than the market failures it seeks to correct.

Fiscal Policy

The principles of a sensible fiscal constitution might be as follows:

Current spending should always be covered by taxation. There is much to be said for the old British Treasury rule that the budget for current spending should be set to balance annually, budget balance providing a surplus (sinking fund) to pay down debt. The current spending budget should include all transfer payments, i.e. social security benefits, pensions, etc.; the more desirable these are regarded as, the higher taxation will need to be. In a recession, sinking fund payments would be reduced or suspended, the resulting deficit being used to finance public works instead. There should be a buffer stock of such works, which would be expanded in a downturn and contracted in an upturn. Providing people with work, even temporarily, is better than paying them to do nothing. Public works schemes should be located in areas of high unemployment and should offer employment at the minimum wage. Whether such schemes add to the nation's stock of assets is immaterial. Much more important is the role they can play in keeping the link to work.

The important fiscal rule for the capital budget is that the state should be prepared to borrow for any beneficial capital spending *additional* to the normal capital outlay of the private sector. The role of the central bank is to enable it to borrow for such purposes as cheaply as possible. The aim should be to restore public investment to about 20 per cent of total investment. The purpose of this is not so much to use public investment as a counter-cyclical tool (though housing construction could fairly easily be expanded and contracted with the cycle), but to provide a sufficiently large and steady stream of demand to smooth out fluctuations in private investment.

In theory, all public investment could be a charge on the state's capital budget. However, where projects are potentially profitable but, for short-termist or other reasons, unattractive to private investors, there is a good case for outsourcing them to independent or quasi-independent institutions, such as a State Investment Bank, run on commercial lines. The reasons for doing so are partly psychological.

Their borrowing would be 'off budget' and so avoid the hostility which attaches to any increase in the government deficit.[8] Public confidence in the value of their investments will be increased if they are seen to be independent of politics. But there are also solid economic reasons. The managers and employees of such an institution would be able to provide technical services and skills which a government bureaucracy lacks. The commercial aim of the Bank would be to earn a rate of return on the average of its investments equal to their cost.

How would it work? The Investment Bank would be capitalized by the state, and empowered to borrow an agreed multiple of its capital for approved purposes; that is, the state would determine the Bank's strategic direction, and the managers would have full operational independence. Depending on the Bank's mandate, such purposes might include investments in energy efficiency, long-term loans to small enterprises and start-up companies through a network of local banks, and support for private venture capital initiatives like FinTech. Being state-owned, the Bank's implicit taxpayer guarantee would enable it to finance projects that would be unviable at the usual risky lending rate. Considered an almost revolutionary innovation in Britain and the United States, public investment banks are up and running in a number of European countries, with good results.[9]

France, Italy and other countries also have state holding companies, operating transport and public utilities. Italy has successful state holding companies (IRI and ENI) involved in a wide range of enterprises, not just natural monopolies. If the railways, water companies and parts of the energy sector are renationalized in the UK, as the Labour Party has proposed, a state holding company, at arm's length from the politicians, would be the right vehicle for public investment in them. The case, though, still needs to be made that public ownership of such companies is superior to regulation.

Where investment projects require a long-term taxpayer commitment, as would be true of new hospitals, schools, colleges and universities, and fundamental scientific research, the state should raise the capital itself, with money for recruiting extra staff being a charge on the capital budget for the period of the loan. Although they lack a calculable social rate of return, such investments may still be, as Adam Smith said, 'in the highest degree advantageous to a great society'.

Taxpayer commitment need not imply a growing taxpayer liability. Although they do not directly 'pay for themselves', they do so indirectly by raising productivity. That the state is, uniquely through its power to tax, in a position to reap such unpriced benefits is probably the strongest argument for increasing the state's share of investment from its present low level.[10] But just because state investment lacks what Janos Kornai called a 'hard budget constraint', it is best to have a rule specifying its limits. The Gordon Brown rule to maintain a constant debt/GDP ratio is still the best on offer, though there is nothing sacrosanct about any particular ratio. Short-term fluctuations round the given ratio are to be expected, but a secular tendency for the ratio to rise would indicate that the social rate of return from public investment was reaching its limits.

The new fiscal constitution might look something like this:[*]

Type of expenditure	Current expenditure	Capital expenditure		
Institution involved	Government current account	Government capital account	National public investment bank	State holding company
Budgetary rule	Balanced budget over the year	Nominal interest rate on borrowing ≤ nominal growth rate	Self-financing (positive portfolio rate of return over cost)	Self-financing (user charges cover borrowing)
Functions	Public administration's costs (salaries, operating costs, transfers etc.); etc.	Building of: a) schools; b) hospitals; c) some infrastructure, e.g. railways, roads; d) fundamental scientific research	Industrial and innovative projects; efficient energy; venture capital; equity support to innovative companies	Investment in utilities (natural monopolies) Competing and co-operating with other firms in certain strategic sectors and economic activities Applied but risky research

* I am indebted to Simone Gasperin for suggesting this sketch.

IV. THE INFLATION PROBLEM

In 1984, the then British Chancellor, Nigel Lawson, announced that the object of macroeconomic policy was the 'conquest of inflation'. This object came to be embodied in mandates given to nearly all central banks over the following years: to hit pre-set 'inflation targets' – usually in the region of 2 per cent annual inflation. To achieve these targets, central banks were given 'operational independence' over interest rates. Today, the urgent need is to 'conquer under-employment'. In this situation, to be left with the 'conquest of inflation' as the only extant macro-policy aim is archaic, indeed nonsensical, when, for the last ten years, the problem has been deflation, not inflation.

Sensible economists, not all of them Keynesians, have recognized the absurdity of macro-policy being uniquely concerned with the price level, and have suggested altering central banks' mandates. Central banks, they say, should be explicitly given a 'dual mandate' to include output as well as inflation. Simon Wren-Lewis, a leading British New Keynesian, has gone further: he suggests that when the central bank's policy rate hits the 'lower bound' – putting orthodox monetary policy out of action – the central bank should be authorized to tell the government that fiscal policy is needed.[11]

It has been objected that broadening the mandates of central banks would destroy their hard-won anti-inflationary credentials by creating uncertainty about the future course of monetary policy. This objection has merit. But neither the proposal to widen central bank mandates nor the argument against it go to the heart of the problem – which is that monetary policy on its own is too weak to ensure the stability of the macroeconomy.

The mainstream analysis was that, provided only that the price of credit was controlled by the central bank, market economies would be cyclically stable at full employment. This was the Wicksellian promise, somewhere between monetarism and Keynesianism, and therefore embraced by New Keynesians as a compromise between the two. The allure of macroeconomic policy a la Wicksell was that it promised to achieve both price stability and full employment by means of a single instrument, Bank Rate, which would impact simultaneously (or after a short lag) on both prices and output.

In the period of the Great Moderation, from 1995 to 2007, this slimmed down machinery of macro-control seemed to run like clockwork. Inflation was stable and low, as was unemployment. Few economists can resist a correlation which seems to confirm their theories. The fact that there was, for a few years, a statistical link between interest rates and prices tells us no more about what caused it than do previous attempts to 'prove' the quantity theory of money. A better explanation of the correlation is the massive entry of cheap Chinese goods into the world market, which subdued inflation and enabled central banks to keep the cost of credit very low. Benefiting from a happy conjunction of events, central bankers attributed the Great Moderation to their own perspicacity.

Then came 2008. Far from being securely in the 'long run' of optimum performance, economies suddenly found themselves in the Keynesian 'short run' of falling output, with only interest rate policy available to fight it. When the policy rate hit the 'lower bound', central banks embarked on quantitative easing. Conventional monetary policy before the crash failed to avert a collapse; unconventional monetary policy after the crash failed to bring about a recovery. What experience since the 1980s suggests is that while dear money can cause a depression, cheap money cannot prevent one.

So what should be the role of central banks and monetary policy in the macroeconomic constitution of the future? If one believes that the collapse of 2008–9 was a one-off event, highly unlikely to be repeated in our lifetimes, then there may be no great case for changing the current central bank mandate. On this view, the permanent danger against which policy needs to guard is the inflation produced by vote-seeking politicians. This remains the mainstream view.

On the other hand, if collapses on the scale of 2008–9 are an ever-present possibility in market economies, as both Marx and Keynes, for different reasons, believed, stabilizing the economy at a high level of activity will require more instruments than just interest rate policy. A central bank can only influence demand indirectly through setting a price for borrowing money; the government can influence it directly through its tax and spend policies. In short, if the economic drama is more Keynesian than Friedmanite or Wicksellian, central bankers should not have the starring role.

The following conclusions suggest themselves:

1. The 'conquest of inflation' is not today's most pressing priority and hardly likely to be so for many years to come. Policy rates are still stuck at very near zero. They cannot quickly be restored as regulators of activity, and most serious people understand that it is lunatic to go on flooding the economy with money which is not spent on currently produced output. In short, monetary policy is as disabled now as fiscal policy was in 2010.

2. The view that central bank interest rate policy can, unaided, prevent inflation or deflation, is a myth. The low inflation of the Great Moderation was due not to the wisdom of central bankers, but to a favourable environment, which importantly included the 'China price'. Strong deflationary forces made it impossible for monetary policy on its own to 'lift' the rate of inflation after the 2008 crisis struck, despite massive injections of central bank cash into the economy. The reason for the relative weakness of monetary policy is that its influence on aggregate demand is indirect.

3. Fiscal and monetary policy should be coordinated, not separated. The idea that 'sound money' is needed to guard against 'fiscal excess' comes from the set of ideas that regards government as the problem, never the solution. But if the problem is the natural volatility of the market system, government is a crucial part of the solution.

4. Because fiscal policy is the more powerful weapon (and because governments, unlike central bankers, are accountable to voters), the government should be the senior partner in macro-policy. Specifically, the trade-off between inflation and unemployment at any one time, or over several years, should be a matter of political judgment. It cannot be outsourced to technicians, whose job should be to advise on the consequence of political choices, not to make them.

5. Central banks would lose their independent control of interest rates. Their mandates should be to support the economic policy of the government. They would advise governments on Bank Rate, not decide it, and they would, uniquely for a state agency,

have the right to publish their dissent. For countries with their own governments and their own currencies, a change in mandate simply requires a change in domestic law. This would, in effect, restore the position to what it generally was before the late 1990s. Such a change in the mandate of the European Central Bank is presently impossible, because there is no central government to tell the European Central Bank what to do.

6. Such a reform would deprive central banks of their policy role, but leave them with the vital task of ensuring the stability of the banking system. Regulatory tools, long in disuse, will need to be revived. Given the culpability of the financial system for the collapse of 2008–9, it is the central bank's regulatory, not its policy, role that needs prioritizing.

V. MAKING BANKING SAFE

The financial system caused the Great Recession, but it was allowed to. Its faults were licensed. Reform of banking that does not include regulating what banks are allowed to do will miss the point. As Professor James Galbraith tells it:

> These are institutions with high fixed costs, with technologies and transnational legal structures that are designed to facilitate tax evasion and regulatory arbitrage, and which face very limited prospects for sustained profitability in activities that correspond to social need. Their entire structure isn't viable in a world of slow growth, except by fostering short-lived booms followed by busts and bailouts. In short, the financial sector as a whole is a luxury we cannot afford.[12]

One could add that a corrupted capitalism is also a political luxury too far, because it is certain to provoke a popular backlash.

Because of the damage they inflict on the economy, banking collapses generally lead to the demand for banking reform. Following the Great Depression of the 1930s, the US Congress passed the Banking Act of 1933, popularly known as the Glass–Steagall Act, which separated deposit-taking from investment banking, and introduced deposit insurance for the former. The 2008–9 banking crisis also led to a reform agenda, aimed at limiting bank failures and hence recourse to the taxpayer for bank bail-outs. The difference between the two reform agendas is that the earlier one was embedded in a much more extensive programme of economic reform, whereas today the consensus view is that, provided only that the banking system can be made more 'resilient to shocks', everything else can continue exactly the same as before. (I abstract from the new world of crypto (encrypted) currencies started outside the banking system. Using digital technology to hide the transactions of their users from regulatory scrutiny, they have so far mainly been useful for speculation and money laundering.)

Functional Separation

The earliest idea for reform was to break up big banks into smaller units – local, neighbourhood, regional. This would eliminate the 'too big to fail' problem, and reconnect banks with their depositors. In fact, the financial crisis has increased the concentration of the banking system, as such crises always do. The ten biggest banks in the US now control 75 per cent of American assets, as opposed to 10 per cent in 1990. So reformist ideas shifted to separating banks by function. This harks back to Glass–Steagall.

The principle of separating retail from speculative banking underlines the Paul Volcker-inspired Dodd–Frank Act in the USA, the Vickers-inspired Financial Services Act in the UK, and the Liikanen Report sponsored by the European Commission.[13] The main idea behind all three is that deposit-taking banks should not also be investment houses. Such separation would reduce 'moral hazard': risky lending would not be publicly insured against loss.

The problem is that the core activity of retail banks has become the mortgage business. It was the retail not the 'shadow banking' sector which initiated the banking crisis of 2007: the British bank Northern Rock, which had to be rescued by the government and nationalized early in 2008, provided mortgages for a quarter of the population. Securitization made this supposedly safe business unexpectedly risky. Functional separation on its own will do little to check the credit cycle generated by mortgage-lending or limit taxpayer liability for its excesses.

Compelling banks to hold mortgages for a period of years, plus a big boost to social house-building, would cool this particular inflammation.

Macroprudential Regulation

More recently, the main aim of reform has been to make banks more 'resilient' to shocks.

Following the crash of 2008, the G20 set up a Financial Stability Board to improve global financial stability. In the UK, a Prudential Regulatory Authority was established in the Bank of England, charged with a 'primary objective of identifying, monitoring and taking action to remove or reduce systemic risks with a view to protecting and enhancing the resilience of the UK financial system'. The EU's Financial Stability Board (FSB) is tasked with implementing a Capital Requirements Directive (CRD), a Bank Recovery and Resolution Directive (BRRD) and a Single Resolution Mechanism (SRM). The main object of these initiatives is to strengthen banks' ability to survive shocks by strengthening their balance sheets *ex ante*. They include beefing up banks' capital and liquidity requirements, regulating the derivatives' market and strengthening creditor liability for bank failure.

The record of augmenting banks' capital stocks, which started with Basel I in 1988 and continued with Basel II in 1994, hardly inspires confidence. Basel I and II required banks to hold 'risk-weighted'[14] capital equal to 8 per cent of their assets. (See Ch. 11, pp. 317–18.) When the crash came, the actual equity of some of the major banks was only 2–3 per cent of their assets. The new minimum capital ratios stipulated by Basel III – up to 30 per cent for systemically important banks – similarly assume that risks are measurable either by the regulator or by the banks themselves. If they are unknown and unknowable, there will always be either too much or too little capital in store for the next turn in the tide of activity. To get round this problem, some central banks now have the authority to vary capital adequacy requirements countercyclically. But this assumes that the regulator can know accurately at what point in the cycle the economy, or any particular sector of it, has reached.

The capital adequacy approach to bank regulation has been predictably condemned by banking spokesmen. A typical complaint is that 'higher bank capital requirements intensified the Great Recession, and renewed calls for tighter requirements threaten to cut the slowly recovering economy off at the knees once more'.[15] A more credible complaint is that, if tougher capital requirements curtail the risky lending of systemically important investment banks, it will migrate to banks not subject to them. The vulnerability of the system as a whole will remain.

Banking 'resilience' is also to be improved by 'stress testing'. Central bank regulators test how banks would fare in the event of another crisis. If they fail to meet their capital requirements relative to their risk-weighted assets, they will have to raise more capital. Mario Draghi, Governor of the ECB, said, 'the ultimate purpose of [stress testing] is to restore or strengthen private sector confidence in the soundness of the banks, in the quality of their balance sheets'.[16] Having spectacularly failed its latest 'stress test', the bailed-out Royal Bank of Scotland announced 'important steps to enhance our capital strength'.[17] Europe's oldest bank, Monte dei Paschi di Siena, was trying to raise €5 billion, after failing its summer 2016 stress test. The problem with stress tests is not so much that banks will find ways to evade them, but that they rely on the same risk-assessment techniques that failed to spot the risks banks were running before 2007.

A more radical-sounding route to 'resilience' is to raise banks' reserve or liquidity requirements. Cash reserves against deposits were run down to almost nothing pre-crash. This caused a credit-crunch when banks stopped lending to each other. Basel III seeks to ensure that at all times banks have enough sufficiently liquid assets to meet all payments due in thirty days. Since 2009, UK-based banks have been required to hold a buffer of central bank reserves or gilts, the amounts to be determined by 'stress tests'. In the USA and China, 10 per cent and 20 per cent liquidity ratios are in force, respectively. The problem with this approach is that it assumes that reserves determine the amount of lending, whereas it is truer to say that lending determines the amount of reserves; that is, the central bank will always supply sufficient reserves to the banking system to prevent liquidity crises and volatile interest rates.

To deal with the threat of insolvency, central banks have set up 'resolution regimes'. Their object is to allow the regulators to intervene early enough in the rake's progress to ensure that the bank can carry on its business, while avoiding the taxpayer having to pick up the bill. This requires that the authorities have the power to restructure a bank before insolvency hits and possess a 'bail-in tool' to ensure that, in any restructuring, the bank's losses are borne by its shareholders and creditors rather than by the taxpayer.[18] The ambitious double aim is to forestall liquidations like Lehman Brothers *and* sovereign debt crises such as afflicted governments in Portugal, Ireland and Greece, when they bailed out their banks.

Such regimes have been enacted in the USA, the UK and the European Union. The EU, largely at Germany's insistence, has gone furthest. Its Single Resolution Board, started on 1 January 2016, decides how much of any bank's losses should be borne by its shareholders and bondholders. At the same time, the Commission agreed to restructure deposit insurance, by setting up a fund that will build up over eight years from *ex ante* contributions from the banking sector, with contributions proportionate to risks.

Since 'resolving' the affairs of a big 'stressed' international bank with hundreds of branches and subsidiaries, many different classes of shareholder, creditor and debtor, and located in dozens of separate jurisdictions, is likely to defy the best efforts of a Single Resolution Board, systemically important banks are being asked to submit 'living wills' to ensure that their mortality will not be at the public's expense. Under the US Dodd–Frank Act, any bank with a capitalization over $50 billion must describe the company's strategy for rapid and orderly resolution (i.e. liquidation) in the event of its failure.

The first eleven such 'wills' submitted by big US banks were deemed inadequate by the regulators. Unsurprisingly, Thomas Hoenig, Vice-Chairman of the Federal Deposit Insurance Corporation, commented: 'The plans provide no credible or clear path through bankruptcy that doesn't require . . . direct or indirect public support.'[19]

Changing Banking Culture

In July 2014, the think-tank ResPublica published a report called 'Virtuous Banking: Placing ethos and purpose at the heart of finance'. It argued that the 'inherent lack of virtue amongst our banking institutions' was the 'root cause of the financial crisis'. It pointed out that fraud continued unabated. The 'self-serving' culture of banks needed to be challenged, as without this, banks would circumvent the regulations.[20] ResPublica proposed a banker's oath, modelled on the Hippocratic oath sworn by doctors, which would enjoin a duty of care on bankers towards their customers.

There are proposals to detach financial compensation from short-term stock-price performance, to fine bankers for unethical practices, and to cap or claw back bonuses. Nick Leeson, the original 'rogue trader' whose exploits brought down Barings Bank in 1995, has cut through the thinness of these precautions: 'If we are going to try and change a banker's bonus structure, I think within 15 minutes they will have a new structure that works in the same way. They have the best accountants and lawyers.'[21] The root of the problem is the greed for money. As long as bankers continue to believe that they can get away with flexible ethical standards, they will do so. Bankers have got off lightly. Banks have been fined enormous sums for frauds that in other professions would result in custodial sentences, but very few bankers are in jail.

Financial Intensity

The global financial system has grown faster than trade; and trade has grown faster than production. This is what Adair Turner means when he talks of the increase of 'financial intensity' – the ratio of financial transactions to total economic transactions. In advanced economies, bank balances as a ratio of GDP – a measure of financial transactions – had risen from 70 per cent in 1980 to over 450 per cent in 2011. Financial intensity is thus a measure of credit creation in excess of the needs of non-financial business. Its growth is what is meant by the 'financialization' of economic life.

Turner writes that 'there is no evidence that advanced economies have become overall more efficient as a result of the post-1970 increase in financial intensity . . . and the development of a bigger and more innovative financial system led to the crisis of 2007–2008 and to a severe recession'.[22] The reason for this is that most credit created by banks is not issued to finance new investment – the creation of new productive assets – but to expand consumption and speculate in real estate, currencies and stock markets. This leads to a volatile, destructive credit cycle.[23]

Proposals to reduce financialization include forcing banks to hold 100 per cent reserves against their loans, and abolishing deposit insurance. Such Hayekian measures to restrict credit creation would simultaneously attack the build-up of over-optimism and moral hazard. However, neither reform gets to the root of the 'excess credit' problem, which, we have suggested, is the stagnation of real earnings. This results in the substitution of speculative for productive investment and easy consumer credit for vanishing welfare entitlements. The globalization of finance amplifies both tendencies, since it gives banks almost unlimited opportunities for regulatory arbitrage.

An aspect of financialization little discussed in polite circles is the extent of its criminality. A sizeable fraction of the money sloshing around the world originates in criminal activity – often Russian and Middle Eastern – which is then 'laundered' through Special Purpose Vehicles set up in offshore tax havens under fake owners. Much of the laundering is done through London, which boasts the most sophisticated financial service industry in the world. Regulators run checks on the origins of deposits, but the volume of transactions defeats them. Closing down offshore deposits, or requiring that they be registered in the name of their real owners, would curb this source of criminality.

Reform proposals have been dogged by bankers' complaints about the unnecessary regulations. These complaints have survived the damage under-regulated banks have done: 'Wholesale capital markets', the bankers declare self-righteously, 'contribute to the efficient allocation of capital. International banks match savers and borrowers across the globe, reducing funding costs, facilitating cross-border investment and financing trade.'[24] It is considered politically impertinent to question this celebration of banking benefactions, so productive of well-deserved profits. In truth, the reform measures proposed, and the even fewer of them enacted, have been palpably insufficient to attain their aim of making banks resilient to shocks. This is because they have not been part of a broader strategy of economic reform.

Banks should be obliged to hold mortgages for a minimum period; financial innovation should be controlled; the flow of footloose capital around the world should be restricted. But such reforms will not be possible without a lessening of the social reliance on bank credit. The economy doesn't work well for the average person, who then has to resort to borrowing to fulfil customary expectation. A more stable economy is the key to safer banking. The neo-liberal project of removing the state from economic management has made economic life less secure; the result of which has been a more speculative financial system. The unsettled question is whether financial regulation can be made sufficiently global to support a global financial system.

VI. INEQUALITY

I have suggested that the deeper cause of the banking collapse of 2007–8 was the growth of inequality. A big expansion in the 'financial circulation' (debt) had been required to sustain mass consumption and to speculate in risky assets in the face of falling real earnings and yields. There is little evidence that these trends have been reversed.

In a cryptic letter to T. S. Eliot in 1945, Keynes envisaged three possible forms post-war economic policy might take:

> . . . the full employment policy by means of investment is only one particularly application of an intellectual theorem. You can produce the result just as well by consuming more or working less. Personally I regard the investment policy as first aid. In U.S. it almost certainly will not do the trick. Less work is the ultimate solution (a 35 hour week in U.S. would do the trick now). How you mix up the three ingredients of a cure is a matter of taste and experience, i.e. of morals and knowledge.[25]

In writing this, Keynes took the standard view that there is no 'optimum' rate of investment for any community. It depends on how wealthy it already is. Neo-classical economic theory tells us that the scarcer the capital stock, the higher the rate of return to capital investment. So poor countries should consume less and save more. Present sacrifice will earn future reward. The moral for rich countries would seem to be the opposite: save less, consume more, work less and learn to enjoy life. Nirvana is the state of not wanting more than one already has.

The nineteenth-century idea of the 'stationary state' was based on the notion of capital saturation. It envisaged a situation in which there were constant 'stocks' of people and capital, and therefore the

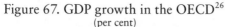

Figure 67. GDP growth in the OECD[26]
(per cent)

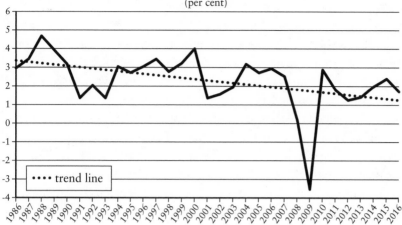

economy simply reproduced itself. In the pessimistic version of Ricardo, the declining marginal fertility of the soil brings growth to an end long before human wants are satiated. Efficiency in production could delay the outcome, but not avert it. The 'limits of nature' argument of modern ecological economics is a contemporary version of Ricardo's argument, though one projected from a much higher base of affluence.

In the optimistic version of John Stuart Mill, echoed by Keynes in his 1930 essay 'Economic Possibilities for our Grandchildren', and shared by John Hicks, the stationary state comes at the point of saturation of human needs. This kind of stationary state was desirable because it would free humanity from the burden of toil. In Keynes's vision, the mores of society would no longer be driven by the need to accumulate capital: for the first time in history most people would be able to devote themselves to the 'art of life' rather than to the 'means of life'.

In the last thirty years the average growth rate of rich societies has slowed down, as Figure 67 shows. In the standard growth model, this reflects a decline in the rate at which the advanced countries are adding to their capital stock. Superficially this suggests that Western societies are approaching their 'bliss point'. Growth deceleration should be regarded not as a problem, but as a culmination. It is possible to interpret the 'stagnation' of Japan as the social choice of a rich society.[27]

However, a more pessimistic view is taken by modern 'secular stagnation' theorists such as Paul Krugman and Larry Summers.[28]

For Krugman, 'persistent shortfalls in demand' for new capital goods are to be explained by the increasingly skewed distribution of income. Because the rich save more of their incomes than do the poor, there will be a persistent tendency, in capitalist societies, for saving to 'run ahead' of investment, causing Keynesian under-employment. The remedies are public investment programmes and income redistribution. The former can plug the investment gap; the latter the consumption gap. Time will determine the relative weights to be attached to the two remedies.

Like Krugman, Larry Summers denies there has been a *secular* collapse in productivity growth; i.e. that rich societies today are close to the 'saturation' or 'bliss' point identified by Mill and Keynes. If, in fact, human wants are insatiable (as most economists believe), the bliss point is bound to be a moving target: the more people have, the more they want. It is just that capitalism, as presently organized, prevents most people from having what they want. Summers attaches particular importance to the 'hysteresis' produced by the collapse of 2008–9 (see p. 239). Thus the theory of secular stagnation is a contemporary version of under-consumption theory.

Market optimists regard the problem as spurious: technology and globalization will keep growth in line with expanding consumer wants, if unfettered by government restrictions. Market pessimists would urge a substantial redistribution of wealth and income from the rich to the poor, both on grounds of social justice and to lessen reliance on debt-fuelled growth.

Optimists and pessimists alike abstract from the problem of automation. Yet Keynes foresaw in 1930 that automation would reduce the demand for human work. As he put it, we will need to 'spread the bread thin on the butter – to make what work there is still to be done as widely shared as possible'.[29] The state's task would be not to guarantee full employment in the current sense, but to enable an orderly transition to a shorter working week: this was the point he made in his letter to Eliot in 1945.

Keynes's prediction hasn't yet materialized, but he may be right in the end. In the past, new technology made some jobs obsolete, but simultaneously made other workers more productive.[30] Likewise, it created, and is still creating, whole new areas of work such as web design, hi-tech engineering, programming, data analysis and so forth. An ageing population will require more looking after. But now machine intelligence is improving at such a rapid rate that the distinction between capital and labour is blurring. New technology may, indeed, create as many jobs as it destroys, but the new workers will be machines, not humans. For the first time in history, human labour may be being made redundant faster than new human employment is being found for it; i.e. the 'technological unemployment' predicted by Wassily Leontief in 1979[31] may be turning into a reality.

If this turns out to be the case, the income equalization which can serve the narrow purposes of the modern secular stagnationist will need to become an essential ingredient of policy in the future. Workers displaced by machines will need to be guaranteed a replacement income. An unconditional basic income guarantee, financed by taxation, will probably be needed in the transition to a less work-intensive future. This raises a whole host of problems which are beyond the scope of this book, but should not be irrelevant to the design of long-term macroeconomic policy.

VII. HYPER-GLOBALIZATION AND ITS DISCONTENTS

In the early 1990s it was usual to say that the world economy was 're-globalizing', or returning to its pre-1914 condition after a seventy-year protectionist detour. Three developments have shattered this optimistic prognosis. The first was the unexpected financial meltdown in East Asia in 1997-8, which, following the Mexican peso crisis of 1995, highlighted the instability of global financial markets and the inadequacy of the world's financial architecture. Second, were the mass protests in Geneva in 1998 and Seattle in 1999 against the setting up of the World Trade Organization (WTO). These marked the start of a popular insurrection against globalization. Insofar as the loose coalition of economic nationalists, anti-capitalists, environmentalists, anarchists and trade unionists had a coherent message, it was that the WTO transferred power from elected governments to multinational corporations. It was a predominantly rich country protest against free trade, though often couched in terms of Western big business exploiting poor countries.[32] The third event was the even more unexpected collapse of the developed world's 'mature' financial system in 2008. This sharpened the sense that globalization was harmful to rich countries. Since the Great Recession of 2008–9, these anti-globalist stirrings have splintered and morphed into populist movements of both right and left. Globalization has, in reaction, created global populism.[33] Our political language finds it hard to keep up. There is still a political divide between right and left, but it is increasingly overshadowed by one between nationalism and globalism.

Twenty years or so ago it was usual to think of globalization as a unified process involving not just economic/technical but also political/cultural transformation. The internet was conceived as the decisive game-changer in both spheres. By changing the technical means by which people communicated with each other it would change the way they related to each other. Now it is increasingly recognized that economic/technical change has been racing ahead of political/cultural change. This explains the upsurge of old-fashioned nationalism.

The globalist typically wants culture to adapt to the imperatives of economic interdependence, and is surprised and disappointed when it hits back in discordant, often ugly ways. France's President Emmanuel Macron has described populism as the politics of those 'left behind'. This is right, as long as it is recognized that the feeling of being left behind is not just economic, but also cultural. At heart the globalist thinks of anti-globalist feeling as a social pathology, which needs to be explained, rather than as a reasonable response to what, for many, are distressing events. Globalists demand that people *adapt* to seemingly irreversible economic changes, without understanding that it is a mutual adaptation which is needed. Societies have very strong adaptive capacities, but they are not infinitely malleable, like bits of putty.

Thus it would be wrong to see anti-globalization as just fuelled by economic discontent. Sociology, anthropology and history have been undermining the economist's understanding of human nature. *Homo economicus*, the man who lives for bread alone, has given way to a more complex understanding of the human as a social animal for whom belonging and eating are interconnected elements of being. Hence the rise of identity politics is not just a protest against job losses, declining wages and rising inequality but – just as importantly – a protest against cultural changes which are robbing people of their need for the familiar and normal. An economics which both minimizes the possibility of non-material forms of flourishing and fails to deliver its own promised goods is ripe for populist demolition.

Donald Trump is the most important populist to have won high office so far (Viktor Orbán, prime minister of Hungary, is the most important European populist in power), but popular opposition to the free movement of goods, capital and labour has stopped globalization in its tracks. Trade and capital flows have recovered from the 2008–9 crisis at about the same pace as output, but no faster. There has been no multilateral trade agreement since 1993; instead there has been a proliferation of bilateral deals. Trump promises to scrap the North American Free Trade Agreement of 1992, and the Trans-Atlantic and Trans-Pacific trade treaties conjured up by President Obama. He announced tariffs on imports from China and the EU in what could well be the opening shots of a new trade war. Capital movements are being restricted de facto on security grounds. Free movement of labour is curtailed in North America and Europe. The most astounding reversion to national economics was the British vote in 2016 to leave the European Union.

The kernel of the problem is that the market system lives by generating systemic upheaval, not just in economic but in social relations, as Marx recognized. Out of the upheaval comes a better life – or so it is claimed. But along the way there is a great deal of human breakage, and in the short-run many losers. That is why a market system, to be generally acceptable, requires a state to curb its excesses, distribute its fruits in an equitable way, and mitigate its hardships. National states were created to do this; they in turn created and enabled unified domestic markets. We have been trying to create a unified global market by diminishing national states without setting up a global state, or even recognizing the need for one. No wonder there has been an explosion of popular resistance.

Karl Polanyi brilliantly analysed the emergence, in the nineteenth century, of the simultaneous double movement towards greater marketization *and* state protection against its consequences, the numerous Factory Acts of the early industrial revolution, to protect children and limit hours of work being one of his main examples. The first great age of globalization in the late 1800s saw the extension of this double movement: the growth of the international market led to the birth of welfare states, the restoration of protective tariffs, and the establishment of central banks to minimize financial crises.

However, such *national* defences against the consequences of globalization were never incorporated into a rule-based international order. Its absence brought the first age of globalization crashing down in 1914. Following the disintegration of the world economy in the 1930s, Allied victory in the Second World War led to the setting up of a more robust set of international institutions and rules, the so-called Bretton Woods system, to underpin a revived liberal market order. Significantly, it allowed, while seeking to relax, the protective national controls over the transnational movement of trade, capital and people left over from the 1930s. What was set up was an 'embedded' liberal trading system as an international counterpart to post-1945 Keynesian social democracy in domestic politics. It fell far short of providing an economic government of the world, however, just as the United Nations failed to provide a political government. In practice, the United States acted as a kind of surrogate government for the free world in both economics and politics (just as the Soviet Union did for its own sphere). The surrogate was more or less legitimate because US hegemony was partly disguised and America provided services deemed indispensable by its beneficiaries. This liberal mix of national leadership, international institutions and markets, backed by hard power where necessary, provided a solid-enough basis for peace and prosperity for thirty years.

The unrepentant resurgence of globalization was made possible by capitalism's triumph over communism. Although in the 1990s the Soviet Union failed to match the economic performance of the capitalist West, for many years the appeal of communism checked the power of the business class. But, since 1990 neo-liberal statecraft has been unchallenged. It scrapped or emasculated the protectionist features of the post-war order which made it politically acceptable. Enslaved by utopian theories and ignorant of history, the ideologues of the free market have been preparing the ground for the Apocalypse.

Di/Trilemma

The conflict between cross-border economic integration and national systems of politics is at the heart of Dani Rodrik's intriguing notion of the 'impossible trinity'. He contends that democracy, national sovereignty and economic integration are mutually incompatible: we can have any two of them, but not the three together. National sovereignty can be combined with economic integration if there is no democracy – as happened in the nineteenth century because there were too few voters to protest against it. We can have national sovereignty and democracy at the expense of economic integration. Or we can have economic integration and democracy together, provided we have democratically accountable supra-national institutions. The argument is over-stylized because at all times rulers have had to pay attention to their people, and most nineteenth-century states were protectionist. The value of Rodrik's exercise is to challenge the conventional wisdom that economic integration is irreversible. His trilemma offers an explanation of why the first wave of globalization was rolled back in 1914, and warns of disaster if we persist in global fantasies that are not anchored in the realities of nation states and their voters. Economics has gone global but politics remains national. The contradiction between the two domains of action explains the rise of populism. Either we create an international social contract or nationalist economics will return.

The Case of Europe

The European Union is a model of a currently failing effort at economic integration. The Treaty of Rome of 1957 committed the founding states to the 'Four Freedoms' – freedom of movement of goods, services, capital and labour. These are the building blocks of the Economic and Monetary Union (EMU), and are held to be indivisible. To enshrine them at the heart of the EU signified the ambition of its founding fathers to create a state, or 'political union'. But the state has not arrived. The competences of the EU's central institutions, the scope of its rules, have been constantly expanded, but their accountability has not kept pace. Instead of democratic accountability there are rules against money creation, fiscal deficits, unfair competition and so on. But strong rules and weak states are a contradiction in terms. Complaints about the 'democratic deficit' have been growing and have exploded in powerful anti-European populist movements.

The rules started to crumble as soon as they were put to the test in 2008–10. The jewel in the EMU's crown was the Single Currency Area, started in 1997. Paul de Grauwe has identified its two main design faults: the lack of a fiscal transfer mechanism, and the lack of a lender of last resort for the banking system. As a result, liquidity crises have spilt over into solvency crises, and solvency crises into sovereign debt crises.[34] 'This dynamic can force countries into a bad equilibrium characterised by increasing interest rates that trigger excessive austerity measures, which in turn lead to a deflationary spiral that aggravates the fiscal crisis.' The only remedy, de Grauwe argues, is a 'budgetary union'. By 'centralising part of the national budgets into a common budget managed by a common political authority, the different increases in budget deficits . . . translate into a budget deficit at the union level' in time of recession. But the 'common political authority' needed for such a construction is 'far off'.[35] De Grauwe's two design flaws can be reduced to one: the lack of a legitimate state. Keynesians spotted the flaw in this reasoning from the start.[36]

Political Union (otherwise a state) was always expected to be built alongside the Economic and Monetary Union. Indeed, the more cynical, or realistic, Europeanists saw the inevitable crises of the EMU as spurs to state-creation – a huge gamble that the integrative forces would prove more powerful than the distintegrative ones.

Today the future is in the balance. In response to the crisis, and its populist reactions, the Commission has proposed a European Monetary Fund and a European Finance Minister as the next instalment of statehood. But the Germans are opposed: they prefer risk prevention by strict rules to risk sharing through monetary and fiscal transfers, understandably from their point of view, since most of the risk will be transferred to them. They oppose a fiscal union for the same reason. A European Finance Minister without a usable budget is a symbol of futility.

Few of the sensible reforms needed to make the EU, and especially the eurozone, work well are feasible, because of the particularly rigid way they have been set up. Paradoxically, the working of this fixed-rule system depends on discretionary action by its leading member, Germany, which has the position, but not yet the outlook, of a Kindlebergian 'underwriter'.

To the threatened implosion of the world's most ambious experiment in stateless economic integration there are two possible reactions: 'One', writes de Grauwe, 'is to despair and to conclude that it would be better to dissolve the monetary union . . . The other reaction is to say, yes, it will be very difficult, and the chances of success are slim, but let's try anyway.'[37]

What Professor de Grauwe fails to explain is how the Eurozone came to be constructed with such a palpable design flaw. The standard answer is that it was part of the political deal that allowed the reunification of Germany. But just as importantly it reflected the view of neo-liberal economics that markets needed rules, not states.

The Case for Protection Revisited

The general presumption in favour of free trade has rarely been questioned since the nineteenth century. Tim Congdon does not beat about the bush: 'Free trade is good for you,' he tells us. 'Nations that adopt it . . . develop and prosper: they outperform nations that restrict imports and limit contact with the rest of the world.'[38] This is bad history, since many nations have prospered under Protection.

Protection is currently defined as 'the setting of trade barriers high enough to discourage foreign imports or to raise their prices sufficiently to enable relatively inefficient domestic producers to compete successfully with foreigners'.[39] The roots of this definition in the doctrine of comparative advantage are clear enough. The Protectionist would say that the primary duty of a government is to protect its own people from danger and misfortune. To do so while benefitting others is best of all. This was Adam Smith's powerful argument for free trade. But a government is not elected to promote the 'welfare of the world' at the expense of its own people. If it tries to, it will soon feel their wrath. Running through the free trade argument is the conviction that free trade is best *in the long-run*. It forgets that what happens in the short-run can blight the lives of a generation and, beyond that, those of their children.

There are seven main arguments for Protection:

1. The 'infant industry' argument, which we have already encountered (p. 89). Friedrich List rejected the static nature of Ricardo's theory. Initial conditions need not be final conditions. Comparative advantages could be consciously created by state policy by steps to foster initially uncompetitive manufactures. Ha-Joon Chang puts it graphically: 'had the Japanese government followed the free-trade economists back in the early 1960s, there would have been no Lexus. Toyota today would, at best, be a junior partner to some western car manufacturer, or worse, have been wiped out. The same would have been true of the entire Japanese economy.'[40] List did not think of Protection as a permanent system: after the 'infant industries' that he wanted protected had achieved maturity, free trade should be the rule. He forgot though that there is no end to economic development, because technology never stops. Today's advanced countries are full of industries, both senile and juvenile, clamouring for Protection.[41]

2. New or Strategic Trade Theory is an offshoot of the infant industry argument. In the standard free trade model, factor endowments – the determinants of comparative advantage – lie outside the model, whereas within the model there are constant returns to scale. New Protectionists like Nicholas Kaldor and Paul Krugman 'endogenized' the factors by postulating increasing returns to scale. Put simply, in a world of imperfect competition, starters' advantage cumulates. Increasing returns are captured by those who are first in the field with a new process or product, making them almost impossible to dislodge thereafter. In principle this can justify Protection for the infant industries of both developed and developing countries.[42] This argument, as can be seen, depends heavily on the persistence of monopoly. It makes little sense in today's world, where being first to build a transport system may lock a country into an obsolete state of the industrial arts.

3. Unemployment. The free trade model assumes full employment both before and after trade. The existence of a state of unemployment therefore provides an argument for Protection. This is a good argument.

378

4. The free trade case developed by Ricardo assumed that capital was mobile within countries, but immobile between countries. He recognized that if capital were free to maximize profit globally, the theory of comparative advantage would not hold 'because in that case international specialization will be determined by absolute costs, like specialization in one country'. There would then be no barrier to the depopulation of regions, even whole countries, if their costs were uncompetitive. Ricardo even hoped that men of property would keep their capital at home and be content with a modest profit.[43] Commenting on Ricardo's position, two authors write: '[T]his is also a question of the *culture* of capitalism. The type of "nativist" tradition which Ricardo expresses is no longer in keeping with the conditions of casino capitalism and its world of financial derivatives.'[44] Today capital exports are closely linked to the export of jobs via the export of technology. This can force higher-paid workers of the capital-exporting countries to compete with lower-wage labour abroad *using the same technology* – a competition which will either cost them their jobs or force down their wages. We should not forget that globalization was *intended* to depress wage growth in the developed world.

5. The 'strategic industry' argument. Protection has been advocated to safeguard war-making capacity. By contrast, free trade presupposes the permanent peace which it claims to help bring about.

6. The argument from diversity. Ricardo's theory required Portugal to concentrate on producing wine, leaving cloth production to Britain. Liberals who rightly value cultural diversity fail to understand that cultural diversity requires economic diversity.

7. Protection as a retaliation or bargaining chip. Tariffs, or their threat, may be used to negotiate 'fair trade' agreements. Only a country or group of countries with monopoly stakes in world trade can hope to deploy muscle for this purpose. The United States has often used protectionist tools to get other countries to limit their exports to the USA or reduce their trade barriers. Trump's Protectionist announcements may or may not be intended to leverage 'good' trade deals with China and Europe. The EU has just announced Protectionist countermeasures to Trump's Tax Cut Bill.[45]

In the orthodox view, all the valid arguments for Protection are 'second best': they presuppose, that is, that the political or economic conditions for beneficial free trade are lacking. But it could be that these conditions are lacking more often than not, in which case there can be no general presumption in favour of free trade.

While free trade remains accepted doctrine, many forms of disguised Protection flourish. Rich countries aim to protect their producers (under the guise of protecting their consumers) by imposing health and safety standards on imported products, or insisting on minimum labour standards for imported goods, often impossible for poor countries to meet. Countries such as China and Germany rely on under-valued currencies to maintain permanent export surpluses, in line with traditional mercantilist statecraft.

The pressure for Protection is growing. The main reason is that domestic protections for the less educated and less skilled have been progressively eroded at the same time as the speculative power of finance has been enlarged. The result is a substantial increase in insecurity. Populists want their own states to do more to protect their populations while at the same time limiting the power of finance to harm them. Traditional American economic nationalism has been re-ignited by the realization that continued reliance on credit from China and other surplus countries to finance American purchases of their goods is hollowing out the once mighty American economy.

Can political demands for a meaningful national 'control of our borders' be met without breaking up the world economy?

Reform of the World's Trading and Monetary Systems

In his Clearing Union plan of 1941, Keynes proposed a payments system to make the world safe for free trade. Its main purpose was to prevent countries running persistent trade surpluses. These, as he saw it, imposed deflation on deficit countries, who would respond by slapping on tariffs or depreciating their currencies. The International Monetary Fund, set up in 1944, rejected Keynes's logic of 'creditor adjustment'. But as a sop to the British it included, in Article 7, a 'scarce currency' clause, which allowed members of the Fund to restrict their purchases of goods from countries whose currency was declared 'scarce', i.e. which ran persistent current account surpluses. Debtor countries would also be protected from capital flight by restrictions on international capital mobility. Keynes understood that a good payments system was essential for 'good' trade.

Article 7 today could reasonably be invoked by the United States against China and by some members of the European Union against Germany. Cutting its trade deficit with China has long been an aim of American policy, but in the Trump Administration words are being translated more vigorously into action. Following the release of US strategy documents on national security, defence and trade late in 2017, which for the first time defined China as a strategic competitor, Trump imposed import duties of 50 per cent on washing machines, and tariffs of up to 30 per cent on solar panels. And in mid-February 2018 the US Commerce Department proposed the tariffs on US imports of steel and aluminium: 25 per cent on steel and 10 per cent on aluminium; China is the world's largest producer for both commodities.[46]

The economist Vladimir Masch has proposed a more coherent strategy of Compensated Free Trade (CFT) for a 'sensible' Trump Administration, which, in its essentials, amounts to unilateral activation by the United States of Article 7 of the Bretton Woods Agreement.[47] The US Administration would decide on the maximum amount of its desired trade deficit each year. In order to achieve its goal, it would impose limits on the surpluses of each important trading partner. This would chiefly affect China, Japan, Germany and Mexico; of the total $677 billion trade deficit of the US in 2016, China contributed $319 billion, Japan, $62 billion, Germany $60 billion and Mexico $59 billion.

It would then be up to the surplus country to limit its exports to the United States to the required amount. Countries could exceed their 'quotas' if they paid the difference between the value of their actual exports and the value of their allowed exports. If they tried to exceed their quotas without paying the 'fine', their surplus exports would be blocked.

As Chi Lo summarizes:

> In the longer-term, both China and the US seem to be striving for onshoring the globalised production chains built over the past three decades, with China doing it through import substitution to minimise

the foreign share of its industrial base and the US via America-first policies. Even partial success of these initiatives could be damaging.[48]

It is inconceivable that the proposed European Monetary Fund would contain an equivalent of Article 7, allowing, say, Greece, Italy and Portugal to limit imports from Germany, because this would be a major breach in the Customs Union.

In 1941 Keynes, while endorsing the case for 'permanent' control of capital movements, went on to say that

> this does not mean that the era of international investment should now be brought to an end ... The object, and it is a vital object, is to have a means of distinguishing (a) between movements of floating funds and genuine new investment for developing the world's resources; and (b) between movements, which will help to maintain equilibrium, from surplus countries to deficiency countries and speculative movements or flights out of deficiency countries, or from one surplus country to another. There is no country which can, in future, safely allow the flight of funds for political reasons or to evade domestic taxation or in anticipation of the owner turning refugee. Equally, there is no country which can safely receive fugitive funds which cannot be safely used for fixed investment and might turn it into a deficiency country against its will and contrary to the real facts.[49]

These considerations remain as valid today as they were in 1941 – the East Asia crisis of 1997–8 and the European financial crisis of 2010–11 both being examples of the harm which can be wreaked by hot money flows. (Hot money flows between states are, of course, the same as hot money flows within states, except that that sovereign states have central banks to act as regulators and lenders of last resort for their banking systems.) What would be best is an agreed set of rules allowing different types of restriction on cross-border capital flows under specified conditions.

Forwards, Backwards or Sideways?

The current wisdom is that, irrespective of populist opposition, the globalizing momentum is irreversible. There is no going back. Global supply chains lock us into free trade. This is unconvincing. What has been offshored can be re-inshored. As Harold James reminds us,

> There have already been highly developed and highly integrated international communities ... But in every case the momentum was lost; the pendulum swung back. In Europe, for instance, the universal Erasmian world of the Renaissance was destroyed by the Reformation and its Catholic counterpart, and separatism, provincialism, and parochialism followed. A more immediate (and perhaps more familiar) precedent is the disintegration of the highly interconnected world of the late nineteenth century.[50]

The catch lies in the word 'disintegration'. If one sees the future as a linear path of progressive global 'integration', then some disintegration is highly likely. But this will not wipe out the integration already achieved in some regions and for some purposes. It is highly unlikely that the European Union will 'disintegrate' in the sense of going back to the Westphalian balance of power system, or the nationalist politics and economics of the 1930s. And the EU could still fulfil its promise as a model of how, over time, different regions can get together, and eventually come together to tackle planetary problems.

The present is never simply a repeat of the past. Populism, 2018 vintage, is not a repeat of fascism. For one thing, we have not been through a massive war, which was the real seedbed for the militarized politics of the interwar years. Secondly, there has been quite a bit of learning since the last set of catastrophes. One indication of this is the co-ordinated response of global leaders that prevented the Great Recession of 2008–9 from turning into another Great Depression. Thirdly, problems of planetary scope – global warming, exhaustion of natural resources – have emerged which were entirely absent a hundred years ago and clamous for collective responses. Although restrictions on migration are sure to be strengthened, taboos against racism, put in place after the Holocaust, still hold. Despite regrettable backslidings, our political and social systems are more sophisticated, more resilient, than those of even the recent past. Populations are better educated and less submissive to the unbridled will of rulers. This in itself militates against a return to a much more primitive political style.

None of this means that globalization should or can continue, heedless of national sentiment. Identity politics is telling us that there are limits to the rule of profit-maximizing capitalism which we ignore at our peril. Economics can help us understand what those limits are. But it has to be a different kind of economics. Specifically, those who think about economics should spell out the economic conditions for a decent migration policy.

VIII. REFORMING ECONOMICS[51]

Economics has a crucial part to pay in preserving the liberal political system. But to do so political liberalism must be detached from neo-liberal economics.

Economic policy is a central element in statecraft. If it helps societies to realize full employment, rising living standards and a fair distribution of opportunities and rewards, it can take a lot of the sting out of populist politics, which trades on economic discontent to push recidivist political agendas.

Voters get annoyed by many things other than economic misfortune. Many don't like immigration or gay rights, but they are normally not sufficiently annoyed by these things to vote for parties promising to cancel them, unless the economy is faltering as well.

In recent decades, mainstream economics has not helped in the fight for political legitimacy. This is because its central doctrines have encouraged the deregulation and de-institutionalization of markets, especially financial markets, thereby increasing volatility and in-equality. Specifically, mainstream economics has been indifferent to levels of unemployment and to the growth of inequality, holding that these may be the justified consequences of market competition, the 'correction' of which would only make things worse.

This book has taken a long glance at aspects of economics crucial to policymaking. Until Keynes, the main trunk of economics was microeconomics: the study of how the separate parts of the system interact in markets to produce economy-wide outcomes. Somewhat awkwardly bolted on to this structure was the theory of money, whose function was to explain the level of *prices*, the level of *activity* being given by barter trade.

Money's role as the 'great deceiver' required the division of economic processes into short-run and long-run. The function of the short-run in mainstream economics was to indicate the extent of the deviation of the economy from its long-run equilibrium position. As such, it protected the central idea of equilibrium from the attacks of those who denied that the economy displayed any such orderly tendency. The short-run was the world of appearances; the long-run the world of reality. David Ricardo had explained to the Revd Malthus early in the nineteenth century that he would put 'the immediate and temporary effects [of a disturbance] quite aside, and fix my whole attention on the permanent state of things which result from them'. The Ricardian vice of abstraction from messy reality has played a dominant role in economics. Throughout the nineteenth century economics waited for mathematics to catch up with its ambition to describe the reality beneath the surface.

Keynes invented macroeconomics, raising it to co-equal status with microeconomics. Keynes's fundamental claim was that there was no automatic realignment of disturbed economic particles, either in the short-run or in the long-run. It made no sense, therefore, to deduce macro outcomes from micro constructions like 'the invisible hand', where the play of individual self-interest of many agents ensures optimal market equilibria.

Keynes argued repeatedly that the future was radically uncertain; it could not be reduced to known probability distributions. We make our own future in ways too complex to be grasped by a precise logic. It was the existence of radical uncertainty which gave money its peculiar economic property. When the future is uncertain, money offers a choice between spending and not-spending. So the actual economy does not follow a path dictated by the Walrasian logic.

In contrast, orthodox economics abstracts from uncertainty by claiming that the economy is as predictable as is the natural world. If so, money has no function at all except as an intermediary. Keynes's insight, that it is through people's attitude to the holding of money that the present moulds the future, was obliterated.

By abstracting from uncertainty, standard economics also minimizes the role of the state. It has concentrated on exposing the predatory role of the state and has ignored its role in limiting the predations of the market. And indeed, if expectations are rational, in the sense posited by the New Classical economics, the state has no beneficially active role. Its macroeconomic interventions are bound to be ineffectual or perverse.

Keynes left the macroeconomy detached from the microeconomy, only more so: it was not just money that could get 'out of order', but the saving and investment relationship as well. The gulf between macro and micro became a chasm.

Theoretically the attempt to bolt macroeconomics on to the classical microeconomics must be judged a failure. The two approaches, coming out of different mental universes, were inconsistent. Microeconomics was designed to show that markets worked; macroeconomics, how they might fail.

If the thesis of this book, that money and government are stars of the economic drama, is accepted, economics will need to give them the appropriate starring roles. At present this is far from being the case.

Since the 1980s a determined attempt has been made to squeeze macroeconomics out of economics. Orthodox economics insists that macroeconomics be properly 'micro-founded' – that is, derived from the optimizing decisions of well-informed, forward-looking rational agents, subject only to the logic of competitive markets. The trouble with this is that, if it is properly 'micro-founded' in the sense required here, there is no need for macroeconomics at all. Microeconomics can do all the explaining needed.

The reinvention of macroeconomics requires inserting *society* into the study of economics. Marx understood this just as much as Keynes – and in some respects better, because he understood that individuals were members of classes, and their behaviour needed to be explained in terms of their class membership.

So we should say that the task is not so much to 'micro-found' macroeconomics as to 'macro-found' microeconomics: that is, to make the macroeconomy the primary unit of analysis. We should start, therefore, with the social structures, relations, norms and institutions through which individual decisionmaking takes place, as Keynes himself did in the *General Theory*. Keynes's approach was to posit uncertainty and then try to understand individual behaviour in an uncertain world. He emphasized in particular the role of norms and conventions, as opposed to correct information, in anchoring beliefs. The discussion should lead on to a proper sociological economics. But Keynes is a good starting point, because instead of proffering the vague notion that individual behaviour is 'shaped' or 'moulded' by society, Keynes links it to a specific property of the macroeconomy: uncertainty.

Karl Polanyi takes us a step further towards a sociological economics, by his stress on the 'embeddedness' of individual behaviour, its dependence on shared beliefs, norms of behaviour, social biology and institutions; in short, on the shared 'rules of the game' or 'heuristics' which define collective life. All individual choices are made in a collective context, whether of family, community, corporation, religion, class or nation: there are no Robinson Crusoes in the real world. Society cannot be marketized; it is what shapes the market. As John Harvey puts it: 'We live, eat, reproduce, grow and die in packs . . . No individual animal in any . . . species chooses to live with the others. It is hard-wired into them because it evolved as a survival mechanism.'[52]

Most people, though not apparently New Classical economists, understand that there is a 'system' which helps you or screws you up, without being able to define exactly what it is. Few ascribe their successes or failures in life entirely to their own rational foresight, and it is a conceit of economics to believe that aggregate economic outcomes can be so explained.

One does not need to understand how the whole economy works to explain how all the individual parts work. Economics is micro-efficient but macro-inefficient. The housewife who knows what she wants, knows what she can afford, is well informed about prices and gets what she wants is a perfectly serviceable unit of analysis. The mistake is to scale up the housewife into a 'representative agent' and try to extract a coherent macro-story out of her shopping basket. General equilibrium models offer no insight into the sources of aggregate malfunctions: the role of uncertainty in the interaction of many markets, the importance of money as a precaution against uncertainty, the prevalence of herd behaviour, the role of entrepreneurship in creating new wants and new products, the part played by advertising in manipulating choices, the fact that the information systems on which we rely transmit rumour and fake news. They shed no light on the dynamics of the market system as agent of both creation and destruction.

A particular source of false reasoning is the use of language from physics, engineering and mechanics to describe economic processes. Thus we are presented with a picture of perfect markets (machines), which may nevertheless exhibits signs of 'imperfection' (e.g. imperfect competition, imperfect information). Economists typically start from a position of optimal equilibrium, introduce 'shocks' (interventions from outside) which disturb the equilibrium, but treat the effect of these 'shocks' as 'transitional'. Following a 'shock', adjustment to a new optimal equilibrium can be delayed, though not ultimately prevented, by the existence of 'frictions' such as 'sticky' wages. The existence of such 'stickiness' or gluey substance means we have to distinguish between the 'short-run' and the 'long-run' effects of any shock. That the gluey substance is, in fact, society is, if noticed at all, to be regretted. Indeed society itself is rather regrettable, being an impediment to the ever-more perfect integration of markets. From the imperfections of the actual world, economic theorists are eager to escape to a more rarefied sphere. The facts trap you in the present: maths opens up eternity.

Many economists will say this is a caricature. At best it applies only to small section of the profession, and to no section in unqualified form. It presents a vulgarized picture of the discipline, the way, perhaps, it is understood by non-economists (including politicians and some badly trained officials), but remote from the mental universe of practising economists. They will also point to the progressive elements in the economists' research programme.

What is called 'behavioural economics' only really took off after the crisis, although in 1984 Robert Shiller, the doyen of behavioural economics, had already labelled the Efficient Market Hypothesis 'one of the most remarkable errors in the history of economic thought'.[53]

Behavioural economics utilizes empirical psychology to explain why individual behaviour does not conform to the neo-classical model of rationality. One might think this is an act of supererogation, were it not for the primitive character of economists' understanding of psychology. Thus behavioural economics studies the emotional factors involved when an investor buys a stock and, unsurprisingly, alights on 'herd behaviour'. Herd behaviour causes speculative bubbles as investors buy on escalating market sentiment rather than underlying stock value. So while rational expectations theory says that investors are always right in aggregate (exceptions are too small to matter), behavioural economics tells us that they can all be wrong at once.

Behavioural economics has other revelations up its sleeve. We learn that people can exhibit cognitive biases such as over-confidence. Robert Nielsen explains how 'many display an "it-won't-happen-to-me" approach. While it is obvious that some people will lose money on the stock market, each individual believes they have above-average talents that mean it won't be them. This ... leads people to take unnecessary risks.' There is also the 'Representativeness Bias', where people attach too much weight to recent experience. Nielsen explains how 'people often presume things will continue the way they are and do not see future changes. For example it had been so long since the last crash and recession that people thought another one wouldn't occur. They assumed that because the market was rising it would stay rising.' And here's another surprise. Experiments conducted by behavioural economists and game theorists show that 'we are a co-operative species every bit as much as a competitive one'.[54]

It surely doesn't need to be emphasized that such revelations come as surprises only to those who have literally taken leave of their senses. Game theory is the attempt of mainstream economics to come to terms with what Keynes called the fallacy of composition: the fact that decisions rational for the individual need not add up to collective rationality. Through games such as the Prisoner's Dilemma, economists have shown that, while cheating may benefit individuals in single games, honesty has a higher pay-off in repeated games (assumed to be the normal social condition). Thus we learn that honesty pays.

The downside of these advances in understanding is that it leads its amazed practitioners to label as 'irrational' or 'non-rational' behaviour that may be perfectly reasonable in the circumstances. Roman Frydman and Michael D. Goldberg correctly point out that economists' models should try to 'incorporate psychological factors without presuming that market participants behave irrationally'.[55] Or, to put it another way: in many situations, being 'irrational' is the rational way to behave.[56]

An economics course should start with the 'rules of the game' of the particular situation, society or period of interest, investigate their origins and then try to understand outcomes in terms of such collectively inspired behavioural norms. It would make no strong *a priori* claims about individual behaviour, calling it neither rational nor irrational, but assuming, rather, that people do the best they can for themselves in the situations into which they are born or find themselves in. And it would certainly refrain from the claim that aggregate economic outcomes can, in general, be understood as the summed behaviour of maximizing individuals: a claim that can lead to the absurd conclusion that unemployment is always voluntary.

I would argue that such a starting point is the only way to make economics practically useful. For economics as it is now too often practised is a drying reservoir of abstractions. To replenish itself it needs to renew its sources. A return to Keynes is one route; a reopening of the discipline to sociology, history, politics and ethics is another, even if at some cost to its prized professionalism. Earlier in its history, all these subjects formed part of the broad church of political economy. They contain rich insights into the working of economies which should be an integral part of public policy discussion. If they are to help us through the next century, economics students should take as exemplars thinkers like Adam Smith, Karl Marx, John Stuart Mill, Thorstein Veblen, Karl Polanyi, Friedrich Hayek, Joseph Schumpeter and John Maynard Keynes, whose greatness, for all their differences, lay in the fact that they were more than economists. Otherwise economics will simply die, and people will turn elsewhere for intellectual nourishment and practical guidance.

Notes

INTRODUCTION

1. Norman Tebbit's advice in 1981; he repeated it in 2011.
2. The Queen's question might have been more accurately posed as 'Why did no one in mainstream economics see it coming?' What follows is about the views of the economists 'in power'. To a number of economists outside the mainstream, such as William Black, Stephen Keen, Randall Wray and James Galbraith, it was obvious that the financial system was on an unsustainable roll. Of those in the mainstream, Raghuram Rajan and Robert Shiller can claim credit for having foreseen a crisis, for various reasons. The general cause of the financial collapse had been previsioned by Hyman Minsky in his 'financial instability hypothesis': see Minsky (1992).
3. Quoted in Kynaston (2017), p. 358. Montagu Norman to Henry Clay.
4. The original is a bit more verbose than the familiar form given above. Ronald Reagan's actual words were: 'In this present crisis, government is not the solution to our problem; government is the problem.' (See Reagan (1981).)
5. Hicks (1976), pp. 208–9.
6. Keynes (1973a (1936)), pp. 383–4.
7. Dasgupta (1985), pp. 1–2.
8. Marx and Engels (1962), p. 52.
9. Dasgupta (1985), p. 4.
10. Lukes (1974).
11. 'Cultural' Marxists hoped that the counterculture of the 1960s would replace the working class as the harbinger of socialism. In practice, the capitalist system has been adept at 'commodifying' cultural goods.
12. Saul (2004).

PART ONE

1. Mill (1967 (1844)), p. 266.
2. Ibid., pp. 276–8; cf. Keynes (1979), pp. 84–5: 'If indeed, it were easily practicable to divert output towards gold on a sufficient scale for the value of the increased output of gold to make good the deficiency in expenditure in other forms of current output, unemployment could not occur . . . '

I. THE MYSTERIES OF MONEY

1. Mill (1965 (1848)), p. 506.
2. For an excellent account of the Cartesian origins of economic thinking, see Mini (1974), ch. 2.
3. Keynes (1973b), pp. 408–9.
4. Smith (1976 (1776)), p. 38.
5. Samuelson (1970 (1948)), p. 50.
6. Innes (1913), quoted in Shaikh (2016), p. 682.
7. Smith (1976 (1776)), p. 328; Innes (1914), p. 161.
8. Mosler (1997/8); introduction, pp. 4–5, to Wray (2015).
9. Martin (2014), chs. 2 and 3. Martin attributes to the Greeks the invention of the concept of an abstract, universal value, derived from the 'equal worth of every member of the tribe' (p. 58). This allowed a decentralized negotiability of value.
10. See Graeber (2011).
11. Keynes (1971 (1923)), p. 36.
12. Ricardo (2005 (1810)), p. 97.
13. Petty (1899 (1682)), p. 441.
14. Thomas Aquinas' *Sententia libri Ethicorum*, quoted in Martin (2014), p. 131.
15. Sedláček (2011), p. 81.
16. Graeber (2015).
17. In 1675 the Welshman Rice Vaughan calculated that the price level in England had risen six to eight times over the preceding century, but this is now thought to be exaggerated. See Vaughan (1856 (1675)).
18. Bodin (1924 (1568)), p. 127.
19. David Laidler traces the start of the QTM to Polish and Prussian monetary policies between 1520 and 1580, when the counsellors to the King of Poland discovered its 'central tenet' that to limit inflation it was necessary to limit the coinage. He traces an earlier disagreement between

Aquinas in the 13th century and Copernicus in the 16th. For Aquinas the supply of a commodity was the factor which determined its price. For Copernicus, bullion had a value 'in itself', independent of its function in market exchange. See: Volckart (1997). Other historians trace the origins of the QTM to contemporaneous Spanish authors in the Spanish School of Salamanca in the mid-1550s. See: Dempsey (1935) and Hamilton (1935). The important thing to note is that it was the coincidence of two real-world events – the influx of gold and silver from the New World and the rise in prices – that started off the modern theory of money.

20 See Martin (2014).

21 Felix Martin (2014), pp. 20–25 gives an example of the Irish economy living on 'tick' for six months in 1970. An industrial dispute closed down the banking system. The supply of cash went down, but the circulation of tick money (in this case uncashable cheques) made up for it.

22 Hicks (1969), p. 78.

23 Kaldor (1985), p. 5.

24 For definitions, see Ryan-Collins et al. (2014 (2011)), pp. 60–61.

25 McLeay, et al. (2014).

26 Quoted in Arendt (1998 (1958)), p. 102.

27 The legend has the god Dionysius granting the king his wish that everything he touched would turn into gold. But then Midas found he couldn't eat or drink as all his food and water turned to gold, so he starved to death. (Or, in happier endings, Dionysius removed the blessing he had bestowed.)

28 Say (1821), p. 49.

29 See Mill (1967 (1844)).

30 Heckscher (1935), p. 103.

31 Hume (1987 (1752)).

32 The mercantilists were puzzled by the paradox of equivalence. 'Fair' trade requires exchange of goods of equivalent value. Therefore it cannot be a source of increased wealth. An increase in wealth requires an increase in money. For a country without domestic sources of money, this requires 'unfair' trade. See: Mirowski (1999 (1989)), pp. 148–9.

33 Hume (1987 (1752)), ¶ II.V.12. Hume assumed fixed exchange rates, based on gold. But his argument holds just as well for floating rates. Instead of domestic prices going up and down in response to imports and exports of money, it is the exchange rate. Running through Hume's argument is the belief that money will always find its 'proper level'.

34 Hume acknowledged that a nation, by selling only and not buying, might amass a great wealth if it hoarded this to prevent the inflow of money

from having its equilibrating effect on prices. But he dismisses this possibility rather cavalierly: 'A weak state, with an enormous treasure, will soon become a prey to some of its poorer, but more powerful neighbours,' so money will flow out again: Hume (1987 (1752)), ¶ II.V.28.

35 Smith denied that an inflow of money could lower the rate of interest. The rate of interest was determined by competition between lenders and borrowers and this was regulated by the rate of profit. Since an increase in the quantity of money would raise all prices and costs, there would be no fall in the rate of interest as there had been no change in the profit of stock – a good example of a long-run argument being used to refute a valid short-run proposition.

36 'The judicious operations of banking,' Smith writes, 'by substituting paper [for] a great part of ... gold and silver, enables the country to convert a great part of this dead stock [of metals] into active and productive stock.' Smith (1976 (1776)), p. 321.

2. THE FIGHT FOR THE GOLD STANDARD

1 Congdon (1980).
2 Longaker (2015).
3 Locke (1824 (1691)), p. 103.
4 Ibid., p. 145. See also Eltis (1995).
5 Ibid., p. 189.
6 Martin (2014), p. 129.
7 Consumer Price Index 1716–1914: Bank of England (2017a).
8 See Martin (2014), p. 145.
9 We can compare a similar, but much more violent, inflationary episode in France. In 1789, the French revolutionary government issued 400m livres (pounds) of debt in the form of *assignats*, secured ('assigned') on land confiscated from the clergy. According to the original plan, the land was to be sold off gradually, with the government burning the debt tickets with the proceeds of the sale. However, once the government failed to retire the whole of the first tranche of sales proceeds, confidence in government finance declined. Interest payable on the debt soared, as gold disappeared into hoards. This required the issue of more and more *assignats*, which were declared legal tender. By 1796, 45bn of *assignats* had been issued, of which 36bn were circulating (against property originally valued at 3bn livres) and the inflation rate reached 300 per cent. The *assignats* were worthless. Napoleon created a new currency, the franc, in 1803. However the government obtained its

finance, speculators bought up the confiscated property at rock-bottom prices, and the real income of everyone else suffered a catastrophic fall.

10 Ricardo (2005 (1810)), p. 76.

11 Ibid., p. 78.

12 Ricardo (2005 (1817)), p. 364.

13 See Asso and Leeson (2012).

14 For the Bank's assertion, see Kynaston (2017), p. 93. A forerunner of the real bills doctrine was put forward by the speculator John Law (1671–1729), loans from whose proposed land bank were to be collateralized on the 'productivity of the soil'.

15 Thornton (1802).

16 Schumpeter (1954), p. 720.

17 Thornton (1802), p. 287.

18 Ibid.

19 Select Committee on the High Price of Gold Bullion (1810), Abstract.

20 Peel (1819), c. 680.

21 Fisher (1922 (1911)), p. 241.

22 Attwood, quoted in Wright and Harlow (1844), p. 383.

23 Ricardo (2005 (1815)), p. 55. To make the currency more efficient, Ricardo would have replaced gold by paper for internal circulation. Bank of England notes were to be convertible only into bullion, not coin. This was considered too radical.

24 Ricardo (2005 (1816)), p. 120.

25 See Laidler (1991), pp. 21–2. Unregulated country banks, issuing their own notes, expanded their loans in the 18th century to finance the industrial revolution. Liam Brunt has argued that they were proto-venture capitalists: see Brunt (2006).

26 Congdon (1980).

27 A related measure required the Scottish banks, which continued to issue their own notes, to back these with holdings of Bank of England notes.

28 Kynaston (2017), p. 141.

29 Orthodox opinion held that it was because silver was being de-monetized in France in parallel with gold discoveries that the increased quantity of gold coming on to the market did not lead to a big inflation.

30 Germany went on to gold in 1871; the Scandinavian Union in 1873; the Netherlands in 1875. Italy, Spain, Egypt, Australia, India, Chile, Venezuela, Costa Rica, Russia, Japan, Peru, Ecuador and Mexico were all on the gold standard by 1905.

31 Data: Bank of England (2017a). Data was rescaled; in the original data series, 100 = CPI in 2005. Graph: author's own.

32 Giffen (1892), p. 98.

33 Fisher (1922 (1911)), p. 325.

34 Before 1914, a gold pound was defined as 113 grains of fine gold; a gold dollar was 23.22 grains, so a paper pound exchanged for 4.87 paper dollars. In the same way, a pound was worth 20 francs and 20 lire, i.e. it could be converted into twenty times more gold than a franc or a lira.

35 Rodrik (2011), p. 35.

36 The Cunliffe mechanism excluded long-term financing of current account deficits. In the extreme case, when no country is able to borrow, the current account balance is necessarily zero.

37 Eichengreen (1995), pp. 5–6.

38 This is a simplified picture. The gold standard creaked and groaned at the edges (particularly in Latin America) as countries went off and came back to gold, and as central banks restricted and expanded convertibility.

39 Eichengreen (1995), p. 6.

40 See ibid., ch. 2; Kindleberger (1986 (1973)).

41 Cain and Hopkins (2016), p. 224.

42 Statistical Office of the United Nations (1962).

43 Michie (2003), p. 258.

44 Kindleberger (1986 (1973)), p. 11.

45 Cairncross (1953), p. 209.

46 Ibid., p. 208.

3. THE QUANTITY THEORY OF MONEY

1 Wicksell (1936 (1898)), p. 4.

2 Leijonhufvud (1979), p. 1.

3 Fisher (1922 (1911)), p. 172.

4 Ibid., p. 157.

5 Ibid., pp. 280–315.

6 See Marshall (1923).

7 Congdon (2007), p. 282.

8 Fisher's *Elementary Principles of Economics* (1912), quoted in Congdon (2007), p. 282.

9 Eshag (1963), p. 54.

10 If a bank, obliged to hold 10 per cent of its deposits in reserves, receives an extra £100, it will lend out £1,000: the money multiplier is 10.

Similarly, if the banking system's reserves as a whole increase, the total amount lent will be a calculable multiple of the original injection.

11 Quoted in Eshag (1963), p. 16.

12 Fisher (1922 (1911)), p. 56.

13 Ibid., p. 66.

14 Ibid., p. 329.

15 Ibid., pp. 329–30.

16 Gårdlund (1996), p. 269.

17 Leijonhufvud (1979), p. 25.

18 Wicksell (1936 (1898)), p. 96.

19 Ibid., pp. 105–6.

20 Ibid., pp. 120–21.

21 Leijonhufvud (1979), p. 27.

22 See Humphrey (1997), pp. 81–5.

23 Ibid., p. 83.

24 Wicksell (1936 (1898)), pp. 192–4.

25 Before the First World War, the Bank of England tried to steer short-term rates a bit below bank rate, so as to limit recourse to its discount facility. It used open-market operations to keep a spread of 1 per cent between bank rate and the short-term market rate. See Bindseil (2004), p. 15.

26 Eshag (1963), p. 24.

27 See Fisher (1922 (1911)), ch. 2.

28 Ibid., p. 6.

29 In his restatement of the QTM, Friedman glosses T (total transactions) as Y (real income). But money is used for many transactions that do not increase real income, such as those involved in financial speculation.

30 See Fisher (1922 (1911)), ch. 3.

4. THEORIES OF THE FERTILE AND BARREN STATE

1 Ricardo (2005 (1817)), p. 244.

2 Ferguson (2001), pp. 16–23.

3 The question was discussed in China during the 'Discourses on Salt and Iron' – see the 'Record of the Debate on Salt and Iron' in de Bary and Bloom (1999), pp. 360–63. For Khaldûn's work, see especially Khaldûn (1967).

4 Smith (1755).

5 Data: UK Public Spending (2017). Graph: author's own.

6 Ibid.

7 O'Brien (1975), p. 27.

8 Quoted in Whittaker (1940), p. 291.

9 Ferguson (2001).

10 Weir (1989).

11 For the historiography of the Hanoverian state, see Daunton (2012) and O'Brien (2011).

12 Daunton (2012), p. 112.

13 Ibid., p. 130. France paid a 'default premium' for most of the 18th century. It ran persistent deficits in the 18th century, even in peacetime, because its political system 'completely separated the privilege of spending from the obligation to pay taxes and at the same time left the public with enough political power to resist taxation' (ibid., p. 124).

14 Perpetual bonds are bonds with no maturity date; the issuer pays coupons (interest) on the bond for ever, but never has to pay the bondholder the principal (the amount borrowed, on which the interest is paid).

15 Ferguson (2001), p. 130.

16 Ibid., p. 193.

17 Smith (1976 (1776)), pp. 464–5, 881.

18 Ibid., p. 660.

19 Smith treated saving and investment as the same: the profit from production produces 'stock', which can either be spent on consumption or devoted to 'improvements' in production.

20 Smith (1976 (1776)), p. 687.

21 Ibid., pp. 723–4.

22 Ibid., p. 912.

23 Ibid., p. 861.

24 Ibid., p. 921.

25 Ibid., p. 929.

26 Ibid., p. 932.

27 Ibid., bk V, ch. III.

28 Ibid., p. 929. There was an implicit, if unprovable, counterfactual: Britain (and other countries) would have been even richer had not so much money been wasted in wars.

29 Ibid., p. 947.

30 Ricardo (2005 (1817)), p. 247.

31 We owe the modern doctrine of Ricardian equivalence to Robert Barro. It can be summarized as follows: governments can pay for spending through either taxes or bonds. Bonds must be repaid, and so represent taxes at a later date. Under Ricardian equivalence, consumers know this and respond to bond-financed government spending by reducing

consumption, so that they can save for this higher tax future. It thus does not matter how the government funds spending; consumption (and investment) will fall either way. See Barro (1974).

32 Ricardo (2005 (1817)), p. 248.

33 But Smith is not entirely consistent: in the *Wealth of Nations*, he writes about the erection of banking companies in Scottish towns and villages, and holds 'that the trade and industry of Scotland ... have increased very considerably ... and that banks have contributed a good deal to this increase, cannot be doubted' (Smith (1976 (1776)), p. 297). He puts this down to the Scottish banks' willingness to lend credit in the form of 'cash accounts' and their '[peculiarly] easy terms of ... repayment', meaning that a merchant in Edinburgh *ceteris paribus* can 'carry on a greater trade and give employment to a greater number of people than a London merchant' (pp. 299–300).

34 Mill (1967 (1844)), p. 262.

35 Stigler (1986 (1962)), p. 87.

36 Peden (2000), p. 38.

37 Data: Abbas, et al. (2010). Graph: author's own.

38 Crafts (2014).

39 H. C. G. Matthew's *Gladstone 1809–1898*, quoted in Daunton (2012), p. 135. Hypothecation was the pledging of different revenues to different uses. This encouraged virement – the use of surpluses from one 'fund' to cover deficits on another. Both principles were rejected by Gladstone's government: instead revenue was treated as a single pool of money, divided up and managed by Commons' votes every year (p. 134).

40 Peacock and Wiseman (1961), p. 190.

41 Peden (1984), (2002). From 1887 the Treasury insisted that, except for war, departmental borrowing be kept separate from the national debt, with interest service and annual repayments being charged to the annual votes for the department (2002, p. 360). As Peden makes clear, there was something fictional about the Victorian record of debt reduction: whereas the national debt fell from £20.11 per head of population in 1887 to £16.18 by 1911, the indebtedness of local authorities rose from £6.21 per head of population in 1887 to £14.02 by 1911 (Peden (2002)).

42 Middleton (1982), p. 51; see also Morgan (1952) for an account of Victorian and Edwardian war finance. It should also be noted that Middleton claims that there was a second exception to the balanced-budget rule, namely for capital projects expected to be remunerative in an accounting sense. Given the low level of public investment by the

central government (as opposed to local government), this was a theoretical rather than a practical exception (Middleton (1982), p. 51).

43 See Mallet (1913), p. 509.

44 Tomlinson (1990), p. 24.

45 For example, O'Brien (2011).

46 List (1909 (1841)), p. 108.

47 Ibid., p. 37.

48 Ibid., p. 141, List's italics removed.

49 Ibid., p. 295.

50 Plumpe (2016), p. 169.

51 Aaronson (2001), pp. 32–5.

52 A typical unsettled question from economic history is whether German and American tariffs helped or hindered growth, or made no difference. On the pro-Protectionist side see Bairoch (1993); for an alternative view, see Irwin (2000).

53 See Ferguson (1999b).

54 Ibid., p. 123.

55 Ibid.

56 Ibid., p. 6.

57 James Rothschild to Gerson Bleichröder, quoted in Ferguson (1999b), p. 91.

58 North (2015), p. 163.

59 In his 30 April 1781 letter to Robert Morris. See also Brock (1974 (1957)).

60 Henderson (2006 (1961)), p. 45.

PART TWO

1 Keynes (1982), p. 239, from his essay 'National Self-Sufficiency'.

2 Eichengreen (1985), p. 22.

3 Webb and Webb (1923), p. 136.

4 Sir Josiah Stamp, reporting the view of the French economist Jacques Rueff, in *The Times*, 11 June 1931. Quoted in Grant (2015), p. 208.

5 Data: Denman and McDonald (1996). graph: author's own. The unemployment figures for the interwar years are those for workers covered by national unemployment insurance, and are significantly higher than unemployment as a percentage of the total workforce, which included workers in agriculture and domestic employment not covered by the insurance scheme. For example, Feinstein (1972), table 58, gives a figure of 17 per cent for 1932, compared with 22.1 per cent in the graph. The pre-1920 figures are based on returns for unemployment among

trade unionists and would probably also be higher than total unemployment. For a consistent unemployment series running from 1870 to 1999,
see Boyer and Hatton (2002), p. 667.

6 The Financial Resolutions of the Genoa Conference, 1922, summarized
in Brown (1940), p. 343.

7 See Laidler (1999).

5. KEYNES'S INTERVENTION

1 Keynes (1971 (1923)), p. 148.

2 Quoted in Peden (1983), p. 281.

3 Keynes (1981), p. 189.

4 Cannan (1969 (1925)), p. xli.

5 Quoted in Skidelsky (1992), p. 164. See pp. 162–4 for a summary of the
Keynes–Cannan debate. Keynes was right. The banks held huge quantities of short-term Treasury bills, issued by the government to finance its
war expenditure, which fell due for repayment after the war. 'This
meant that after the war the banks could supplement their cash reserves
by not subscribing for new Treasury bills when the old ones matured,
and consequently the monetary authorities had been powerless to prevent a great expansion of credit during the postwar boom of 1919–20'
(Peden (1993), p. 228).

6 See Keynes (1971 (1923)), pp. 61–9.

7 Keynes supposed that the public held 'an amount of money having a
purchasing power over k consumption units', the latter being 'made up
of a collection of specified quantities of their standard articles of consumption or other objects of expenditure' such as those used in the
formulation of price indices; k is thus a measure of an agent's *real* purchasing power held in money, and depends 'partly on their wealth,
partly on their habits' (Keynes (1971 (1923)), pp. 62–3).

8 Ibid., pp. 35, 148.

9 Ibid., p. 138.

10 Kindleberger (1986 (1973)), p. 289.

11 Keynes (1971 (1930a)) and (1971 (1930b)).

12 Keynes (1983), pp. 424–5. See 'Credit Control' in this volume (pp. 420–27),
and also the 'Dual Method of Credit Control' section of his 1924 address
to the League of Nations, Keynes (1981), pp. 188–90. Keynes considered
that while bank rate policy may be best suited to maintaining international
equilibrium, open market operations were the more powerful in influencing the rate of investment. See Keynes (1971 (1930b)), p. 225.

13 Keynes (1971 (1930a)), p. 153.

14 See Bindseil (2004), pp. 19–20.

15 For the two contrasting positions see Skidelsky (1992), pp. 340–41.

16 Friedman and Schwartz (1965), p. x.

17 Congdon (2017a), p. 2.

18 Keynes (1971 (1930b)), p. 347. Open-market operations, as advocated by Keynes, had nothing to do with nominal interest rates having fallen to zero, as they did in 2009. Rather, they were the treatment for an economy failing to respond to a low bank rate. Their aim was to bring down long-term rates 'to the limiting point', i.e. to get the spread between bank rate and investment rate to what had been normal before the slump.

19 Quoted in Kaldor (1970), p. 13.

20 Ibid., pp. 14–15.

21 See Laidler (2014).

22 Peden (2000), p. 148.

23 Niemeyer (1921), quoted in Skidelsky (1981), pp. 171–2.

24 For accounts of the background and effects of the Geddes Axe, see Burrows and Cobbin (2009). The spending cuts were partially offset by cuts in income tax.

25 Middlemas and Barnes (1969), p. 127.

26 The Treasury in the 1920s pretended it was 'balancing the budget' by resorting to fiscal 'window-dressing'. For an example, see Peden (2000), pp. 148–9.

27 For details see Sloman (2015) and Skidelsky (1994 (1967)), pp. 52–5. £250 million constituted just over 5 per cent of nominal GDP.

28 Keynes (1978), pp. 86–125.

29 Hawtrey (1925).

30 Hawtrey (1913), p. 260.

31 Pigou (1913).

32 Hawtrey (1925), p. 40.

33 Ibid., p. 44. This would not be true if the government borrows funds which would otherwise have gone into foreign investment (p. 46), a view also championed by Keynes. Hawtrey's argument presupposes that the central bank has it in its power to 'create credit' independently of the demand for credit.

34 Winston Churchill, Budget speech of 1929, quoted in Peden (2004), p. 57.

35 'The Means to Prosperity', in Keynes (1978), pp. 335–66.

36 Crafts and Mills (2013).

37 One big difference between Nazi Germany and the UK was that Germany was much nearer to being a closed economy, from which the

multiplier effect of public expenditure was prevented from seeping away through imports.

38 Data: Boyer and Hatton (2002), p. 667; Darby (1976), p. 8; Corbett (1991). Graph: author's own.

39 Quoted in Peden (2000), p. 226. See also Skidelsky (1994 (1967)).

40 The deficit projected by the May Committee was as inaccurately (and ideologically) alarmist as similar projections in 2010. It counted all borrowing for the Unemployment and Road funds (not then part of the budget) as current expenditure, as well as £50 million a year for debt redemption.

41 Middleton (1985), pp. 85–6.

42 Ibid., p. 82; see also Clarke (1998), pp. 66–7, and Tomlinson (1990), p. 77.

43 Macmillan Committee (1929–31), qq. 3382, 7690, 7783, 7647, 7653, 7836, 7662, 7835, 7841–3, 7847. For Clay's comment see Clay (1930), quoted in Skidelsky (1992), p. 357.

44 Keynes's Halley-Stewart Lecture of 4 February 1932, quoted in Skidelsky (1992), p. 441.

45 See Skidelsky (1992), pp. 356–62 for further details of these encounters and quotation sources. For debates on the Treasury View, see also Clarke (1988), ch. 3.

46 Krugman (2010).

47 In a letter to Alick de Jeune, 22 November 1934. Quoted in Skidelsky (1992), p. 511.

48 Keynes (1973a (1936)), ch. 11, 'The Marginal Efficiency of Capital', esp. pp. 143–6.

49 Krugman (2007), p. xxx.

50 Keynes (1973c), pp. 115–16. This quotation is originally from Keynes's article 'The General Theory of Employment', *Quarterly Journal of Economics*, February 1937. This article is crucial testimony for what Keynes 'really meant', since in it he set out to summarize 'the comparatively simple ideas which underlie my theory'.

51 Keynes (1973c), pp. 114–15.

52 Keynes (1973a (1936)), pp. 161–2.

53 Ibid., pp. 155–6.

54 Paul Davidson has been the most persistent advocate of the view that Keynes's economics is rooted in the problem of knowledge, and Davidson rejects what he calls the 'ergodic hypothesis'. See Davidson (1978).

55 Keynes (1973a (1936)), p. 167; Keynes (1973c), p. 110.

56 Keynes (1973a (1936)), pp. 293, 294.

57 Ibid., p. 9.

58 Ibid., p. 12.

59 Ibid., p. 265.

60 Keynes's own explanation of the downward stickiness of money, or nominal, wages relied on the assertion that workers were accustomed to a certain scale of wage relativities, so that no group would be the first to accept a wage cut (Keynes (1973a (1936)), pp. 13–15). But this fact from the real world depended on a particular institutional structure of wage determination.

61 Ibid., pp. 378–9.

62 Keynes (1979), p. 179. The argument is that the interest rate only comes into play at the bottom of the slump when capital has become so cheap that investment prospects are improved. This leads to a decline in liquidity preference, and it is this which brings about a fall in the rate of interest. But this will not be enough to revive profit expectations sufficiently to pull the economy back to full employment. So the economy oscillates round a position of 'under-employment equilibrium'.

63 In his futuristic 'Economic Possibilities for our Grandchildren' (1930), Keynes thought that three hours' work a day would be quite enough to 'satisfy the old Adam in us'. In Keynes (1978), pp. 321–32.

64 Keynes (1982), p. 389.

65 Keynes (1973a (1936)), pp. 199–201.

66 From 'The Means to Prosperity', in Keynes (1978), p. 346.

67 Keynes (1973a (1936)), pp 129–31.

68 Keynes (1980a), p. 28.

69 Ibid., p. 74.

70 See ibid., esp. pp. 1–144.

71 It could be said that Keynes's ideas themselves came out of pre-scientific, common-sense economics. In the *General Theory* he devoted ch. 23 to precursors, which led Roy Harrod to accuse him of glorifying cranks and imbeciles.

72 Roosevelt (1936). It is a tenable argument that Roosevelt's deficits, while being too small to bring about complete recovery until the Second World War, dented business confidence sufficiently to produce little net effect. So some 'crowding out' may have been going on, despite the mass of unused resources.

73 Lowe (1965), p. 192.

74 Viner (1936), p. 149.

75 Keynes (1945), p. 385.

76 Allsopp and Mayes (1985), pp. 374, 370.

77 This is an immediate result of pure neo-classical theories, but also one in the IS/LM model when the LM curve is not flat (i.e. 'liquidity trap') or when monetary policy is not accommodating fiscal expansion.

6. THE KEYNESIAN ASCENDANCY

1 Letter to Bernard Shaw, 1 January 1935. Quoted in Skidelsky (1992), pp. 520–21.
2 More precisely: AD = AS balance should include both full employment and external balance (stable foreign exchange reserves).
3 Tobin (1987), p. 41.
4 Hicks (1937). For further details, see p. 173 in Chapter 7.
5 Keynes was not keen on nationalization, but he believed the state should play a larger role in the direction and financing of production, as well as being 'insurer of last resort'.
6 See Schumpeter (1997 (1952)), ch. 10, esp. pp. 274–5.
7 The acronym is from Maddison (1983).
8 Gerber (1994). Andy Storey writes that 'German economic policy was a hybrid of ordoliberalism ... Bismarckian state planning, Keynesian economic thinking, and Rhenish-Catholic corporatism allied (in part) to a resurgent (also largely corporatist) trade union movement.' (In 'The Myth of Ordoliberalism', draft paper, 2017.)
9 This was a very general conclusion. On the other hand, full employment in wartime Britain was a curious example of full employment. There were fewer civilian jobs than in 1938, and the external balance did not matter as long as the Americans took care of it through Lend-Lease. This simply shows that results achieved in conditions of war cannot be readily translated into outcomes available in peacetime.
10 Ministry of Reconstruction (1944), foreword, ¶ 39, 55–6.
11 Ibid., ¶ 74.
12 Tomlinson (1990), p. 246.
13 J. C. R. Dow, quoted in Congdon (2007), p. 88.
14 Stein (1948), p. 475.
15 Samuelson (1970 (1948)), pp. 332–4.
16 Chantrill (2017).
17 Phillips (1958).
18 Holmans (1999), pp. 41–51.
19 From a Treasury & Bank memo, 'Monetary Organisation', dated 25 June 1956. Quoted in Holmans (1999), p. 244.

20 Radcliffe Committee (1959). The Report accepted the cost-push theory of inflation and denied any close connection between bank rate and bank lending. See ¶ 489, 498.

21 See Holmans (1999), pp. 248–9.

22 Samuelson (1991 (1966)), pp. 1329–30.

23 McCracken, et al. (1977), p. 42.

24 Labour Party statement, quoted in Beckerman (1972), p. 44.

25 Among the growth-promoting institutions set up in the 1960s were the National Economic Development Council (in 1962), industrial training boards established by the Industrial Training Act (1964), the Department of Economic Affairs (1964) and the Industrial Reorganisation Corporation (1967).

26 Kaldor (1966).

27 Se Constantini (2015).

28 Tobin (1966), p. 19.

29 Data: The Maddison Project (2013). Growth in 1990 Int. GK$ per capita. Graph: author's own.

30 Tobin (1987), p. 5.

31 Matthews (1968), p. 556.

32 Quoted in Clarke (1998), p. 65.

33 Jowett and Hardie (2014), p. 6. Four quarter moving average. Negative values for PSCBD and PSNB represent surpluses in the current and overall budgets respectively. E.g. in 1968, the government ran a large current budget surplus, but still had an overall budget deficit due to high levels of capital spending (net investment).

34 Data: UK Public Spending (2017); UK Public Revenue (2018). Graph: author's own.

35 Zweig (1976), p. 7.

36 Abramovitz (1986), p. 385.

37 Ibid., p. 395.

38 Ibid., pp. 395–6.

39 Hicks (1974), p. 3.

40 Quoted in Skidelsky (2000), pp. 502–3.

41 Kaldor (1971).

42 Triffin (1960).

43 McCracken, et al. (1977).

44 Ibid., p. 47.

45 Ibid., p. 56.

46 Ibid., pp. 60–65.

47 Ibid., p. 66.
48 Ibid., pp. 11–14, 37–80.
49 Goodhart (2014), p. 11.
50 Balogh (1972).
51 Callaghan (1976). The speech was drafted by his son-in-law Peter Jay, economics editor of *The Times*.
52 Keynesian policy did not expire overnight. An example of a late flowering was the abortive Mitterrand expansion of 1981–3 in France, which ended with the devaluation of the franc and imposition of austerity measures. See Arnone (1995).

7. THE THEORY AND PRACTICE OF MONETARISM

1 Samuelson (1964 (1963)), p. 332.
2 Muth (1961), p. 316.
3 Constantini (2015), p. 34.
4 Prominent among these was the 'Pigou effect'. A fall in money-wages (and prices) would increase the real value of financial wealth, including savings. Individuals would need to save less in order to reach their 'real' savings targets, and therefore they would consume more. The increased consumption brought about by the fall in prices would restore full employment, provided wages were flexible. For a detailed account of the Pigou effect, see Morgan (1978), pp. 48–57.
5 For a sparkling account of these early skirmishes, see Leijonhufvud (1993 (1969)).
6 Hicks (1937).
7 Coddington (1983), pp. 66–7.
8 Quoted in Skidelsky (2003), p. 547.
9 Samuelson (1955 (1948)), p. 212.
10 Hayek (2001 (1944)), pp. 110, 126, 213.
11 Keynes (1980b), pp. 385–8.
12 Quoted in Cherrier (2011), p. 1.
13 Friedman's 'permanent income' acts as a proxy for wealth in the demand for money.
14 See Friedman (1957), esp. ch. 3, 'The Permanent Income Hypothesis', pp. 20–37. In fact, Keynes also thought that over a short period, a decline in income might cause consumption to exceed people's income as they used up their reserves (see Keynes (1973a (1936)), p. 98). He also allowed for the 'windfall effects' of a decline in money prices, similar to the Pigou effect.

But he did not believe these effects had anything to do with people attempting to smooth their consumption over their lifetimes. He thought that uncertainty about future income was too great for people to base spending decisions on calculations of permanent income. Maintaining consumption in face of falling income was much more to do with habitual consumption patterns. See Keynes (1973a (1936)), pp. 89–106 for further discussion.

15 Friedman (1956). Friedman's relation to earlier versions of the QTM is discussed in Wood (1995).

16 Friedman and Schwartz (1963).

17 Friedman and Schwartz (1982).

18 Hendry and Ericsson (1991).

19 Friedman and Schwartz write that a 'more sophisticated analysis [than the simple quantity theory] reveals the existence of a stable demand function for money covering the whole of the period we examine' (1982, p. 624). Hendry and Ericsson found that the same evidence 'refutes constancy in Friedman and Schwartz's reported model' (Hendry and Ericsson (1991), p. 14). As for the exogeneity of money, Friedman and Schwartz in their earlier work claimed their data showed that 'monetary changes have often had an independent origin; they have not been simply a reflection of changes in economic activity' (Friedman and Schwartz (1963), p. 676). Later, they would say: 'the nominal quantity of money . . . is an exogenous variable' (Friedman and Schwartz (1982), p. 35). Hendry and Ericsson responded that 'the money stock appears to be endogenously determined by the decisions of the private sector since the Bank of England in effect acts as a lender of the first resort by standing ready to rediscount first-class bills at the going Bank Rate . . . ' Hendry and Ericsson (1991), p. 27.

20 Friedman quoted in Wood (1995), p. 107.

21 Friedman (1970), p. 24.

22 Friedman (1968), p. 6.

23 Ibid. The attack on Phillips Curve Keynesian was the joint work of Milton Friedman and Edward Phelps.

24 Friedman (1968), p. 8.

25 Ibid., pp. 12–13.

26 Friedman (1951).

27 A point forcefully made by Coddington (1983), p. 43.

28 Cf. Congdon: 'The relationship between belief in the importance of money in the economy and support for market mechanisms [by economists] . . . is almost an empirical regularity in itself.' (Congdon (2007), p. 17.)

29 Wood (1995), p. 97.

30 Ibid.
31 As advocated by Hawtrey (1938).
32 Congdon (2007), p. 150.
33 Ibid.
34 Silber (2012).
35 Laidler (1985).
36 Minford (1988), p. 97.
37 In the USA, the Full Employment and Balanced Budget (Humphrey–Hawkins) Act of 1978 gave the Federal Reserve Board the dual mandate of price stability and full employment. This was in line with the American tradition.
38 Hammond (2009), p. 2.
39 CPI data: Bank of England (2017a). Oil price data: BP (2016). Growth in yearly average of oil prices in nominal US$ per barrel (1971–1983: Arabian Light posted at Ras Tanura; 1984–1990: Brent dated). Graph: author's own.
40 For the Laffer curve discussion see Fullerton, et al. (1994), pp. 174–7.
41 Blyth (2013), esp. pp. 165–7.
42 Quoted in Clarke (1998), p. 77.
43 In his Fifth Mais lecture, 18 June 1984, quoted in Lawson (1992), pp. 414–15.
44 Ibid., p. 298.
45 Ibid., p. 813.
46 Quoted in Clarke (1998), p. 62.
47 Lucas (1972).
48 Lucas (1976). This is known as the 'Lucas critique'.
49 Which in one way brought it closer to the Keynesian idea of multiple equilibria, but without any implication that one equilibrium is superior to another.
50 Quoted in Skidelsky (1992), p. 457.
51 Presidential address to the American Economic Association: Lucas (2003), p. 1.
52 New Keynesian models incorporated one or all of: efficiency wages, staggered wage setting, incomplete markets, search and bargaining, imperfect competition, liquidity constraints and co-ordination failures.
53 Wren-Lewis (2012).
54 Thus market interest rates will react to what the central bank is expected to do, rather than what it does, which means it needs to do very little. However, for the rule to work people must believe not only that the rule will be followed, but also that it is correct.

55 Congdon (2007), p. 14.

56 Jones (2012), p. 262.

57 Lindbeck (1976), p. 31.

58 North and Thomas (1970).

59 For a summary of public choice theory, see Mitchell and Green (1988).

60 Adapted from Woodford (2009).

61 Lucas (1980).

62 Phillips (1958), p. 296. This curve showed a stable 'trade-off' between unemployment and money-wage growth (proxied as the inflation rate).

63 Haberler quoted in Shaw (1984), p. vii.

64 Blume, et al. (1982), p. 314.

65 Evans and Honkapohja (2005), p. 4.

66 Wickens (2012), p. 4.

67 Romer (2011), p. 204.

68 Blanchard (2008), pp. 8–9, describes the three key New Keynesian equations.

69 Wren-Lewis (2012), p. 278.

70 Woodford (2003).

71 Taylor (1993).

PART THREE

1 International Monetary Fund (2016). Gross domestic output growth at constant prices and inflation in average consumer prices for 'advanced economies'.

2 Data: International Monetary Fund (2016). Graph: author's own.

3 Data: International Monetary Fund (2016). Graph: author's own.

4 Minsky (2008 (1986)), p. 237.

5 The European Commission invoked a legal waiver based on Article 107 (3B) of the Maastricht Treaty, allowing state aid whenever there was a serious disturbance in the economy of a member state.

6 Data and graph from Eichengreen and O'Rourke (2010). Notice that the first year of slide was equally steep in both periods, but the slide went on for 38 months in the Great Depression, but for only 12 months in the recent one.

7 Giles (2017).

8 G20 (2009), pp. 1–2.

8. THE DISABLEMENT OF FISCAL POLICY

1 Cameron (2013).

2 HM Treasury (2006), p. 18.

3 For data and discussion see Sawyer (2007).

4 Data: Rogers (2013a, 2013b). Graph: author's own.

5 For an account see Skidelsky (2010), reviewing Gordon Brown's *Beyond the Crash*.

6 Data: International Monetary Fund (2017a). Graph: author's own.

7 Data: International Monetary Fund (2017a). Graph: author's own. Net debt = gross debt minus financial assets corresponding to debt instruments. No data is given for Greece by the IMF in light of controversy over measurement of net debt.

8 Darling (2011), p. 264.

9 See International Monetary Fund (2010), p. 9.

10 Quoted in Wolf (2010b).

11 Obama: 'We must . . . learn from the consequential mistakes of the past when stimulus was too quickly withdrawn.' Quoted in Beattie and Giles (2010). For Schäuble, see Bibow (2010).

12 For examples of journalism against 'consolidation', see e.g. Wolf (2010a, 2010b), Stiglitz (2010), Shiller (2010) and DeLong (2010), the latter advocating 'expansionary fiscal, monetary, and banking policy . . . on a titanic scale'. Anatole Kaletsky, economic columnist of *The Times*, did not cover himself in glory by suggesting that governments were failing to address the long-term threats to their solvency from healthcare and pension liabilities (*The Times*, 12 July 2010).

13 Wolf (2010b).

14 For the 'cruise missile' quotation, see Watt (2008); for the invitation to speculate, see Stephens (2010).

15 Office for Budget Responsibility (2017).

16 Data: HM Treasury (2010, 2014). Graph: author's own.

17 Blanchard and Leigh (2013), p. 6.

18 When policy rates hit the zero lower bound following the financial crisis, this led to a 'rediscovery' of the multiplier. In a much cited piece in the *Journal of Political Economy*, Christiano et al. (2011) argued that, when interest rates cannot be lowered any further to induce private consumers to spend more, there was a role for fiscal policy; and they came up with an estimated multiplier of 3.7.

19 Larry Summers happily called this phrase an 'oxymoron'. See e.g. Summers (2011).

20 Blyth (2013), p. 175 (my italics).

21 Alesina (2010).

22 Reinhart and Rogoff (2011 (2009)), p. xxv.

23 Reinhart and Rogoff (2010b), p. 573.

24 Krugman (2015) summarizing Herndon, et al. (2014).

25 Reinhart and Rogoff (2010a).

26 In response to a question by the author in a House of Lords committee.

27 See *Evening Standard* (2009).

28 Quoted in Skidelsky (2009), p. 49.

29 Specifically, he said: 'Businesses and individuals look to the future, and while they are not the perfectly rational creatures assumed by the theory of Ricardian equivalence, uncertainty over the future paths of tax rates and government spending does play an important role in their behaviour.' Perhaps the proviso of the people not being 'perfectly rational' was inserted by his specialist advisers. http://www.totalpolitics.com/print/speeches/35193/george-osborne-mais-lecture-a-new-economic-model.html.

30 The fairy is the satirical creation of Paul Krugman (Krugman (2010)) to depict the unsubstantial character of this argument.

31 Mackenzie (2010). The 'short view' of Mackenzie's title accurately describes the view of bond-market traders.

32 'You should have just asked a Swabian housewife,' said Angela Merkel in October 2008, in response to a question about the collapse of Lehman Brothers.

33 The distributional effects may not be considered desirable, but they do not impose a net burden on the future generation considered as a whole.

34 Office for Budget Responsibility (2012), p. 33.

35 Data: International Monetary Fund (2008, 2012, 2017a). Graph: author's own.

36 HM Treasury (2010), p. 8.

37 Blanchard and Summers (1986). In this paper, Blanchard and Summers use a neo-classical framework in which persisting unemployment is the result of sticky money-wages. Sticky wages in turn result from the power of 'insiders' (who want to maintain wages) over 'outsiders' (who will accept wage reductions to boost their chances of gaining employment).

38 Average loss of potential output over 23 OECD countries between 2008 and 2015 has been estimated at 8.4 per cent; Ollivaud and Turner (2014), p. 10.

39 Personal correspondence.

40 Data: International Monetary Fund (2016). (Real) GDP at the start of the period shown is indexed to 100 for each country/bloc. The graph thus shows the development of output relative to its pre-crisis peak. Here we see how misleading the promise of a rapid 'V-shaped' recovery was.

41 Council of Economic Advisers (2010).

42 The relatively expansionary American fiscal record reflected peculiarities in the US fiscal constitution. The president may propose, but Congress disposes. The Bush stimulus of 2008 ran on into the Obama period for its mandated length, until it encountered the 'fiscal cliff' at the end of 2012.

43 Heimberger (2017). See also Radice (2014).

44 Since the Eurozone crisis of 2010, the fiscal rules have been strengthened. Budgets must be in balance or surplus, with a maximum structural deficit of 0.5 per cent, and automatic sanctions for non-compliance.

45 Parker and Barker (2010).

46 Bland (2016).

47 International Monetary Fund (2016).

48 Jordà and Taylor (2013), p. 27.

49 Wren-Lewis (2017).

50 Carney (2016), p. 12. This built on the estimates of Blanchard and Leigh (2013).

51 In 2016, 6.3 per cent of those employed in the UK were in 'time-related underemployment' (ILOSTAT (2017)). With an unemployment rate of 4.9 per cent, that means that $0.063*(1-0.049)$, i.e. about 6 per cent, of the total potential workforce were in time-related under-employment. This, plus those who are unemployed, comes to 11 per cent.

52 'Supply-side Keynesianism' became popular in the 1980s through the work of Arthur Laffer, whose 'curve' showed how government revenues could be boosted if top marginal tax rates were cut, by inducing a greater work effort from the wealthy. But the American preference for tax-cutting to spending Keynesianism goes back to Beardsley Rummel in the New Deal period, as Herbert Stein has shown in his book *The Fiscal Revolution in America* (1969). A recent offering in this genre is a paper by Christina and David Romer, which estimates an American 'tax multiplier' of 3 – $1 of tax cuts raises GDP by $3: Romer and Romer (2010).

53 Bernanke (2016).

54 Turner (2015); Pettifor (2017), p. 122.

55 Shaikh (2016), p. 680.

9. THE NEW MONETARISM

1 Brittan (2010).
2 Brookings Institution (2014).
3 May (2016).
4 Draghi (2016).
5 Section 11 of the Bank of England Act 1998; Bank of England (2015), p. 50.
6 'Bank Rate', 'base rate', 'official rate' and 'policy rate' are used interchangeably. They mean the same thing. The US equivalent is the 'federal funds rate'.
7 King (2012), p. 2.
8 Bank of England Monetary Policy Committee (1999), p. 11.
9 'Though a change in the official rate unambiguously moves other short-term rates in the same direction . . . the impact on longer-term interest rates can go either way . . . A rise in the official rate could, for example, generate an expectation of lower future interest rates, in which case long rates might fall in response to an official rate rise.' Ibid., p. 4.
10 The Pensions Regulator (2016), p. 5.
11 Derived from Bank of England Monetary Policy Committee (1999), p. 3. For simplicity not all interactions between variables are shown here, but these can be important.
12 Ibid., p. 6.
13 King (2005). If inflation deviates from the target by more than 1 per cent in either direction, the Bank of England Governor must write an open letter to the Chancellor explaining why this is the case.
14 Ibid., p. 12.
15 Taken from Carney (2017).
16 Carney recently proposed the addition of a term representing financial stability to this equation in light of the financial crisis (ibid.).
17 The ECB's mandate is asymmetric. It defines price stability as inflation 'below but close to 2%'.
18 Data: International Monetary Fund (2017b). Graph: author's own.
19 Roger Bootle has drawn attention to the 'China price' in his book *The Death of Inflation*: Bootle (1996).
20 In the typically coded language of the central banker, Mervyn King, Governor of the Bank of England for much of the period, concluded that 'during the Great Stability [New Keynesian] models proved useful in forecasting the relatively small fluctuations in output and inflation that characterised the period before the crisis. But during the crisis they performed poorly.' (King (2016), p. 305.)

21 Quoted in Cohen (2017).

22 Data: Bank of England (2017b) – 'Statistical Interactive Database – official Bank Rate history'; European Central Bank (2017b); Federal Reserve [US] (2017a, 2017b [used only for the 2002 value]). The values for each year are taken from the interest rates of the central banks at the end of that year; where the Fed gives its rate within a 0.5 per cent range, the mid-point is represented. Graph: author's own.

23 King (2009), p. 7.

24 Bernanke (2004).

25 The Troubled Asset Relief Program (TARP) introduced shortly before QE in the US was a Treasury, not a Fed, initiative.

26 Bernanke (2009).

27 Ricketts and Waller (2014).

28 Wolfers (2014).

29 In 'repo' transactions, the central bank gives commercial banks short-term collateralized loans.

30 See European Central Bank (2017a) for ECB balance sheet, and Eurostat (2017) for Eurozone GDP in current prices, €m.

31 We concentrate here on these three central banks. Liquidity injections in China were carried out through various short-term reverse repurchase procedures and by a long-forgotten tool in the Western world – lowering banks' reserve ratio requirements. Since this stood at 20 per cent, far higher than the near-zero level in Western banks, it gave the People's Bank of China a great deal of flexibility. The Bank of Japan, having tried QE from 2001 to 2006, without any success, did not re-embark on QE proper until 2013 as part of 'Abenonomics', when it announced that it was pursuing 'aggressive monetary easing through its commitment to continue with a virtually zero interest-rate policy and purchases of financial assets for as long as the Bank judges appropriate' to achieve its 2 per cent inflation target (Morimoto (2013), p. 5).

32 Robert Lucas, quoted in Skidelsky (2009), p. 47.

33 Congdon (2007), p. 282.

34 A simple illustration is given in Ryan-Collins, et al. (2014 (2011)), p. 19.

35 Kaldor (1983a), p. 21. This is Kaldor's restatement of the law of reflux (see above, p. 46).

36 Keynes (1973a (1936)), p. 173.

37 Ibid.; or, as neo-classical economists would put it, if there was no perceived opportunity cost in holding money.

38 In the *Treatise on Money*, Keynes defines the activity of finance as the 'business of holding and exchanging existing titles to wealth', pointing

out that it has 'no close connection with the volume of output' (Keynes (1971 (1930a)), pp. 217, 222. This is made clearer if one thinks of the original QTM equation $MV = PT$, where T stands for all transactions in a given period, e.g. it could include purchases of Old Masters.

39 Haldane, et al. (2016), p. 5.
40 Source: Bank of England, taken from Goodhart and Ashworth (2012), p. 662.
41 Haldane, et al. (2016), p. 13.
42 BBC (2014).
43 Haldane, et al. (2016), p. 17.
44 Ryan-Collins, et al. (2013), p. 15.
45 Joyce, et al. (2011a).
46 Meaning and Warren (2015). For further quantitative studies of the impacts of QE, see e.g. Gagnon, et al. (2011a, 2011b), Neely and Dey (2010) and D'Amico and King (2013).
47 Wright (2012). Wright stresses that the effect was only temporary.
48 Miles (2012), p. 6.
49 Haldane, et al. (2016), p. 15.
50 Ibid., p. 17.
51 Bank of England (2017b).
52 Draghi (2011).
53 Data: Bank of England (2017b), interactive database. Series no. LPM-VWVP, seasonally adjusted. Graph: author's own.
54 Churm, et al. (2012), p. 306.
55 *Der Spiegel* (2016).
56 There is an exception; negative rates can be expansionary even if they do not feed into lending rates, if they lead to a devaluation of the currency. Carney: 'From an individual country's perspective this might be an attractive route to boost activity . . . [but] for the world as a whole, this export of excess saving and transfer of demand weakness elsewhere is ultimately a zero-sum game.' (Schomberg (2016).)
57 Bech and Malkhozov (2016).
58 For an explanation of the latter, see Skidelsky (2016).
59 See e.g. Joyce, et al. (2011a); Christensen and Rudebusch (2012).
60 Data: ONS (2017). BoP: current account balance as per cent of GDP (quarterly); time series ID: aa6h. Monthly average, effective exchange rate index, sterling (Jan. 2005 = 100); time series ID: bk67. Graph: author's own.
61 'Operation Twist' was the nickname given to the Fed's strategy to lower long-term yields by selling the short-end Treasuries and using the

proceeds to buy the long end. This term was an homage to the song 'Let's Twist Again' by Chubby Checker.

62 Bank of England (2017b), interactive database. Series nos. LPMVQUU, LPQVQJW, LPQVWVP; monthly [narrow money] and quarterly [M4, M4 lending] 12-month growth rate, seasonally adjusted. Note, 'narrow money' refers to total sterling notes and coin in circulation outside the Bank of England, seasonally adjusted; 'M4' refers to monetary financial institutions' sterling M4 liabilities to the private sector, seasonally adjusted; 'M4 Lending' refers to monetary financial institutions' sterling net lending to the private sector, seasonally adjusted.

63 Data: Bank of England (2017b), series no. LPMVQLC; monthly year-on-year growth rate of M4, not seasonally adjusted. Graph: author's own.

64 Joyce, et al. (2011b).

65 Bank of England (2012), p. 254.

66 Haldane, et al. (2016), p. 23.

67 HM Treasury (2017).

68 Keynes (1973 (1936)), p. 203.

69 Data: ONS (2017), series no. d7g7, CPI: Consumer Price Index (% change). Graph: author's own.

70 Bank of England (2012), p. 259.

71 Data: ONS (2017), series no. d7g7, CPI: Consumer Price Index (% change). Investing.com (2017), monthly Brent oil price. Graph: author's own.

72 Bank of England (2012), p. 259.

73 Carney (2017), passim.

74 Data: International Monetary Fund (2017b). (Real) GDP at the start of the period shown is indexed to 100 for each country/bloc. The graph thus shows the development of output relative to its pre-crisis peak.

75 Driffill and Miller (2013).

76 Kang, et al. (2016).

77 Ibid.

78 See Dale (2012).

79 Bridges and Thomas (2012), chart 23.

80 Congdon (2011), pp. 100–101.

81 McLeay, et al. (2014), p. 2.

82 'With the quantity of money 20 to 25 per cent less, the equilibrium levels of national income and wealth in nominal terms would also have been 20 to 25 per cent less, roughly speaking.' (Congdon (2017a), p. 58.)

83 Ibid., p. 24.

84 Private correspondence.

85 Private correspondence.

86 McLeay, et al. (2014).

87 Congdon (2017a), p. 40.

88 Ibid., p. 5.

89 Ibid., p. 6.

90 Thomas (2017), p. 90.

91 Congdon (2017a), p. 41.

92 Ibid., p. 23.

93 Ibid., passim.

94 He condemns, for example 'the drastic and hurried tightening of bank regulation from October 2008', and 'applauds central bank action to boost the quantity of money from spring 2009' (ibid., p. 47).

95 Thomas (2017), p. 90.

96 Ibid.

97 Congdon (2017a), p. 47. Congdon singles out the enforced raising of minimum capital/asset ratios in October 2008. See Congdon (2017b): 'if banks' capital/asset ratios are increased in a hurry, and the amount of capital is given, banks' assets – and hence their deposit liabilities (i.e., money) – must fall'.

98 See Fisher in Chapter 3.

99 Congdon (2017a), p. 38.

100 Ibid.

101 Ibid.

102 Ibid., pp. 41–2.

103 Private correspondence.

104 Congdon (2011), pp. 405–6.

105 Ibid., p. 204.

106 Congdon (2017a), p. 24.

107 Ibid. (my italics).

10. DISTRIBUTION AS A MACROECONOMIC PROBLEM

1 Clark (1899).

2 Piketty (2014 (2013)); Scheidel (2017).

3 *Inequality For All* (2013), based on Reich (2010).

4 Pigou (1912).

5 Edgeworth (1961 (1881)), p. 101.

6 Samuelson (1970 (1948)), p. 609.

7 In fact, Samuelson's theoretical summary, as quoted here, was challenged in the 'Cambridge capital controversy' of the 1960s and 1970s,

which pitted Cambridge (UK) against Cambridge (Massachusetts). The Cambridge UK economists Piero Sraffa, Joan Robinson and Nicholas Kaldor denied the neo-classical doctrine (represented in this controversy by Samuelson and others of Cambridge, Massachusetts) that capital was a separate factor of production, contributing a separate marginal product, deserving of its reward. They argued that while the prices of different kinds of capital reflect relative scarcities, the rate of profit as a whole reflects the power of the owners of capital. However, though they were deemed to have won the theoretical battle, no one at the time took any notice.

8 Quoted in Córdoba and Verdier (2007), p. 3.

9 See Rawls (1971). Rawls argues that inequality is justified only to the extent that it improves the position of the least well-off.

10 Though Michael Bleaney denies that Malthus and Luxemburg were truly under-consumptionists: Bleaney (1976).

11 On Hobson, see Nemmers (1956).

12 Hobson and Mummery (1889), p. v.

13 Hobson (1922), p. 12; Hobson (1910 (1909)), p. 303.

14 Hobson (1902).

15 See Lenin (1970 (1917)).

16 Hobson (1896, 1900).

17 The most detailed examination of Hobson's doctrines is to be found in Lee (1970). D. K. Fieldhouse finds that of the big four capital exporters before 1914 (the UK, France, Germany and the USA), only the USA and Germany showed marked signs of capital concentration; see Fieldhouse (1973), pp. 47–53.

18 Marx's *Das Kapital* (vol. III, ch. 30) quoted in Blaug (1996), p. 270.

19 'Fear the Boom and Bust', a Hayek vs Keynes rap anthem (2010), quoted in Durand (2017), p. 43.

20 See Skidelsky (1992), pp. 454–9. 'The wildest farrago of nonsense yet' was Keynes's comment on a draft of Hayek's paper 'Capital Consumption', published in German in 1932. See also Durand (2017), pp. 46–8.

21 Keynes (1973a (1936)), p. 371.

22 Ibid., pp. 367–8.

23 Ibid., p. 370.

24 Ibid., p. 376.

25 Ibid., pp. 376–7.

26 Ibid., p. 374.

27 Eccles (1951), p. 76.

28 Devine (1994).

29 Piketty (2014 (2013)).

30 Mishel, et al. (2012).

31 Luttwak (2015).

32 Data: Institute for Fiscal Studies (2016). Gini coefficient calculated using net equivalized household income before deduction of housing costs. Absolute equality is zero; absolute inequality (one person owning all the income) is 1. Graph: author's own.

33 Data: Federal Reserve Bank of St Louis (2015). Graph: author's own.

34 Data: ILOSTAT (2017). Graph: author's own.

35 Piketty (2014 (2013)). This is also the argument of Walter Scheidel (2017), for whom war is history's 'Great Leveller'.

36 Piketty (2014 (2013)), p. 292.

37 Giles (2014). See also the critique of the way Piketty presents his data in his graphs by Noah Wright: Wright (2015).

38 Reed (2014).

39 Ibid., p. 145.

40 Galbraith (2014). More specifically, Piketty glosses over and mis-characterizes the Cambridge capital controversies (see n. 7, above).

41 Abstract, Palley (2001).

42 Ibid.

43 Weeks (2011).

44 Palley (2009).

11. WHAT WAS WRONG WITH THE BANKS?

1 Volcker (2011).

2 Turner (2016), p. 87.

3 Pettifor (2017), p. 11.

4 Clinton (1995), p. 808.

5 van Steenis (2016).

6 Harrison, et al. (2005), p. 43.

7 Ibid., fig. 3.1, p. 24.

8 King (2016), p. 315.

9 Skypala (2015).

10 Ryan-Collins, et al. (2014 (2011)), p. 51.

11 Fama (1991), p. 1575.

12 Fama (1995 (1965)), p. 76. Formally, 'market efficiency requires that in setting the prices of securities at any time t-1, the market correctly uses all available information. For simplicity, assume that the prices at t-1 depend only on the characteristics of the joint distribution of prices to

be set at t. Market efficiency then requires that in setting prices at t-1, the market correctly uses all available information to assess the joint distribution of prices at t. Formally, in an efficient market, $f(P_t | \varphi_{t-1}) = f_m(P_t | \varphi_{t-1}^m)$, where $P_t = (p_{1t}, ..., p_{nt})$ is the vector of prices of securities at time t, φ_{t-1} is the set of information available at t-1, φ_{t-1}^m is the set of information used by the market, $f_m(P_t | \varphi_{t-1}^m)$ is the market assessed density function for P_t, and $f(P_t | \varphi_{t-1})$ is the true density function implied by φ_{t-1}.'

13 Unless the government has private information, but under the EMH it would be best for government to release this information to the public so that it could be processed by the superior brain of the market.

14 The compromise made was that 'the market is just close enough to perfect efficiency that the returns available for exploiting any inefficiency are equal to the cost of the skill and effort that goes into discovering it'. This allowed for the coexistence of the EMH *and* huge returns in a booming financial sector: Quiggin (2010), p. 41.

15 Cassidy (2010).

16 Nocera (2009a).

17 One needn't cast one's mind back too far in time. In the decade before the Great Recession, the dotcom bubble had burst in Western countries and there had been a string of financial crises in emerging markets that had embraced financial market liberalism (notably in Argentina and in East Asia); these alone ought to have cast more doubt on the efficient market hypothesis.

18 Quiggin (2010), p. 22. See Minsky (2008 (1986)).

19 The horizontal axis shows a range of potential values (W) of a portfolio in three months' time. Wo represents the value of the portfolio today. The total area under the curve is 1. For any given value of W, the area under the curve to the left of W is the probability that the portfolio will have a value below W at the three-month point. At the point W where the area to its left totals 0.01 (or 1 per cent), there is therefore a 1 per cent chance of the portfolio being below that value of W in three months. The VaR relative to today's value is the movement between the value today (Wo) and that W – a movement represented in Figure 60 by the double arrow.

20 David Einhorn, quoted in Nocera (2009b).

21 Larsen (2007).

22 Dowd, et al. (2008).

23 Ostry, et al. (2016), p. 39.

24 For an early account of the consequences of the IMF's capital liberalization programme, see Stiglitz (2002).

25 Ostry, et al. (2016), p. 39.

26 Ibid., p. 41.

27 Technically part of the 1933 Banking Act.

28 Reed (2015).

29 Wolf (2008).

30 'The Basel Committee on Banking Supervision (BCBS) has formulated recommendations concerning required bank capital. The Committee is a private body of central banks and regulators linked to the Bank for International Settlement (BIS). Commonly referred to as the Basel Accord, the BCBS rules, while formally non-binding on any national regulatory, are in practice adopted by national and European Union financial regulatory authorities and thus have become binding on banks.' (Ryan-Collins et al. (2014 (2011)), p. 93.)

31 Turner (2009), p. 39.

32 Ibid., p. 87.

33 'It would have been impossible to create these weird derivatives without access to very powerful computers.' (Ford (2009), p. 46.)

34 Buiter (2009).

35 Soros (2009b).

36 Quoted in BBC News (2003).

37 Davies (2010).

38 Utzig (2010).

39 See Kingsley (2012).

40 Turner (2009), pp. 77–8.

12. GLOBAL IMBALANCES

1 King (2012).

2 Adaptation of Fig. 10.1 from Reinhart and Rogoff (2011 (2009)), p. 156. The percentage of countries in banking crises series is calculated by summing the percentages of countries in financial crisis in each of the three years up to the given year.

3 Harvey (2009), p. 2, quoted in Kishore (2014), p. 49. Data of trade and financial flows from Kishore's pp. 46–7.

4 Quoted in Balls (2005).

5 International Monetary Fund (2017a).

6 Ibid.

7 Wolf (2004), p. 184.

8 Wolf (2007a).

9 Wolf (2007b).

10 Working Group on Long-term Finance (2013), p. 42; constant 2011 exchange rates. Flows defined as net purchases of domestic assets by non-residents; total capital inflows comprised of inward foreign direct investment, and portfolio and lending inflows.

11 Dani Rodrik, quoted in Ostry, et al. (2016), p. 39.

12 International Monetary Fund (2009), Appendix I, p. 1.

13 Pettis (2013). See also Chi Lo (2015). Lo's argument in a nutshell is that China has reached the end of the line of the Deng Xiaoping development model based on export-led growth through an under-valued exchange rate, continued political monopoly of the Communist Party and a repressed financial system that funnels Chinese savings into loss-making state-owned enterprises. It needs to be rebalanced towards serving domestic consumer needs. But each step of reform challenges the powerful vested interests attached to the old system – elements of the central leadership itself, local governments, state-owned industries and banks – and sharpens the contradictions between the old and the new.

14 Publisher's account of Rajan (2010).

15 See Calleo (2009).

16 Greenspan (2007), pp. 471–2.

17 For details see Lazonick (2015), p. 36.

18 de Grauwe (2011).

19 See Borio and Disyatat (2015).

13. REINVENTING POLITICAL ECONOMY

1 Hutchison (1978), p.125

2 Marx and Engels (1967), p. 83.

3 See Mazzucato (2013).

4 Mazzucato (2016), p. 104.

5 The British Treasury has belatedly accepted the need for start-up capital by setting up a 'patient capital' unit. 'The patient capital review is an initiative funded by HM Treasury, which seeks to consider all aspects of the financial system affecting the provision of long-term finance to growing innovative firms . . . looking to scale up.' (Report, August 2017.) It is a long-overdue attempt to overcome the shortage of venture capital, the so-called 'Macmillan gap', identified in 1931 by the Macmillan Report on Finance and Industry.

6 Keynes (1973a (1936)), p. 164.

7 Data: ONS (2012). Graph: author's own.

8 Keeping certain kinds of public investment 'off budget' should be distinguished from privatizing the institutions which make the investment, as has been common in the UK; e.g. housing associations have been reclassified as private institutions, removing more than £60 billion of debt from the government's balance sheet (*Financial Times*, 16 November 2017).

9 For details see Skidelsky, et al. (2012). The European Investment Bank is a major source of venture capital, mainly in the EU. Britain already has two public investment banks – the Green Investment Bank and the British Business Bank – but they have no power to borrow, crippling their investment potential.

10 See Atkins, et al. (2017).

11 https://mainlymacro.blogspot.com/2018/06/a-new-mandate-for-monetary-policy.html.

12 Galbraith (2017).

13 The Dodd–Frank Wall Street Reform and Consumer Protection Act was passed in 2010. Based on the so-called Volcker rule, it bans proprietary trading – i.e. using customer deposits to make investments on behalf of the banks' proprietors and owners – for deposit-taking banks. The 2013 Financial Services Act implemented the report of Sir John Vickers, which proposed 'ring-fencing' the retail from the investment departments of banks, without separating ownership. The Liikanen Report proposed a similar system of ring-fencing for banks in the European Union, but has yet to be legislated.

14 'Riskier' assets – loans held by the bank where the borrowers had higher chances of defaulting – were given a larger weighting than 'safer' assets, such as cash or government bonds.

15 Congdon and Hanke (2017).

16 Riecher and Black (2013); see also Wallace (2013).

17 Prynn (2016).

18 Foreword to 'The Bank of England's approach to resolution', Bank of England (2017d).

19 Hoenig (2014).

20 Restoring 'virtue' in banking is defined as the 're-introduction of purpose into banking as both an economic need and a moral necessity' and to promote the ethos required to inculcate that purpose 'into all of the industries' operations and behaviour'.

21 Nick Leeson, quoted in Baxter (2014).

22 Lord Turner, quoted in Private Debt Project (2015).

23 For an individual bank, lending against real estate seems more secure, but system-wide 'lending against real estate – and in particular against existing real estate whose supply cannot be easily increased – generates self-reinforcing cycles of credit supply, credit demand, and asset prices' (ibid.).

24 Woods (2017).

25 Keynes (1980b), p. 384.

26 Source: World Bank (2017d).

27 The stationary state was later developed into the idea of balanced growth, with population and wealth increasing at the same rate, and unchanged tastes.

28 Summers (2013, 2014); Krugman (2013a, 2013b).

29 Keynes (1978), p. 328. From Keynes's 'Economic Possibilities for our Grandchildren'.

30 This naturally has effects on distribution: see Autor, et al. (2015).

31 Leontief (1952, 1979).

32 For detailed statements, see Aaronson (2001), ch. 1, and Stiglitz (2006).

33 'Populism' was originally used to describe the opposition of farmers to the moneyed power of the industrialists and 'robber barons' in late 19th-century America. Later the label was attached to a style of Latin American anti-United States politics. With its strong emphasis on *caudillismo* (strongman leadership) and mixture of right- and left-wing rhetoric, it was influenced by interwar European fascism. Peronism and Chavinism are the best-known instances. Now it is routinely attached to a style of demagogic politics outside the established political parties. The Dutch political scientist Cas Mudde has called it 'an illiberal democratic response to undemocratic liberalism'.

34 de Grauwe (2011); de Grauwe and Ji (2016).

35 de Grauwe and Ji (2016).

36 A prescient critic was Giorgio La Malfa: see Malfa (2000).

37 de Grauwe and Ji (2016).

38 Congdon (2017c).

39 By the Office of the United States Trade Representative in 1982. Notice the dependence of the definition on the theory of comparative advantage.

40 Chang (2007), p. 3.

41 For a modern infant industry argument, see Ho (2012).

42 For a review of New Trade Theory (NTT) see Sen (2010). See also Davey (2017).

43 Ricardo, quoted in Went (2002), pp. 15–16. See also Steve Keen, who writes that Ricardo 'assumed a crucial *false* equivalence between physical machinery and monetary capital that has bedevilled economics ever since,

treating the specialized machinery in different countries as if it were as liquid . . . as the money with which it had been produced' (Keen (2017)).

44 Alvater and Mahnkopf, *Grenzen der Globalisierung: Ökonomie, Ökologie und Politik in der Weltgesellschaft*, 1996, p. 206, quoted in Went (2002), p. 16.

45 *Financial Times*, 12 December 2017.

46 Lo (2018).

47 Masch (2017).

48 Lo (2018).

49 Keynes (1980a), p. 53.

50 James (2002), p. 1.

51 For an excellent survey of what needs to be reconsidered in economics, see Lavoie (2018).

52 Harvey (2015), p. 111.

53 Milner (2009).

54 Nielsen (2012).

55 Frydman and Goldberg (2011).

56 Professor Richard Thaler received a Nobel Prize in economics in 2017 for 'nudge' theory. This identifies behaviours which fall short of rational: enrolment in private pension plans is increased when people are given the option to opt out rather than opt in, which is clearly irrational if an objective assessment of the benefits of the plans is available. The behavioural bias towards inertia has long been known and exploited for policy purposes. For example, trade unions in the UK, backed by Labour governments, have always favoured forcing their members to 'opt out' of the political levy to the Labour Party; Conservative governments have passed legislation forcing them to 'opt in'. According to the *Financial Times* on 10 October 2017, 'Professor Thaler's catch-all advice is, whether you are a business or a government, if you want people to do something, make it easy.' It is hard to avoid surmising that the Nobel Prize is being awarded, not for any new insight, but for technical prowess in making an old insight acceptable to the economics profession.

Bibliography

Aaronson, S. A. (2001), *Taking Trade to the Streets: The Lost History of Public Efforts to Shape Globalization*. Michigan: Michigan University Press.

Abbas, S. A., Belhocine, N., El Ganainy, A. and Horton, M. (2010), A historical public debt database. *IMF Working Paper* (WP/10/245).

Abramovitz, M. (1986), Catching up, forging ahead, and falling behind. *Journal of Economic History*, 46 (2), pp. 385–406.

Alesina, A. (2010), Fiscal Adjustments and the Recession. Available at: http://voxeu.org/article/fiscal-adjustments-and-recession [Accessed 5 July 2017].

Allen, K. (2017), Employment statistics tell us skewed story about UK jobs market. *Guardian*, 6 August.

Allsopp, C. J. and Mayes, D. (1985), Demand management policy: theory and measurement. In: D. Morris (ed.), *The Economic System in the UK*. Oxford: Oxford University Press, pp. 366–97.

Arendt, H. (1998 (1958)). *The Human Condition*. 2nd edn. Chicago, Ill.: University of Chicago Press.

Arnone, M. (1995), French macroeconomic policy under President Mitterrand: an assessment. *Rivista Internazionale di Scienze Sociali*, 103 (4), pp. 743–56.

Asso, P. F. and Leeson, R. (2012), Monetary policy rules: from Adam Smith to John Taylor. In: E. F. Koenig, R. Leeson and G. A. Khan (eds.), *The Taylor Rule and the Transformation of Monetary Policy*. Stanford, Calif.: Hoover Institute Press.

Atkins, G., Davies, N. and Bishop, T. K. (2017), *How to Value Infrastructure: Improving Cost Benefit Analysis*. London: Institute for Government. Available at: https://www.instituteforgovernment.org.uk/publications/value-infrastructure-september-2017 [Accessed 21 December 2017].

Autor, D., Dorn, D. and Hanson, G. (2015), Untangling trade and technology: evidence from local labour markets. *The Economic Journal*, 125 (May), pp. 621–46.

Bagehot, W. (1873), *Lombard Street: A Description of the Money Market.* London: Henry S. King & Co.

Bairoch, P. (1993), *Economics and World History: Myths and Paradoxes.* New York: Harvester Wheatsheaf.

Baldwin, R. and Giavazzi, F. (2015), Introduction. In: R. Baldwin and F. Giavazzi (eds.), *The Eurozone Crisis: A Consensus View of the Causes and a Few Possible Solutions.* London: CEPR Press, pp. 18–62.

Balls, A. (2005), Bernanke likely to be tough on inflation. *Financial Times,* 27 October.

Balogh, T. (1972), Unemployment: the real cause. *New Statesman,* 28 January.

Bank of England (1933), *Bank of England Papers,* EID 4/103, 30 June, s.l.: s.n.

Bank of England (2012), *Quarterly Bulletin, 2013 Q3: The distributional effects of asset purchases,* pp. 254–66. Available at: https://www.bankofengland.co.uk/quarterly-bulletin/2012/q3/the-distributional-effects-of-asset-purchases [Accessed 9 May 2018].

Bank of England (2015), *The Bank of England Act 1998: The Charters of the Bank and related documents.* Available at: http://www.bankofengland.co.uk/about/Documents/legislation/1998act.pdf [Accessed 10 July 2017].

Bank of England (2016), *Monetary Policy Summary.* Available at: http://www.bankofengland.co.uk/publications/minutes/Documents/mpc/mps/2016/mpsaug.pdf [Accessed 10 July 2017].

Bank of England (2017a), *Dataset – Three Centuries of Data, Version 3.* London: Bank of England.

Bank of England (2017b), *How Does Monetary Policy Work?* Available at: http://www.bankofengland.co.uk/monetarypolicy/Pages/how.aspx [Accessed 10 July 2017].

Bank of England (2017c), *Statistical Interactive Database: Bank of England.* Available at: http://www.bankofengland.co.uk/boeapps/iadb/newintermed.asp [Accessed 11 July and 23 November 2017].

Bank of England (2017d), *The Bank Return: Bank of England.* Available at: http://www.bankofengland.co.uk/publications/Pages/bankreturn/default.aspx [Accessed 11 July 2017].

Bank of England (2017e), *The Bank of England's Approach to Resolution.* Available at: https://www.bankofengland.co.uk/financial-stability/resolution [Accessed 19 December 2017 – page updated periodically].

Bank of England Monetary Policy Committee (1999), *The Transmission Mechanism of Monetary Policy.* Available at: http://www.bankofengland.co.uk/publications/Documents/other/monetary/montrans.pdf [Accessed 10 July 2017].

Barro, R. J. (1974), Are government bonds net wealth? *Journal of Political Economy*, 82 (6), pp. 1095–117.

Baxter, D. (2014), The big interview: Nick Leeson, the original rogue trader. *Business Reporter.* 3 August. Available at: https://staging.business-reporter.co.uk/2014/08/03/the-big-interview-nick-leeseon-the-original-rogue-trader-on-regrets-and-revival/ [Accessed 6 December 2017].

BBC (2010), Irish deficit balloons after new bank bail-out. Available at: http://www.bbc.co.uk/news/business-11441473 [Accessed 4 July 2017].

BBC (2014), Q&A: What is 'forward guidance'? Available at: http://www.bbc.co.uk/news/business-23145755 [Accessed 10 July 2017].

BBC News (2003), Buffett warns on investment 'time bomb'. Available at: http://news.bbc.co.uk/1/hi/2817995.stm [Accessed 31 July 2017].

Beattie, A. and Giles, C. (2010), Obama urges G20 to boost demand. *Financial Times*, 18 June.

Bech, M. and Malkhozov, A. (2016), How have central banks implemented negative policy rates? *BIS Quarterly Review*, March, pp. 31–44.

Beckerman, W. (1972), *The Labour Government's Economic Record: 1964–1970*. London: Duckworth.

Bernanke, B. (2004), Remarks by Governor Ben S. Bernanke at the H. Parker Willis Lecture in Economic Policy, Washington and Lee University, Lexington, Va. Available at: https://www.federalreserve.gov/boarddocs/speeches/2004/200403022/ [Accessed 10 July 2017].

Bernanke, B. (2005), The Global Saving Glut and the U.S. Current Account Deficit: Sandridge Lecture, Virginal Association of Economists. Available at: https://www.federalreserve.gov/boarddocs/speeches/2005/200503102/ [Accessed 01 August 2017].

Bernanke, B. (2009), Speech at the National Press Club Luncheon, National Press Club, Washington DC. Available at: https://www.federalreserve.gov/newsevents/speech/bernanke20090218a.htm [Accessed 10 July 2017].

Bernanke, B. (2016), What Tools Does The Fed Have Left? Part 3: Helicopter Money. Brookings: Blogs. 14 April. Available at: https://www.brookings.edu/blog/ben-bernanke/2016/04/11/what-tools-does-the-fed-have-left-part-3-helicopter-money/ [Accessed 14 December 2017].

Bernstein, J. (2010), Deficit reduction is not the enemy of jobs. *Financial Times*, 28 June.

Bibow, J. (2010), It is worrying that the German view of austerity is now Europe's. *Financial Times*, 28 June.

Bindseil, U. (2004), *The Operational Target of Monetary Policy and the Rise and Fall of Reserve Position Doctrine*. European Central Bank Working Paper Series No. 372.

Blanchard, O. (2008), *The State of Macro*. NBER Working Paper No. 14259.

Blanchard, O. and Leigh, D. (2013), Growth forecast errors and fiscal multipliers. *IMF Working Paper* (WP/13/1).

Blanchard, O. J. and Summers, L. (1986), *Hysteresis and the European Unemployment Problem*. NBER Working Paper No. 1950.

Blanchflower, D. (2013), Decoding the unemployment figures exposes the truth behind the coalition's spin. *New Statesman*, 28 February.

Bland, A. (2016), George Osborne meets Yuval Harari: 'I didn't show enough vulnerability'. *Guardian*, 26 November.

Blaug, M. (1996), *Economic Theory In Retrospect*. 5th edn. Cambridge: Cambridge University Press.

Bleaney, M. (1976), *Under-Consumption Theories: A History and Critical Analysis*. New York: International Publishers.

Blume, L. E., Bray, M. M. and Easley, D. (1982), Introduction to the stability of rational expectations equilibrium. *Journal of Economic Theory*, 26, pp. 313–17.

Blyth, M. (2013), *Austerity: The History of a Dangerous Idea*. New York: Oxford University Press.

Bodin, J. (1924 (1568)), The dearness of things. In: A. E. Monroe (ed.), *Early Economic Thought: Selections from Economic Literature prior to Adam Smith*. Cambridge, Mass.: Harvard University Press.

Bootle, R. P. (1996), *The Death of Inflation*. London: Nicholas Brealey.

Borio, C. and Disyatat, P. (2015), *Capital Flows and the Current Account: Taking Financing (More) Seriously*. Bank for International Settlements, Working Paper No. 525.

Boyer, G. R. and Hatton, T. (2002), New estimates of British unemployment, 1870–1913. *Journal of Economic History*, 62 (3), pp. 643–75.

BP (2016), *BP Statistical Review of World Energy Workbook*. Available at: http://www.bp.com/content/dam/bp/excel/energy-economics/statistical-review-2016/bp-statistical-review-of-world-energy-2016-workbook.xlsx [Accessed 4 July 2017].

Bridges, J. and Thomas, R. (2012), *The Impact of QE on the UK Economy – Some Supportive Monetarist Arithmetic*. Bank of England Working Paper No. 442.

Brittan, S. (2010), Are these hardships necessary? *Financial Times*, 17 June.

Brock, H. W. (2012), *American Gridlock: Why the Right and the Left are Both Wrong*. Hoboken: John Wiley & Sons.

Brock, W. R. (1974 (1957)), The ideas and influence of Alexander Hamilton. In: L. W. Levy and C. Siracusa (eds.), *Essays on the Early Republic: 1789–1815*. New York: Holt, Rinehart & Winston.

Brookings Institution (2014), A Discussion with Federal Reserve Chairman Ben Bernanke. Available at: https://www.brookings.edu/wp-content/uploads/2014/01/20140116_bernanke_remarks_transcript.pdf [Accessed 10 July 2017].

Brown, W. A. (1940), *The International Gold Standard Reinterpreted 1914–1934*. New York: National Bureau of Economic Research.

Brunt, L. (2006), Rediscovering risk: Country banks as proto-venture capital firms in the first industrial revolution. *Journal of Economic History*, 66 (1), pp. 74–102.

Buiter, W. (2009), Should you be able to sell what you do not own? *Financial Times*. Available at: http://blogs.ft.com/maverecon/2009/03/should-you-be-able-to-sell-what-you-do-not-own/#axzz4oQNGTIje [Accessed 31 July 2017].

Burrows, G. and Cobbin, P. (2009), Controlling government expenditure by external review: the 1921–2 'Geddes Axe'. *Accounting History*, 14 (3), pp. 199–220.

Cain, P. J. and Hopkins, A. G. (2016), *British Imperialism: 1688–2015*. 3rd edn. Oxford: Routledge.

Cairncross, A. K. (1953), *Home and Foreign Investment, 1870–1913: Studies in Capital Accumulation*. Cambridge: Cambridge University Press.

Callaghan, J. (1976), Political Speeches. Available at: http://www.britishpoliticalspeech.org/speech-archive.htm?speech=174 [Accessed 27 June 2017].

Calleo, D. (2009), *Follies of Power: America's Unipolar Fantasy*. Cambridge: Cambridge University Press

Cameron, D. (2013), Speech on the Economy: Available at: https://www.gov.uk/government/speeches/economy-speech-delivered-by-david-cameron [Accessed 4 July 2017].

Cannan, E. (1969 (1925)), *The Paper Pound*. 2nd edn. London: Frank Cass & Co.

Carney, M. (2016), The Spectre of Monetarism. Roscoe Lecture: Liverpool John Moores University, 5 December.

Carney, M. (2017), Lambda: Speech given at the London School of Economics. Available at: http://www.bankofengland.co.uk/publications/Documents/speeches/2017/speech954.pdf [Accessed 10 July 2017].

Cartwright, N. (1999), *The Dappled World*. Cambridge: Cambridge University Press.

Cassidy, J. (2010), Interview with Eugene Fama. *New Yorker* Magazine, 13 January.

Chang, H.-J. (2007), *Bad Samaritans: The Myth of Free Trade and the Secret History of Capitalism*. London: Bloomsbury.

Chantrill, C. (2017), *US Government Debt*. Available at: usgovernment-debt.us [Accessed 26 June 2017].

Cherrier, B. (2011), *The Lucky Consistency of Milton Friedman's Science and Politics, 1933–1963*. Available at: https://beatricecherrier.files.word-press.com/2011/11/friedman-cherrier-final.pdf [Accessed 3 July 2017].

Christensen, J. H. E. and Rudebusch, G. D. (2012), The response of interest rates to US and UK quantitative easing. *The Economic Journal*, 122, pp. F385–414.

Christiano, L., Eichenbaum, M. and Rebelo, S. (2011), When is the government spending multiplier large? *Journal of Political Economy*, 119 (1), pp. 78–121.

Churm, R. et al. (2012), The funding for lending scheme. *Bank of England Quarterly Bulletin*, Q4, pp. 306–19.

Clark, J. B. (1899), *Distribution of Wealth*. London: Macmillan.

Clark, T. and Heath, A. (2015), *Hard Times: Inequality, Recession, After-math*. New Haven, Conn.: Yale University Press.

Clarke, P. F. (1988), *The Keynesian Revolution in the Making, 1924–1936*. Oxford: Clarendon Press.

Clarke, P. F. (1998), *The Keynesian Revolution and its Economic Conse-quences*. Cheltenham: Edward Elgar.

Clay, H. (1930), Memorandum: bank rate, credit, and employment. 17 May. Bank of England Papers (Archive), EID 1/2.

Clinton, W. J. (1995), *Public Papers of the Presidents of the United States: William J. Clinton, 1995. Book I – January 1 to June 30*. Washington, DC: United States Printing Office.

Coddington, A. (1983), *Keynesian Economics: The Search for First Prin-ciples*. London: George Allen & Unwin.

Cohen, B. J. (2017), How Stable is the Global Financial System? *Project Syn-dicate: On Point*. 29 September. Available at: https://www.project-syndicate.org/onpoint/how-stable-is-the-global-financial-system-by-benjamin-j-cohen-2017-09?barrier=accesspaylog [Accessed 15 December 2017].

Collini, S. (2009), Impact on Humanities, *Times Literary Supplement*, 13 November.

Congdon, T. (1980), The monetary base debate: another instalment in the Currency School vs Banking School controversy. *National Westminster Bank Quarterly Review*, August.

Congdon, T. (2007), *Keynes, the Keynesians and Monetarism*. Chelten-ham: Edward Elgar.

Congdon, T. (2011), *Money in a Free Society: Keynes, Friedman, and the New Crisis in Capitalism*. New York: Encounter Books.

Congdon, T. (2017a), *Money in the Great Recession: Did a Crash in Money Growth Cause the Global Slump?* Gloucester: Edward Elgar.

Congdon, T. (2017b), Monthly monetary update: were big banks to blame for the Great Recession? And what are the implications for banks' capital requirements? *Institute of International Monetary Research.* September. Available at: https://www.mv-pt.org/viewdocument.php?Filename=38_iimr_monthly_newsletter_september_2017 [Accessed 15 December 2017].

Congdon, T. (2017c), Our Best Brexit Policy is All-Out Free Trade. *Standpoint*, June 2017. Available at: http://standpointmag.co.uk/node/6854 [Accessed 18 December 2017].

Congdon, T. and Hanke, S. (2017), More bank capital could kill the economy. *Wall Street Journal*, 13 March.

Constantini, O. (2015), *The Cyclical Adjusted Budget: History and Exegesis of a Fateful Estimate.* Institute for New Economic Thinking, Working Paper No. 24.

Corbett, D. (1991), The nature of unemployment in interwar Germany. In: Unemployment in Interwar Germany. Unpublished PhD thesis, Harvard University. Available at: http://davidcorbettlaw.com/yahoo_site_admin/assets/docs/Dissertation--chapter_one.118160805.pdf [Accessed 8 January 2018].

Córdoba, J.-C. and Verdier, G. (2007), Lucas vs. Lucas: on inequality and growth. *IMF Working Paper* (WP/07/17).

Council of Economic Advisers (2010), *Recovery Act Fourth Quarterly Report – Executive Summary.* Available at: https://obamawhitehouse.archives.gov/administration/eop/cea/factsheets-reports/economic-impact-arra-4th-quarterly-report/summary [Accessed 5 July 2017].

Crafts, N. (2014), *Reducing High Public Debt Ratios: Lessons from UK Experience.* The University of Warwick Centre for Competitive Advantage in the Global Economy, Working Paper No. 199.

Crafts, N. and Mills, T. C. (2013), Rearmament to the rescue? New estimates of the impact of 'Keynesian' policies in 1930s Britain. *Journal of Economic History*, 73 (4), pp. 1077–104.

Dale, S. (2011), Prospects for monetary policy: learning the lessons from 2011. Speech at Bloomberg, London. Available at: http://www.bankofengland.co.uk/archive/Documents/historicpubs/speeches/2011/speech537.pdf [Accessed 12 July 2017].

Dale, S. (2012), Spencer Dale warns on QE: full speech. *Daily Telegraph.* Available at: http://www.telegraph.co.uk/finance/economics/9530138/Spencer-Dale-warns-on-QE-full-speech.html [Accessed 12 July 2017].

D'Amico, S. and King, T. (2013), Flow and stock effects of large-scale treasury purchases: evidence on the importance of local supply. *Journal of Financial Economics*, 108 (2), pp. 425–48.

Darby, M. R. (1976), Three-and-a-half million U.S. employees have been mislaid: or, an explanation of unemployment, 1934–1941. *Journal of Political Economy*, 84 (1), pp. 1–16.

Darling, A. (2011), *Back From the Brink: 1000 Days at Number 11*. London: Atlantic Books

Dasgupta, A. K. (1985), *Epochs of Economic Theory*. Oxford: Basil Blackwell.

Daunton, M. (2012), The politics of British taxation, from the Glorious Revolution to the Great War. In: B. Yun-Casalilla and P. K. O'Brien (eds.), *The Rise of Fiscal States: A Global History, 1500–1914*. Cambridge: Cambridge University Press, pp. 111–42.

Davey, B. (2017), Specialisation and trade: David Ricardo versus Fredrich List. *Credo*. Available at: www.credoeconomics.com/specialisation-and-trade-david-ricardo-versus-frederich-list/ [Accessed 7 May 2018].

Davidson, P. (1978), *Money and the Real World*. 2nd edn. London: Palgrave Macmillan

Davidson, P. (1999), The case for capital regulation. In: R. Skidelsky, M. Lawson, J. Flemming, M. Desai and P. Davidson, *Capital Regulation: For and Against*. London: Social Market Foundation.

Davies, H. (2010), Regulation since the crisis: what has changed and is it enough? *ICEF Seminar, HSE Cultural Centre*, 29 November.

de Bary, W. T. and Bloom, I. (1999), *Sources of Chinese Tradition*, Vol. 1: *From Earliest Times to 1600*. 2nd edn. New York: Columbia University Press. Relevant exerpt available online: http://afe.easia.columbia.edu/ps/cup/debate_salt_iron.pdf [Accessed 8 March 2018].

de Grauwe, P. (2011), Eurozone bank recapitalisations – pouring water into a leaky bucket. *Centre for European Policy Studies*. Available at: https://www.ceps.eu/system/files/book/2011/10/Oct_PDG_on_Bank_recapitalisation.pdf [Accessed 1 August 2017].

de Grauwe, P. and Ji, Y. (2016), *How to Reboot the Eurozone and Ensure its Long-Term Survival*. VoxEU.org – CEPR's policy portal. Available at: http://voxeu.org/article/how-reboot-eurozone-and-ensure-its-long-term-survival [Accessed 18 December 2017].

DeLong, B. (2010), It is far too soon to end expansion. *Financial Times*, 19 July.

Dempsey, B. W. (1935), The historical emergence of Quantity Theory. *Quarterly Journal of Economics*, 50 (1), pp. 174–84.

Denman, J. and McDonald, P. (1996), *Unemployment Statistics from 1881 to the Present Day*. Available at: http://www.ons.gov.uk/ons/rel/lms/

labour-market-trends--discontinued-/january-1996/unemployment-since-
1881.pdf [Accessed 2017 June 20].

Der Spiegel (2016), *Bayerische Sparkassen wollen überschüssiges Geld vor
EZB verstecken* (Bavarian savings banks want to hide excess money from
the ECB). *Der Spiegel*, 3 March.

Devine, J. (1994) The causes of the 1929–33 Great Collapse: a Marxian
interpretation. *Research in Political Economy*, 14, pp. 119–94.

Dobbs, R., Lund, S., Koller, T. and Shwayder, A. (2013), QE and ultra-low
interest rates: distributional effects and risks. *McKinsey Global Institute*.
Available at: http://www.mckinsey.com/global-themes/employment-and-
growth/qe-and-ultra-low-interest-rates-distributional-effects-and-risks
[Accessed 12 July 2017].

Dowd, K., Cotter, J., Humphrey, C. and Woods, M. (2008), *How Unlucky is 25-
Sigma*. Available at: https://arxiv.org/ftp/arxiv/papers/1103/1103.5672.pdf
[Accessed 31 July 2017].

Draghi, M. (2011), The Euro, Monetary Policy and the Design of a Fiscal Compact: Ludwig Erhard Lecture, Berlin. Available at: https://www.ecb.europa.
eu/press/key/date/2011/html/sp111215.en.html [Accessed 11 July 2017].

Draghi, M. (2016), Stability, Equity and Monetary Policy. 2nd DIW Europe
Lecture, Berlin, 25 October.

Driffill, J. and Miller, M. (2013), Liquidity when it matters: QE and Tobin's
q. *Oxford Economic Papers*, 65, pp. i1115–45.

Durand, C. (2017), *Fictitious Capital: How Finance is Appropriating Our
Future* (trans. David Broder). London: Verso.

Eccles, M. S. (1951), *Beckoning Frontiers, Public and Personal Recollec-
tions*. New York: Alfred A. Knopf.

Edgeworth, F. Y. (1961 (1881)), *Mathematical Physics: An Essay on the
Application of Mathematics to the Moral Sciences*. New York: Augustus
M. Kelly.

Eichengreen, B. (1985), *The Gold Standard in Theory and History*. London:
Methuen.

Eichengreen, B. (1995), *Golden Fetters: The Gold Standard and the Great
Depression, 1919–1939*. Oxford: Oxford University Press.

Eichengreen, B. and O'Rourke, K. (2010). What do the new data tell us? *Vox*,
8 March. Available at: http://voxeu.org/article/tale-two-depressions-what-
do-new-data-tell-us-february-2010-update [Accessed 8 January 2018].

Eltis, W. (1995), John Locke, the quantity theory of money and the establishment of a sound currency. In: M. Blaug (ed.), *The Quantity Theory of
Money: From Locke to Keynes to Friedman*. Aldershot: Edward Elgar,
pp. 4–26.

Eshag, E. (1963), *From Marshall to Keynes: An Essay on the Monetary Theory of the Cambridge School*. Oxford: Blackwell.

European Central Bank (2017a), *Consolidated Financial Statement of the Eurosystem*. Available at: https://www.ecb.europa.eu/press/pr/wfs/2017/html/ecb.fs170705.en.html [Accessed 10 July 2017].

European Central Bank (2017b), *Key ECB Interest Rates*. Available at: https://www.ecb.europa.eu/stats/policy_and_exchange_rates/key_ecb_interest_rates/html/index.en.html [Accessed 23 November 2017].

Eurostat (2017), *Eurostat*. Available at: http://ec.europa.eu/eurostat [Accessed 10 July 2017].

Evans, G. W. and Honkapohja, S. (2005), An Interview with Thomas J. Sargent. *UCL Economics*. Available at: http://www.econ.ucl.ac.uk/downloads/denardi/Sargent_Interview.pdf [Accessed 4 July 2017].

Evening Standard (2009), Darling forecast savaged by IMF's dire predictions. *Evening Standard*, 22 April.

Fama, E. F. (1991), Efficient capital markets: II. *Journal of Finance*, 46 (5), pp. 1575–617.

Fama, E. F. (1995 (1965)), Random walks in stock market prices. *Financial Analysts Journal*, 51 (1), pp. 75–80. Reprinted from *Financial Analysts Journal*, September/October 1965, 21 (5), pp. 55–9.

Fazi, T. (2015), QE in the Eurozone has failed. *Pieria*. Available at: http://www.pieria.co.uk/articles/qe_in_the_Eurozone_has_failed [Accessed 11 July 2017].

Febrero, E. and Uxó, J. (2013), *Understanding TARGET2 Imbalances from an Endogenous Money View*. Universidad de Castilla-La Mancha, Working Paper DT-DAEF 2013/2.

Federal Reserve Bank of St Louis (2015), *The Mean vs. the Median of Family Income: FRED blog*. Available at: https://fredblog.stlouisfed.org/2015/05/the-mean-vs-the-median-of-family-income/ [Accessed 28 July 2017].

Federal Reserve [US] (2017a), *Monetary Policy: Open Market Operations*. Available at: https://www.federalreserve.gov/monetarypolicy/openmarket.htm [Accessed 23 November 2017].

Federal Reserve [US] (2017b), *Monetary Policy: Open Market Operations Archive*. Available at: https://www.federalreserve.gov/monetarypolicy/openmarket_archive.htm [Accessed 23 November 2017].

Feinstein, C. (1972), *National Income, Expenditure and Output of the United Kingdom 1855–1965*. Cambridge: Cambridge University Press.

Ferguson, N. (1999a), *The House of Rothschild: Money's Prophets 1798–1848*. London: Penguin.

Ferguson, N. (1999b), *The House of Rothschild: The World's Banker 1849–1999*. New York: Viking.

Ferguson, N. (2001), *The Cash Nexus*. New York: Basic Books.

Ferguson, T. and Galbraith, J. K. (1999), The American wage structure, 1920–1947. *Research in Economic History*, 19, pp. 205–57.

Fieldhouse, D. K. (1973), *Economics and Empire 1830–1914*. Ithaca, NY: Cornell University Press.

Fisher, I. (1922 (1911)), *The Purchasing Power of Money*. 2nd edn. New York: The Macmillan Co.

Ford, M. (2009), *The Lights in the Tunnel: Automation, Accelerating Technology and the Economy of the Future*. United States: Acculant.

Friedman, M. (1951), Neo-Liberalism and its prospects. *Farmand*, 17 February, pp. 89–93.

Friedman, M. (1956) The Quantity Theory of Money – a restatement. In: M. Friedman (ed.), *Studies in the Quantity Theory of Money*. Chicago, Ill.: University of Chicago Press, pp. 3–21.

Friedman, M. (1957), *A Theory of the Consumption Function*. Princeton, NJ: Princeton University Press.

Friedman, M. (1968), The role of monetary policy. *The American Economic Review*, 58 (1), pp. 1–17.

Friedman, M. (1970), *The Counter-Revolution in Monetary Theory*. London: The Wincott Foundation for the Institute of Economic Affairs.

Friedman, M. and Schwartz, A. (1963), *A Monetary History of the United States, 1867–1960*. Princeton, NJ: Princeton University Press.

Friedman, M. and Schwartz, A. (1982), *Monetary Trends in the United States and the United Kingdom*. Chicago, Ill.: University of Chicago Press.

Friedman, M. and Schwartz, A. J. (1965), *The Great Contraction: 1929–1933*. New York: National Bureau of Economic Research.

Frydman, R. and Goldberg, M. (2011), *Beyond Mechanical Markets*. Princeton, NJ: Princeton University Press.

Fullerton, D., Walker, C. E. and Long, R. B. (1994), Tax policy. In: M. Feldstein (ed.), *American Economic Policy in the 1980s*. Chicago, Ill.: University of Chicago Press, pp. 165–233.

Gagnon, J. E., Raskin, M., Remache, J. and Sack, B. P. (2011a), Large-scale asset purchases by the Federal Reserve: did they work? *Federal Reserve Bank of New York Economic Policy Review*, 17 (1), pp. 41–59.

Gagnon, J. E., Raskin, M., Remache, J. and Sack, B. P. (2011b), The financial market effects of the Federal Reserve's large-scale asset purchases. *International Journal of Central Banking*, 7 (1), pp. 3–43.

Galbraith, James K. (1998), *Created Unequal: The Crisis in American Pay*. New York: Free Press.

Galbraith, James K. (2014), 'Kapital' for the twenty-first century. *Dissent.* Spring.

Galbraith, James K. (2017), Can Trump overcome secular stagnation? *Real-World Economics Review*, 78, pp. 20–27.

Galbraith, John K. (1952), *American Capitalism: The Concept of Countervailing Power.* London: Harper Publications.

Gårdlund, T. (1996), *The Life of Knut Wicksell.* Cheltenham: Edward Elgar.

Gasperin, S. (2016), *Integration is Disintegrating: Financial and Structural Causes of the Eurozone Crisis.* Available at: https://etd.adm.unipi.it/t/etd-09122016-222239/ [Accessed 1 August 2017].

Gerber, D. J. (1994), Constitutionalizing the economy: German neo-liberalism, competition law and the 'new' Europe. *American Journal of Comparative Law*, 42 (1), pp. 25–84.

Giffen, R. (1892), *The Case Against Bimetallism.* London: George Bell & Sons.

Giles, C. (2014), Data problems with capital in the 21st century. *Financial Times.* Available at: http://blogs.ft.com/money-supply/2014/05/23/data-problems-with-capital-in-the-21st-century/ [Accessed 28 July 2017].

Giles, C. (2017), Setting policy in the dark. *Financial Times*, 12 October.

Goodhart, C. A. E. (2014), Competition and credit control. *LSE Financial Markets Group Special Paper No. 229.*

Goodhart, C. A. E. and Ashworth, J. P. (2012), QE: a successful start may be running into diminishing returns. *Oxford Review of Economic Policy*, 28 (4), pp. 640–70.

Graeber, D. (2011), *Debt: The First 5,000 Years.* New York: Melville House Publishing.

Graeber, D. (2015), The meaning of money. In: E. Skidelsky and R. Skidelsky (eds.), *Are Markets Moral?* London: Palgrave Macmillan, pp. 125–37.

Grant, J. (2015), *The Forgotten Depression.* New York: Simon & Schuster.

Greenspan, A. (2007), *The Age of Turbulence: Adventures in a New World.* London: Allen Lane.

G20 (2009), Leaders' statement, Pittsburgh, 24–25 September. Available at: https://www.treasury.gov/resource-center/international/g7-g20/Documents/pittsburgh_summit_leaders_statement_250909.pdf [Accessed 14 December 2017].

Guardian (2010), The austerity agenda must not go unopposed (Editorial). *Guardian*, 20 June.

Haldane, A. G., Roberts-Sklar, M., Wieladek, T. and Young, C. (2016), *QE: The Story So Far.* Bank of England Staff Working Paper No. 624.

Hamilton, E. (1935), Comments. *Quarterly Journal of Economics*, 50 (1), pp. 185–92.

Hammond, G. (2009), *Inflation Targeting in the UK: Bank of England presentation at the Banco Central do Brasil.* Available at: http://www.bcb.gov.br/pec/depep/seminarios/2009_xisemanualmetasinflbcb/arquivos/2009_xisemanualmetasinflbcb_gillhammond.pdf [Accessed 4 July 2017].

Harrison, R. et al. (2005), *The Bank of England Quarterly Model.* Available at: https://www.researchgate.net/publication/247789825 [Accessed 31 July 2017].

Harvey, J. (2009), *Currencies, Capital Flows and Crises: A Post Keynesian Analysis of Exchange Rate Determination.* Abingdon: Routledge.

Harvey, J. (2015), *Contending Perspectives in Economics: A Guide to Contemporary Schools of Thought.* Cheltenham: Edward Elgar.

Hawtrey, R. G. (1913), *Good and Bad Trade: An Inquiry into the Causes of Trade.* London: Longmans.

Hawtrey, R. G. (1925), Public expenditure and the demand for labour. *Economica*, 13, pp. 38–48.

Hawtrey, R. G. (1938), *A Century of Bank Rate.* New York: Longman, Green.

Hayek, F. A. (2001 (1944)), *The Road to Serfdom.* London: Routledge.

Heckscher, E. F. (1935), *Mercantilism, Vol. II.* London: George Allen & Unwin.

Heimberger, P. (2017), Did fiscal consolidation cause the double-dip recession in the euro area? *Review of Keynesian Economics*, 5 (3), pp. 439–58.

Heller, W. W. (1966), *New Dimensions of Political Economy.* Cambridge, Mass.: Harvard University Press.

Henderson, W. O. (2006 (1961)), *The Industrial Revolution on the Continent: Germany, France, Russia 1800–1914.* Oxford: Routledge.

Hendry, D. F. and Ericsson, N. R. (1991), An econometric analysis of U.K. money demand in *Monetary Trends in the United States and the United Kingdom* by Milton Friedman and Anna J. Schwartz. *American Economic Review*, 81 (1), pp. 8–38.

Herndon, T., Ash, M. and Pollin, R. (2014), Does high public debt consistently stifle economic growth? A critique of Reinhart and Rogoff. *Cambridge Journal of Economics*, 38 (2), pp. 257–79.

Hicks, J. (1935), A suggestion for simplifying the theory of money. *Economica*, 2 (5), pp. 1–19.

Hicks, J. (1969), *A Theory of Economic History.* Oxford: Oxford University Press.

Hicks, J. (1974), *The Crisis in Keynesian Economics.* New York: Basic Books.

Hicks, J. (1976), 'Revolutions' in economics. In: S. Latsis (ed.), *Method and Appraisal in Economics.* New York: Cambridge University Press, pp. 207–18.

Hicks, J. (1977), *Economic Perspectives: Further Essays on Money and Growth*. Oxford: Oxford University Press.

Hicks, J. R. (1937), Mr. Keynes and the 'Classics'; a suggested interpretation. *Econometrica*, 5 (2), pp. 147–59.

Hirschman, D. (2016), Stylized facts in the social sciences. *Sociological Science*. Available at: https://www.sociologicalscience.com/articles-v3-26-604/ [Accessed 5 July 2017].

HM Treasury (2006), *Budget 2006 (HC 968)*. London: The Stationery Office.

HM Treasury (2010), *Budget 2010 (HC 61)*. London: The Stationery Office.

HM Treasury (2014), *Autumn Statement 2014 (Cm 8961)*, December. London: The Stationery Office.

HM Treasury (2017), *Pocket Databank, October*. London: The Stationery Office.

Ho, P. (2012), Revisiting Prebisch and Singer: beyond the declining terms of trade thesis and on to technological capability development. *Cambridge Journal of Economics*, 36 (4), July, pp. 869–93.

Hobson, J. A. (1896), *The Problem of the Unemployed*. London: Methuen & Co.

Hobson, J. A. (1900), *The Economics of Distribution*. London: Macmillan.

Hobson, J. A. (1902), *Imperialism*. New York: James Pott Co.

Hobson, J. A. (1910 (1909)), *The Industrial System: An Inquiry into Earned and Unearned Income*. 2nd edn. London: Longman, Green & Co.

Hobson, J. A. (1922), *The Economics of Unemployment*. London: George Allen Unwin.

Hobson, J. A. and Mummery, A. F. (1889), *The Physiology of Industry*. London: John Murray.

Hoenig, T. M. (2014), Credibility of Living Wills. Federal Deposit Insurance Corporation, 5 August. Available at: https://www.fdic.gov/news/news/speeches/spaug0514a.pdf [Accessed 19 December 2017].

Holmans, A. E. (1999), *Demand Management in Britain 1953–58*. London: Institute for Contemporary British History.

Hume, D. (1987 (1752)), Political Discourses. In: E. F. Miller (ed.), *David Hume: Essays, Moral, Political and Literary*. Indianapolis, Ind.: Liberty Fund.

Humphrey, T. M. (1997), Fisher and Wicksell on the Quantity Theory. *Federal Reserve Bank of Richmond Economic Quarterly*, 83 (4), Fall, pp. 71–90.

Hutchison, T. W. (1978), *On Revolutions and Progress in Economic Knowledge*. Cambridge: Cambridge University Press.

ILOSTAT (2017), *SDG Labour Market Indicators*. Available at: http://www.ilo.org/ilostat/faces/ilostat-home/home?_adf.ctrl-state=c04kb9iu4_4&_afrLoop=196666878792954#! [Accessed 23 November 2017].

Inequality for All (2013), [Film] Directed by Jacob Kornbluth. United States: 72 Productions.

Innes, A. M. (1913), What is money? *Banking Law Journal*, May, pp. 377–408.

Innes, A. M. (1914), Credit theory of money. *Banking Law Journal*, January, pp. 151–68.

Institute for Fiscal Studies (2016), *Living Standards, Inequality and Poverty Spreadsheet*. Available at: https://www.ifs.org.uk/tools_and_resources/incomes_in_uk [Accessed 28 July 2017].

International Monetary Fund (2008), *World Economic Outlook October 2008*. Washington, DC: IMF.

International Monetary Fund (2009), *IMF Annual Report*. Washington, DC: IMF.

International Monetary Fund (2010), Global Economic Prospects and Policy Challenges: Meetings of G-7 Finance Ministers and Central Bank Governors. Iqaluit, Canada. Available at: https://www.imf.org/external/np/g7/020510.pdf [Accessed 4 July 2017].

International Monetary Fund (2012), *World Economic Outlook October 2012*. Washington, DC: IMF.

International Monetary Fund (2016), *World Economic Outlook April 2016 Dataset*. Available at: https://www.imf.org/external/pubs/ft/weo/2016/01/weodata/index.aspx.

International Monetary Fund (2017a), *World Economic Outlook April 2017 Dataset*. Available at: https://www.imf.org/external/pubs/ft/weo/2017/01/weodata/index.aspx.

International Monetary Fund (2017b.) *World Economic Outlook October 2017 Dataset*. Available at: http://www.imf.org/external/datamapper/datasets/WEO.

Investing.com (2017), *Brent Oil*. Available at: https://uk.investing.com/commodities/brent-oil-historical-data [Accessed 11 July 2017].

Irwin, D. (2000), *Tariffs and Growth in Late 19th Century America*. Hanover: Dartmouth College. Available at: http://www.dartmouth.edu/~dirwin/docs/Growth.pdf [Accessed 8 March 2018].

James, H. (1996), *International Monetary Cooperation Since Bretton Woods*. Washington, DC: International Monetary Fund and Oxford: Oxford University Press.

James, H. (2002), *The End of Globalization: Lessons from the Great Depression*. Cambridge, Mass.: Harvard University Press.

Johnson, P. (2016), *Autumn Statement 2016: IFS Briefing*. Available at: https://www.ifs.org.uk/uploads/budgets/as2016/as2016_pj.pdf [Accessed 5 July 2017].

Jones, D. S. (2012), *Masters of the Universe: Hayek, Friedman and the Birth of Neoliberal Politics*. Princeton, NJ: Princeton University Press.

Jordà, Ò. and Taylor, A. (2013), *The Time for Austerity: Estimating the Average Treatment Effect of Fiscal Policy*. National Bureau of Economic Research, Working Paper 19414.

Jowett, A. and Hardie, M. (2014), *Longer-term Trends – Public Sector Finance: Office for National Statistics*. Available at: http://webarchive.national-archives.gov.uk/20160105160709/http://www.ons.gov.uk/ons/dcp171766_386187.pdf [Accessed 27 June 2017].

Joyce, M., Lasaosa, A., Stevens, I. and Tong, M. (2011a), The financial market impact of quantitative easing. *International Journal of Central Banking*, 7 (3), pp. 113–61.

Joyce, M., Tong, M. and Woods, R. (2011b), The United Kingdom's quantitative easing policy: design, operation and impact. *Bank of England Quarterly Bulletin*, Q3, pp. 200–212.

Kaldor, N. (1966), *Causes of the Slow Rate of Economic Growth of the United Kingdom*. Cambridge: Cambridge University Press.

Kaldor, N. (1970), The new monetarism. *Lloyds Bank Review*, July, pp. 1–18.

Kaldor, N. (1971), The sea-change of the dollar. *The Times*, 6 September.

Kaldor, N. (1983a), Keynesian economics after fifty years. In: D. Worswick and J. Trevithick (eds.), *Keynes and the Modern World*. Cambridge: Cambridge University Press, pp. 1–28.

Kaldor, N. (1983b). *The Economic Consequences of Mrs. Thatcher: Speeches 1979–82*. London: Fabian Society.

Kaldor, N. (1985), How monetarism failed. *Challenge*, 28 (2), pp. 4–13.

Kang, D. W., Ligthart, N. and Mody, A. (2016), *The ECB and the Fed: A Comparative Narrative*. Bruegel. Available at: http://bruegel.org/2016/01/the-ecb-and-the-fed-a-comparative-narrative/ [Accessed 12 July 2017].

Keen, S. (2017), Ricardo's vice and the virtues of industrial diversity. *American Affairs*, 1 (3), Fall, pp. 17–30.

Keynes, J. M. (1945), Letter to S. G. Macfarlane, 5 June 1945, reproduced in the *Collected Writings of John Maynard Keynes*, Vol. XXVII, 1980. Cambridge: Cambridge University Press for the Royal Economic Society.

Keynes, J. M. (1971 (1923)), *The Collected Writings of John Maynard Keynes (IV) Tract on Monetary Reform*. London: Macmillan.

Keynes, J. M. (1971 (1930a)), *The Collected Writings of John Maynard Keynes (V) A Treatise on Money: The Pure Theory of Money*. London: Macmillan.

Keynes, J. M. (1971 (1930b)), *The Collected Writings of John Maynard Keynes (VI) A Treatise on Money: The Applied Theory of Money.* London: Macmillan.

Keynes, J. M. (1973a (1936)), *The Collected Writings of John Maynard Keynes (VII) The General Theory of Employment, Interest and Money.* Cambridge: Cambridge University Press for the Royal Economic Society.

Keynes, J. M. (1973b), *The Collected Writings of John Maynard Keynes (XIII) The General Theory and After, Part I: Preparation.* Cambridge: Cambridge University Press for the Royal Economic Society.

Keynes, J. M. (1973c), *The Collected Writings of John Maynard Keynes (XIV) The General Theory and After, Part II: Defence and Development.* Cambridge: Cambridge University Press for the Royal Economic Society.

Keynes, J. M. (1978), *The Collected Writings of John Maynard Keynes (IX) Essays in Persuasion.* Cambridge: Cambridge University Press for the Royal Economic Society.

Keynes, J. M. (1979), *The Collected Writings of John Maynard Keynes (XXIX) The General Theory and After: A Supplement.* Cambridge: Cambridge University Press for the Royal Economic Society.

Keynes, J. M. (1980a), *The Collected Writings of John Maynard Keynes (XXV) Activities 1940–1944: Shaping the Post-War World, The Clearing Union.* Cambridge: Cambridge University Press for the Royal Economic Society.

Keynes, J. M. (1980b), *The Collected Writings of John Maynard Keynes (XXVII) Activities 1940–1946, Shaping the Post-War World: Employment and Commodities.* Cambridge: Cambridge University Press for the Royal Economic Society.

Keynes, J. M. (1981), *The Collected Writings of John Maynard Keynes (XIX) Activities 1922–1929: The Return to Gold and Industrial Policy.* Cambridge: Cambridge University Press for the Royal Economic Society.

Keynes, J. M. (1982), *The Collected Writings of John Maynard Keynes (XXI) Activities 1931–1939: World Crises and Policies in Britain and America.* Cambridge: Cambridge University Press for the Royal Economic Society .

Keynes, J. M. (1983), *The Collected Writings of John Maynard Keynes (XI) Economic Articles and Correspondence: Academic.* Cambridge: Cambridge University Press for the Royal Economic Society.

Khaldûn, I. (1967 (1377)), *The Muqaddimah: An Introduction to History.* Abridged and ed. by N. J. Dawood, trans. Franz Rosenthal. Princeton, NJ: Princeton University Press.

Kindleberger, C. P. (1986 (1973)), *The World in Depression, 1929–1939.* London: University of California Press.

King, M. (2005), Monetary Policy: Practice Ahead of Theory. Mais Lecture. Available at: http://www.bankofengland.co.uk/archive/Documents/historicpubs/speeches/2005/speech245.pdf [Accessed 10 July 2017].

King, M. (2009), Speech given to the CBI Dinner, Nottingham. Available at: http://www.bankofengland.co.uk/archive/Documents/historicpubs/speeches/2009/speech372.pdf [Accessed 10 July 2017].

King, M. (2011), Global imbalances: the perspective of the Bank of England. *Banque de France Financial Stability Review*, 15, pp. 73–80.

King, M. (2012), *Twenty Years of Inflation Targeting*. Available at: http://www.bis.org/review/r121010f.pdf [Accessed 10 July 2017].

King, M. (2016), *The End of Alchemy*. London: Little, Brown.

Kingsley, P. (2012). How credit ratings agencies rule the world. *Guardian*, 15 February.

Kishore, V. (2014), *Ricardo's Gauntlet: Economic Fiction and the Flawed Case for Free Trade*. London: Anthem Press.

Knapp, G. F. (1924 (1905)), *The State Theory of Money*. London: Macmillan.

Krugman, P. (1998), It's baaack: Japan's slump and the return of the liquidity trap. *Brookings Papers on Economic Activity*, 2, pp. 137–205.

Krugman, P. (2007), Introduction to new edition. In: J. M. Keynes, *The General Theory of Employment, Interest and Money*. 2nd edn. Basingstoke: Palgrave Macmillan, pp. xxv–xxxviii.

Krugman, P. (2010), Myths of austerity. *New York Times*, 2 July. Available at: http://www.nytimes.com/2010/07/02/opinion/02krugman.html [Accessed 21 June 2017].

Krugman, P. (2013a), Bubbles, regulation and secular stagnation. *New York Times*, 25 September. Available at: https://krugman.blogs.nytimes.com/2013/09/25/bubbles-regulation-and-secular-stagnation/?_r=0 [Accessed 21 December 2017].

Krugman, P. (2013b), Secular stagnation, coalmines, bubbles, and Larry Summers. *New York Times*, 16 November. Available at: https://krugman.blogs.nytimes.com/2013/11/16/secular-stagnation-coalmines-bubbles-and-larry-summers/?_r=3 [Accessed 21 December 2017].

Krugman, P. (2014), Nobody understands the liquidity trap, still. *New York Times*, 4 October.

Krugman, P. (2015), The austerity delusion. *Guardian*, 29 April.

Kynaston, D. (2017), *Till Time's Last Stand: A History of the Bank of England 1694–2013*. London: Bloomsbury.

Laidler, D. (1985), Monetary policy in Britain: successes and shortcomings. *Oxford Review of Economic Policy*, 1 (1), pp. 35–43.

Laidler, D. (1991), *The Golden Age of the Quantity Theory*. Princeton, NJ: Princeton University Press.

Laidler, D. (1999), *Fabricating the Keynesian Revolution: Studies of the Inter-war Literature on Money, the Cycle, and Unemployment*. Cambridge: Cambridge University Press.

Laidler, D. (2014), *Reassessing the Thesis of the Monetary History*. University of Western Ontario Economic Policy Research Institute Working Paper #2013-5.

Larsen, P. T. (2007), Goldman pays the price of being big. *Financial Times*, 13 August.

Lavelle, A. (2016 (2008)), *The Death of Social Democracy: Political Consequences in the 21st Century*. Abingdon: Routledge.

Lavoie, M. (2018), Rethinking macroeconomic theory before the next crisis. *Review of Keynesian Economics*, 6 (1), pp. 1–21.

Lawson, N. (1992), *The View from No. 11: Memoirs of a Tory Radical*. London: Bantam Press.

Lazonick, W. (2015), How maximising shareholder value stops innovation. In: Mariana Mazzucato and Caetano C. R. Penna (eds.), *Mission-Oriented Finance for Innovation: New Ideas for Investment-Led Growth*. London: Rowman & Littlefield, pp. 31–8.

Lee, A. J. (1970), The Social and Economic Thought of J. A. Hobson. PhD thesis, University of London.

Leijonhufvud, A. (1979), *The Wicksell Connection: Variations on a Theme*. UCLA Economics Working Paper No. 165.

Leijonhufvud, A. (1993 (1969)), Keynes and the Classics. In: W. Allan (ed.), *A Critique of Keynesian Economics*. Basingstoke and London: Macmillan, pp. 81–114.

Lenin, V. I. (1970 (1917)), Imperialism, the Highest Stage of Capitalism. In: *V. I. Lenin, Selected Works (I)*. Moscow: Progress Publishers, pp. 667–768.

Leontief, W. (1952), Machines and man. *Scientific American*, 187 (3), pp. 150–60.

Leontief, W. (1979), Is technological unemployment inevitable? *Challenge*, 22 (4), pp. 48–50.

Lindbeck, A. (1976), *Stabilization Policy in Open Economies with Endogenous Politicians*. Seminar Paper 54, Institute for International Economic Studies, University of Stockholm.

List, F. (1909 (1841)), *The National System of Political Economy*. London: Longman, Green & Co.

Lo, C. (2015). *China's Impossible Trinity: The Structural Challenges to the 'Chinese Dream'*. Basingstoke: Palgrave Macmillan.

Lo, C. (2018), *Implications of Sino-US trade frictions*. BNP Paribas Asset Management.

Locke, J. (1824 (1691)), *The Works of John Locke in Nine Volumes (IV) Economic Writings and Two Treatises of Government*. 12th edn. London: Rivington.

Lohr, S. (2004), An elder challenges outsourcing's orthodoxy. *New York Times*, 9 September.

Longaker, M. G. (2015), *Rhetorical Style and Bourgeois Virtue: Capitalism and Civil Society in the British Enlightenment*. University Park, Pa.: Penn State University Press.

Lowe, A. (1965), *On Economic Knowledge: Toward a Science of Political Economics*, New York: Harper & Row.

Lucas, R. (1990), Why doesn't capital flow from rich to poor countries? *American Economic Review*, 80 (2), pp. 92–6.

Lucas, R. E. (1972), Expectations and the neutrality of money. *Journal of Economic Theory*, 4 (2), pp. 103–24.

Lucas, R. E. (1976), Econometric policy evaluation: a critique. In: K. Brunner and A. Meltzer (eds.), *Carnegie Rochester Conference Series on Public Policy, Vol. 1*. New York: Elsevier, pp. 19–46.

Lucas, R. E. (1980), The death of Keynesian economics. *Issues and Ideas*, Winter.

Lucas, R. E. (2003), Macroeconomic priorities. *American Economic Review*, 93 (1), pp. 1–14.

Lukes, Steven (1974), *Power – A Radical View* (reissued 2005). London: Palgrave Macmillan.

Luttwak, E. N. (2015), Too high a bill. *Times Literary Supplement*, 23 September.

McCracken, P. W. et al. (1977), *Towards Full Employment and Price Stability*. s.l.: OECD.

Mackenzie, M. (2010), The short view. *Financial Times*, 21 July.

McLeay, M., Radia, A. and Thomas, R. (2014), Money creation in the modern economy. *Bank of England Quarterly Bulletin*, Q1, pp. 14–27.

Macmillan Committee (1929–31), T 200. Committee on Finance and Industry: Minutes of evidence. Held by The National Archives, Kew. Available at: http://discovery.nationalarchives.gov.uk/details/r/C1851843.

Maddison, A. (1983), Economic stagnation since 1973, its nature and causes: a six country survey. *De Economist*, 131 (4), pp. 585–608.

Madjd-Sadjadi, Z. (2015), China: 2,500 years of economic thought. In: V. Barnett (ed.), *Routledge Handbook of the History of Global Economic Thought*. New York: Routledge, pp. 294–305.

Malfa, G. L. (2000), *L'Europa legata, i rischi dell'Euro*. Milano: Rizzoli. Recently re-edited as: Malfa, G. L. (2011), *La crisi dell'Euro, Bagno a Ripoli*. Florence: Passigli Editori.

Mallet, B. (1913), *British Budgets 1887/88 to 1912/13*. London: Macmillan.

Marshall, A. (1923), *Money, Credit and Commerce*. London: Macmillan.

Martin, F. (2014), *Money: The Unauthorised Biography*. London: Vintage.

Marx, K. (1909 (1894)), *Capital: A Critique of Political Economy (III) The Process of Capitalist Production as a Whole*. Chicago, Ill.: Charles H. Kerr & Co.

Marx, K. and Engels, F. (1962), *Selected Works*. London: Lawrence & Wishart.

Marx, K. and Engels, F. (1967), *The Communist Manifesto* (intro. A. J. P. Taylor). Harmondsworth: Penguin.

Masch, V. (2010), An application of risk-constrained optimization (RCO) to a problem of international trade. *International Journal of Operations and Quantitative Management*, 16 (4), pp. 415–65.

Masch, V. (2015), Shifting 'the dodo paradigm': to be or not to be. *World Journal of Social Sciences*, 5 (3), September, pp. 123–42.

Masch, V. A. (2017), Balancing global trade: 'compensated free trade'. *World Journal of Social Sciences*, 7 (1), March, pp. 49–63.

Matthews, R. C. O. (1968), Why has Britain had full employment since the war? *The Economic Journal*, 78 (311), pp. 555–69.

May, T. (2016), Keynote speech to Tory party conference, 5 October.

Mazzucato, M. (2013), *The Entrepreneurial State: Debunking Public vs Private Sector Myths*. London and New York: Anthem Press.

Mazzucato, M. (2016), 'Innovation, the state and patient capital', in M. Jacobs and M. Mazzucato (eds.), *Rethinking Capitalism: Economics and Policy for Sustainable and Inclusive Growth*. Chichester: The Political Quarterly Publishing Co. and Wiley-Blackwell.

Meaning, J. and Warren, J. (2015), The transmission of unconventional monetary policy in UK government debt markets. *National Institute Economic Review*, 234, pp. R40–R47.

Michie, R. C. (2003), The City of London and British banking, 1900–1939. In: C. Wigley (ed.), *A Companion to Early Twentieth-Century Britain*. Oxford: Blackwell, pp. 249–69.

Middlemas, K. and Barnes, A. J. L. (1969), *Baldwin: A Biography*. London: Weidenfeld & Nicolson.

Middleton, R. (1982), The Treasury in the 1930s: political and administrative constraints to acceptance of the 'new' economics. *Oxford Economic Papers*, 34 (1), pp. 48–77.

Middleton, R. (1985), *Towards the Managed Economy*. London: Methuen.

Miles, D. (2012), Government debt and unconventional monetary policy: Speech at the 28th NABE Economic Policy Conference, Virginia. Available at: http://www.bankofengland.co.uk/archive/Documents/historicpubs/speeches/2012/speech559.pdf [Accessed 11 July 2017].

Mill, J. S. (1965 (1848)), *The Collected Works of John Stuart Mill (III) Principles of Political Economy with Some of Their Applications to Social Philosophy, Part II*. London: Routledge & Kegan Paul.

Mill, J. S. (1967 (1844)), Essays on Some Unsettled Questions of Political Economy. In: J. M. Robson (ed.), *The Collected Works of John Stuart Mill (IV) Essays on Economics and Society, Part I*. London: Routledge & Kegan Paul, pp. 229–341.

Milner, B. (2009), Sun finally sets on notion that markets are rational. *The Globe and Mail*, 3 July. Available at: http://www.theglobeandmail.com/globe-investor/investment-ideas/features/taking-stock/sun-finally-sets-on-notion-that-markets-are-rational/article14301916.

Minford, P. (1988), Mrs. Thatcher's economic reform programme. In: R. Skidelsky (ed.), *Thatcherism*. London: Chatto & Windus, pp. 93–106.

Mini, P. V. (1974), *Philosophy and Economics: The Origins and Development of Economic Theory*. Gainesville, Fla.: University Presses of Florida.

Ministry of Reconstruction (1944), *Employment Policy (Cmd. 6527)*. London: HMSO.

Minsky, H. (1992), *Financial Instability Hypothesis*. Levy Economics Institute of Bard College, Working Paper No. 74.

Minsky, H. (2008 (1986)), *Stabilizing an Unstable Economy*. New York: McGraw-Hill Education.

Mirowski, P. (1999 (1989)), *More Heat than Light: Economics as Social Physics, Physics as Nature's Economics*. Cambridge: Cambridge University Press.

Mishel, L., Bivens, J., Gould, E. and Shierholz, H. (2012), *The State of Working America*. 12th edn. Ithaca, NY: Cornell University Press.

Mitchell, W. C. and Green, D. G. (1988), *Government As It Is*. London: Institute for Economic Affairs.

Morgan, B. (1978), *Monetarists and Keynesians: Their Contribution to Monetary Theory*. London: Macmillan.

Morgan, E. V. (1952), *Studies in British Financial Policy, 1914–25*. London: Macmillan.

Morimoto, Y. (2013), *Economic Activity and Prices in Japan and Monetary Policy*. BIS. Available at: http://www.bis.org/review/r130319b.pdf [Accessed 20 July 2017].

Mosler, W. (1997/8), Full employment and price stability. *Journal of Post-Keynesian Economics*, 20 (2), Winter.

Muellbauer, J. (2014), *Combatting Eurozone Deflation: QE for the People*. Available at: http://voxeu.org/article/combatting-Eurozone-deflation-qe-people [Accessed 12 July 2017].

Muellbauer, J. (2016), *Helicopter Money and Fiscal Rules*. Available at: http://voxeu.org/article/helicopter-money-and-fiscal-rules [Accessed 5 July 2017].

Munchau, W. (2010), Even Eurozone optimists are not optimistic. *Financial Times*, 11 July.

Muth, J. F. (1961), Rational expectations and the theory of price movements. *Econometrica*, 29 (3), pp. 315–35.

Neely, C. J. and Dey, S. R. (2010), A survey of announcement effects on foreign exchange returns. *Federal Reserve Bank of St. Louis Review*, 92 (5), pp. 417–63.

Nemmers, E. E. (1956), *Hobson and Underconsumption*. Amsterdam: North Holland.

Nielsen, R. (2012), *The Nonsense of the Efficient Market Hypothesis*. Whistling in the Wind, 9 August. Available at: https://whistlinginthewind.org/2012/08/09/the-nonsense-of-the-efficient-market-hypothesis/ [Accessed 10 January 2018].

Niemeyer, O. (1921), Memorandum to Chancellor. PRO T 172/1208, 5 October.

Nocera, J. (2009a), Poking holes in a theory of markets. *New York Times*, 5 June.

Nocera, J. (2009b), Risk mismanagement. *New York Times*, 2 January.

North, D. C. and Thomas, R. P. (1970), An economic theory of the growth of the western world. *Economic History Review*, 23 (1), pp. 1–17.

North, M. (2015), Finances and power in the German state system. In: B. Yun-Casalilla and P. K. O'Brien (eds.), *The Rise of Fiscal States: A Global History, 1500–1914*. Cambridge: Cambridge University Press, pp. 145–63.

O'Brien, D. P. (1975), *The Classical Economists*. Oxford: Clarendon Press.

O'Brien, P. K. (2011), The nature and historical evolution of an exceptional fiscal state and its possible significance for the precocious commercialization and industrialization of the British economy from Cromwell to Nelson. *Economic History Review*, 64 (2), pp. 408–46.

Office for Budget Responsibility (2012), *Economic and Fiscal Outlook, December*. Available at: http://obr.uk/efo/economic-and-fiscal-outlook-december-2012/ [Accessed 7 May 2018].

Office for Budget Responsibility (2016), *Forecast Evaluation Report – October 2016*. s.l.: s.n.

Office for Budget Responsibility (2017), *Historical Official Forecasts Database*. Available at: http://budgetresponsibility.org.uk/data/ [Accessed 28 August 2017].

Ollivaud, P. and Turner, D. (2014), *The Effect of the Global Financial Crisis on OECD Potential Output*. OECD Economics Department Working Paper No. 1166.

ONS (2012), *United Kingdom National Accounts: The Blue Book, 2012 Edition*. Newport: Office for National Statistics. Available at: http://webarchive.nationalarchives.gov.uk/20160106152309/http://www.ons.gov.uk/ons/rel/naa1-rd/united-kingdom-national-accounts/the-blue-book--2012-edition/index.html [Accessed 10 January 2018].

ONS (2017), *Office for National Statistics*. Available at: https://www.ons.gov.uk/ [Accessed 10 July 2016].

Osborne, G. (2013), *Autumn Statement*, 5 December. s.l.: s.n.

Ostry, J. D., Loungani, P. and Furceri, D. (2016), Neoliberalism: oversold? *IMF Finance and Development*, 53 (2), pp. 38–41.

Palley, T. (2001), *Contradictions Coming Home to Roost? Income Distribution and the Return of the Aggregate Demand Problem*. Levy Economics Institute of Bard College, Working Paper No. 332.

Palley, T. (2008), The debt delusion. *Guardian*, 8 February.

Palley, T. (2009), *America's Exhausted Paradigm: Macroeconomic Causes of the Financial Crisis and Great Recession*. Institute for International Political Economy Berlin, Working Paper No. 02/2009.

Palley, T. (2014), The accidental controversialist: deeper reflections on Thomas Piketty's 'Capital'. *Real-World Economics Review*, Issue 67, pp. 143–6.

Palley, T. (2015), The Federal Reserve and shared prosperity: a guide to the policy issues and institutional challenges. *Real-World Economics Review*, Issue 70, pp. 27–48.

Parker, G. and Barker, A. (2010), Osborne tells Commons recovery is on track. *Financial Times*, 29 November.

Patinkin, D. (2008), John Maynard Keynes. In: S. N. Durlauf and L. E. Blume (eds.), *The New Palgrave Dictionary of Economics, Second Edition (IV)*. Basingstoke: Palgrave Macmillan, pp. 687–716.

Peacock, A. T. and Wiseman, J. (1961), *The Growth of Public Expenditure in the United Kingdom*. Princeton, NJ: Princeton University Press.

Peden, G. C. (1983), Sir Richard Hopkins and the 'Keynesian Revolution' in employment policy, 1929–1945. *Economic History Review*, 36 (2), pp. 281–96.

Peden, G. C. (1984), The 'Treasury View' on public works and employment in the interwar period. *Economic History Review*, 37 (2), pp. 167–81.

Peden, G. C. (1993), The road to and from Gairloch: Lloyd George, unemployment, inflation, and the 'Treasury View' in 1921. *Twentieth Century British History*, 4 (3), pp. 224–49.

Peden, G. C. (2000), *The Treasury and British Public Policy, 1906–1959*. Oxford: Oxford University Press.

Peden, G. C. (2002), From cheap government to efficient government: the political economy of public expenditure in the United Kingdom, 1832–1914. In: Donald Winch and Patrick K. O'Brien (eds.), *The Political Economy of British Historical Experience, 1688–1914*. Oxford: Oxford University Press, pp. 351–78.

Peden, G. C. (2004), *Keynes and His Critics: Treasury Responses to the Keynesian Revolution, 1925–1946*. Oxford: Oxford University Press.

Peel, R. (1819), HC Deb. 24 May 1819. London: Hansard.

Pettifor, A. (2017), *The Production of Money: How to Break the Power of Bankers*. London: Verso Books.

Pettis, M. (2013), *The Great Rebalancing: Trade, Conflict, and the Perilous Road Ahead for the World Economy*. Princeton, NJ: Princeton University Press.

Petty, W. (1899 (1682)), Quantulumcunque concerning Money. In: C. H. Hull (ed.), *The Economic Writings of Sir William Petty II*. Cambridge: The University Press, pp. 437–48.

Phillips, A. W. (1958), The relation between unemployment and the rate of change of money wage rates in the United Kingdom, 1861–1957. *Economica*, 25 (100), pp. 283–99.

Pigou, A. C. (1912), *Wealth and Welfare*. London: Macmillan.

Pigou, A. C. (1913), Review of R. G. Hawtrey, *Good and Bad Trade*, *The Economic Journal*, 23, pp. 580–83.

Piketty, T. (2014 (2013)), *Capital in the Twenty-First Century*. Cambridge, Mass.: Harvard University Press.

Piketty, T. (2017), *Chronicles: On our Troubled Times*. London: Penguin.

Plumpe, W. (2016), *German Economic and Business History in the 19th and 20th Centuries*. London: Palgrave Macmillan.

Private Debt Project (2015), *Conversation with Lord Adair Turner*. Available at: http://privatedebtproject.org/view-articles.php?An-Interview-With-Lord-Adair-Turner-6 [Accessed 6 December 2017].

Prynn, J. (2016), RBS forced to draw up £2bn action plan after spectacular 'stress test' failure. *Evening Standard*, 30 November. Available at: https://www.standard.co.uk/news/uk/rbs-forced-to-draw-up-2bn-action-plan-after-spectacular-stress-test-failure-a3408381.html [Accessed 19 December 2017].

Quiggin, J. (2010), *Zombie Economics*. Princeton, NJ and Oxford: Princeton University Press.

Radcliffe Committee (1959), *Report of the Committee on the Working of the Monetary System*. London: HMSO.

Radice, H. (2014), Enforcing austerity in Europe: the structural deficit as a policy target. *Journal of Contemporary European Studies*, 22 (3), pp. 318–28.

Rajan, R. G. (2010), *Fault Lines: How Hidden Fractures Still Threaten the World Economy*. Princeton, NJ: Princeton University Press.

Rawls, J. (1971), *A Theory of Justice*. Cambridge, Mass.: Belknap.

Reagan, R. (1981), Inaugural Address, 20 January. In: G. Peters and J. Woolley, *The American Presidency Project*. Available at: http://www.presidency.ucsb.edu/ws/?pid=43130 [Accessed 01 December 2017].

Reed, H. (2014), Piketty, Chris Giles and wealth inequality: it's all about the discontinuities. *Guardian*, 29 May. Available at: https://www.theguardian.com/news/datablog/2014/may/29/piketty-chris-giles-and-wealth-inequality-its-all-about-the-discontinuities [Accessed 28 July 2017].

Reed, J. (2015), We were wrong about universal banking. *Financial Times*, 11 November.

Reich, R. (2010), *Aftershock: The Next Economy and America's Future*. New York: Alfred A. Knopf.

Reinhart, C. M. and Rogoff, K. S. (2010a), *Debt and Growth Revisited*. Available at: http://voxeu.org/article/debt-and-growth-revisited [Accessed 5 August 2017].

Reinhart, C. M. and Rogoff, K. S. (2010b), Growth in a time of debt. *American Economic Review*, 100 (2), pp. 573–8.

Reinhart, C. M. and Rogoff, K. S. (2011 (2009)), *This Time Is Different: Eight Centuries of Financial Folly*. Princeton, NJ: Princeton University Press.

Ricardo, D. (2005 (1810)), The High Price of Bullion, A Proof of the Depreciation of Bank Notes. In: P. Sraffa (ed.), *The Works and Correspondence of David Ricardo (III) Pamphlets and Papers 1809–11*. Indianapolis, Ind.: Liberty Fund, pp. 47–128.

Ricardo, D. (2005 (1815)), *The Works and Correspondence of David Ricardo (IV) Pamphlets and Papers 1815–1823*. Indianapolis, Ind.: Liberty Fund.

Ricardo, D. (2005 (1816)), *The Works and Correspondence of David Ricardo (VII) Letters 1816–1818*. Indianapolis, Ind.: Liberty Fund.

Ricardo, D. (2005 (1817)), *The Works and Correspondence of David Ricardo (I) On the Principles of Political Economy and Taxation*. Indianapolis, Ind.: Liberty Fund.

Ricketts, L. R. and Waller, C. J. (2014), *The Rise and (Eventual) Fall in the Fed's Balance Sheet*. Federal Reserve Bank of St. Louis. Available at: https://www.stlouisfed.org/publications/regional-economist/january-2014/the-rise-and-eventual-fall-in-the-feds-balance-sheet [Accessed 10 July 2017].

Riecher, S. and Black, J. (2013), Draghi says ECB won't hesitate to fail banks in stress tests. *Bloomberg*, 13 October. Available at: https://www.bloomberg.com/news/articles/2013-10-23/draghi-says-ecb-won-t-hesitate-to-fail-banks-in-stress-tests [Accessed 19 December 2017].

Robbins, L. (1971), *Money, Trade and International Relations*. London: Palgrave Macmillan.

Robinson, J. and Wilkinson, F. (1985), Ideology and logic. In: F. Vicarelli (ed.), *Keynes's Relevance Today*. London and Basingstoke: Macmillan, pp. 73–98.

Rodrik, D. (2011), *The Globalization Paradox*. Oxford: Oxford University Press.

Rogers, S. (2013a), Budget 2013 datablog. Tax receipts since 1963. *Guardian*, 18 March. Available at: https://www.theguardian.com/news/datablog/2010/apr/25/tax-receipts-1963#data [Accessed 9 January 2018].

Rogers, S. (2013b), Budget 2013 datablog. UK public spending since 1963. *Guardian*, 18 March. Available at: https://www.theguardian.com/news/datablog/2010/apr/25/uk-public-spending-1963#data [Accessed 9 January 2018].

Romer, C. D. and Romer, D. H. (2010), The macroeconomic effects of tax changes: estimates based on a new measure of fiscal shocks. *American Economic Review*, June, 100 (3), pp. 763–801.

Romer, D. (2011), *Advanced Macroeconomics*. 4th edn. New York: McGraw-Hill.

Roosevelt, F. D. (1936), Address at Forbes Field, Pittsburgh, Pa. *The American Presidency Project*. Available at: http://www.presidency.ucsb.edu/ws/?pid=15149 [Accessed 21 June 2017].

Ryan-Collins, J., Greenham, T., Werner, R. and Jackson, A. (2014 (2011)), *Where Does Money Come From?* 2nd edn. London: New Economics Foundation.

Ryan-Collins, J., Werner, R., Greenham, T. and Bernardo, G. (2013), *Strategic Quantitative Easing: Stimulating Investment to Rebalance the Economy*. Available at: http://neweconomics.org/2013/07/strategic-quantitative-easing/ [Accessed 10 July 2017].

Samuelson, P. A. (1955 (1948)), *Economics*. 3rd edn. New York: McGraw-Hill.

Samuelson, P. A. (1964 (1963)), A brief survey of post-Keynesian developments. In: R. Lekachman (ed.), *Keynes' General Theory: Reports of Three Decades*. London: Palgrave Macmillan, pp. 331–47.

Samuelson, P. A. (1970 (1948)), *Economics*. 8th edn. New York: McGraw-Hill.

Samuelson, P. A. (1973), *The Samuelson Sampler*. Glen Ridge, NJ: Thomas Horton.

Samuelson, P. A. (1991 (1966)), *The Collected Scientific Papers of Paul A. Samuelson (II)*. Cambridge, Mass.: MIT Press.

Samuelson, P. A. (2004), Where Ricardo and Mill rebut and confirm arguments of mainstream economists supporting globalization. *Journal of Economic Perspectives*, 18 (3), Summer, pp. 135–46.

Sandbu, M. (2015), Free lunch: Germany's incredible shrinking surplus. *Financial Times*, 9 December.

Saul, J. R. (2004), The collapse of globalism. *Harper's Magazine*, March.

Sawyer, M. (2007), Fiscal policy under New Labour. *Cambridge Journal of Economics*, 31 (6), pp. 885–99.

Say, J. B. (1821), *Letters to Mr. Malthus on Several Subjects of Political Economy and the Cause of the Stagnation of Commerce*. London: Sherwood, Neely & Jones.

Scheidel, W. (2017), *The Great Leveler: Violence and the History of Inequality from the Stone Age to the Twenty-First Century*. Princeton, NJ: Princeton University Press.

Schlesinger Jr, A. (1986), *The Cycles of American History*. Boston, Mass.: Houghton Mifflin.

Schomberg, W. (2016), Bank of England's Carney warns of zero-sum game from negative rates. Reuters. Available at: http://uk.reuters.com/article/uk-g20-china-carney-idUKKCN0VZ14A [Accessed 11 July 2017].

Schumpeter, J. A. (1954), *History of Economic Analysis*. London: Routledge.

Schumpeter, J. A. (1997 (1952)), *Ten Great Economists: From Marx to Keynes*. London: Routledge.

Sedláček, T. (2011), *Economics of Good and Evil: The Quest for Economic Meaning from Gilgamesh to Wall Street*. New York: Oxford University Press.

Select Committee on the High Price of Gold Bullion (1810), *Report of the Select Committee of the House of Commons on the High Price of Gold Bullion*. London: House of Commons.

Sen, S. (2010), *International Trade Theory and Policy: A Review of the Literature*. Levy Economics Institute of Bard College, Working Paper No. 635, November. Available at: http://www.levyinstitute.org/pubs/wp_635.pdf [Accessed 18 December 2017].

Shaikh, A. (2016), *Capitalism: Competition, Conflict, Crisis*. Oxford: Oxford University Press.

Shaw, G. K. (1984), *Rational Expectations: An Elementary Exposition*. Brighton: Wheatsheaf Books.

Shiller, R. J. (2010), What would Roosevelt do? *New York Times*, 31 July.

Silber, W. (2012), *How Volcker Created a Gold Standard Without Gold*. Bloomberg View. Available at: https://www.bloomberg.com/view/articles/2012-08-21/how-volcker-created-a-gold-standard-without-gold [Accessed 3 July 2017].

Skidelsky, R. (1981), Keynes and the Treasury View: the case for and against an active unemployment policy, 1920–1929. In: W. J. Mommsen (ed.), *The Emergence of the Welfare State in Britain and Germany, 1850–1950*. Beckenham: Croom Helm, pp. 167–87.

Skidelsky, R. (1992), *John Maynard Keynes: The Economist as Saviour 1920–1937*. London: Macmillan.

Skidelsky, R. (1994 (1967)), *Politicians and the Slump*. London: Papermac.

Skidelsky, R. (2000), *John Maynard Keynes: Fighting for Freedom, 1937–1946*. London: Penguin.

Skidelsky, R. (2003), *John Maynard Keynes 1883–1946: Economist, Philosopher, Statesman*. London: Penguin.

Skidelsky, R. (2009), *Keynes: The Return of the Master*. London: Allen Lane.

Skidelsky, R. (2010), *Beyond the Crash: Overcoming the First Crisis of Globalization* by Gordon Brown – review. *Guardian*, 12 December.

Skidelsky, R. (2015), *The Essential Keynes*. London: Penguin.

Skidelsky, R. (2016), *The Case for UK Import Substitution*. Project Syndicate. Available at: https://www.project-syndicate.org/commentary/case-for-uk-import-substitution-by-robert-skidelsky-2016-10 [Accessed 11 July 2017].

Skidelsky, R., Martin, F. and Wigstrom, F. M. (2012), *Blueprint for a British Investment Bank*. Centre for Global Studies. Available at: http://globalstudies.org.uk/publications/blueprint-for-a-british-investment-bank/ [Accessed 21 December 2017].

Skypala, P. (2015), The reality gap in the role of the banks. *Financial Times*, 8 June.

Sloman, P. (2015), *The Liberal Party and the Economy, 1929–1964*. Oxford: Oxford University Press.

Smith, A. (1755), *Adam Smith on the need for 'peace, easy taxes, and a tolerable administration of justice'*. Online Library of Liberty. Available at: http://oll.libertyfund.org/quote/436 [Accessed 25 August 2017].

Smith, A. (1976 (1776)), *The Glasgow Edition of the Works and Corre-spondences of Adam Smith (Vol. II) An Inquiry into the Nature and Causes of the Wealth of Nations (Vols. I & II)*. Oxford: Clarendon Press.

Soros, G. (2009a), General theory of reflexivity. *Financial Times*, 26 October.

Soros, G. (2009b), One way to stop bear raids. *Wall Street Journal*, 24 March.

Statistical Office of the United Nations (1962), *International Trade Statistics: 1900–1960*. New York: United Nations.

Stein, H. (1948), The C.E.D. on Budget Policy. *Proceedings of the Annual Conference on Taxation under the Auspices of the National Tax Association*, 41, pp. 472–80.

Stein, H. (1969), *The Fiscal Revolution in America*. Chicago, Ill.: University of Chicago Press.

Stephens, P. (2010), The tensions behind Cameron's puff and PR. *Financial Times*, 14 June.

Stigler, G. (1986 (1962)), The Intellectual and the Marketplace. In: K. R. Leube and T. G. Moore (eds.), *The Essence of Stigler*. Stanford, Calif.: Hoover Institution Press, pp. 79–88.

Stiglitz, J. E. (1989), On the economic role of the state. In: Arnold Heertje (ed.), *The Economic Role of the State*. Oxford: Blackwell.

Stiglitz, J. E. (2002), *Globalization and its Discontents*. London: Penguin.

Stiglitz, J. E. (2006), *Making Globalization Work*. New York: W. W. Norton.

Stiglitz, J. E. (2010), Needed: a new economic paradigm. *Financial Times*, 19 August.

Stieglitz, J. E. (2012), *The Price of Inequality*. New York: W. W. Norton.

Stiglitz, J. E. (2014), *Europe's Austerity Zombies*. Project Syndicate. 26 September. Available at: https://www.project-syndicate.org/commentary/joseph-e--stiglitz-wonders-why-eu-leaders-are-nursing-a-dead-theory?barrier=accessreg [Accessed 23 March 2018].

Summers, L. (2011), Five grim and essential lessons for world leaders. *Financial Times*, 2 November.

Summers, L. (2013), Speech given in the IMF Fourteenth Annual Research Conference in Honor of Stanley Fischer. Washington, DC, 8 November. Available at: http://larrysummers.com/imf-fourteenth-annual-research-conference-in-honor-of-stanley-fischer/ [Accessed 21 December 2017].

Summers, L. (2014), U. S. economic prospects: secular stagnation, hysteresis, and the zero lower bound. *Business Economics*, 49 (2), pp. 65–73.

Taylor, J. B. (1993), Discretion versus policy rules in practice. *Carnegie-Rochester Conference Series on Public Policy*, 39, pp. 195–214.

The Economist (2012), *The Lo Down*. Available at: http://www.economist. com/node/21542781 [Accessed 31 July 2017].

The Maddison Project (2013), *The New Maddison Project Database*. Available at: http://www.ggdc.net/maddison/maddison-project/home.htm [Accessed 27 June 2017].

The Pensions Regulator (2016), *An Introduction to Investment: Tutorial 5 of 9, Capital Markets and Economic Cycles*. Available at: https://trustee toolkit.thepensionsregulator.gov.uk/pluginfile.php/133/mod_data/content/ 2543/intro-to-investment-tutorial-five.pdf [Accessed 23 March 2018].

Thomas, R. (2017), UK broad money growth and nominal spending during the Great Recession: an analysis of the money creation process and the role of money demand. In: T. Congdon (ed.), *Money in the Great Recession: Did a Crash in Money Growth Cause the Global Slump?* Gloucester: Edward Elgar, pp. 78–100.

Thornton, H. (1802), *An Enquiry Into the Nature and Effects of the Paper Credit of Great Britain*. London: J. Hatchard.

Tieben, B. (2009), *The Concept of Equilibrium in Different Economic Traditions: A Historical Investigation*. Amsterdam: Rozenberg Publishers.

Tobin, J. (1966), *The Intellectual Revolution in U.S. Economic Policy-Making: The Second Noel Buxton Lecture of the University of Essex*. London: Longmans for the University of Essex.

Tobin, J. (1987), *Policies for Prosperity: Essays in a Keynesian Mode* (ed. P. M. Jackson). Cambridge, Mass.: MIT Press.

Tomlinson, J. (1990), *Public Policy and the Economy Since 1900*. Oxford: Clarendon Press.

Triffin, R. (1960), *Gold and the Dollar Crisis*. New Haven, Conn.: Yale University Press.

Turner, A. (2009), *The Turner Review: A Regulatory Response to the Global Banking Crisis*. London: Financial Services Authority.

Turner, A. (2014), Too Much of the Wrong Type of Capital Flow. Speech in New Delhi, 13 January.

Turner, A. (2015), The Case for Monetary Finance – An Essentially Political Issue. Washington, DC: IMF. 16th Jacques Polak Annual Research Conference, 5 November. Available at: https://www.imf.org/external/np/res/ seminars/2015/arc/pdf/adair.pdf [Accessed 15 December 2017].

Turner, A. (2016), *Between Debt and the Devil: Money, Credit, and Fixing Global Finance*. Princeton, NJ and Oxford: Princeton University Press.

Turner, G. (2008), *The Credit Crunch: Housing Bubbles, Globalisation and the Worldwide Economic Crisis*. London: Pluto.

UK Public Revenue (2018), *Total Direct Revenue: Fiscal Years 1900–2020*. Available at: https://www.ukpublicrevenue.co.uk/revenue_chart_1900_2020UKp_XXc1li111tcn_Fot#copypaste [Accessed 8 February 2018].

UK Public Spending (2017), *UK Public Spending Data Series 1692–2020*. Available at: http://www.ukpublicspending.co.uk/download_raw [Accessed 15 June 2017].

Utzig, S. (2010), *The Financial Crisis and the Regulation of Credit Rating Agencies: A European Banking Perspective*. Asian Development Bank Institute, Working Paper No. 188.

van Steenis, H. (2016), Why central banks need some friction in their models. *Financial Times*, 1 November.

Vaughan, R. (1856 (1675)), A Discourse of Coin and Coinage. In: J. R. McCulloch (ed.), *A Select Collection of Scarce and Variable Tracts on Money*. London: Printed for the Political Economy Club, pp. 4–120.

Viner, J. (1936), Mr. Keynes on the causes of unemployment. *Quarterly Journal of Economics*, 51 (1), November, pp. 147–67.

Vives, V. (1969), *Economic History of Spain*. Princeton, NJ: Princeton University Press.

Volckart, O. (1997), Early beginnings of the quantity theory of money and their context in Polish and Prussian monetary policies. *Economic History Review*, 50 (3), pp. 430–49.

Volcker, P. (2011), Financial reform: unfinished business. *New York Review of Books*, 24 November.

Walker, F. A. (1878), *Money*. New York: Henry Holt & Co.

Wallace, T. (2013), States blocked from tweaking EU stress tests. *City AM*, 22 October. Available at: http://www.cityam.com/article/1382402969/states-blocked-tweaking-eu-s-stress-tests [Accessed 19 December 2017].

Walras, L. (1874), *Éléments d'économie politique pure; ou, Théorie de la richesse sociale*. Lausanne: L. Corbaz.

Watt, N. (2008), Britain 'faces harder bump than in 1990s'. *Guardian*, 1 November.

Webb, S. and Webb, B. P. (1923), *The Decay of Capitalist Civilisation*. 3rd edn. Westminster: The Fabian Society.

Weeks, J. (2011), Mean, median and mode of impoverishment: why to Occupy Wall Street. *Social Europe*. Available at: https://www.socialeurope.eu/mean-median-and-mode-of-impoverishment-why-to-occupy-wall-street [Accessed 28 July 2017].

Weir, D. R. (1989), Tontines, public finance, and revolution in France and England, 1688–1789. *Journal of Economic History*, 49, pp. 95–124.

Went, R. (2002), *The Enigma of Globalization: A Journey to a New Stage of Capitalism*. London: Routledge.

Whittaker, E. (1940), *A History of Economic Ideas*. London: Longman, Green & Co.

Wickens, M. (2012), *Macroeconomic Theory: A Dynamic General Equilibrium Approach*. 2nd edn. Princeton, NJ: Princeton University Press.

Wicksell, K. (1936 (1898)), *Interest and Prices*. New York: Sentry Press.

Wolf, M. (2004), *Why Globalization Works*. New Haven, Conn. and London: Yale University Press.

Wolf, M. (2007a), Risks and rewards of today's unshackled global finance. *Financial Times*, 26 June.

Wolf, M. (2007b), The Federal Reserve must prolong the party. *Financial Times*, 21 August.

Wolf, M. (2008), Regulators should intervene in bankers' pay. *Financial Times*, 15 January.

Wolf, M. (2009), *Fixing Global Finance*. Baltimore, Md: Johns Hopkins University Press.

Wolf, M. (2010a), Fear must not blind us to deflation's dangers. *Financial Times*, 8 June.

Wolf, M. (2010b), Why the battle is joined over tightening. *Financial Times*, 18 July.

Wolfers, J. (2014). The Fed has not stopped trying to stimulate the economy. *New York Times*, 29 October.

Wood, G. E. (1995), The quantity theory in the 1980s: Hume, Thornton, Friedman and the relation between money and inflation. In: M. Blaug (ed.), *The Quantity Theory of Money: From Locke to Keynes and Friedman*. Aldershot: Edward Elgar.

Woodford, M. (2003), *Interest and Prices: Foundations of a Theory of Monetary Policy*. Princeton, NJ: Princeton University Press.

Woodford, M. (2009), Convergence in macroeconomics: elements of the new synthesis. *American Economic Journal: Macroeconomics*, 1 (2), pp. 267–79.

Woods, S. (2017), Speech: Geofinance. 4 October. London: Bank of England. Available at: https://www.bankofengland.co.uk/-/media/boe/files/speech/2017/geofinance-speech-by-sam-woods.pdf?la=en&hash=1B7B8C099846ED4D305128BBB265F7BB71A354BA [Accessed 18 December 2017].

Working Group on Long-term Finance (2013), *Long-term Finance and Economic Growth*. Washington, DC: Group of Thirty.

World Bank (2017a), GDP (current US$). Available at: http://data.world-bank.org/indicator/NY.GDP.MKTP.CD [Accessed 5 July 2017].

World Bank (2017b), GDP per capita (constant 2010 US$). Available at: http://data.worldbank.org/indicator/NY.GDP.PCAP.KD [Accessed 4 July 2017].

World Bank (2017c), Unemployment, total (% of labor force) (modeled ILO estimate). Available at: http://data.worldbank.org/indicator/SL.UEM.TOTL.ZS [Accessed 5 July 2017].

World Bank (2017d), GDP growth (annual %). Available at: https://data.worldbank.org/indicator/NY.GDP.MKTP.KD.ZG [Accessed 21 December 2017].

Wray, L. R. (2015), *Modern Money Theory: A Primer on Macroeconomics for Sovereign Monetary Systems.* 2nd edn. Basingstoke: Palgrave Macmillan.

Wren-Lewis, S. (2012), *What Have Microfoundations Ever Done For Us?* Available at: https://mainlymacro.blogspot.co.uk/2012/03/what-have-microfoundations-ever-done.html [Accessed 4 July 2017].

Wren-Lewis, S. (2017), *Could Austerity's Impact be Persistent?* Available at: https://mainlymacro.blogspot.co.uk/2017/06/could-austeritys-impact-be-persistent.html [Accessed 5 July 2017].

Wright, J. H. (2012), What does monetary policy do to long-term interest rates at the zero lower bound? *The Economic Journal*, 122, pp. F447–F466.

Wright, N. (2015), *Data Visualization in 'Capital in the 21st Century'.* The University of Texas Inequality Project, WP #70.

Wright, T. B. and Harlow, J. (1844), *The Currency Question: The Gemini Letters.* London: Simpkin, Marshall & Co.

Zweig, K. (1976), *Germany Through Inflation and Recession: An Object Lesson in Economic Management, 1973–1976.* London: Centre for Policy Studies.

Index

Italic figures refer to graphs and charts

initial signs of recovery (2009),
218–19, 225, 226
monetary interpretation of, 105, 106
'premature withdrawal' of fiscal
stimulus, 219–20, 223–36,
245, 352
reform agenda after, 361–8
rise in inequality in lead-up to,
289–90, 299–300
see also financial collapse (2007–8)
Greece
and Eurozone debt crisis, 32, 224,
224–5, 226, 233, 235, 242–3,
243, 337, 341, 365
in gold standard era, 59
Greenspan, Alan, 188, 313

Hamilton, Alexander, 88, 90, 92
Hammond, Philip, 236, 352
Hannover Re scandal, 329
Harrison, George, 105
Harrod, Roy, 123
Harvey, John, 333, 387
Hawtrey, Ralph, 109–10, 280
Hayek, Friedrich, 33, 46, 177, 195,
350, 367
founds Mont Pelerin Society, 176
'over-consumption' theory, 296
The Road to Serfdom (1944),
16, 175–6
on Wall Street Crash, 104
Heath, Edward, 167–8
Heckscher, Eli, 37
Help to Buy programme, 265, 266
Henderson, Hubert, 109
Henderson, W. O., 92
Hendry, D. F., 179
Hicks, John, 7–8, 34, 138, 158–9, 369
IS/LM model, 173, 199, 203,
203–4, 204
Hitler, Adolf, 111, 129–30
Hobson, J. A., 294–7
Hoenig, Thomas, 365

homo economicus, 24, 372
Hoover, Herbert, 53
Hopkins, Sir Richard, 112, 116–17
housing market
boom before 2007 crash, 239,
304, 331
British boom (1931), 125
British boom (1980s), 187
Coalition government subsidy
programmes, 265–6
as core activity of retail banks, 362–3
post-crash recovery in, 265
social house-building, 363
speculative boom and bust in, 331
US sub-prime mortgage market, 3,
216, 304–5, 309, 323, 328, 341
Howe, Geoffrey, 186–7, 192
Hume, David, 22, 37–8, 53, 54, 84,
104, 181, 285, 332, 336
Hutchison, Terence, 349
hysteresis (Blanchard and Summers
term), 239–41, 240, 241, 370

Ibn Khaldun, 73
India, 35–6
inequality
assault on Piketty's framework, 302–3
and austerity policies, 245–6
causes of disequalization, 300–306
and crisis of conservative
economics, 17
as deeper cause of banking
collapse, 299–306, 368
and deregulation of financial
markets, 384
fall in wage share of national income,
299–300, *301*, 303, 304, 305
in Great Moderation years, 4
and Keynes, 127, 297
macroeconomic impact of, 11,
289–90, 299–300, 303–6, 370
and new macroeconomic
constitution, 352